DILEMMAS
OF
POLITICS

Every time that I have approached a question, I have found that my enquiries ended by giving rise to new problems, and the farther I pushed my investigations the more disquieting these new problems became. But philosophy is after all perhaps only the recognition of the abysses which lie on each side of the footpath that the vulgar follow with the serenity of somnambulists.

GEORGES SOREL, *Reflections on Violence*

DILEMMAS
OF
POLITICS

By Hans J. Morgenthau

THE UNIVERSITY OF CHICAGO PRESS

Library of Congress Catalog Card Number: 58-11722

THE UNIVERSITY OF CHICAGO PRESS, CHICAGO & LONDON
The University of Toronto Press, Toronto 5, Canada

© 1958 by The University of Chicago. Published 1958
Second Impression 1962. Composed and printed by
THE UNIVERSITY OF CHICAGO PRESS,
Chicago, Illinois, U.S.A.

To my mother

FRIEDA BACHMANN MORGENTHAU

Preface

The essays which comprise this book were written during a period of almost twenty years for different publications on different occasions about different subjects. But they have been written by the same author, for whose unchanged philosophy and intellectual preoccupations they have furnished an opportunity for expression. They have been brought up to date and partly rewritten. Additions have been made primarily for the purpose of emphasizing the common concern of all these essays in what has been described here as the dilemmas of politics.

I gratefully acknowledge the permission of the following publications and publishers to use copyrighted materials on which this book is based: *American Journal of International Law, American Political Science Review, Bulletin of the Atomic Scientists, Chicago Law Review, Commentary,* Committee for Economic Development, *Encounter,* Harper & Brothers, *International Social Science Review, Iowa Law Review, Yearbook of World Affairs,* Northwestern University Press, *Review of Metaphysics, Review of Politics, World Politics, Yale Review.*

H. J. M.

Table of Contents

Introduction: Dilemmas of Politics   1

PART I. *Dilemmas of Political Understanding*

  1. The State of Political Science   7

  2. The Commitments of Political Science   27

PART II. *Dilemmas of Understanding International Politics*

  3. The Commitments of a Theory of International Politics   47

  4. The Problem of the National Interest   54

  5. International Relations as an Academic Discipline   88

PART III. *The Burden of an Obsolescent Tradition*

  6. Freedom   104

  7. The New Despotism and the New Feudalism   116

  8. Separation of Powers   123

  9. Nationalism   170

  10. Neutrality and Neutralism   185

  11. International Law   210

PART IV-A. *Dilemmas of Political Action: The Autonomy of Political Action*

  12. The Escape from Power   239

  13. The Moral Dilemma of Political Action   246

  14. The Military Displacement of Politics   256

  15. The Disparagement of Diplomacy   270

  16. The Decline of Democratic Government   281

ix

PART IV-B. *Dilemmas of Political Action: The Integrity of Political Action*

17. The Decline of the Democratic Process   295

18. The Corruption of Patriotism   305

19. The Subversion of Foreign Policy   324

PART V. *Dilemmas of Restoration*

20. The Corruption of Liberal Thought: Harold Laski   343

21. The Surrender to the Immanence of Power: E. H. Carr   350

22. The Evocation of the Past: Bertrand de Jouvenel   358

23. The Rediscovery of Imagination and Religion: Arnold Toynbee   368

24. The Revival of Objective Standards: Walter Lippmann   377

INDEX

Index   383

Introduction: Dilemmas of Politics

The history of political thought is a dialogue between the teachings of tradition and the demands of the contemporary world. Creative political thought illuminates the political experience of the day—and of all days—by discovering within it the perennial forces, problems, and patterns of interaction, of which political life consists. Both the tradition of political thought and the contemporary experience of political life, then, contain two elements: one contingent and ephemeral, the other necessary and perennial. Each epoch of history has the task to disengage from the tradition of political thought those truths which fit its own experience and, in turn, to separate out of the welter of its own experience the perennial configurations of political life. It must test yesterday's dogmas against the facts of today and today's orthodoxies against the perennial truths. It must liberate itself from the dead hand of tradition without falling victim to new dogma or else being lost in the labyrinth of uncomprehended experience.

This task confronts political thought with an inescapable dilemma. What of the tradition is perennially true, and what is but the outgrowth of particular interests and circumstances? And what in the political experience of the contemporary world is the ephemeral product of historic accident, and what is a manifestation of the eternal verities of politics? The history of political thought is the story of the gropings with which successive generations have searched for answers to these questions. They had to beware of two temptations which are indeed the horns of the dilemma: either to smother the contemporary world with obsolescent dogma or else to exchange the wisdom of the ages for the innovations of the age.

Until the French Revolution of 1789, political thought has tended to err on the side of dogma and tradition. Finding the perennial truths of politics imbedded in the shell of historic contingencies, each generation is tempted by its prideful or spiteful identification with its own times to give the contingent the appearance of the perennial. Theocracies have claimed for themselves a monopoly of truth, denying to rival theocracies any part of it. The philosophers of the Greek city-state fashioned out of their limited historic experience a model of political perfection. Imperial Rome saw in its constitution the repository of eternal truth and, hence, thought it would last forever. Both the feudal order of the Middle Ages and the absolute monarchy following it claimed to apply the truth of religion to the political sphere. In our own time, both liberal democracy and divers totalitarianisms have laid claim to being true democracies, both assuming that the truth of politics is to be found only in democracy, however defined.

While thus in the past the great source of error has been the unresisted temptation to clothe a particular political position or tradition with the dignity of absolute truth, our own time has to come to terms with the opposite temptation, that is, to throw all tradition overboard and either to deny the existence of objective political truth altogether or else to seek it in some novel political arrangement or device, apparently unencumbered by past political experience. That new temptation results from the successful attack to which the tradition of Western political thought has been exposed in the last two centuries.

In the realm of immediate experience, a succession of technological revolutions has transformed the natural and social environment of man almost beyond recognition and has radically changed man's experience of himself A succession of political revolutions opened the doors of the political arena to the masses which before the French Revolution had been excluded from active participation in political life. The Western tradition appeared to be incapable of coping in thought or deed with these novel experiences, and in the face of their novelty it appeared to be hopelessly out of date. Thus intellectual movements arose which tried to absorb these experiences by being openly or surreptitiously at odds with the Western tradition. Rousseau undermined it by substituting for the transcendent and substantive standards of the tradition an immanent and formal standard, the General Will, as the source of political truth. Marx destroyed it by making truth a function of political power.

Since in every epoch political thought is but the particular manifestation and application of a general philosophy, this destruction of the political tradition must be seen in the context of the general intellectual trend of the times. What Rousseau and Marx did to politics, Kierkegaard did to religion, Nietzsche to philosophy, and Freud to the image of man. These attacks upon the very foundations of Western civilization have left the received systems of thought empty of content and, in any event, without conviction. They live on as ritualistic incantations and ideological justifications and rationalizations, proclaiming their truth loudly but without rational vitality. Religion has become an organized social activity and the public demonstration of official piety, permeated with doubt and disbelief. Philosophy has set itself the task of proving that the very enterprise of philosophy is absurd and limits itself to clarifying the meaning of concepts. The image of man has disintegrated into a bundle of impulses with an infinite capacity for self-deception and an infinite need for expert management. And of politics nothing is left but the struggle of individuals and groups for access to the levers of power, in terms either of majority or oligarchic rule, crying out again either for expert management or else for utopian reform, oblivious of the distinction of what is desirable and what is possible and of the ineluctability of power itself.

The dilemma which confronts us today, then, is twofold. We must come to terms with the dilemma which grows from the very nature of political thought and which every epoch must try to solve anew: the tension between the political ideas which have come to us from the past, claiming to tell us the truth about ourselves, and the political experiences of the age which, at the very least, question this claim. Yet before we face this perennial dilemma of political thought we must cope with the attitude peculiar to our age which denies the value of tradition to help us understand and master the problems of contemporary politics and therefore denies the existence of the perennial dilemma itself.

This book indeed assumes, as shown in particular in the first chapter, not only the continuing value of the tradition of political thought for the contemporary world but also the need for the restoration of its timeless elements. It is especially concerned with the restoration of politics as an autonomous sphere of thought and action. Beyond this preliminary task of restoration, it subjects a number of traditional political ideas and institutions to the test of their contemporary relevance, discarding, affirming, and refashioning as the situation may require. Finally, it gives a critical account of some representative attempts at re-creating a relevant system of political thought.

The result is bound to be tentative and fragmentary. For the disintegration of the great intellectual systems from which the Western world used to receive its meaning has not spared even our sense of reality. As modern physics has destroyed the reliability and relevance of the sensory perception of our natural environment, so do Marxism and psychoanalysis and their derivatives deny the reliability of consciousness of ourselves and of our social environment. Things natural and social are not what they seem to be. What parades as truth in matters political is but a delusion of self and of others or a pretense, masking interests of class and the desires of self. This is no doubt so, sometimes or even often. But the whole history of the race and our own inner experience militates against the assumption that it is so always. When is it so and when is it not? When is truth in matters political not a delusion or a pretense?

This is the crucial question which faces political philosophy, as it has faced general philosophy since Plato inquired into the difference between truth and opinion. Given the present state of philosophic and political thought, this question cannot be answered today in any systematic fashion. Yet from a piecemeal examination of concrete issues there might at least emerge an awareness of the dilemma in its perennial and contemporary configuration.

4

PART I

DILEMMAS
OF POLITICAL
UNDERSTANDING

1 *The State of Political Science*

In Plato's *Theaetetus* Socrates develops the character of the philosopher, the man of knowledge, in contrast to the atheoretical, practical man. He endeavors to demonstrate the distinctive qualities of the philosopher by emphasizing his peculiar attitude toward the political sphere.

First, the philosopher has no political ambitions, and he does not care about what is going on in the political sphere. The philosophers have never, from their youth upwards, known their way to the Agora, or the dicastery, or the council, or any other political assembly; they neither see nor hear the laws or decrees, as they are called, of the State written or recited; the eagerness of political societies in the attainment of offices—clubs, and banquets, and revels, and singing-maidens—do not enter even into their dreams. Whether any event has turned out well or ill in the city, what disgrace may have descended to any one from his ancestors, male or female, are matters of which the philosopher no more knows than he can tell, as they say, how many pints are contained in the ocean.

Second, the philosopher is ignorant about political matters and incapable of acting effectively on the political plane. He "is wholly unacquainted with his next-door neighbor; he is ignorant, not only of what he is doing, but he hardly knows whether he is a man or an animal. . . . His awkwardness is fearful, and gives the impression of imbecility. When he is reviled, he has nothing personal to say in answer to the civilities of his adversaries, for he knows no scandals of anyone, and they do not interest him. . . ."

Third, the philosopher is morally uncommitted and indifferent to the values of politics.

When he hears a tyrant or king eulogized, he fancies that he is listening to the praises of some keeper of cattle—a swineherd, or shepherd, or perhaps a cowherd, who is congratulated on the quantity of milk which he squeezes from them; and he remarks that the creature whom they tend, and out of whom they squeeze the wealth, is of a less tractable and more insidious nature. Then again, he observes that the great man is of necessity as ill-mannered and uneducated as any shepherd—for he has no leisure, and he is surrounded by a wall, which is his mountain-pen. Hearing of enor-

7

mous landed proprietors of ten thousand acres and more, our philosopher deems this to be a trifle, because he has been accustomed to think of the whole earth; and when they sing the praises of family, and say that some one is a gentleman because he can show seven generations of wealthy ancestors, he thinks that their sentiments only betray a dull and narrow vision in those who utter them and who are not educated enough to look at the whole, nor to consider that every man has had thousands and ten thousands of progenitors, and among them have been rich and poor, kings and slaves, Hellenes and barbarians, innumerable. And when people pride themselves on having a pedigree of twenty-five ancestors, which goes back to Heracles, the son of Amphitryon, he cannot understand their poverty of ideas. Why are they unable to calculate that Amphitryon had a twenty-fifth ancestor, who might have had a fiftieth, and so on? He amuses himself with the notion that they cannot count, and thinks that a little arithmetic would have got rid of their senseless vanity.

This political indifference and incapacity is the reflection of the philosopher's positive nature. The philosopher's

outer form . . . only is in the city. His mind, disdaining the littlenesses and nothingnesses of human things, is "flying all abroad" as Pindar says, measuring earth and heaven and the things which are under and on the earth and above the heaven, interrogating the whole nature of each and all in their entirety, but not condescending to anything which is within reach. . . . He is searching into the essence of man, and busy in enquiring what belongs to such a nature to do or suffer different from any other. . . .

This commitment to the search for the truth for its own sake and, concomitant with it, his divorcement—morally and intellectually, in judgment and action—from the political sphere makes the man of theory a scandal in the eyes of the multitude. He "is laughed at for his sheepishness. . . . He seems to be a downright idiot." He "is derided by the vulgar, partly because he is thought to despise them, and also because he is ignorant of what is before him and always at a loss." Socrates tells "the jest which the clever witty Thracian handmaid is said to have made about Thales, when he fell into a well as he was looking up at the stars. She said, that he was so eager to know what was going on in heaven, that he could not see what was before his feet." And Socrates adds: "This is a jest which is equally applicable to all philosophers."

Yet the philosopher has his revenge.

But, O my friend, when he draws the other into upper air, and gets him out of his pleas and rejoinders into the contemplation of justice and injustice in their own nature and in their difference from one another and from all other things; or from the commonplaces about the happiness of a king or a rich man to the consideration of government, and of human happiness and misery in general—what they are, and how a man is to attain the one and avoid the other—when that narrow, keen, little legal mind is called to account about all this, he gives the philosopher his revenge; for dizzied by the height at which he is hanging, whence he looks down into space, which is a strange experience to him, he being dismayed, and lost, and stammering broken words, is laughed at, not by Thracian handmaidens or any other uneducated persons, for they have no eye for the situation but by every man who has not been brought up a slave.

We may well recognize in this juxtaposition of the philosopher with the practitioner the archetypes of a perennial conflict between the theoretical man who thinks for the sake of finding the truth and the practical man who thinks for the sake of finding solutions to practical problems. Yet neither can we fail to recognize the limitations of the Platonic analysis, which is too neat, too "Greek" in its classical simplicity to satisfy us. While what Plato says is true, it is not the whole truth of the matter. There is, as we shall see, in the political thinker's place within the society about which he thinks an ambiguity—intellectual and moral—of which the ancients knew—and perhaps were bound to know—nothing. Yet with all its limitations Plato's statement conveys an insight into the nature of philosophy, theory, and science which, in turn, sheds an illuminating light upon the state of political science in America.

The impulse to which American political science owes its existence was overwhelmingly practical. It was nourished from two roots, one of which it has in common with all of modern political science, while the other is peculiar to itself.

Political science as an academic discipline everywhere in the Western world owes its existence to the disintegration, after their last flowering in the early nineteenth century, of the great philosophic systems which had dominated Western thought and to the concomitant development of the empirical investigation of the social world. All the social sciences are the fruit of the emancipation of the Western mind from metaphysical systems which had made the social world primarily a subject for metaphysical speculation and ethical postulates. In certain fields, such as economics, that emancipation occurred early; in others, such as political science, it occurred relatively late (for reasons which, as we shall see, are inherent in the nature of political science).

This antispeculative and empirical tendency of Western thought, as it developed in the second half of the nineteenth century, could not but find a ready and, as it were, natural response in the propensities of the American mind. Yet while European political thought continued to combine an antimetaphysical position with concern for theory, American political science was overwhelmed by the practical promises of the new discipline. The first departments of political science were established in America in the eighties of the last century, not for the purpose of theoretical understanding, let alone philosophic speculation, but primarily for the purpose of meeting the practical exigencies of the day.

It is illuminating in this context, and it is in a sense a moving experience, to read the address that was delivered on October 3, 1881, at the opening of the School of Political Science at the University of Michigan by its first dean, Charles Kendall Adams.[1] Of the perennial problems of politics, such as power, legitimacy, authority, freedom, forms of government, natural law, sovereignty, revolution, tyranny, majority rule, this address makes no mention. The only problems which concern it are the practical problems of the day, and the case it tries to make for political science in America rests exclusively upon the contribution the new discipline promises to make to the solution of these problems. Looking abroad, Dean Adams finds that the rapid recovery of France after 1871 was primarily due to the instruction in political science. "The close of their war was six years later than the close of ours; and yet long before we had gained our financial equilibrium, France was the most prosperous nation in Europe." In England, "political instruction . . . has been given by men, some of whom have been thought worthy of high places in Parliament, in the diplomatic service, and in the Cabinet. . . . Their pupils are all about them in Parliament and in the diplomatic service." In diplomacy and, more particularly, in economic reform the influence of university instruction has been persuasive. Dean Adams finds the same beneficial results in Germany. "Graduates of these schools [of political science] found their way into administration positions of influence

[1] *The Relations of Political Science to National Prosperity* (Ann Arbor, 1881).

in all parts of Germany. . . . Commissioner White . . . uses these words: 'In conversation with leading men in Southern Germany I have not found one who did not declare this and similar courses of instruction the main cause of the present efficiency in the German administration.' "

Having thus made a case for the advantages that political science has brought to the practice of European governments, Dean Adams must now dispose of the argument that American political institutions are superior to those of Europe and that, therefore, America has no need of political science. The argument is revealing in its exclusive emphasis upon the practical benefits to be expected.

Is it certain that our municipal governments are better than theirs? Are our systems of taxation more equitably adjusted than theirs? Do our public and private corporations have greater respect for the rights of the people than theirs? Can we maintain that our legislatures are more free from corruption and bribery than theirs? Was our financial management at the close of our war wiser than that of France at the close of hers? If these questions can be answered in the affirmative, and without the shadow of a doubt, I concede that an argument may be built upon them in favor of what may be called intuitive methods.

After passing in systematic review the operations of the three branches of government which are in need of improvement, Dean Adams turns to "several other fields of activity in which great influence is exerted." He singles out journalism and speechmaking, which political science can help to improve. He sums up his argument in favor of political science by saying:

It is for the purpose of aiding in the several directions that have been hinted at, and in others that would be mentioned if there were time, that the School of Political Science in the University of Michigan has been established. It finds its justification where the other schools of the University find theirs: in the good of the people and the welfare of the State.

This exclusive concern with practical improvements is by no means an isolated instance. It dominates the virtually simultaneous establishment of a School of Political Science at Columbia University. The objective of that school was as practical as that of Michigan; yet while the latter's appeal was one of boundless vocationalism, the former's practical interests were narrowly confined to a particular profession, that of the civil servant. When President

Barnard submitted the proposal for the establishment of the school to the trustees of Columbia University, he called it "Proposed School of Preparation for the Civil Service." Reflecting the philosophy of John W. Burgess, the driving spirit behind the proposal, we find the purpose of the school defined as "to prepare young men for public life whether in the Civil Service at home or abroad, or in the legislatures of the States or of the nation; and also to fit young men for the duties and responsibilities of public journalists."[2]

The first departments of political science in this country, then, did not grow organically from a general conception as to what was covered by the field of political science, nor did they respond to a strongly felt intellectual need. Rather they tried to satisfy practical demands, which other academic disciplines refused to meet. For instance, in that period the law schools would not deal with public law. It was felt that somebody ought to deal with it, and thus it was made part of political science. There was a demand for instruction in journalism, but there was no place for it to be taught; thus it was made part of political science. There was a local demand for guidance in certain aspects of municipal administration; and thus a course in that subject was made part of the curriculum of political science.

In other words, political science grew, not by virtue of an intellectual principle germane to the field, but in response to pressures from the outside. What could not be defined in terms of a traditional academic discipline was defined as political science. This inorganic growth and haphazard character of political science is strikingly reflected in the curriculums of the early departments of political science, such as those of Michigan, Columbia, and Harvard. In the address from which we have quoted, Dean Adams mentions the following subjects which were to form part of the curriculum of the School of Political Science: General History, The History of Political Institutions, The Recent Political History of Europe, The Political and Constitutional History of England, The Political and Constitutional History of the United States; several courses in political economy; under the general heading of "Sanitary Science": The Laws of Physiological Growth and Decay, The Varieties and

[2] R. Gordon Hoxie *et al., A History of the Faculty of Political Science, Columbia University* (New York: Columbia University Press, 1955), p. 13.

Adaptabilities of Foods, The Best Methods of Supplying Pure Water and Air, The Causes of Infectious Diseases, The Proper Disposal of Decomposing Matter, The Proper Functions of Boards of Health and Health Officers; under the general heading of "Social Science": The Prevalence of Crime and the Most Efficient Means of Diminishing and Preventing It, The Best Methods of Treating our Criminals, The Care of the Insane and the Management of Asylums, The Proper Treatment of the Poor and the Proper Superintendence of Almshouses, The Place and the Proper Equipment and Control of Hospitals; courses in forestry and political ethics; and finally "crowning the whole": The Idea of the State; The Nature of Individual, Social, and Political Rights; The History of Political Ideas; The Government of Cities; Theories and Methods of Taxation; Comparative Constitutional Law; Comparative Administrative Law; Theories of International Law; and The History of Modern Diplomacy. "Such," Dean Adams concludes, "in the briefest outline, is what it is the purpose of the school at present to teach. Additions to the corps and the courses of instruction will be added, from time to time, as the necessity is revealed."

While this program is but an extreme example of the practicality of early American political science, the list of courses which formed the curriculum of the School of Political Science of Columbia University from 1880 to 1887 is typical of its eclecticism. According to Burgess, the "School of Political Science" was "the collective name which we give the graduate or university courses in history, philosophy, economy, public law, jurisprudence, diplomacy, and sociology."[3] These are the courses which were then taught: Physical and Political Geography, Ethnology, General Political and Constitutional History of Europe, Political and Constitutional History of England, Political and Constitutional History of the United States, Bibliography of the Political Sciences, History of Roman Law to the Present Day, Comparative Constitutional Law of the Principal European States and of the United States, Statistical Science—Methods and Results, Comparative Jurisprudence of the Principal European Systems of Civil Law, Comparative Constitutional Law of the Several Commonwealths of the American Union,

[3] John W. Burgess, "The Study of the Political Sciences in Columbia College," *International Review,* XII (1882), 348.

History of Diplomacy, Comparative Administrative Law of the Principal States of Europe and of the United States, Comparative Administrative Law of the Several Commonwealths of the American Union, Private International Law; social sciences: Communistic and Socialistic Theories; political economy: History of Politico-Economic Institutions, Taxation and Finance; philosophy: History of Political Theories from Plato to Hegel.[4]

Similarly, the courses differentiated in 1892–93 at Harvard under the heading of "Government" comprised: Constitutional Government; Elements of International Law (which included history of diplomacy); History and Institutes of Roman Law; Federal Government—Historical and Comparative; Leading Principles of Constitutional Law—Selected Cases American and English; History of Political Theories, with particular reference to the origin of American institutions; Government and Political Methods in the United States; and International Law as Administered by the Courts.[5]

In its further development political science as an academic discipline has undergone a process of both contraction and expansion. On the one hand, new schools and departments have absorbed much of the subject matter that was formerly taught in departments of political science because there was no other place in the university to teach them. On the other hand, however, new practical interests have continued to call for the inclusion of new subjects of instruction in the curriculum.

Thus today the curriculum of political science still bears the unmistakable marks of its haphazard origin and development. To pick out at random some courses from two departments of political science with which I am familiar, what have "Plato's Political Philosophy and Its Metaphysical Foundation" and "The Politics of Conservation" in common, or "General Principles of Organization and Administration" and "International Law," or "Conduct of American Foreign Relations" and "Introduction to Jurisprudence," or "Nationalism" and "Political Behavior and Public Policy," or "Russian Political and Economic Institutions" and "Public Personnel Administration"? The only common denominator which

[4] Hoxie *et al., op. cit.,* pp. 305–6.

[5] Anna Haddow, *Political Science in American Colleges and Universities, 1636–1900* (New York: Appleton-Century, 1939), p. 175.

now ties these courses loosely together is a general and vague orientation toward the nature and activities of the state and toward activities which have in turn a direct bearing upon the state. Beyond that orientation toward a common subject matter, defined in the most general terms, contemporary political science has no unity of method, outlook, and purpose.

As concerns method, political science is split five ways, and four of these methodological positions have hardly anything in common. Their disparity is such that there is hardly even a possibility of fruitful discourse among the representatives of the different approaches beyond polemics which deny the very legitimacy of the other approaches. These approaches can be classified as philosophic theory, empirical theory, empirical science, description, and practical amelioration.

These five methodological approaches are not peculiar to political science. They have appeared in other social sciences as well—such as psychology, economics, and sociology—yet with two significant differences. First of all, the other social sciences have traditionally shown a much greater awareness of the existence, nature, and separate functions of these approaches than has political science. Second, they have been able, at least at times, to rid themselves in good measure of the ameliorative and vocational approach which has by itself only a minimum of intellectual relevance. Political science, on the other hand, has never squarely faced the methodological problem in terms of the intrinsic character of these different approaches and the functions which they are able to perform for the understanding of its subject matter. These five approaches have rather coexisted without clear distinction within the departments of political science, one to be emphasized over the others at different times and places according to the pressures of supply and demand. Here, too, the development has been haphazard and subject to accident rather than guided by certain fundamental requirements of theory.

Thus political science has not generally been able to make that distinction which is a precondition for the development of any true science: the distinction between what is worth knowing intellectually and what is useful for practice. It is this distinction which economics and sociology accomplished some decades ago when schools of business, home economics, retailing, social work, and the like took over the practical concerns which at best develop practical uses for theoretical knowledge or else have but the most tenuous connection with it. Political science has taken a similar step in some instances by organizing the practical uses of political science for the amelioration of government activities in schools of administration and the like. But not only has this separation been exceptional rather than typical, it has also been made as a matter of convenience rather than in application of a generally accepted theoretical principle. In consequence, improvement of the processes of government is still generally considered not only a worthwhile activity to be engaged in by political scientists but also a legitimate, and sometimes even the only legitimate, element of political science as an academic discipline, to be taught under any of the course headings composing its curriculum.

It should be pointed out in passing that we are dealing here not with a specific subject matter but with a particular method, a particular intellectual approach. This approach will naturally manifest itself most frequently and typically in those fields of political science which have a direct relevance to the operations of government, such as public administration, but it is by no means limited to them. The other fields of political science, such as international relations, American government, constitutional law, and parties, have at times been dominated by the practical approach seeking practical remedies for conditions regarded as being in need of amelioration.

Yet it is exactly this commitment of modern political science to practical ends which has powerfully contributed to its decline as theory. Modern political science has been largely committed to the practical goals of liberal reform. Each major achievement in the direction of one of these goals was expected to bring society that much closer to solving once and for all one of the perennial problems of politics, such as inequality, insecurity, conflict, violence, power itself—and none ever did. The old problems reappeared in a new garb, mocking the scientific pretenses and eschatological expectations of liberal political science, and yesterday's hope and today's achievement became tomorrow's illusion. To this succession of blows which liberal politics suffered at the hands of experience must be attributed in good measure its disenchantment with reform and its decline in creative thought and action. The grand ameliorative schemes of liberal political science petered out in proposals for piecemeal improvements from which no great things can be expected.

Thus description is today the method most widely used in political science. Factual information arranged according to certain traditional classifications still dominates most of the textbooks in the field. While it is unnecessary to argue the case for the need for factual information, it ought to be no more necessary to argue that factual description is not science but a mere, however indispensable, preparation for the scientific understanding of the facts. It may, however, point toward a theoretical awakening that descriptive political science tends to dress up descriptive accounts of facts in theoretical garb and to use fancy classifications and terminologies in order to conceal the mere descriptive character of its substance. While the theoretical pretense of factual accounts shows an awareness of the need for theoretical understanding, that understanding itself requires more than the demonstrative use of an elaborate apparatus of classification and terminology.

With this last type of descriptive political science which overlays its descriptive substance with theoretical pretense, we are in the borderland where description and empirical science merge. Empirical science is today the most vigorous branch of political science and tends to attract many of the abler and more inventive students. Taking its cue from the natural sciences, or what it thinks the natural sciences are, it tries to develop rigorous methods of quantitative verification which are expected in good time to attain the same precision in the discovery of uniformities and in prediction to which the natural sciences owe their theoretical and practical success.

I have argued elsewhere against this analogy between the social and the natural sciences,[6] and this is not the place to resume the controversy. It must suffice here to state dogmatically that the object of the social sciences is man, not as a product of nature but as both the creature and the creator of history in and through

[6] *Scientific Man vs. Power Politics* (Chicago: University of Chicago Press, 1946).

which his individuality and freedom of choice manifest themselves. To make susceptibility to quantitative measurement the yardstick of the scientific character of the social sciences in general and of political science in particular is to deprive these sciences of that very orientation which is adequate to the understanding of their subject matter.

The inadequacy of the quantitative method to the subject matter of political science is demonstrated by the limitation of its success to those types of political behavior which by their very nature lend themselves to a certain measure of quantification, such as voting, and the barrenness of the attempts to apply the quantitative method to phenomena which are determined by historic individuality, rational or moral choice. As concerns these phenomena, the best quantification can achieve is to confirm and refine knowledge which theory has already discovered. It will not do to argue that this limitation is due to the "backwardness" of political science which could be overcome if only more and better people would spend more time and money for quantification. For that argument to be plausible, the limitation is too persistent, and it becomes ever more spectacular as more and better people spend more time and money to make it a success.

Once quantification has left that narrow sphere where it can contribute to relevant knowledge, two roads are open to it. Either it can try to quantify phenomena which in their aspects relevant to political science are not susceptible to quantification, and by doing so obscure and distort what political science ought to know; thus much of quantitative political science has become a pretentious collection of trivialities. Or, dimly aware of this inadequacy, quantification may shun contact with the empirical phenomena of political life altogether and try to find out instead what the correct way of quantifying is. Basic to this methodological concern is the assumption that the failure of quantification to yield results in any way proportionate to the effort spent follows from the lack of a correct quantitative method. Once that method is discovered and applied, quantification will yield the results in precise knowledge its adherents claim for it.

However, it is obvious that these methodological investigations, patently intended for the guidance of empirical research, have hardly exerted any influence upon the latter. This divorce of methodology from empirical investigation is not fortuitous. For it points not only to the inadequacy of the quantitative method for the understanding of much of the subject matter of political science, an inadequacy which must become particularly striking when quantification is confronted in its pure theoretical form with the actuality of political life. That divorce also illuminates a tendency, common not only to all methodological endeavors in the social sciences but to general philosophy as well, to retreat ever more from contact with the empirical world into a realm of self-sufficient abstractions. Logical positivism and general semantics owe their existence as independent branches of philosophy to this "new scholasticism," as it has been aptly called.[7] General sociological theory is dominated by it, and it has left its impact also upon political science. The new scholastic dissolves the substance of knowledge into the processes of knowing; he tends to think about how to think and to conceptualize about concepts, regressing ever further from empirical reality until he finds the logical consummation of his endeavors in mathematical symbols and other formal relations. And it is not fortuitous that the apparent precision of his formal categories tends to go hand in hand with an often shocking imprecision of his vestigial substantive thought; for, to the extent that objective reality demands qualitative evaluation, formalism either misses the point altogether or else distorts it.

A remarkable example of this new political science—remarkable by virtue of the reputation of its authors and of its own claims—is Lasswell and Kaplan, *Power and Society: A Framework for Political Inquiry*.[8] This book claims to be "a book of political theory, not an analysis of the contemporary or impending political situation" (p. ix). Critical of the German *Staatslehre* and of De Tocqueville and Bryce, it finds itself "much closer to the straightforward empirical standpoint of Machiavelli's *Discourses* or Michels' *Political Parties*" (p. x). "The present work is an attempt to formulate the basic concepts and hypotheses of political science" (p. xi). Its purpose is "to provide a framework for political science" (p. xiii). There can

[7] Barrington Moore, Jr., "The New Scholasticism and the Study of Politics," *World Politics*, VI (1953), 122–38.

[8] New Haven: Yale University Press, 1950.

be no doubt that the authors present this work as a major contribution to political theory.

The book consists of a series of definitions and propositions, with commentary, under the following headings: persons, perspectives, groups, influence, power, symbols, practices, functions, structures, process. What do these definitions and propositions contribute to knowledge? We open the book at random and read on page 13 the following definitions: "A *personality trait* is a kind of act characteristic of a self. The *personality* is the totality of the personality traits pertaining to an actor. A person is an actor characterized as to personality." This is hardly more meaningful than Gertrude Stein's "Rose is a rose is a rose is a rose," and does not have even its primitive phonetic charm. On page 154, we read the following proposition: "Acquisition and maintenance of leadership is a function of the prestige of the leaders." On page 187, the rulers are defined as "those supreme in the body politic." On page 218, information is conveyed in the form of the following definition: "*Autocracy* is the form of rule in which the weight of power is chiefly in the hands of one person; *oligarchy*, in the hands of a group of rulers; a *republic*, distributed throughout the domain." On page 234, democracy and despotism are defined as follows: "A *democracy* is a libertarian, juridical commonwealth; a *despotism* is a nondemocratic rule." These definitions are obviously either platitudinous, circular, or tautological, and at best convey information which Aristotle would have taken for granted.

However, what vitiates this book as a major contribution to political theory is a thorough misunderstanding of the nature of political theory and of its relationship to empirical research. The authors believe that political science can be "straightforward empirical" and that Machiavelli and Michels so conceived it. We shall not deal here with the case of Michels. But do the authors not recognize the fact that Machiavelli was a political philosopher steeped in the ancient tradition, that his empirical inquiry is inclosed within a philosophical framework resting upon the pillars of *fortuna* and *virtu*, concepts which come straight from classical antiquity, and that his work, far from being "straightforward empirical," is a philosophic protest against the scholastic tradition in an attempt to reassert the political philosophy of the ancients? Are the authors unaware of the fact that in this sense Machiavelli is no more an empiricist in politics than Raphael and Michelangelo are naturalists in art? Their purpose, as that of the Renaissance as a whole, was philosophic and not merely descriptive. Are the authors unfamiliar with the literature which has uncovered the philosophic system behind the seemingly empirical surface of Machiavelli's writings?

One error, perhaps inconsequential in itself, but characteristic of the authors' method, will illustrate the point. The authors express their criticism of the metaphysical speculation of the "German *Staatslehre* tradition, so influential at the turn of the century" (p. x). As an example they quote J. K. Bluntschli and give as the date of his *Theory of the State* the year 1921. It so happens that Bluntschli was a Hegelian who died in 1881 and whose work, referred to by the authors, was published in 1851 and 1852. What the authors cite is the third edition of the English translation, the first of which appeared in 1885 (the year of the last German one), the second in 1895. Neither Bluntschli's organismic brand of Hegelianism nor metaphysical speculation in general had any considerable influence on German political thought at the turn of the century, having been replaced by the theories of social and legal historians such as Gierke, or of constitutional and comparative lawyers such as Laband, Gneist, and Jellinek. In 1921 Bluntschli and his metaphysical speculations were a mere historic recollection, and the epic struggle between Kelsen, the philosopher of the pure theory of law, and his politically oriented enemies provided the great issues in political science.

The authors are not only careless about the incontestable facts of political theory; they are also given to sweeping judgments barely supported by evidence. Let us examine the following statement: "Many of the most influential political writings—those of Plato, Locke, Rousseau, the *Federalist*, and others—have not been concerned with political inquiry at all, but with the justification of existent or proposed political structures. We say such works formulate *political doctrine* rather than propositions of *political science*" (p. xi). What is correct in this statement is that the great writings of political theory had as their ultimate purpose the justification of a certain political system. This is true of Plato and Locke, as it is of Machiavelli and Michels. There have been thinkers who were "not concerned with political inquiry at all," as there were and are those who are concerned with nothing but political science conceived in "straightforward empirical" terms; most of them for that very reason have been, and will be, forgotten. What makes it today worth reading Plato, Locke, Rousseau, the *Federalist*, and above all Aristotle (whom the authors have omitted from their list) is exactly that, within the framework of a political doctrine, they have given us the results of political inquiry in the form of propositions of political science, more profound and more illuminating by far than anything that a "straightforward empirical standpoint" has to offer. The authors are unable to see that a political science inclosed in nothing but an empirical framework is a contradiction in terms and a monstrosity. The intellectual barrenness of the present work, its logical aimlessness and diffuseness, and its excessive concern with verbal artifices are the results of this fundamental misunderstanding.

Every student approaches the political scene, whether as a thinker or as an actor, with certain intellectual and moral preconceptions regarding it. His thoughts and actions are determined by those preconceptions. In other words, he looks at the political scene from a perspective which is determined by his philosophy and which he will share with some but not with other observers. Whether or not he approves of it, whether or not he realizes it, he is a political philosopher before he is a political scientist. All observers of politics, then, bring to their observations a framework of political philosophy, however inarticulate and fragmentary it may be. It is only within such a philosophical framework that an empirical framework of political inquiry can have meaning and that empirical inquiry can become fruitful. Of the realization in theory and practice of that necessary relationship between political philosophy and empirical inquiry, Aristotle provides the unrivaled example.

Our authors have subjected Aristotle to a kind of content analysis and have found, on the basis of a sample of three hundred sentences, that the proportion of "political philosophy (demand statements and evaluations) to political science (statements of facts and empirical hypotheses)" (p. 118 n.) is 25 to 75. We shall not compete with the authors in a mechanical exercise of this kind and shall not even raise the question of whether the three hundred sentences chosen were "representative samples." We only call attention to the basic proposition that in politics empirical inquiry without a philosophic framework must needs be blind, as political philosophy without empirical verification must needs be wholly speculative. To have understood this makes Aristotle a great political scientist, regardless of the quantitative proportions of different kinds of statements in his work.

We have said that all men dealing with the political realm bring of necessity to their field of inquiry or action a political philosophy, and our authors are no exception. Their philosophy is that of freedom (pp. xiii–xxiv). Yet the difference between the layman and the dilettante, on the one hand, and the political scientist worthy of the name, on the other, is determined by whether the individual has made his political philosophy articulate and whether he has brought it into organic relationship with his empirical inquiry. In this respect all the great political thinkers of the past, from Plato and Aristotle onward, stand on one side; our authors, together with many academic political scientists of the day, stand on the other. The latter take the democratic values of freedom for granted and do not ask themselves what the content of those values and what the relations among those values and between them and other values of a non-democratic character must be under the conditions of the contemporary world. Nor are they aware—and they cannot be, in view of their preconceptions—of the necessary relationship between those questions of political philosophy and the framework and content of empirical political inquiry. As their political philosophy is inarticulate and fragmentary, so their empirical inquiry is bound to be without direction and barren of meaning.

This spectacle of two superbly endowed minds failing so thoroughly in spite of great ability and great effort contains an element of tragedy. That tragedy is not so much the tragedy of two men as the tragedy of political science and of philosophy in America. For as Mr. Lasswell is the product of a school of political science which was, if not hostile, in any case indifferent, to the necessary contribution which political philosophy must make to empirical inquiry, so Mr. Kaplan is the product of a school of philosophy which sees in the history of philosophy primarily a history of errors. These authors are among the most gifted representatives of schools which at present ride the crest of the wave. Yet in truth they represent an obsolescent point of view. This book perhaps constitutes the most extreme, and therefore self-defeating, product of the fundamental errors of those schools. It may well contribute to their demise by virtue of its own absurdity.

There is a revealing similarity, pointing to a common root in the disorders of our culture, between abstract modern political science and abstract modern art. Both retreat from empirical reality into a world of formal relations and abstract symbols, which either on closer examination reveal themselves to be trivial or else are unintelligible, except to the initiated. Both share in the indifference to the accumulated achievements of mankind in their respective fields; Plato and Phidias, St. Thomas and Giotto, Spinoza and Rembrandt have no message for them. That divorcement from reality, contemporary and historic, deprives both of that wholesome discipline which prevents the mind from indulging its fancies without regard to some relevant objective standards. Thus one fashion, intellectual or artistic, follows the other, each oblivious of what has gone before, each relegated to limbo by its successors. Both abstract political science and abstract modern art tend to become esoteric, self-sufficient, and self-perpetuating cults, clustered around a "master," imitating his "style," and conversing in a lingo intelligible only to the members. Yet common sense, trying to penetrate the mysteries of these abstractions, cannot help wondering whether even the initiated understand each other and themselves. Perhaps, common sense continues wondering, some of the "masters" are just pulling the legs of their followers, who must pretend to understand in order to remain intellectually "up to date." "Enlightened people," to quote Georges Sorel, "dare not admit that they cannot understand arguments that are presented in very sophisticated language by an illustrious writer."

With this emphasis upon theoretical abstractions which have no relation to political reality, the methodology of political science joins a school which from the beginning to this day has occupied an honored but lonely place in the curriculum of political science: political theory. Political theory as an academic discipline has been traditionally the history of political philosophies in chronological succession, starting with Plato and ending, if time permits, with Laski. As an academic discipline, political theory has been hardly more than an account of what writers of the past, traditionally regarded as "great," have thought about the traditional problems of politics, with hardly a systematic attempt being made to correlate that historic knowledge to the other fields of political science and to the contemporary political world. "The danger," in the words of Sir Ernest Barker, "of some subjects of speculation—I would cite in evidence literary criticism as well as political theory—is that they may be choked, as it were, by the history of their own past."[9] Thus political theory as an academic discipline has been intellectually sterile, and it is not by accident that some of the most important contributions to contemporary political theory have been made not by professional political scientists but by theologians, philosophers, and sociologists.

Political theory remained an indispensable part of the curriculum, not because of the vital influence it was able to exert upon our thinking, but rather because of a vague conviction that there was something venerable and respectable in this otherwise useless exercise. Thus the academic concern with political theory tended to become an intellectually and practically meaningless ritual which one had to engage in for reasons of tradition and prestige before one could occupy one's self with the things that really mattered.

The awareness of this contrast between the prestige of political theory and its actual lack of relevance for the understanding of contemporary political problems has led theory closer to the contemporary political world. On the other hand, the awareness of the meagerness of the insights to be gained from strictly empirical investigations has made empirical political science search for a theoretical framework. Avoiding the limitations of the traditional approaches and fusing certain of their elements, contemporary political science is in the process of reviving a tradition to which most of the classics of political science owe their existence and influence. The intent of that tradition is theoretical: it wants to understand political reality in a theoretical manner, that is, by bringing to bear upon it propositions of both objective and general validity. These propositions claim to be objective in that their validity is not affected by the subjective limitations of the observer. They claim to be general in that their validity is not affected by the peculiar circumstances of time and place of the subject matter.

[9] *The Study of Political Science and Its Relation to Cognate Studies* (Cambridge: Cambridge University Press, 1929), pp. 25–26.

The subject matter of this theoretical concern is the contemporary political world. This branch of political science, which we call empirical theory, reflects in theoretical terms upon the contemporary political world. The political world, however, poses a formidable obstacle to such understanding. This obstacle is of a moral rather than an intellectual nature. Before we turn to the requirements of such an empirical theory and its central concept, we have to dispose of the moral problem with which political science must come to terms.

2 *The Commitments of Political Science*

The moral position of the political scientist in society is ambivalent; it can even be called paradoxical. For the political scientist is a product of the society which it is his mission to understand. He is also an active part, and frequently he seeks to be a leading part, of that society. To be faithful to his mission he would, then, have to overcome two limitations: the limitation of origin, which determines the perspective from which he looks at society, and the limitation of purpose, which makes him wish to remain a member in good standing of that society or even to play a leading role in it.

The mind of the political scientist is molded by the society which he observes. His outlook, his intellectual interests, and his mode of thinking are determined by the civilization, the national community, and all the particular religious, political, economic, and social groups of which he is a member. The "personal equation" of the political scientist both limits and directs his scholarly pursuits. The truth which a mind thus socially conditioned is able to grasp is likewise socially conditioned. The perspective of the observer determines what can be known and how it is to be understood. In consequence, the truth of political science is of necessity a partial truth.[1]

Upon a mind which by its very nature is unable to see more than part of the truth, society exerts its pressures, which confront the scholar with a choice between social advantage and the truth. The stronger the trend toward conformity within the society and the stronger the social ambitions within the individual scholar, the greater will be the temptation to sacrifice the moral commitment to the truth for social advantage. It follows that a respectable political science—respectable, that is, in terms of the society to be investigated—is in a sense a contradiction in terms. For a political science

[1] Cf. below, pp. 37 ff., the comment on the changing perspectives of political science. The views, expressed here necessarily in an aphoristic form, develop further what was said in *Scientific Man vs. Power Politics* (Chicago: University of Chicago Press, 1946), pp. 166–67.

which is faithful to its moral commitment of telling the truth about the political world cannot help telling society things it does not want to hear. The truth of political science is the truth about power, its manifestations, its configurations, its limitations, its implications, its laws. Yet one of the main purposes of society is to conceal these truths from its members. That concealment, that elaborate and subtle and purposeful misunderstanding of the nature of political man and of political society, is one of the cornerstones upon which all societies are founded.[2]

In his search for truth, the political scientist is hemmed in by society in three different ways: with regard to the objects, the results, and the methods of his inquiry. In so far as the political scientist yields to these pressures, he violates his moral commitment to discovering the truth of society.

In all societies certain social problems cannot be investigated at all, or only at grave risk to the investigator. The basic philosophic assumptions by which a society lives are beyond scientific investigation. For to question them is tantamount to questioning the worth of society itself, its justice, its rationality, its very right to exist. Thus a theocratic society cannot permit the scientific investigation of its religious beliefs. A Marxist society cannot tolerate scientific inquiry into dialectic materialism. In a society based upon racial discrimination, race problems are beyond the ken of social science. The profit motive and free enterprise are taboo in capitalistic societies, and the popular control of government will be taken for granted rather than questioned in democracies.

Similarly, in all societies certain results are beyond the reach of scientific inquiry, or they can be reached only at great personal risks. No Russian economist is likely to conclude publicly that capitalism is superior to communism, nor is an American professor of economics likely to maintain the reverse position. Social scientists in monogamic societies are not likely to see virtue in polygamy, and in a scientific civilization, they will emphasize the advantages of science rather than its liabilities.

What is true of the objects and results of scientific investigation is true likewise of its methods. In a humanistically or religiously

[2] For an elaboration of this theme see *ibid.*, pp. 155 ff.; *Politics among Nations* (2d ed.; New York: Alfred A. Knopf, 1954), pp. 80 ff.

oriented society, quantitative methods and experimental methods in general will be at a disadvantage. The same fate will befall the methods of philosophic inquiry and rational deduction in a scientifically oriented society. Thus different societies put the stamp of social approval or disapproval upon different methods of inquiry, and the political scientist is again confronted with a dilemma between his commitment to the truth and his concern with social convenience and advancement.

No lengthy explanation is needed to show that those different pressures against which the political scientist must maintain his moral commitment are multiplied in the actual situation in which he must make his decisions. For the political scientist to be a member of a pluralistic society, such as America, means actually to be a member of a multiplicity of sectional societies of a religious, political, social, and economic character, all exerting parallel or contradictory pressures upon him. All these groups are committed to a particular social "truth," and the political scientist cannot help deviating from one or the other of these "truths," if he does not want to forego his moral commitment to discovering *the* truth of society altogether.

These pressures account for the enormous positive and negative influence which foundations exert upon the objects, results, and methods of research. They reward certain types of research by supporting them and stimulate more research of the same type by promising to support it. On the other hand, they thwart or make impossible other types of research by not supporting them. The political scientist who wants to share in these rewards and, by doing so, gain prestige and power within the profession cannot help bring influenced by these positive and negative expectations in his concept of the social truth, of the methods by which to seek it, and of the relevant results to be expected from it.

A political science that is true to its moral commitment ought at the very least to be an unpopular undertaking. At its very best, it cannot help being a subversive and revolutionary force with regard to certain vested interests—intellectual, political, economic, social in general. For it must sit in continuous judgment upon political man and political society, measuring their truth, which is in good part a social convention, by its own. By doing so, it is not only an embarrassment to society intellectually, but it becomes also a political threat to the defenders or the opponents of the status quo or to both; for the social conventions about power, which political science cannot help subjecting to a critical—and often destructive—examination, are one of the main sources from which the claims to power, and hence power itself, derive.

It stands to reason that political science as a social institution could never hope even to approach this ideal of a completely disinterested commitment to the truth. For no social institution can completely transcend the limitations of its origin; nor can it endeavor to free itself completely from its commitments to the society of which it forms a part, without destroying itself in the attempt. Only rare individuals have achieved the Socratic distinction of unpopularity, social ostracism, and criminal penalties, which are the reward of constant dedication to the relevant truth in matters political. Yet while political science as a social institution cannot hope to approach the ideal, it must be aware of its existence; and the awareness of its moral commitment to the truth must mitigate the limitations of origin as well as the compromises between the moral commitment and social convenience and ambition, both of which no political scientist can fully escape. It is the measure of the degree to which political science in America meets the needs of society rather than its moral commitment to the truth that it is not only eminently respectable and popular, but—what is worse—that it is also widely regarded with indifference.

A political science that is mistreated and persecuted is likely to have earned that enmity because it has put its moral commitment to the truth above social convenience and ambition. It has penetrated beneath the ideological veil with which society conceals the true nature of political relations, disturbing the complacency of the powers-that-be and stirring up the conscience of society. A political science that is respected is likely to have earned that respect because it performs useful functions for society. It helps to cover political relations with the veil of ideologies which mollify the conscience of society; by justifying the existing power relations, it reassures the powers-that-be in their possession of power; it illuminates certain aspects of the existing power relations; and it contributes to the improvement of the technical operations of government. The relevance of this political science does not lie primarily in the discovery of the truth about politics but in its contribution to the stability of society.

A political science that is neither hated nor respected, but treated with indifference as an innocuous pastime, is likely to have retreated into a sphere that lies beyond the positive or negative interests of society. The retreat into the trivial, the formal, the methodological, the purely theoretical, the remotely historical—in short the politically irrelevant—is the unmistakable sign of a "non-controversial" political science which has neither friends nor enemies because it has no relevance for the great political issues in which society has a stake. History and methodology, in particular, become the protective armor which shields political science from contact with the political reality of the contemporary world. Political science, then, resembles what Tolstoi said modern history has become: "a deaf man answering questions which no one has asked him."

By being committed to a truth which is in this sense irrelevant, political science distorts the perspective under which the political world is seen. Certain eminent exceptions notwithstanding, it tends to pass in silence over such burning problems as the nature of power and of the truth about it, political ideologies, the political power of economic organizations, alternative foreign policies, the relations between government and public opinion, between tyranny and democracy, between objective truth and majority rule, as well as most of the other fundamental problems of contemporary democracy. By doing so, it makes it appear as though these problems either did not exist or were not important or were not susceptible to theoretical understanding. By its predominant concern with the irrelevant, it devaluates by implication the really important problems of politics.

Thus the political scientist, oblivious of his moral commitment, has completed his descent. The custodian of the truth and disturber of society's complacent conscience first descends to the role of the ideologue of society and mollifier of its conscience. This role still requiring a social commitment, not to the truth but to society as it is, and, hence, implying a long-term risk, the political scientist who wants to play absolutely safe must take another downward step. In this final role, concerning himself with issues in which nobody has a stake, he avoids the risk of social disapproval by foregoing the chance of social approbation. In the end, then, the concern with social convenience triumphs over social ambition. The commitment to the truth in matters political is dangerous all the time, while carrying within it the promise of ultimate triumph and spiritual perfection. The commitment to society as it is may be dangerous in the long run, carrying within it the promise of social rewards. Retreat from any commitment, to truth or to society, is free of danger, carrying within it no other reward but that freedom from danger itself.

What, then, ought a political science to be like, which does justice both to its scientific pretense and to its subject matter? The answer to this question, in so far as it concerns the scientific pretense of political science, derives from three basic propositions: the importance of political philosophy for political science, the identity of political theory and political science, the ability of political science to communicate objective and general truth about matters political.

Political science, like all science, is both in the general conception of its scope and method and in its particular concepts and operations a—largely unavowed—reflection of philosophic propositions. Even the most antiphilosophic science of politics is founded upon a philosophic understanding of the nature of man and society and of science itself. That understanding is philosophic in that its validity does not derive from its being capable of empirical verification (although it may be so verified) but rather from its logical consistency with certain general propositions which claim to present the true nature of reality. Political science needs neither to prove nor disprove the philosophic validity of these propositions but must assume the fallacy of some and the validity of others. The choice of these philosophic assumptions cannot but limit the scope, outlook, method, and purpose of political science. Political science is of necessity based upon, and permeated by, a total world view—religious, poetic as well as philosophic in nature—the validity of which it must take for granted.

During most of the history of Western political thought, the functions of political philosophy and political science were united in the same persons. The great political philosophers were also the great political scientists deriving concrete, empirically verifiable propositions from abstract philosophic ones. If the disintegration of the great political systems in the nineteenth century and the concomitant development of a separate political science to which we have referred above had led only to a division of labor between political philosophy and political science, no objection on principle would have been in order. However, the denial of the legitimacy and relevance of political philosophy for political science, prevalent in our day, is quite a different matter. For by denying that legitimacy and relevance, political science cuts itself off from the very roots to which it owes its life, which determine its growth, and which give it meaning. A political science that knows nothing but its own subject matter cannot even know that subject matter well. Contemporary political science, predominantly identified with a positivistic philosophy which is itself a denial of virtually all of the philosophic traditions of the West, has, as it were, mutilated itself by refusing itself access to the sources of insight available in the great philosophic systems of the past. Yet without that access it cannot even recognize, let alone understand, some of the perennial problems of politics which contemporary experience poses with almost unprecedented urgency.

Why is it that all men lust for power; why is it that even their noblest aspirations are tainted by that lust? Why is it that the political act, in its concern with man's power over man and the concomitant denial of the other man's freedom, carries within itself an element of immorality and puts upon the actor the stigma of guilt? Why is it, finally, that in politics good intentions do not necessarily produce good results and well-conceived plans frequently lead to failure in action, and why is it, conversely, that evil men have sometimes done great good in politics and improvident ones have frequently been successful? Here we are in the presence of the mystery, the sin, and the tragedy of politics. The problems that these questions raise are not scientific but philosophic in nature. Yet without the awareness of their legitimacy and relevance political science is precluded from even raising certain problems essential to the scientific understanding of politics.[3]

The same antiphilosophic position, prevalent in contemporary political science, is responsible for the common distinction between

[3] Cf. on this general problem the discussion on values in the social sciences in *America,* Vol. XCII (Oct. 9, 30, 1954).

political theory and political science. Theory, being by definition useless for practical purposes, was assigned that honorific but ineffectual position to which we have referred before, and main emphasis was placed upon science whose immediate usefulness for society the natural sciences seemed to have demonstrated.

Perhaps no event has had a more disastrous effect upon the development of American political science than this dichotomy between political theory and political science. For it has made political theory sterile by cutting it off from contact with the contemporary issues of politics, and it has tended to deprive political science of intellectual content by severing its ties with the Western tradition of political thought, its concerns, its accumulation of wisdom and knowledge. When American political science became sporadically aware of that impoverishment suffered by its own hands, it resorted to the remedy of adding more courses in political theory to the curriculum, or making them compulsory, or requiring knowledge of political theory in examinations. However, the remedy has been of no avail; for it derives from that very dichotomy between political theory and political science, which is at the root of the disease itself.

Of that disease, the plight of comparative government as an academic discipline provides a striking example. The comparison of different political institutions and systems requires logically a *tertium comparationis*, that is, a proposition which provides a standard for comparison. That standard, in order to be meaningful, cannot be merely empirical but must have a theoretical significance pointing to propositions of general validity. Comparative government, in order to be an academic discipline at all, then, requires a theory of politics that makes meaningful comparisons possible. In the absence of such a theory, it is not fortuitous that comparative government is hardly more than the description of, or at best a series of theories about, individual political institutions and systems without comparison.

The very distinction between political theory and political science is untenable. Historically and logically, a scientific theory is a system of empirically verifiable, general truths, sought for their own sake. This definition sets theory apart from practical knowledge, common-sense knowledge, and philosophy. Practical knowledge is interested only in truths which lend themselves to immediate practical application; common-sense knowledge is particular, fragmentary, and unsystematic; philosophic knowledge may be, but is not of necessity, empirically verifiable. What else, then, is scientific knowledge if not theory? It follows that political science cannot be made more theoretical by increasing emphasis upon the separate field of political theory but only by infusing all branches of political science susceptible of theoretical understanding with the spirit of theory.

The same philosophic position which has made political science disparage philosophy and separate itself from theory has also made it deny the existence and intelligibility of objective, general truths in matters political. That denial manifests itself in different ways on different levels of discourse. On the level of the general theory of democracy, it leads to the conclusion that the decision of the majority is the ultimate datum beyond which neither analysis nor evaluation can go. On the level of the analysis of political processes and decisions, it reduces political science to the explanation of the ways by which pressure groups operate and the decisions of government are reached. A political science thus conceived limits itself to the descriptive analysis of a complex of particular historic facts. Its denial of the existence and intelligibility of a truth about matters political that exists regardless of time and place implies a denial of the possibility of political theory both in its analytical and normative sense. What a political science of the past has discovered to be true, then, is true only in view of the peculiar and ephemeral historic circumstances of the time, carrying no lesson for us or any other period of history, or else is a mere reflection of the subjective preferences of the observer. The political science of the past is thus reduced, in so far as it seeks empirical analysis, to the description of an ephemeral historic situation and, as normative theory, becomes undistinguishable from political ideology.

This being so, contemporary political science is caught in the same relativistic dilemma and is no more able to transcend the limitations of time and place than were its predecessors. Either it will be tempted to overcome the limits of its relativist assumptions, whose nihilistic consequences it is unable to face, by taking flight in a subjective dogmatism that identifies the perspective and preferences of the observer with objective, general truth. Thus it becomes the ideology of a particular view of society, reflecting particular social interests. Or else political science will travel the relativistic road to the end and surrender the very concept of objective, general truth, concluding from the subjectivity of its own insights that there is nothing but opinion and that one opinion is as good as another, provided society does not object to it.

We cannot here enter into a detailed discussion of this fundamental problem; two observations must suffice. Political science, like any science, presupposes the existence and accessibility of objective, general truth. If nothing that is true regardless of time and place could be said about matters political, political science itself would be impossible. Yet the whole history of political thought is a living monument to that possibility. The relevance for ourselves of insights which political scientists of the past, reflecting upon matters political under the most diverse historic circumstances, considered to be true, points toward the existence of a store of objective, general truths which are as accessible to us as they were to our predecessors. If it were otherwise, how could we not only understand, but also appreciate, the political insights of a Jeremiah, a Kautilya, a Plato, a Bodin, or a Hobbes?

The content of political science is not to be determined a priori and in the abstract. A theory is a tool for understanding. Its purpose is to bring order and meaning to a mass of phenomena which without it would remain disconnected and unintelligible. There is a strong tendency in contemporary political science to force theory into a Procrustean bed by judging it by its conformity with certain pre-established methodological criteria rather than by its intrinsic contribution to knowledge and understanding. The result is an academic formalism which in its concern with methodological requirements tends to lose sight of the goal of knowledge and understanding which method must serve. One is reminded of the answer which Galileo is reported to have received when he invited some of his critics to look through a telescope at an astronomical phenomenon the existence of which they had denied; they said that there was no need for them to use this empirical instrument since according to Aristotle such a phenomenon could not exist. One is also reminded of the tendencies of the French literature of the seventeenth, the German literature of the eighteenth, and the French art of the nineteenth centuries to make the compliance with certain formal requirements the ultimate standard of literary and artistic value. And one takes heart from the impotence of such attempts to prevent for long the human mind from seeking and finding what is important in science, literature, and art.

The validity of a theory, then, does not depend upon its conformity with a priori assumptions, methodological or otherwise. It is subject to a purely pragmatic test. Does this theory broaden our knowledge and deepen our understanding of what is worth knowing? If it does, it is good, and if it does not, it is worthless, regardless of its a priori assumptions.

The content of theory, then, must be determined by the intellectual interest of the observer. What is it we want to know about politics? What concerns us most about it? What questions do we want a theory of politics to answer? The replies to these three questions determine the content of political science and the replies may well differ, not only from one period of history to another, but from one contemporaneous group of observers to another.

Hypothetically one can imagine as many theories of politics as there are legitimate intellectual perspectives from which to approach the political scene. But in a particular culture and a particular period of history, there is likely to be one perspective which for theoretical and practical reasons takes precedence over the others. At one time theoretical interest was focused upon the constitutional arrangements within which political relations take place; in view of the theoretical and practical problems to be solved, this was then a legitimate interest. At another time in the history of political science, theoretical interest was centered upon political institutions and their operations; in view of what was worth knowing and doing at that time, this theoretical interest was again legitimate. Thus political science is like a spotlight which, while trying to illuminate the whole political world, focuses in one period of history upon one aspect of politics and changes its focus in accordance with new theoretical and practical concerns.[4]

In our period of history, the justice and stability of political life is threatened, and our understanding of the political world is challenged, by the rise of totalitarianism on the domestic and international scene. The novel political phenomenon of totalitarianism

[4] Cf. the discussion of international relations below, pp. 98 ff.

37

puts in doubt certain assumptions about the nature of man and of society which we took for granted. It raises issues about institutions which we thought had been settled once and for all. It disrupts and overwhelms legal processes on which we had come to look as self-sufficient instruments of control. In one word, what has emerged from under the surface of legal and institutional arrangements as the distinctive, unifying element of politics is the struggle for power, elemental, undisguised, and all-pervading.[5] As recently as at the end of the Second World War, it was still held by conservatives, liberals, and Marxists alike either that the struggle for power was at worst a raucous pastime, safely regulated by law and channeled by institutions, or that it had been replaced in its dominant influence by economic competition, or that the ultimate triumph of liberal democracy or the classless society, which were expected to be close at hand, would make an end to it altogether. These assumptions and expectations have been refuted by the experience of our age. It is to the challenge of this refutation that political science must respond, as political practice must meet the challenge of that experience.

Yet while political science must thus come to terms with the problem of power, it must adapt its emphasis to the ever changing circumstances of the times. When the times tend to depreciate the element of power, it must stress its importance. When the times incline toward a monistic conception of power in the general scheme of things, it must show its limitations. When the times conceive of power primarily in military terms, it must call attention to the variety of factors which go into the power equation and, more particularly, to the subtle psychological relation of which the web of power is fashioned. When the reality of power is being lost sight of over its moral and legal limitations, it must point to that reality. When law and morality are judged as nothing, it must assign them their rightful place.

It may be pointed out in passing that all great contributions to political science, from Plato, Aristotle, and Augustine to *The Federalist* and Calhoun, have been responses to such challenges arising from political reality. They have not been self-sufficient theoretical developments pursuing theoretical concerns for their own sake.

[5] Cf. W. A. Robson, *The University Teaching of Social Sciences: Political Science* (Paris: UNESCO, 1954), pp. 17, 63.

Rather, they were confronted with a set of political experiences and problems which defied understanding with the theoretical tools at hand. Thus they had to face a new political experience, unencumbered by an intellectual tradition which might have been adequate to preceding experiences but which failed to illuminate the experience of the contemporary world. Thus they were compelled to separate in the intellectual tradition at their disposal that which is historically conditioned from that which is true regardless of time and place, to pose again the perennial problems of politics, and to reformulate the perennial truths of politics, in the light of the contemporary experience. This has been the task of political science throughout its history and this is the task of political science today.[6] There is, then, in political science what might be called a "higher practicality," which responds to practical needs not by devising practical remedies, but by broadening and deepening the understanding of the problems from which the practical needs arose.

By making power its central concept, a theory of politics does not presume that none but power relations control political action. What it must presume is the need for a central concept which allows the observer to distinguish the field of politics from other social spheres, to orient himself in the maze of empirical phenomena which make up that field, and to establish a measure of rational order within it. As economics is centered upon the concept of interest defined as wealth, its accumulation and distribution, so political science is centered upon the concept of interest defined as power, its accumulation, distribution, and control. A central concept, such as power, then provides a kind of rational outline of politics, a map of the political scene. Such a map does not provide a complete description of the political landscape as it is in a particular period of history. It rather provides the timeless features of its geography distinct from their ever changing historic setting. Such a map, then, will tell us what are the rational possibilities for travel from one spot on the map to another, and which road is most likely to be taken by certain travelers under certain conditions. Thus it imparts a measure of rational order to the observing mind and, by doing so, establishes one of the conditions for successful action.

[6] Cf. Alfred Cobban's important article, "The Decline of Political Theory," *Political Science Quarterly,* LXVIII (1953), 321–32.

A theory of politics, by the very fact of painting a rational picture of the political scene, points to the contrast between what the political scene actually is and what it tends to be, but can never completely become. The difference between the empirical reality of politics and a theory of politics is like the difference between a photograph and a painted portrait. The photograph shows everything that can be seen by the naked eye. The painted portrait does not show everything that can be seen by the naked eye, but it shows one thing that the naked eye cannot see: the human essence of the person portrayed. Thus a theory of politics must seek to depict the rational essence of its subject matter.

By doing so, a theory of politics cannot help implying that the rational elements of politics are superior in value to the contingent ones and that they are so in two respects. They are so in view of the theoretical understanding which theory seeks; for its very possibility and the extent to which it is possible depend upon the rationality of its subject matter. A theory of politics must value that rational nature of its subject matter also for practical reasons. It must assume that a rational policy is of necessity a good policy; for only such a policy minimizes risks and maximizes benefits and, hence, complies both with the moral precept of prudence and the political requirement of success. A theory of politics must want the photographic picture of the political scene to resemble as much as possible its painted portrait.

Hence, a theory of politics presents not only a guide to understanding but also an ideal for action. It presents a map of the political scene not only in order to understand what that scene is like but also in order to show the shortest and safest road to a given objective. The use of theory, then, is not limited to rational explanation and anticipation. A theory of politics also contains a normative element.

A curriculum of political science which would try to put such a theoretical understanding of politics into practice for the purposes of teaching would have to eliminate all those subjects which do not serve this theoretical understanding. It would also have to add subjects which at present are not included but which are essential to such understanding.

The process of elimination must move on two fronts. First, it

40

must affect those subjects which have been traditionally included in the field but which have no organic connection with its subject matter or with the perspective from which contemporary political science ought to view it. In this category belong, for instance, all the legal subjects with which political science concerns itself because the law schools at one time did not. However, this practical consideration is unfounded today when law schools offer courses in jurisprudence and administrative, constitutional, and international law. Political science is not interested in any legal subject per se, yet it has indeed a vital interest in the interrelations between law and politics. It must look at law not as a self-contained system of rules of conduct, but rather as both the creation and the creator of political forces.

Second, there has been a strong tendency in political science to add to the curriculum subjects which happen to be of practical importance at a particular moment, regardless of their theoretical relevance. However, what is worth knowing for practical reasons is not necessarily worth knowing on theoretical grounds. A certain innovation in municipal administration or international organization may attract at one time wide attention by virtue of the practical results it promises, or the political developments in a certain area of the world may become a matter of topical interest for public opinion. It still remains to be shown on theoretical grounds that such topics ought to be included as independent subjects in the curriculum of political science. On a limited scale this problem raises again the issue of liberal versus vocational education.

The additions to the curriculum of political science, too, must be of two different kinds. On the one hand, the curriculum must take into account the fact that its central concept is a general social phenomenon which manifests itself most typically in the political sphere but is not limited to it. The phenomenon of power and the social configurations to which it gives rise play an important, yet largely neglected, part in all social life. A configuration, such as the balance of power, is a general social phenomenon to be found on all levels of social interaction. The theoretical understanding of specifically political phenomena and configurations requires the understanding of the extent to which these political phenomena and configurations are merely the specific instances of general social phenomena and configurations and the extent to which they grow out of their specific political environment. One of the cornerstones of the curriculum of political science, then, ought to be political sociology, which deals with the phenomenon of power and the social configurations to which it gives rise in general, with special reference, of course, to those in the political sphere.[7]

On the other hand, the contemporary political scene is characterized by the interaction between the political and economic spheres. This interaction runs counter to the liberal assumption and requirement of actual separation, which is reflected in the academic separation of the two fields. This interaction reverts to a situation which existed before political science was established as an academic discipline and which was reflected by the academic fusion of the two fields in the form of political economy. The curriculum of political science must take theoretical notice of the actual development of private governments in the form of giant corporations and labor unions. These organizations exercise power within their own organizational limits, in their relations to each other, and in their relations to the state. The state, in turn, exercises power over them. These power relations constitute a new field for theoretical understanding.[8]

Yet what political science needs above all changes in the curriculum—even though it needs them too—is the restoration of the intellectual and moral commitment to the truth about matters political for its own sake. That restoration becomes the more urgent in the measure in which the general social and the particular academic environment tends to discourage it. Society in general and that particular society of which he is a professional member pull and push the political scientist toward being useful here and now and playing it safe forever. If the political scientist cannot resist these pushes and pulls by repairing to the vision of the searcher for the political truth, which Plato brought to the world, and of the professor of the political truth, which the prophets exemplified, what will become of him as a scholar, and what will become of a society which has deprived

[7] Cf. the important but largely neglected monograph by Frederick Watkins, *The State as a Concept of Political Science* (New York: Harper & Bros., 1934), esp. pp. 81 ff.

[8] See below, chapter 7.

itself of the ability to measure the conflicting claims of interested parties against the truth, however dimly seen?

A society which has thus closed its eyes to the truth about itself has cut its tie with what connects it with the mainsprings of civilization. For without at least the assumption that objective, general truth in matters political exists and can be known, order and justice and truth itself become the mere by-products of ever changing power relations. In such a society the political scientist has still an important part to play: he becomes the ideologue who gives the appearance of truth and justice to power and the claim for it.

Political science, as we have tried to show before, can indeed not help performing such an ideological function. Yet it is the measure of the awareness and fulfilment of its mission as a science of politics that it is conscious of the existence of an objective, general truth behind ideological rationalizations and justifications and that it seeks the comprehension of that truth. In order to fulfil that mission the political scientist must live within the political world without being of it. He must watch it with intense interest and sympathy; yet the gaze of his mind and the impulse of his will must transcend it. He must understand it as well and better than does the politician, and yet his ambition has nothing in common with the latter's. His primary moral commitment is not to society but to the truth and, hence, to society only in so far as it lives up to the truth. Only so can he at least approach the ideal of political justice, he alone among those concerned with political matters; for in the words of Goethe: "The actor is always unjust; nobody has justice but the observer."

At such impracticality in action and ambivalence in moral commitment, the Socratic handmaids of all ages, the born servants of society, can only laugh. Of them, however clever and witty they may be, history reports nothing but laughter. Yet what they laugh at is the moral and intellectual outlook from which stems our heritage of political knowledge and wisdom.

PART **II**

DILEMMAS

OF UNDERSTANDING

INTERNATIONAL POLITICS

3 The Commitments of a Theory of International Politics

With these dilemmas all attempts at a theoretical understanding of politics must come to terms. The intensity of the dilemma is proportional to the political involvement of the observer and to the political relevance of the subject matter. Under present conditions, it is likely to be greater in the field of economic policy than in the field of municipal government. That intensity is greatest in the sphere of international politics, and it is compounded by the presence of a dilemma which is peculiar to that sphere.

One basic fact distinguishes international politics from all other types of politics and exerts a persuasive influence on the practice of international politics as well as upon its theoretical understanding. That fact concerns the relationship between international society and its constituent members, the nation states. The constituent members of domestic society, individuals and subnational groups, live in an integrated society, which holds supreme power and is the repository of the highest secular values and the recipient of the ultimate secular loyalties. Yet these domestic societies are the constituent members of international society which must defer to them in terms of power, values, and loyalties. What sets international society apart from other societies is the fact that its strength—political, moral, social—is concentrated in its members, its own weakness being the reflection of that strength.

A theory of international politics has the task, in applying the general principles of politics to the international sphere, to reformulate, modify, and qualify these principles in the light of that distinctive quality of international politics. A theory of international politics plays, as it were, the tune which the general theory of politics provides, but it plays it in a key and with variations which stem from the peculiarities of international society. The national interest defined in terms of power, the precarious uncertainty of the international balance of power, the weakness of international morality,

47

the decentralized character of international law, the deceptiveness of ideologies, the inner contradictions of international organization, the democratic control of foreign policy, the requirements of diplomacy, the problem of war—of these phenomena and problems of international politics theory must take account in terms of the general principles of politics which reveal themselves on the international scene in peculiar manifestations, owing to the peculiar character of international society.

This is obviously not the place to attempt a demonstration of the correctness of this view; for such a demonstration would require the development of a substantive theory of international politics. Since the attempt to do this has been made elsewhere and since this chapter deals with the requirements and problems of such a theory rather than with its substance, it must suffice here to point to the great and peculiar difficulties which stand in the way of the development of such a theory and to the relatively narrow limits within which it seems to be possible. Two facts deserve special attention in this context: the implicit rather than explicit character of past attempts at a theory of international politics; and the peculiar difficulties impeding theoretical understanding which arise from the relationship of power, morality, and the national interest as it reveals itself on the international scene.

That men throughout the ages have thought little of a theory of international politics is borne out by the fact that but rarely an explicit attempt to develop such a theory has been made; as rare instances of such atempts, Kautilya and Machiavelli come to mind. Men have generally dealt with international politics on one of three levels, all alien to theory: history, reform, or pragmatic manipulation. That is to say, they have endeavored to detect the facts and meaning of international politics through the knowledge of the past; or they have tried to devise a pattern of international politics more in keeping with an abstract ideal than the empirical one; or they have sought to meet the day-by-day issues of international politics by trial and error.

Yet each of these approaches presupposes, and in actuality reveals, a theoretical conception of what international politics is all about, however fragmentary, implicit, and unavowed such a theoretical conception may be. In historians with a philosophic bent, such as

Thucydides and Ranke, the history of foreign policy appears as a mere demonstration of certain theoretical assumptions which are always present beneath the surface of historical events to provide the standards for their selection and to give them meaning. In such historians of international politics, theory is like the skeleton which, invisible to the naked eye, gives form and function to the body. What distinguishes such a history of international politics from a theory is not so much its substance as its form. The historian presents his theory in the form of a historical recital using the historic sequence of events as demonstration of his theory. The theoretician, dispensing with the historical recital, makes the theory explicit and uses historic facts in bits and pieces to demonstrate his theory.

What holds true of the historian of international politics applies also to the reformer. He is, as it were, a "forward-looking" theoretician. His scheme of reform provides an explicit theory of what international politics ought to be, derived from an explicit or implicit theory of what international politics actually is. What has prevented William Penn, the Abbé de St. Pierre, or contemporary World Federalists from developing a complete theory of international politics is their primary concern with practical reform rather than the absence of theoretical elements in their thinking.

This same practical concern has prevented the practitioners of international politics from developing an explicit theory of what they are doing. Even a perfunctory perusal of the speeches, state papers, and memoirs of such diverse types of statesmen as Bismarck, Wilson, Churchill, and Stalin, shows that their relationship to theory is even closer than we found that of the historian to be. For the great statesman differs from the run-of-the-mill diplomatist and politician exactly in that he is able to see the issues confronting him as special cases of general and objective—that is, theoretical—propositions. Here again it is not the substance of his thinking but the form in which it manifests itself, which distinguishes the statesman from the theoretician of international politics. Here again it is his practical concern, not his alienation from theory as such, which prevents him from becoming a theoretician. Yet it illuminates the theoretical essence of the statesman's thinking that whenever practical concerns receded into the background or seemed best served by theoretical considerations, the four great statesmen mentioned above naturally transformed themselves from practitioners into theoreticians, making explicit in systematic or aphoristic form the theoretical foundations of their statecraft.

These observations support the case for the possibility and even the necessity of the theoretical understanding of international politics. However, by showing the scarcity of explicit, systematic theories of international politics, they point to the difficulties which stand in the way of the development of such a theory. The relationship of power, morality, and the national interest constitutes one of these difficulties.

On the domestic plane, the relationship of power, morality, and interest is so obvious as to be hardly open to controversy. In domestic politics, individuals pursue their interests defined in terms of power. These interests, in view of their relation to power, have three outstanding characteristics. First, the interests to which power attaches itself and which it serves are as varied and manifold as are the possible social objectives of the members of a given society. Second, these interests shift continuously from the center of political attention and emphasis to its margin until they may fade out of the political picture altogether, only to come back again when circumstances change. Third, measured by the interests of society as a whole, these interests are partial in nature, and their existence within a transcendent whole both limits their nature and the manner of their pursuit. The very nature of the interests with which the member of a domestic society may identify himself is determined by the "common good" as society as a whole understands it, and so are the means by which he may pursue those interests.

The relationship between interest and power is different on the international plane. Here power is wedded to the interests of a particular nation. And while it is true, as will be pointed out in the next chapter, that it has not always been so and it is not likely to be so forever, the relatively constant relationship between power and the national interest is the basic datum for purposes of both theoretical analysis and political practice. The content of the national interest is likewise constant over long periods of history. All the ideal and material elements which make up that content are subordinated at the very least to those requirements—not susceptible to rapid change—upon which the survival of the nation and the preservation of its identity depend. Finally—and most importantly—the national interest is not a fraction of a transcendent, comprehensive social interest to which it is subordinated and by which it is limited both as to content and to the means employed for its realization. The period of history when the national interest could be said to be so subordinated and limited has been replaced by one in which the nation has become the highest secular social organization and its interest the common focus of secular social interests.

However, it is not these characteristics of the national interest which make theoretical understanding difficult. Quite to the contrary, the constancy and supremacy of the national interest, taken by themselves, favor theoretical analysis. Theoretical complications arise from the relationship which exists between morality, on the one hand, power and the national interest, on the other. Here again it is revealing to trace the different manifestations of the same theoretical structure in the domestic and international sphere.

The relationship between morality, on the one hand, power and interest, on the other, is threefold. First, morality limits the interests that power seeks and the means that power employs to that end. Certain ends cannot be pursued and certain means cannot be employed in a given society within a certain period of history by virtue of the moral opprobrium that attaches to them. Second, morality puts the stamp of its approval upon certain ends and means which thereby not only become politically feasible but also acquire a positive moral value. These moral values, then, become an intrinsic element of the very interests that power seeks. Third, morality serves interests and power as their ideological justification.

In the domestic sphere morality performs all these three functions effectively. It directs the choice of the means and ends of power away from what society considers to be harmful to its purposes and toward what it regards to be beneficial to them. What we call a civilized political community is the result of the efficiency with which morality performs these negative and positive functions. Yet civilization requires more than the negative and positive limitations of the means and ends of politics. It also requires the mitigation of the struggle for power by glossing over power interests and power relations and making them appear as something different than what they actually are.

This ideological function, which morality performs on the domestic scene together with the other two, has become its main function for international politics. On the international scene, the individual nation is by far the strongest moral force, and the limitations which a supranational morality is able to impose today upon international politics are both fewer and weaker than they were almost at any time since the end of the Thirty Years' War. The individual nation, thus having become virtually the highest moral unit on earth, has naturally been tempted to equate its own moral values with morality as such, and especially the most powerful nations have found it hard to resist that temptation. In consequence, the main function which morality performs today for international politics is ideological. It makes it appear as though the interests and policies of individual nations were the manifestations of universal moral principles. The part aspires to become the whole, and there is very little to counteract that aspiration. It is not so much morality which limits individual interests, as it is the individual interests which identify themselves with morality.

This identification of the interests and power of the nation with universal morality confronts theoretical understanding with formidable difficulties. The distinction between ideology and morality becomes blurred as does the distinction between ideology and theory. The advocate of the national crusade appears not only to promote universal moral values but also to have discovered theoretical truth. By contrast, the theoretician who seeks the truth hidden beneath these veils of ideology cannot help being in an intellectually and morally awkward position. His very probing of the moral pretenses of national interest and national power in the name of a higher truth and a higher morality makes him suspect of being indifferent to all truth and all morality. Thus to write a theory of international politics is not an easy thing. Perhaps this is why we have so many ideologies, and so few theories, of international politics.

The difficulties which stand in the way of the theoretical understanding of international politics have grown more formidable with the ever more intensive identification of national purposes and policies with absolute truth and universal morality. Yet at the same time the need for such understanding has become paramount in an age in which the nation, deeming itself intellectually and morally self-sufficient, threatens civilization and the human race itself with extinction. To look in such circumstances at one's own nation and its relations with other nations objectively, dispassionately, critically has never been more difficult, hazardous, and necessary than it is today. This task presents a theory of international politics with its supreme intellectual and moral challenge. Its performance would constitute not only an intellectual and moral but a political triumph as well. For it would indicate that at least the mind of man has succeeded in mastering that blind and potent monster which in the name of God or history is poised for universal destruction.

4 *The Problem of the National Interest*

We have suggested that a theory of politics, domestic or international, requires a central concept. For a general theory of politics, the concept of interest defined as power serves as the central focus, while a theory of international politics must be focused on the concept of the national interest. The controversy which has arisen since the end of the Second World War around the concept of the national interest differs from the great historical debates on American foreign policy in that it raises not necessarily a specific issue of American foreign policy but the fundamental issue of the nature of all foreign policy and of all politics as well.

The great debates of the past, such as the one over intervention versus neutrality in 1793, expansion versus the status quo before the Mexican and after the Spanish-American War, international cooperation versus isolation in the twenties, intervention versus abstention in the late thirties—all evolved around clear-cut issues of foreign policy. In 1793 you were in favor of going to war on the side of France or of remaining neutral. In the 1840's you approved of the annexation of Texas or you did not. At the turn of the century you supported overseas expansion or you were against it. In the twenties you advocated joining the League of Nations or staying out of it. In the late thirties you wanted to oppose the Axis Powers by all means short of war or you wanted to abstain from intervening. While what separates the two schools of thought, the "utopian" and the "realist," which have developed around the concept of the national interest can sometimes be expressed in terms of alternative foreign policies, more often it cannot. Frequently and typically, the very same policies can be and are being supported by both schools of thought. What sets them apart is not necessarily a matter of practical judgment but of philosophies and standards of thought.

The issue the present debate raises concerns the nature of all politics and, more particularly, of the American tradition in foreign policy. The history of modern political thought is the story of a contest between two schools which differ fundamentally in their conception of the nature of man, society, and politics. One believes that a rational and moral political order, derived from universally valid abstract principles, can be achieved here and now. It assumes the essential goodness and infinite malleability of human nature and attributes the failure of the social order to measure up to the rational standards to lack of knowledge and understanding, obsolescent social institutions, or the depravity of certain isolated individuals or groups. It trusts in education, reform, and the sporadic use of force to remedy these deficiencies.[1]

The other school believes that the world, imperfect as it is from the rational point of view, is the result of forces inherent in human nature. To improve the world one must work with those forces, not against them. This being inherently a world of opposing interests and of conflict among them, moral principles can never be fully realized, but at best approximated through the ever temporary balancing of interests and the ever precarious settlement of conflicts. This school, then, sees in a system of checks and balances a universal principle for all pluralist societies.[2] It appeals to historic precedent rather than to abstract principles and aims at achievement of the lesser evil rather than of the absolute good.

The conflict between two basic conceptions of man and politics is at the bottom of the present controversy. It provided in the sixteenth, seventeenth, and eighteenth centuries the issue for the debate on the reason of state of which Friedrich Meinecke has given the definitive account. It separated on the occasion of the neutrality proclamation of 1793 Washington and Hamilton from their opponents, and Hamilton has indeed given in the "Pacificus" and "Americanus" letters the classic American formulation of the philosophy of the national interest. In general philosophic terms it found its

---

[1] This is the ideal type of the utopian position rather than the empirical description of any particular historic type. In actuality, and this is true particularly of the present, the utopian position in international affairs is not always consistent with its philosophic premises.

[2] It ought not to need special emphasis that a principle of social conduct, in contrast to a law of nature, allows of, and even presupposes, conduct in violation of the principle. Robert W. Tucker, in "Professor Morgenthau's Theory of Political 'Realism,'" *American Political Science Review,* XLVI (March, 1952), 214–24, has missed this and many other points in his zeal to find contradictions where there are none.

classic expression in the polemic of Burke against the philosophy of the French Revolution.

In order to refute a theory which pretends to be scientific, it is first necessary to understand what a scientific theory is. A scientific theory, as pointed out before, is an attempt to bring order and meaning to a mass of phenomena which without it would remain disconnected and unintelligible. Anyone who disputes the scientific character of such a theory either must produce a theory superior in these scientific functions to the one attacked or must, at the very least, demonstrate that the facts as they actually are do not lend themselves to the interpretation that the theory has put upon them. When a historian tells us that the balance of power is not a universal principle of politics, domestic and international, that it was practiced in Europe only for a limited period and never by the United States, that it ruined the states that practiced it,[3] it is incumbent upon him to tell us how we can dispose by means of theory of the historic data by which, for instance, David Hume demonstrated the universality of the balance of power and Paul Scott Mowrer[4] and Alfred Vagts[5] its practice by the United States; what Kautilya was writing about in the fourth century B.C. when he summarized the theoretical and practical tradition of Indian statecraft in terms of the balance of power; what the Greek city-states, the Roman republic, and the medieval emperors and popes were doing if they did not apply the principles of the balance of power; and how the nations that either neglected these principles or applied them wrongly suffered political and military defeat and even extinction, while the nation that applied these principles most consistently and consciously, that is, Great Britain, enjoyed unrivaled power for an unparalleled length of time.

The historian who wishes to replace the balance of power as the guiding principle of American foreign policy with the "humanitarian and pacific traditions" of the "coördinate state"[6] must first of

---

[3] Tannenbaum in "The Balance of Power versus the Coördinate State," *Political Science Quarterly*, LXVII (June, 1952), 173, and in "The American Tradition in Foreign Relations," *Foreign Affairs*, XXX (October, 1951), 31–50.

[4] *Our Foreign Affairs* (New York: E. P. Dutton & Co., 1924), pp. 246 ff.

[5] "The United States and the Balance of Power," *Journal of Politics*, III (November, 1941), 401–49.

[6] Tannenbaum, "The Balance of Power versus the Coördinate State," p. 173.

all explain how it has come about that the thirteen original states expanded into the full breadth and a good deal of the length of a continent, until today the strategic frontiers of the United States run parallel to the coastline of Asia and along the River Elbe. If such are the results of policies based upon "humanitarian and pacific traditions," never in the history of the world has virtue been more bountifully rewarded! Yet our historian must explain not only the great sweep of American expansion but also the specific foreign policies which in their historic succession make up that sweep. Is it easier to explain the successive shifts of American support from Great Britain to France and back again from the beginning of King George's War in 1744 to the War of 1812 in terms of the "coördinate state" than in terms of the balance of power? The same question might be asked about the postponement of the recognition of the independence of the Spanish colonies until 1822, when the Floridas had been acquired from Spain and Spain had thereby been deprived of the ability to challenge the United States from within the hemisphere. The same question might be asked about the Monroe Doctrine itself, about Lincoln's policies toward Great Britain and France, and about our successive policies with regard to Mexico and the Caribbean. One could go on and pick out at random any foreign policy pursued by the United States from the beginning to the First World War, and one would hardly find a policy, with the exception perhaps of the War of 1812, that could not be made intelligible by reference to the national interest defined in terms of power—political, military, and economic—rather than by reference to the principle of the "coordinate state." This inevitable outcome of such an inquiry is well summarized in these words:

Ease and prosperity have made us wish the whole world to be as happy and well to do as ourselves; and we have supposed that institutions and principles like our own were the simple prescription for making them so. And yet, when issues of our own interests arose, we have not been unselfish. We have shown ourselves kin to all the world, when it came to pushing an advantage. Our action against Spain in the Floridas, and against Mexico on the coasts of the Pacific; our attitude toward first the Spaniards, and then the French, with regard to the control of the Mississippi; the unpitying force with which we thrust the Indians to the wall wherever they stood in our way, have suited our professions of peacefulness and justice and liberality no better than the aggressions of other nations that were strong and not to be gainsaid. Even Mr. Jefferson, philanthropist and champion of peaceable and modest government though he was, exemplified this double temper of the people he ruled. "Peace is our passion," he had declared; but the passion abated when he saw the mouth of the Mississippi about to pass into the hands of France. Though he had loved France and hated England, he did not hesitate then what language to hold. "There is on the globe," he wrote to Mr. Livingston at Paris, "one single spot the possessor of which is our natural and habitual enemy. The day that France takes possession of New Orleans seals the union of two nations, who, in conjunction, can maintain exclusive possession of the sea. From that moment we must marry ourselves to the British fleet and nation." Our interests must march forward, altruists though we are; other nations must see to it that they stand off, and do not seek to stay us.

This realist appraisal of the American tradition in foreign policy was published in 1901 in the *Atlantic Monthly*. Its author was a professor of jurisprudence and political economy at Princeton by the name of Woodrow Wilson.[7]

Nothing more needs to be said to demonstrate that facts do not support a revision of American diplomatic history that tries to substitute "humanitarian and pacifist traditions" and the "coördinate state" for power politics and the balance of power as the guiding principle of American foreign policy. What, then, does support it? Three things: the way American statesmen have spoken about American foreign policy; the legal fiction of the "coördinate state"; finally, and foremost, an emotional urge to justify American foreign policy in humanitarian, pacifist terms.

It is elementary that the character of a foreign policy can be ascertained only through the examination of the political acts performed and of the foreseeable consequences of these acts. Thus we can find out what statesmen have actually done, and from the foreseeable consequences of their acts we can surmise what their objectives might have been. Yet examination of the facts is not enough. To give meaning to the factual raw material of history, we must approach historical reality with a kind of rational outline, a map which suggests to us the possible meanings of history. In other words, we put ourselves in the position of a statesman who must meet a certain problem of foreign policy under certain circumstances and ask ourselves: what are the rational alternatives from which a statesman

---

[7] "Democracy and Efficiency," *Atlantic Monthly*, LXXXVII (March, 1901), 293–94.

may choose who must meet this problem under these circumstances, presuming always that he acts in a rational manner, and which of these rational alternatives was this particular statesman, acting under these circumstances, likely to choose? It is the testing of this rational hypothesis against the actual facts and their consequences which gives meaning to the facts of history and makes the scientific writing of political history possible.

In the process of writing the history of foreign policy the interpretations by statesmen of their own acts, especially if they are made for public consumption, must needs have a strictly subsidiary place. The public self-interpretation by actors on the political scene is itself, of course, a political act which seeks to present a certain policy to its presumed supporters in terms of their moral and political folklore and to those against which it is directed in terms which intend to embarrass and deceive. Such declarations may indeed shed light upon the character and objectives of the policy pursued if they are considered in conjunction with, and in subordination to, rational hypotheses, actions, and likely consequences. Yet it is quite a different matter to interpret the American tradition of foreign policy in the light of a collection of official statements which, like most such statements, present humanitarian and pacifist justifications for the policies pursued. If anybody should be bold enough to write a history of world politics with so uncritical a method he would easily and well-night inevitably be driven to the conclusion that from Timur to Hitler and Stalin the foreign policies of all nations were inspired by the ideals of humanitarianism and pacifism. The absurdity of the result is commensurate with the defects of the method.

It is only from a method that accepts the declarations of statesmen as evidence of the character of the policies pursued that the principle of the "coördinate state" receives a semblance of plausibility. Statesmen and international lawyers have been wont to speak of the "equal dignity" of all states, regardless of "wealth, power, size, population or culture,"[8] which I take the principle of the "coördinate state" to mean. It is also referred to as the principle of "federalism in international relations."[9] As its prime examples are cited the relations amongst the states of the Union, the states of the American

[8] Tannenbaum, "The Balance of Power versus the Coördinate State," p. 177.
[9] *Ibid.*

system, the members of the Commonwealth of Nations, and the members of the Swiss Confederation. If the whole world were organized in accordance with this principle, as are already these four political entities, it is assumed that the freedom, dignity, and peace of all nations would then be assured.

There is no need to examine the theoretical and practical merits of the principle of the "coördinate state," because for none of the four political entities mentioned does the idea of the "coördinate state" provide the principle of political organization. The equality of the states as the political foundation of the United States became obsolescent when Chief Justice Marshall's Supreme Court resolved the ambiguity of the Constitution in favor of the federal government, and it became obsolete when the Civil War proved Chief Justice Marshall's point. The equality of the states survives today only in the shadow and by virtue of the federal government's political supremacy, and without the cohesive force of that supremacy there would be no union of equal states to begin with. That these powers of the federal government are limited and qualified by the principle of federalism, that is, by the constitutionally granted powers of the states, is quite a different matter; it concerns the distribution of powers between federal government and states within a general system of checks and balances, but has nothing to do with the equality of the states as the alleged political foundation of the American system of government. With the exception of the equality of senatorial representation, the principle of the equality of the states is today, as it has been for almost a century, devoid of political content. It serves only as a principle of regional organization, of administrative decentralization, and, above all, of constitutional rhetoric. What it really signifies was pointed out more than fifty years ago by W. A. Dunning when he summarized his answer to the question "Are the states equal under the Constitution?" by saying that "the theory of equal states falls to the ground."[10]

Similarly, the federalism of Switzerland is the result of a long series of civil wars, the last one fought a little more than a century ago, which established the predominance of the German-speaking cantons within the confederation. Here too, it is the existence of

[10] William Archibald Dunning, *Essays on the Civil War and Reconstruction and Related Topics* (New York: P. Smith, 1931), p. 351.

predominant power, located in one segment of the federal system, which makes federalism possible in the first place.

By the same token, the unchallengeable supremacy of the United States within the Western Hemisphere has throughout been the backbone of the system of American states. As long as this supremacy is secure, there is, on the one hand, no need for the United States to assert it in the political and military sphere, and, taking it for granted, the United States can well afford to pursue a policy of the Good Neighbor; and there is, on the other hand, no opportunity for the other members of the system to challenge that supremacy effectively. This is what the principle of the "coördinate state" amounts to in the Western Hemisphere. Consequently, whenever there was even a remote possibility that the supremacy of the United States might be challenged, generally through instigation from outside the hemisphere, the United States asserted its superior power within the hemisphere and acted as all states must act under similar conditions.

Whatever possibility for common political action there remains among the members of the Commonwealth of Nations is the result of the interests which these members may have in common. In other words, the member states may work together or each of them may work with other nations, as their interests dictate. Their membership in the Commonwealth, as the examples of India, South Africa, Australia, and New Zealand clearly show, has no influence upon this decision; that membership is but a faint remembrance of the times when Great Britain could secure co-operation among the member states on its terms by virtue of its superior power.

What, then, have these four examples of the "coördinate state" in common which would establish them as a distinct type of interstate relationship, and what conclusions can be drawn from them for the organization of the world? The only thing that these four examples seem to have really in common is the legal stipulation of the equality of the members of the respective systems, and this characteristic is not peculiar to them, but a general principle of international law applicable to all sovereign states. In the political sphere they seem to have nothing in common at all. What they tend to show, however, is the decisive importance of the distribution of political power for the operation of federal and egalitarian relations among states. The political cohesion of a federal system is the result of superior power located in some part of it. It is by virtue of its superior power that the predominant part can afford to grant the other members of the federal system a measure of equality in the non-political sphere. These observations bring us back to power politics and the balance of power to which the principle of the "coördinate state" was supposed to be the alternative.

In truth, it is not the disinterested consideration of facts which has given birth to the theory of the "coördinate state." That theory is rather the response to an emotional urge, and since this emotion is not peculiar to a particular author but typical of a popular reaction to the new role which the United States must play in world affairs, it deserves a brief analysis.

One of the great experiences of our time which have impressed themselves upon the American mind is the emergence of the United States as a nation among other nations, exposed to the same opportunities, temptations, risks, and liabilities to which other nations have been traditionally exposed. This experience becomes the more shocking if it is compared with the expectation with which we fought the Second World War. We expected from that war a reaffirmation of the secure, detached, and independent position in world affairs which we had inherited from the founding fathers and which we had been successful in preserving at least to the First World War. By avoiding what we thought had been Wilson's mistakes, we expected to emerge from that war if not more independent, certainly more secure than we were when we entered it. In fact, not even in the early days of the Republic were we more exposed to danger from abroad than we are today, and never had we less freedom of action in taking care of our interests than we have today.

It is naturally shocking to recognize that a happy chapter in the history of the nation and in one's own way of life has come to an end. There are those who reconcile themselves to the inevitable, albeit with sorrow rather than with glee, and try to apply the lessons of the past to the tasks at hand. There are others who try to escape from a disappointing and threatening reality into the realm of fantasy. Three such escapist fantasies have arisen in our midst in response to the challenge of American world leadership and power: the fantasy of needless American participation in war, the fantasy of American treason, and the fantasy of American innocence.

The first of these fantasies presumes that the present predicament is a result not of necessity but of folly, the folly of American statesmen who needlessly intervened in two world wars. The second of these fantasies attributes the present predicament to treason in high places whereby the fruits of victory were handed to the enemy. The third of these fantasies denies that the predicament is real and prefers to think of it as an intellectual fraud perpetrated upon the American people. To suport this fictional denial of the actualities of the present, it draws upon a fictional account of the past. The United States does not need to bear at present the intellectual, moral, and political burdens which go with involvement in power politics and the maintenance of the balance of power; for it has never borne them in the past, never having been thus involved. The golden age of past political innocence sheds its glow upon a but seemingly less innocent present and promises a future in which all the world will follow the example of America, forswear power politics and the balance of power, and accept the principle of the "coördinate state." Our alliances, we are told, have nothing to do with the balance of power but aim at the "organization of as much of the world as we can upon the basis of the coördinate state. . . . It may prove impossible under present conditions to build such a system without having to fight a war with Russia, but then at least we will be fighting, as we did before, for the thing we consider worth defending with our lives and treasure."[11] Thus a fictional account of the American past, begun as an act of uncalled-for patriotic piety, issues in an ideology for a third world war. Escape we must from the unfamiliar, unpleasant, and dangerous present, first into the political innocence of the past and from there into the immediate future of a third world war, beyond which the revived and universalized innocence of the more distant future will surely lie.

We have said that to present the American tradition in foreign policy as having been free from concern with power politics and the balance of power is not warranted by the facts of American history. Yet it might still be argued, and it is actually being argued, that, regardless of the evidence of history, the American people will not be reconciled to power politics and the balance of power and

[11] Tannenbaum, "The Balance of Power versus the Coördinate State," pp. 195–96.

will support only policies based upon abstract moral principles. While in the past the United States might have pursued balance-of-power policies and while it might be a good thing if it did do so again, the American people will not stand for it. Here the emotional appeal to patriotic piety is joined by calculations of political expediency. Yet the case for misrepresenting American history has nothing to gain from either.

There is a strong tendency in all historiography to glorify the national past, and in popular presentations that tendency takes on the aspects of the jingoist whitewash. Even so penetrating a mind as John Stuart Mill's could deliver itself of an essay in which he proved, no doubt to the satisfaction of many of his English readers but certainly of few others, that Great Britain had never interfered in the affairs of European nations and had interfered in those of the Indian states only for their own good.[12] Yet it is the measure of a nation's maturity to be able to recognize its past for what it actually is. Why should we not admit that American foreign policy has been generally hardheaded and practical and at times ruthless? Why should we deny Jefferson's cunning, say, in the Puget Sound affair, the cruelty with which the Indians were treated, and the faithlessness with which the treaties with the Indians were cast aside? We know that this is the way all nations are when their interests are at stake—so cruel, so faithless, so cunning. We know that the United States has refrained from seeking dominions beyond the seas not because it is more virtuous than other nations but because it had the better part of a continent to colonize.

As has been pointed out elsewhere at greater length, the man in the street, unsophisticated as he is and uninformed as he may be, has a surer grasp of the essentials of foreign policy and a more mature judgment of its basic issues than many of the intellectuals and politicians who pretend to speak for him and cater to what they imagine his prejudices to be. During the Second World War the ideologues of the Atlantic Charter, the Four Freedoms, and the United Nations were constantly complaining that the American soldier did not know what he was fighting for. Indeed, if he was fighting for

[12] "A Few Words on Non-Intervention," *Dissertations and Discussions: Political, Philosophical, and Historical* (London: Longmans, Green, Reader and Dyer, 1875), pp. 153–78.

some utopian ideal, divorced from the concrete experiences and interests of the country, then the complaint was well grounded. However, if he was fighting for the territorial integrity of the nation and for its survival as a free country where he could live, think, and act as he pleased, then he had never any doubt about what he was fighting for. Ideological rationalizations and justifications are indeed the indispensable concomitants of all political action. Yet there is something unhealthy in a craving for ideological intoxication and in the inability to act and to see merit in action except under the stimulant of grandiose ideas and far-fetched schemes. Have our intellectuals become, like Hamlet, too much beset by doubt to act and, unlike Hamlet, compelled to still their doubts by renouncing their sense of what is real? The man in the street has no such doubts. It is true that ideologues and demagogues can sway him by appealing to his emotions. But it is also true, as American history shows in abundance, that responsible statesmen can guide him by awakening his latent understanding of the national interest.

Yet what is the national interest? How can we define it and give it the content which will make it a guide both for understanding and for action? This is one of the relevant questions to which the current debate has given rise.

It has been frequently argued against the realist conception of foreign policy that its key concept, the national interest, does not provide an acceptable standard for either thought or action. This argument is in the main based upon two grounds: the elusiveness of the concept and its susceptibility to interpretations, such as limitless imperialism and narrow nationalism, which are not in keeping with the American tradition in foreign policy. The argument has substance as far as it goes, but it does not invalidate the usefulness of the concept.

The concept of the national interest is similar in two respects to the "great generalities" of the Constitution, such as the general welfare and due process. It contains a residual meaning which is inherent in the concept itself, but beyond these minimum requirements its content can run the whole gamut of meanings that are logically compatible with it. That content is determined by the political traditions and the total cultural context within which a nation formulates its foreign policy. The concept of the national interest, then, contains two elements, one that is logically required and in that sense necessary, and one that is variable and determined by circumstances. The former is, then, of necessity relatively permanent while the latter will vary with circumstances.

The relative permanency of what one might call the hard core of the national interest stems from three factors: the nature of the interests to be protected, the political environment within which the interests operate, and the rational necessities which limit the choice of ends and means by all actors on the stage of foreign policy. Any foreign policy that operates under the standard of the national interest must obviously have some reference to the physical, political, and cultural entity which we call a nation. In a world where a number of sovereign nations compete with and oppose each other for power, the foreign policies of all nations must necessarily refer to their survival as their minimum requirement. Thus all nations do what they cannot help but do: protect their physical, political, and cultural identity against encroachments by other nations.

The nature of the threat to which the national interest is exposed remains equally constant over long periods of history. Throughout the centuries the main threat to Great Britain has come from the hegemonic aspirations of one or the other of the European nations. Russia has traditionally been threatened by a great power having access to the plains of eastern Europe. France and Germany, regardless of their changing political forms, have threatened each other throughout the ages.

The relative permanency of interest and threat is surpassed by the virtual immutability of the configurations through which the reason of man transforms the abstract concept of the national interest into foreign policy. Faced with the necessity to protect the hard core of the national interest, that is, to preserve the identity of the nation, all governments have resorted throughout history to certain basic policies, such as competitive armaments, the balance of power, alliances, and subversion, intended to make of the abstract concept of the national interest a viable political reality. Governments might have been wise or unwise in their choice of policies, successful or unsuccessful in their execution; they could not have escaped the rational necessity of selecting one of a limited number of avenues through which to bring the power of their nation to bear upon the power of other nations on behalf of the national interest.

The possibility both to reconstruct past foreign policies through the writing of history and to understand the contemporary foreign policies of one's own and other nations derives from this rational character of the national interest. If one could not assume that this rationality is identical throughout history and ubiquitous on the contemporary scene, however diminished and distorted by the irrationality of men and nations, one would be lost in a maze of unconnected data, to be explained perhaps in terms of psychology and sociology but not in terms conducive to the understanding of foreign policy. It is this assumption of the universality of the national interest in time and space which enables us to understand the foreign policies of Demosthenes and Caesar, of Kautilya and Henry VIII, of the statesmen of contemporary Russia and China. Regardless of all the differences in personality, social environment, convictions, and preferences, their thinking was predetermined and their actions could take place only within a narrow range, when they were faced with the task of protecting and promoting the rational core of the national interest. By thinking as they must have thought we can understand their thoughts, and by putting their thoughts into the context of their personalities and social environment we can understand their actions as well.

It has been suggested that this reasoning erects the national state into the last word in politics and the national interest into an absolute standard for political action. This, however, is not quite the case. The idea of interest is indeed of the essence of politics and, as such, unaffected by the circumstances of time and place. Thucydides' statement, born of the experiences of ancient Greece, that "identity of interest is the surest of bonds whether between states or individuals" was taken up in the nineteenth century by Lord Salisbury's remark that "the only bond of union that endures" among nations is "the absence of all clashing interests." The perennial issue between the realist and utopian schools of thought over the nature of politics, to which we have referred before, might well be formulated in terms of concrete interests versus abstract principles. Yet while the concern of politics with interest is perennial,

67

the connection between interest and the national state is a product of history.

The national state itself is obviously a product of history and as such is destined to yield in time to different modes of political organization. As long as the world is politically organized into nations, the national interest is indeed the last word in international politics. When the national state has been replaced by another mode of organization, foreign policy must then protect the interest in survival of that new organization. For the benefit of those who insist upon discarding the national state and constructing supranational organizations by constitutional fiat, it must be pointed out that these new organizational forms will either come into being through conquest or else through consent based upon the mutual recognition of the national interests of the nations concerned; for no nation will forego its freedom of action if it has no reason to expect proportionate benefits in compensation for that loss. This is true of treaties concerning commerce or fisheries as it is true of the great compacts, such as the European Coal and Steel Community, through which nations try to create supranational forms of organization. Thus, by an apparent paradox, what is historically conditioned in the idea of the national interest can be overcome only through the promotion in concert of the national interest of a number of nations.

These reflections have been made particularly relevant by the atomic age. It has been said that the atomic age has rendered obsolete the idea of the national interest and the conception of foreign policy derived from it. This is too sweeping a statement to be correct. What has become obsolete is the historically conditioned connection between interest and a passing historic phenomenon, the nation state; what has not, and could not have, become obsolete is the logically required connection between interest and foreign policy. The point can indeed be made—and it will be made in greater detail in chapter 9—that the technological revolutions of our age, of which the atomic revolution is the most spectacular one, have made the political organization of the world into nation states as obsolete as the first industrial revolution did the political organization based upon the feudal state. Yet the techniques by which new and wider interest must be given a politically viable expression have not been affected by those revolutionary changes. Thus the supranational control of atomic energy is today in the national interest of all nations; for while the present bipolarity of atomic power is dangerous to all nations, the acquisition of uncontrolled atomic power by an indefinite number of nations is likely to prove fatal to civilized life on this planet. In consequence, the nations of the world are faced with, and must overcome, the dilemma that the pursuit of their interests, conceived in national terms, is incompatible with modern technology, which requires supranational political organization.

The survival of a political unit, such as a nation, in its identity is the irreducible minimum, the necessary element of its interests vis-à-vis other units. Taken in isolation, the determination of its content in a concrete situation is relatively simple; for it encompasses the integrity of the nation's territory, of its political institutions, and of its culture. Thus bipartisanship in foreign policy, especially in times of war, has been most easily achieved in the promotion of these minimum requirements of the national interest. The situation is different with respect to the variable elements of the national interest. All the crosscurrents of personalities, public opinion, sectional interests, partisan politics, and political and moral folkways are brought to bear upon their determination. In consequence, the contribution which scientific analysis can make to this field, as to all fields of policy formation, is limited. It can identify the different agencies of the government which contribute to the determination of the variable elements of the national interest and assess their relative weight. It can separate the long-range objectives of foreign policy from the short-term ones which are the means for the achievement of the former and can tentatively establish their rational relations. Finally, it can analyze the variable elements of the national interest in terms of their legitimacy and their compatibility with other national values and with the national interest of other nations. We shall address ourselves briefly to the typical problems with which this analysis must deal.

The legitimacy of the national interest must be determined in the face of possible usurpation by subnational, other-national, and supranational interests. On the subnational level we find group interests, represented particularly by ethnic and economic groups, which tend to identify themselves with the national interest. Charles A. Beard has emphasized, however one-sidedly, the extent to which the economic interests of certain groups have been presented as those of the United States.[13] Group interests exert, of course, constant pressure upon the conduct of our foreign policy, claiming their identity with the national interest. It is, however, doubtful that, with the exception of a few spectacular cases, they have been successful in determining the course of American foreign policy. It is much more likely, given the nature of American domestic politics, that American foreign policy, in so far as it is the object of pressures by sectional interests, will normally be a compromise between divergent sectional interests. The concept of the national interest, as it emerges from this contest of conflicting sectional interests as the actual guide for foreign policy, may well fall short of what would be rationally required by the over-all interests of the United States. Yet this concept of the national interest is also more than any particular sectional interest or their sum total. It is, as it were, the lowest common denominator where sectional interests and the national interest rationally conceived meet in an uneasy compromise which may leave much to be desired in view of all the interests concerned.

The national interest can be usurped by other-national interests in two typical ways. The case of treason by individuals, either out of conviction or for pay, needs only to be mentioned here; for in so far as treason is committed on behalf of a foreign government rather than a supranational principle, it is significant for psychology, sociology, and criminology but not for the theory of politics. The other case, however, is important not only for the theory of politics but also for its practice, especially in the United States.

National minorities in European countries, ethnic groups in the United States, ideological minorities anywhere may identify themselves, either spontaneously or under the direction of the agents of a foreign government, with the interests of that foreign government and may promote these interests under the guise of the national interest of the country whose citizens they happen to be. The activities of the German-American Bund in the United States in the thirties and of Communists everywhere are cases in point. Yet the issue of the national interest versus other-national interests masquer-

[13] *The Idea of National Interest: An Analytical Study in American Foreign Policy* (New York: Macmillan Co., 1934).

ading as the national interest has arisen constantly in the United States in a less clear-cut fashion.

A country that had been settled by consecutive waves of "foreigners" was bound to find it particularly difficult to identify its own national interest against alleged, seeming, or actual other-national interests represented by certain groups among its own citizens. Since virtually all citizens of the United States are, as it were, "more or less" foreign born, those who were "less" so have frequently not resisted the temptation to use this distinction as a polemic weapon against latecomers who happened to differ from them in their conception of the national interest of the United States. Frequently, this rationalization has been dispensed with, and a conception of foreign policy with which a writer happened to disagree has been attributed outright to foreign sympathy or influence or worse. British influence and interests have served as standard arguments in debates on American foreign policy. Madison, in his polemic against Hamilton on the occasion of Washington's neutrality proclamation of 1793, identified the Federalist position with that of "the foreigners and degenerate citizens among us, who hate our republican government, and the French revolution,"[14] and the accusation met with a favorable response in a majority of Congress and of public opinion. However, these traditional attempts to discredit dissenting opinion as being influenced by foreign interests should not obscure the real issue, which is the peculiar vulnerability of the national interest of the United States to usurpation by the interests of other nations.

This problem has become in our time particularly acute in the form of Communist subversion. The transference of an individual's allegiance from his own nation to another one, the Soviet Union, is here made peculiarly attractive by the identification of the interests of the Soviet Union with the interests of humanity, that is, the supranational interest par excellence. As the testimony before the royal commission investigating the Gouzenko case clearly shows, the sincere Communist identifies the interests of the Soviet Union with those of humanity and, hence, experiences his betrayal of the

---

[14] "Helvidius, in Answer to Pacificus, on President Washington's Proclamation of Neutrality," in *Letters and Other Writings of James Madison* (Philadelphia: J. B. Lippincott Co., 1867), I, 611.

interests of his own nation not as treason but rather as the establishment of the correct priority between lower and higher interests, the lower one having to yield in case of conflict to those that are superior.

The genuine usurpation of the national interest by supranational interests can derive in our time from two sources: religious bodies and international organizations. The competition between church and state for determination of certain interests and policies, domestic and international, has been an intermittent issue throughout the history of the nation state. Here, too, the legitimate defense of the national interest against usurpation has frequently, especially in the United States, degenerated into the demagogic stigmatization of dissenting views as being inspired by Rome and, hence, being incompatible with the national interest. Yet here, too, the misuse of the issue for demagogic purposes must be considered apart from the legitimacy of the issue itself.

The more acute problem arises at the present time from the importance which the public and government officials, at least in their public utterances, attribute to the values represented and the policies pursued by international organizations either as alternatives or supplements to the values and policies for which the national government stands. It is frequently asserted that the foreign policy of the United States pursues no objectives apart from those of the United Nations, that, in other words, the foreign policy of the United States is actually identical with the policy of the United Nations. This assertion cannot refer to anything real in actual politics to support it. For the constitutional structure of international organizations, such as the United Nations, and their procedural practices make it impossible for them to pursue interests apart from those of the member states which dominate their policy-forming bodies. The identity between the interests of the United Nations and the United States can only refer to the successful policies of the United States within the United Nations through which the support of the United Nations is being secured for the policies of the United States. The assertion, then, is mere polemic, different from the one discussed previously in that the identification of a certain policy with an assumed supranational interest does not seek to reflect discredit upon the former but to bestow upon it a dignity which the national interest pure and simple is supposed to lack.

The real issue in view of the problem that concerns us here is not whether the so-called interests of the United Nations, which do not exist apart from the interests of its most influential members, have superseded the national interest of the United States, but for what kind of interests the United States has secured United Nations support. While these interests cannot be United Nations interests, they do not need to be national interests either. Here we are in the presence of that modern phenomenon which has been variously described as "utopianism," "sentimentalism," "moralism," the "legalistic-moralistic approach." The common denominator of all these tendencies in modern political thought is the substitution for the national interest of an assumed supranational standard of action which is generally identified with an international organization. The national interest is here not being usurped by subnational or supranational interests which, however inferior in worth to the national interest, are nevertheless real and worthy of consideration within their proper sphere. What challenges the national interest here is a mere figment of the imagination, a product of wishful thinking, which is postulated as a valid norm for international conduct, without being valid either there or anywhere else. At this point we touch the core of the present controversy between utopianism and realism in international affairs; we shall return to it later.

The national interest as such must be defended against usurpation by non-national interests. Yet once that task is accomplished, a rational order must be established among the values which make up the national interest and among the resources to be committed to them. While the interests which a nation may pursue in its relation with other nations are of infinite variety and magnitude, the resources which are available for the pursuit of such interests are necessarily limited in quantity and kind. No nation has the resources to promote all desirable objectives with equal vigor; all nations must therefore allocate their scarce resources as rationally as possible. The indispensable precondition of such rational allocation is a clear understanding of the distinction between the necessary and variable elements of the national interest. Given the contentious manner in which in democracies the variable elements of the national interest are generally determined, the advocates of an extensive conception of the national interest will inevitably present certain variable elements of the national interest as though their attainment were necessary for the nation's survival. In other words, the necessary elements of the national interest have a tendency to swallow up the variable elements so that in the end all kinds of objectives, actual or potential, are justified in terms of national survival. Such arguments have been advanced, for instance, in support of the rearmament of West Germany and of the defense of Formosa. They must be subjected to rational scrutiny which will determine, however tentatively, their approximate place in the scale of national values.

The same problem presents itself in its extreme form when a nation pursues, or is asked to pursue, objectives that are not only unnecessary for its survival but tend to jeopardize it. Second-rate nations which dream of playing the role of great powers, such as Italy and Poland in the interwar period, illustrate this point. So do great powers which dream of remaking the world in their own image and embark upon world-wide crusades, thus straining their resources to exhaustion. Here scientific analysis has the urgent task of pruning down national objectives to the measure of available resources in order to make their pursuit compatible with national survival.

Finally, the national interest of a nation that is conscious not only of its own interests but also of that of other nations must be defined in terms compatible with the latter. In a multinational world this is a requirement of political morality; in an age of total war it is also a condition for survival.

Two mutually exclusive arguments have been brought to bear upon this problem. On the one hand, it has been argued against the theory of international politics here presented that the concept of the national interest revives the eighteenth-century concept of enlightened self-interest, presuming that the uniformly enlightened pursuit of their self-interest by all individuals, as by all nations, will of itself be conducive to a peaceful and harmonious society. On the other hand, the point has been made that the pursuit of their national interest by all nations makes war the permanent arbiter of conflicts among them. Neither argument is well taken.

The concept of the national interest presupposes neither a naturally harmonious, peaceful world nor the inevitability of war as a consequence of the pursuit by all nations of their national interest.

Quite to the contrary, it assumes continuous conflict and threat of war, to be minimized through the continuous adjustment of conflicting interests by diplomatic action. No such assumption would be warranted if all nations at all times conceived of their national interest only in terms of their survival and, in turn, defined their interest in survival in restrictive and rational terms. As it is, their conception of the national interest is subject to all the hazards of misinterpretation, usurpation, and misjudgment to which reference has been made above. To minimize these hazards is the first task of a foreign policy that seeks the defense of the national interest by peaceful means. Its second task is the defense of the national interest, restrictively and rationally defined, against the national interests of other nations which may or may not be thus defined. If they are not, it becomes the task of armed diplomacy to convince the nations concerned that their legitimate interests have nothing to fear from a restrictive and rational foreign policy and that their illegitimate interests have nothing to gain in the face of armed might rationally employed.

We have said before that the utopian and realist positions in international affairs do not necessarily differ in the policies they advocate, but that they part company over their general philosophies of politics and their way of thinking about matters political. It does not follow that the present debate is only of academic interest and without practical significance. Both camps, it is true, may support the same policy for different reasons. Yet if the reasons are unsound, the soundness of the policies supported by them is a mere coincidence, and these very same reasons may be, and inevitably are, invoked on other occasions in support of unsound policies. The nefarious consequences of false philosophies and wrong ways of thinking may for the time being be concealed by the apparent success of policies derived from them. You may go to war, justified by your nation's interests, for a moral purpose and in disregard of considerations of power; and military victory seems to satisfy both your moral aspirations and your nation's interests. Yet the manner in which you waged the war, achieved victory, and settled the peace cannot help reflecting your philosophy of politics and your way of thinking about political problems. If these are in error, you may win victory on the field of battle and still assist in the defeat of both your moral principles and the national interest of your country.

Any number of examples could illustrate the real yet subtle practical consequences which follow from the different positions taken. We have chosen two: collective security in Korea and the liberation of the nations that are captives of communism. A case for both policies can be made from both the utopian and the realist positions, but with significant differences in the emphasis and substance of the policies pursued.

Collective security as an abstract principle of utopian politics requires that all nations come to the aid of a victim of aggression by resisting the aggressor with all means necessary to frustrate his aims. Once the case of aggression is established, the duty to act is unequivocal. Its extent may be affected by concern for the nation's survival; obviously no nation will commit outright suicide in the service of collective security. But beyond that elemental limitation no consideration of interest or power, either with regard to the aggressor or his victim or the nation acting in the latter's defense, can qualify the obligation to act under the principle of collective security. Thus high officials of our government have declared that we intervened in Korea not for any narrow interest of ours but in support of the moral principle of collective security.

Collective security as a concrete principle of realist policy is the age-old maxim, "Hang together or hang separately," in modern dress. It recognizes the need for nation A under certain circumstances to defend nation B against attack by nation C. That need is determined, first, by the interest which A has in the territorial integrity of B and by the relation of that interest to all the other interests of A as well as to the resources available for the support of all those interests. Furthermore, A must take into account the power which is at the disposal of aggressor C for fighting A and B as over against the power available to A and B for fighting C. The same calculation must be carried on concerning the power of the likely allies of C as over against those of A and B. Before going to war for the defense of South Korea in the name of collective security, an American adherent of political realism would have demanded an answer to the following four questions: First, what is our interest in the preservation of the independence of South Korea;

second, what is our power to defend that independence against North Korea; third, what is our power to defend that independence against China and the Soviet Union; and fourth, what are the chances for preventing China and the Soviet Union from entering the Korean War?

In view of the principle of collective security, interpreted in utopian terms, our intervention in Korea was a foregone conclusion. The interpretation of this principle in realist terms might or might not, depending upon the concrete circumstances of interest and power, have led us to the same conclusion. In the execution of the policy of collective security the utopian had to be indifferent to the possibility of Chinese and Russian intervention, except for his resolution to apply the principle of collective security to anybody who would intervene on the side of the aggressor. The realist could not help weighing the possibility of the intervention of a great power on the side of the aggressor in terms of the interests engaged and the power available on the other side.[15]

The Truman administration could not bring itself to take resolutely the utopian or the realist position. It resolved to intervene in good measure on utopian grounds and in spite of military advice to the contrary; it allowed the military commander to advance to the Yalu River in disregard of the risk of the intervention of a great power against which collective security could be carried out only by means of a general war, and then refused to pursue the war with full effectiveness on the realist grounds of the risk of a third world war. Thus Mr. Truman in 1952 was caught in the same dilemma from which Mr. Baldwin could extricate himself in 1936 on the occasion of the League of Nations sanctions against Italy's attack upon Ethiopia only at an enormous loss to British prestige. Collective security as a defense of the status quo short of a general war can be effective only against second-rate powers. Applied against a major power, it is a contradiction in terms, for it means necessarily a major war. Of this self-defeating contradiction Mr. Baldwin

[15] The difference in these two attitudes is well illustrated by the following passage from a Moon Mullins cartoon. An elderly representative of the utopian school asks little Kayo: "Remember the golden rule. Now, supposing that boy slapped you on the right cheek, what would you do?" Whereupon Kayo replies realistically: "Jest how big a boy are you supposin'?"

was as unaware in the thirties as Mr. Truman seemed to be in 1952. Mr. Churchill put Mr. Baldwin's dilemma in these cogent terms: "First, the Prime Minister had declared that sanctions meant war; secondly, he was resolved that there must be no war; and thirdly, he decided upon sanctions. It was evidently impossible to comply with these three conditions." Similarly Mr. Truman had declared that the effective prosecution of the Korean War meant the possibility of a third world war; he resolved that there must be no third world war; and he decided upon intervention in the Korean War. Here, too, it was impossible to comply with these three conditions.

Similar contradictions are inherent in the proposals which would substitute for the policy of containment the liberation of the nations presently the captives of Russian communism. This objective can be compatible with the utopian or realist position, but the policies designed to secure it will be fundamentally different according to whether they are based upon one or the other position. A clear case for the utopian justification of such policies was made by Representative Charles J. Kersten of Wisconsin, who pointed to these four "basic defects" of the "negative policy of containment and negotiated coexistence":

> It would be immoral and unchristian to negotiate a permanent agreement with forces which by every religious creed and moral precept are evil. It abandons nearly one-half of humanity and the once free nations of Poland, Czechoslovakia, Hungary, Rumania, Bulgaria, Albania, Lithuania, Latvia, Estonia and China to enslavement of the Communist police state.
>
> It is un-American because it violates the principle of the American Declaration of Independence, which proclaims the rights of all people to freedom and their right and duty to throw off tyranny.
>
> It will lead to all-out World War III because it aligns all the forces of the non-Communist world in military opposition to and against all the forces of the Communist world, including the 800,000,000 peoples behind the Iron Curtain.
>
> The policy of mere containment is uneconomic and will lead to national bankruptcy.[16]

This statement is interesting for its straightforwardness and because it combines in a rather typical fashion considerations of abstract morality and of expediency. The captive nations must be liberated not only because their captivity is immoral, unchristian,

---

[16] *New York Times*, August 14, 1952, p. 1.

and un-American, but also because its continuation will lead to a third world war and to national bankruptcy. To what extent, however, these considerations of expediency are invalidated by their utopian setting will become obvious from a comparison between the utopian and the realist positions.

From the utopian point of view there can be nó difference between the liberation of Estonia or Czechoslovakia, of Poland or China; the captivity of any nation, large or small, close or far away, is a moral outrage which cannot be tolerated. The realist, too, seeks the liberation of all captive nations because he realizes that the presence of the Russian armies in the heart of Europe and their cooperation with the Chinese armies constitute the two main sources of the imbalance of power which threatens our security. Yet before he formulates a program of liberation, he will seek answers to a number of questions such as these: While the United States has a general interest in the liberation of all captive nations, what is the hierarchy of interests it has in the liberation, say, of China, Estonia, and Hungary? And while the Soviet Union has a general interest in keeping all captive nations in that state, what is the hierarchy of its interests in keeping, say, Poland, East Germany, and Bulgaria captive? If we assume, as we must on the historic evidence of two centuries, that Russia would at present not give up control over Poland without being compelled by force of arms, would the objective of the liberation of Poland justify the ruin of Western civilization, that of Poland included, which would be the certain result of a third world war? What resources does the United States have at its disposal for the liberation of all captive nations or some of them? What resources does the Soviet Union have at its disposal to keep in captivity all captive nations or some of them? Are we more likely to avoid national bankruptcy by embarking upon a policy of indiscriminate liberation with the concomitant certainty of war or by continuing the present policy of containment?

It might be that in a particular instance the policies suggested by the answers to these questions will coincide with Representative Kersten's proposals, but there can be no doubt that in its over-all character, substance, emphasis, and likely consequences a utopian policy of liberation differs fundamentally from a realist one.

The issue between liberation as a utopian principle of abstract morality versus the realist evaluation of the consequences which a policy of liberation would have for the survival of the nation has arisen before in American history. Abraham Lincoln was faced with a dilemma similar to that which confronts us today. Should he make the liberation of the slaves the ultimate standard of his policy even at the risk of destroying the Union, as many urged him to do, or should he subordinate the moral principle of universal freedom to considerations of the national interest? The answer Lincoln gave to Horace Greeley, a spokesman for the utopian moralists, is timeless in its eloquent wisdom. "If there be those," he wrote on August 22, 1862,

who would not save the Union unless they could at the same time save slavery, I do not agree with them. If there be those who would not save the Union unless they could at the same time destroy slavery, I do not agree with them. My paramount object in this struggle *is* to save the Union, and is *not* either to save or to destroy slavery. If I could save the Union without freeing *any* slave I would do it, and if I could save it by freeing *all* the slaves, I would do it; and if I could save it by freeing some and leaving others alone I would also do that. What I do about slavery, and the colored race, I do because I believe it helps to save the Union; and what I forbear, I forbear because I do *not* believe it would help to save the Union. I shall do *less* whenever I shall believe what I am doing hurts the cause, and I shall do *more* whenever I shall believe doing more will help the cause. I shall try to correct errors when shown to be errors; and I shall adopt new views so fast as they shall appear to be true views.

I have here stated my purpose according to my view of *official* duty; and I intend no modification of my oft-expressed *personal* wish that all men everywhere could be free.

The foregoing discussion ought to shed additional light, if this is still needed, upon the moral merits of the utopian and realist positions. This question, more than any other, seems to have agitated the critics of realism in international affairs. Disregarding the voluminous evidence, some of them have picked a few words out of their context to prove that realism in international affairs is unprincipled and contemptuous of morality. To mention but one example, one eminent critic summarizes my position, which he supposes to deny the possibility of judging the conduct of states by moral criteria, in these words: "And one spokesman finds 'a profound and neglected truth,' to use his words, in the dictum of Hobbes that 'there is neither morality nor law outside the state.' "[17] These are indeed my words, but not all of them. What I actually said was this: "There is a profound and neglected truth hidden in Hobbes's extreme dictum that the state creates morality as well as law and that there is neither morality nor law outside the state. Universal moral principles, such as justice or equality, are capable of guiding political action only to the extent that they have been given concrete content and have been related to political situations by society."[18]

It must be obvious from this passage and from all my other writings on the subject that my position is the exact opposite from what this critic makes it out to be.[19] I have always maintained that the actions of states are subject to universal moral principles, and I have been careful to differentiate my position in this respect from that of Hobbes. Five points basic to my position may need to be emphasized again.

The first point is what one might call the requirement of cosmic humility with regard to the moral evaluation of the actions of states. To know that states are subject to the moral law is one thing; to pretend to know what is morally required of states in a particular situation is quite another. The human mind tends naturally to identify the particular interests of states, as of individuals, with the moral purposes of the universe. The statesman in the defense of the nation's interests may, and at times even must, yield to that tendency; the scholar must resist it at every turn. For the lighthearted assumption that what one's own nation aims at and does is morally good and that those who oppose that nation's policies are evil is morally

[17] A. H. Feller, "In Defense of International Law and Morality," *Annals of the American Academy of Political and Social Science*, CCLXXXII (July, 1952), 80.

[18] *In Defense of the National Interest: A Critical Examination of American Foreign Policy* (New York: Alfred A. Knopf, 1951), p. 34.

[19] See, for instance, "The Machiavellian Utopia," *Ethics*, LV (January, 1945), 145–47; "Ethics and Politics," in *Approaches to Group Understanding* (Sixth Symposium of the Conference on Science, Philosophy and Religion), ed. Lyman Bryson *et al.* (New York, 1947), pp. 319–41; *Scientific Man vs. Power Politics* (Chicago: University of Chicago Press, 1946), chaps. 7, 8; "Views of Nuremberg: Further Analysis of the Trial and Its Importance," *America*, LXXVI (December 7, 1946), 266–67; "The Twilight of International Morality," *Ethics*, LVIII (January, 1948), 79–99; *Politics among Nations* (2d ed.; New York: Alfred A. Knopf, 1954), chap. 16; "National Interest and Moral Principles in Foreign Policy: The Primacy of the National Interest," *American Scholar*, XVIII (Spring, 1949), 207–12. See also below, chap. 13.

indefensible and intellectually untenable and leads in practice to that distortion of judgment, born of the blindness of crusading frenzy, which has been the curse of nations from the beginning of time.

The second point which obviously needs to be made again concerns the effectiveness of the restraints which morality imposes upon the actions of states.

A discussion of international morality must guard against the two extremes either of overrating the influence of ethics upon international politics or else of denying that statesmen and diplomats are moved by anything else but considerations of material power.

On the one hand, there is the dual error of confounding the moral rules which people actually observe with those they pretend to observe as well as with those which writers declare they ought to observe. . . .

On the other hand, there is the misconception, usually associated with the general depreciation and moral condemnation of power politics, discussed above, that international politics is so thoroughly evil that it is no use looking for ethical limitations of the aspirations for power on the international scene. Yet, if we ask ourselves what statesmen and diplomats are capable of doing to further the power objectives of their respective nations and what they actually do, we realize that they do less than they probably could and less than they actually did in other periods of history. They refuse to consider certain ends and to use certain means, either altogether or under certain conditions, not because in the light of expediency they appear impractical or unwise, but because certain moral rules interpose an absolute barrier. Moral rules do not permit certain policies to be considered at all from the point of view of expediency. Such ethical inhibitions operate in our time on different levels with different effectiveness. Their restraining function is most obvious and most effective in affirming the sacredness of human life in times of peace.[20]

In connection with this passage we gave a number of historic examples showing the influence of moral principles upon the conduct of foreign policy. An example taken from contemporary history will illustrate the same point. There can be little doubt that the Soviet Union could have achieved the objectives of its foreign policy at the end of the Second World War without antagonizing the nations of the West into that encircling coalition which has been the nightmare of Bolshevist foreign policy since 1917. It could have mitigated cunning for its own sake and the use of force with persuasion, conciliation, and a trust derived from the awareness of a partial community of interests and would thereby have minimized the dan-

[20] Morgenthau, *Politics among Nations,* pp. 210–16.

gers to itself and the rest of the world which are inherent in the objectives of its policies. Yet the Soviet Union was precluded from relying upon these traditional methods of diplomacy by its general conception of human nature, politics, and morality. In the general philosophy of Bolshevism there is no room for honest dissent, the recognition of the intrinsic worth of divergent interests, and genuine conciliation between such interests. On all levels of social interaction opposition must be destroyed by cunning and violence, since it has no right to exist, rather than be met halfway in view of its intrinsic legitimacy. This being the general conception of the political morality of Bolshevism, the foreign policy of the Soviet Union is limited to a much more narrow choice of means than the foreign policies of other nations.

The United States, for instance, has been able, in its relations with the nations of Latin America, to replace military intervention and dollar diplomacy with the policy of the Good Neighbor. That drastic change was made possible by the general conception of political morality which has been prevalent in the United States from its very inception. The United States is a pluralist society which presupposes the continuing existence and legitimacy of divergent interests. These interests are locked in a continuing struggle for supremacy to be decided by force only as a last resort but, normally, through a multitude of institutions which are so devised as to allow one or the other interest a temporary advantage but none a permanent supremacy at the price of the destruction of the others. This morality of pluralism allows the United States, once it is secure in that minimum of vital interests to which we have referred above, to transfer those principles of political morality to the international scene and to deal with divergent interests there with the same methods of genuine compromise and conciliation which are a permanent element of its domestic political life.

The third point concerns the relations between universal moral principles and political action. I have always maintained that these universal moral principles cannot be applied to the actions of states in their abstract universal formulation but that they must be, as it were, filtered through the concrete circumstances of time and place. The individual may say for himself: *Fiat justitia, pereat mundus;* the state has no right to say so in the name of those who are in its care.

Both individual and state must judge political action by universal moral principles, such as that of liberty. Yet while the individual has a moral right to sacrifice himself in defense of such a moral principle, the state has no moral right to let its moral disapprobation of the infringement of liberty get in the way of successful political action, itself inspired by the moral principle of national survival. There can be no political morality without prudence, that is, without consideration of the political consequences of seemingly moral action. Classical and medieval philosophy knew this and so did Lincoln when he said: "I do the very best I know how, the very best I can, and I mean to keep doing so until the end. If the end brings me out all right, what is said against me won't amount to anything. If the end brings me out wrong, ten angels swearing I was right would make no difference." The issue between utopianism and realism, as it bears on this point, has been put most succinctly by Edmund Burke, and what he has to say in the following passage about revolution, that is, civil war, may well be applied *mutatis mutandis* to all war.

Nothing universal can be rationally affirmed on any moral or any political subject. Pure metaphysical abstraction does not belong to these matters. The lines of morality are not like the ideal lines of mathematics. They are broad and deep as well as long. They admit of exceptions; they demand modifications. These exceptions and modifications are not made by the process of logic, but by the rules of prudence. Prudence is not only the first in rank of the virtues political and moral, but she is the director, the regulator, the standard of them all. Metaphysics cannot live without definition; but Prudence is cautious how she defines. Our courts cannot be more fearful in suffering fictitious cases to be brought before them for eliciting their determination on a point of law than prudent moralists are in putting extreme and hazardous cases of conscience upon emergencies not existing. Without attempting, therefore, to define, what never can be defined, the case of a revolution in government, this, I think, may be safely affirmed—that a sore and pressing evil is to be removed, and that a good, great in its amount and unequivocal in its nature, must be probable almost to a certainty, before the inestimable price of our own morals and the well-being of a number of our fellow-citizens is paid for a revolution. If ever we ought to be economists even to parsimony, it is in the voluntary production of evil. Every revolution contains in it something of evil.[21]

[21] *The Works of The Right Honorable Edmund Burke* (4th ed.; Boston: Little, Brown & Co., 1871), IV, 80–81. Cf. also Burke, "Speech on a Bill for Shortening the Duration of Parliaments, May 8, 1780," *ibid.*, VII, 73: "I must see,

Fourth, the realist recognizes that a moral decision, especially in the political sphere, does not imply a simple choice between a moral principle and a standard of action which is morally irrelevant or even outright immoral. A moral decision implies always a choice among different moral principles, one of which is given precedence over others. To say that a political action has no moral purpose is absurd; for political action can be defined as an attempt to realize moral values through the medium of politics, that is, power. The relevant moral question concerns the choice among different moral values, and it is at this point that the realist and the utopian part company again. If an American statesman must choose between the promotion of universal liberty, which is a moral good, at the risk of American security and, hence, of liberty in the United States, on the one hand, and the promotion of American security and of liberty in the United States, which is another moral good, to the detriment of the promotion of universal liberty, on the other, which choice ought he to make? The utopian will not face the issue squarely and will deceive himself into believing that he can achieve both goods at the same time. The realist will choose the national interest on both moral and pragmatic grounds; for if he does not take care of the national interest nobody else will, and if he puts American security and liberty in jeopardy the cause of liberty everywhere will be impaired.

Finally, the political realist distinguishes between his moral sympathies and the political interests which he must defend. He will distinguish with Lincoln between his "*official* duty" which is to protect the national interest and his "*personal* wish" which is to see universal moral values realized throughout the world.

The issue has been admirably put by Father Wilfred Parsons of Catholic University in defending Mr. Kennan's position:

Mr. Kennan did not say state behavior is not a fit subject for moral judgment, but only that it should not sway our realization of the realities with

---

to satisfy me, the remedies; I must see, from their operation in the cure of the old evil, and in the cure of those new evils which are inseparable from all remedies, how they balance each other, and what is the total result. The excellence of mathematics and metaphysics is, to have but one thing before you; but he forms the best judgment in all moral disquisitions who has the greatest number and variety of considerations in one view before him, and can take them in with the best possible consideration of the middle results of all."

which we have to deal. Msgr. Koenig continues: "Should we accept power realities and aspirations without feeling the obligation of moral judgment?" And he appeals to the present writer and other political scientists to say whether this doctrine agrees with Pope Pius XII's messages on peace.

I am sure that most political scientists, and also Mr. Kennan, would agree with the Monsignor that we should not accept those realities "without feeling the obligation of moral judgment." But there is a difference between *feeling* this obligation (and even expressing it) and allowing this feeling to sway our actions in concrete negotiations that deal with the national or world common good. We can still feel and yet deal.

To make my meaning clearer, I understood Mr. Kennan to hold that we went off the beam with Woodrow Wilson, when we began to make our moral disapprobation an *essential part* of our foreign relations, even sometimes at the expense of our own and the world's common good. Logically, such an attitude would inhibit our dealing with Britain, France and a host of countries. Pius XI, speaking of Mussolini after the Lateran Treaty, said he would deal with the devil himself if he must. Here was moral disapprobation, but it was not "carried over into the affairs of states."

This relative position, and not the absolute one of Msgr. Koenig (with which in itself I agree), is, I think, the issue raised by Mr. Kennan, and it is worth debating on that basis.[22]

The contest between utopianism and realism is not tantamount to a contest between principle and expediency, morality and immorality, although some spokesmen for the former would like to have it that way. The contest is rather between one type of political morality and another type of political morality, one taking as its standard universal moral principles abstractly formulated, the other weighing these principles against the moral requirements of concrete political action, their relative merits to be decided by a prudent evaluation of the political consequences to which they are likely to lead.[23]

[22] *America,* LXXXVI (March 29, 1952), 700. See also Algernon Cecil, "The Foreign Office," in *The Cambridge History of British Foreign Policy, 1783–1919* (Cambridge: Cambridge University Press, 1923), III, 605, concerning Lord Salisbury: "Always, however, the motive of his policy was to be found in the political interests as opposed to the political sympathies of Great Britain; and in this way his treatment of Foreign Affairs is at the opposite policy from that of Palmerston and Gladstone." Cf. also the general remarks in Alexander H. Leighton, *Human Relations in a Changing World* (New York: E. P. Dutton & Co., 1949), pp. 155 ff.

[23] See, on this point, Shirley R. Letwin, "Rationalism, Principles, and Politics," *Review of Politics,* XIV (July, 1952), 367–93; L. Susan Stebbing, *Ideals and Illusions* (London: Watts & Co., 1951); Vernon H. Holloway, *Religious Ethics and the Politics of Power* (New York: Church Peace Union and World Alliance for International Friendship through Religion, 1951); and Dorothy Fosdick,

These points are re-emphasized by the foregoing discussion. Which attitude with regard to collective security and to the liberation of the captive nations, the utopian or the realist, is more likely to safeguard the survival of the United States in its territorial, political, and cultural identity and at the same time to contribute the most to the security and liberty of other nations? This is the ultimate test—political and moral—by which utopianism and realism must be judged.

"Ethical Standards and Political Strategies," *Political Science Quarterly,* LVII (1942), 214 ff.

5 International Relations as an Academic Discipline

The assumption that a central concept is necessary for the theoretical understanding of politics has been disputed implicitly through the development of theories of politics which are lacking in such a central concept and explicitly in the form of an attack upon the suggested central concept of power. The question of whether such a central concept is necessary at all and, if so, which one it ought to be has divided opinion on all levels of theory and practice. It has done so also on the level of academic curriculum and organization. The controversy about the nature and the proper place of international relations and area studies as academic disciplines is a manifestation of that division of opinion concerning the fundamental problem of understanding politics.

These two novel academic disciplines must solve the same basic problems. If one wants to put the issue in epigrammatic and, therefore, oversimplified form, one might say that the main problem, as yet unsolved, that confronts these two academic "disciplines" is that they have not been able to acquire intellectual discipline. They have no intellectually valid focus which could give unity to their intellectual endeavors, and they have no common method by which the results of their investigations could be tested. These deficiencies have been as obvious in the study of international relations as they are in area studies. They are the more obvious in the latter, since area studies have made integration their main claim for recognition as an academic discipline. Area studies are in the process of showing —and the most mature discussion of their problems shows it with particular clarity—that they stand and fall with the precise formulation of a relevant problem to which different academic disciplines are to contribute. If area studies can demonstrate in practice that success in international studies, area or otherwise, depends upon the precise definition of a common problem and the sharp focus of all relevant research upon that problem, they will indeed have made an outstanding contribution to the study of international relations.

When after the First World War the study of international relations gained recognition as an independent academic discipline, it had three main intellectual interests: history, international law, and political reform. It is not by accident that the first two occupants of the first chair of international politics, the one which was founded in 1919 at the University of Wales, were distinguished historians, Professors Zimmern and Webster. There can of course be no doubt that knowledge of history and, more particularly, of diplomatic history forms an indispensable element of international relations; but, as will be shown later, while the student of international relations must have a thorough knowledge of history, his intellectual interest is not identical with that of the historian.

Obviously, the intellectual interest of international relations is in the present and the future rather than in the past and, especially in the interwar years, that interest was conceived in terms of international law. International relations were considered to move on two different levels: the legal one which presented the rules by which states were supposed to act, and the empirical one which showed how they actually did act in view of the rules of international law. Thus general history, diplomatic history, and international law became three cornerstones of the study of international relations.

The fourth cornerstone of the study of international relations is less easy to identify. For it is formed by the aspirations for a better world, morally respectable in themselves but vaguely conceived and identified with whatever remedy seems to be fashionable at a particular time. Thus we find that the focus of academic interest changes continuously in accordance with the preferences of public opinion, centering on disarmament one day, the League of Nations or the United Nations another, world government or regional federation another again.

The interstices between those four cornerstones are filled in with an incoherent collection of fragmentary knowledge ranging the whole gamut of academic disciplines and having only one thing in common: that they transcend the boundaries of a particular nation. The tone is set in the letter offering in 1919 a chair of international politics to the University of Wales and describing its purposes as "the study of those related problems of law and politics, of ethics and economics, which are raised by the project of a League of Nations, and for the encouragement of a truer understanding of civilizations other than our own." Reading the voluminous proceedings of the International Institute of Intellectual Co-operation, which in the interwar years dedicated much of its work to the discussion of international relations as an academic discipline, one cannot but be struck by the amorphousness of the discussion and the vagueness of the results. One speaker seems to have well summarized the consensus of those meetings when he said:

The science of international relations has primarily a descriptive character. It is somewhat in the order of the contemporary history of nations, covering all fields: economics, trade, exchange, movement of production, of goods, of currency, as well as politics and culture. . . . The factor uniting the problems which form the science of international relations is their international character, that is to say, the tie which is created among all domains of social life when that life transgresses the limits of one single nation and influences the relations among nations.[1]

The same consensus is reflected in the ironic comment, rare in its critical detachment, of another speaker who expressed himself thus:

One can without doubt call international any phenomenon because it belongs to all countries. Anything one wants to then becomes international. From this point of view, seasickness is an international fact; not only does one experience it on all oceans; but there are societies against that disease, and one can conceive of an international league whose purpose it is to do research and compare the methods with which to combat the disease. Yet the question remains outside our field of inquiry until one concerns oneself with the conclusion of an international convention obligating vessels to equip themselves with certain medicines which are recognized as necessary for the protection against seasickness.

I beg your pardon for having chosen that imaginary example. I wanted only to indicate the need for a narrow definition of international studies.[2]

The organization of academic teaching and research in international relations has largely reflected the vagueness and eclecticism of the theoretical conception of international relations as an academic discipline. There has been a general tendency to divide the field of international relations into a number of subdivisions whose common denominator is their transcendence of national boundaries either geographically or functionally. These subdivisions were selected

[1] Antoni Deryng, in *Coopération intellectuelle*, No. 68–69 (Paris, 1936), p. 33. Translated from the French by the author.

[2] Paul Mantoux, in *Coopération intellectuelle*, No. 57–58 (Paris, 1935), p. 490. My translation.

from the traditional academic disciplines either *in toto,* such as international law and international economics, or rearranged through the selection of individual courses taken from different disciplines. Thus all the courses which, for instance, had a reference to Russia in their title would be grouped under the area heading of Russia.

It could not have passed unnoticed that the intellectual unity of an academic field, thus established, was bound to be of a most superficial nature and that where there occurred real integration and cross-fertilization among several academic disciplines, credit was due to the creative process occurring in the minds of outstanding students rather than to the academic organization of the field. Attempts have therefore been made to give international relations the unity of an academic discipline by buttressing the eclectic organization of the field with a general or "core" course or number of courses which are supposed to present the distinctive characteristics of international relations as an academic discipline. This core generally covers the fields of international law, international organization, international politics, international economics, international geography, American and European diplomatic history, with such additions as meet the preferences of individual institutions. Most textbooks in the field reflect the eclectic character of this core. For such a core, if it has no focus other than that of the "international" character of international relations, cannot help being as eclectic and disparate as the field itself.

The problems with which area studies must cope are similar, *mutatis mutandis,* to those with which the academic discipline of international relations has dealt thus far without spectacular success. The central problem is again that of focus and method. Area studies, both historically and analytically, form a part of the field of international relations. The type of area study which is prevalent today owes its existence to the practical need to prepare members of the armed forces for service in foreign countries during the Second World War. Those who were expected to take responsible positions in foreign countries had to get acquainted as quickly as possible with the language, geography, culture, and history of those countries. Not only were these training courses successful in their immediate purpose; they also put into sharp focus a foreign area not in terms of the traditional academic disciplines but, as it were, in terms of the characteristics and problems of the area itself upon which the methods of all the relevant disciplines would be brought to bear. The process by which this objective is to be accomplished is generally called "integration"; the effect of this process upon the minds of the student goes by the name of "cross-fertilization."

Practical needs, if on a higher intellectual level, still provide one of the major arguments in favor of area studies; they are also apparrent in the selection of the areas most frequently studied. Russia and Asia vie with each other for the attention of students and the commitment of resources. It is not by accident that it is with those areas that American foreign policy is primarily concerned and that knowledge of them is fragmentary and the supply of experts available for government service falls drastically below demand. Nor is it an accident that the areas around which area studies are centered are generally defined in terms which coincide with the areas of political interest.

Aside from the training of prospective government officials, area studies are frequently motivated by the recognition of America's predominant place in world affairs, which necessitates a knowledge of the world with which the United States must deal as friend or foe. This higher level of practicality entails the desire to learn all the facts about all the regions of the world. Since the regions of prime political importance seem already to be adequately covered, latecomers among university administrations have been known to search for empty spaces on the map which they might cover with an institute for area studies. Underlying this tendency is the conviction that knowledge of unknown areas is useful in itself and that the more knowledge of this kind there is, the better will we be able to understand the world and discharge our responsibilities toward it.

The purely intellectual objectives which are connected with area studies—generally in theory and sometimes also in practice—number three. One stands on the borderline between theory and practice, one is conceived from the perspective of the social sciences, and one from that of the humanities. Area studies are aimed at conveying the experience of cultural relativity which will enable us to do justice to foreign cultures in our intellectual judgment, moral evaluation, and aesthetic appreciation and will at the same time enable us to deal effectively with foreign areas, that is, on their own terms rather than through the imposition of our culture on theirs. Furthermore, area studies are expected to contribute to the development of a universal social science which will arise from the isolation, analysis, and comparison of similar phenomena in different cultures. Finally, they are supposed to provide the intellectual and aesthetic satisfaction that comes from the understanding of any culture in all its manifestations.

These different objectives of area studies are not necessarily incompatible with one another. Yet it is obviously impossible to plan for all of them with equal emphasis at the same time. If they are all achieved at once, some of them are bound to be the by-products of those for the sake of which the studies were undertaken. There can be little doubt that in practice, as concerns the delimitation and selection of areas as well as the development of concrete research projects, practical considerations have generally prevailed over purely intellectual ones.

An interdisciplinary science of areas, in order to be theoretically valid and practically useful, must be mindful of seven principles which apply to all social sciences but which have been insufficiently heeded by area studies in particular and by international relations in general:

First, a non-directive, "objective" social science is, as we have seen, a contradiction in terms. All social sciences, in so far as they deserve the name of science at all, cannot fail to reflect both the social *Standort* and the particular intellectual interest of the observer. A social science which strives for unattainable objectivity can at best collect the raw materials of science in the form of a mass of unrelated or but superficially and irrelevantly related facts. Social science is of necessity science from a certain point of view, and that point of view is determined by the over-all outlook of the scholar as well as by the particular interest with which the scholar approaches the segment of social reality which he intends to investigate.

Second, it follows that the quantity of facts collected is not necessarily proportionate to the quantity of truth discovered. In order to understand a particular area it is not necessary, even if it were possible, to know all the facts about it. Nor is it true that our knowledge of the world around us increases necessarily with the number of areas investigated and the number of facts known about those areas.

Third, regardless of whether the immediate purpose of area research is theoretical or practical, only a theoretical approach to area research can assure useful, practical results, which are not useful merely by accident. A non-theoretical approach to area research can do no more than elaborate upon the common-sense approach which the layman uses when he must solve a practical problem. An area study, to be useful not only for the practical problems raised by yesterday's news but for a whole series of practical problems to be expected in the future, must rest on theoretical foundations which are able to support a whole series of practical solutions by virtue of their theoretical nature.

Fourth, an area for research is not necessarily identical with a geographical, political, or cultural area. The definition of the area and of the problems to be investigated within the area is a function of the intellectual interest of the scholar. Theoretically, then, one can imagine as many definitions of areas and of area problems as there are scholars interested in that particular region. In practice, of course, the number of area definitions and problem selections is limited by the number of legitimate intellectual interests with which members of a certain culture will approach other areas at a particular time. Obviously, scholarly interest in the Soviet Union today is focused in a certain way by the general intellectual interests of our culture in which all potentially interested scholars partake.

Fifth, it follows from this observation that the interdisciplinary approach to area studies that is likely to proceed by way of integration and to result in cross-fertilization must be more than the addition of a number of different disciplines concerned with the same area and the same problems within that area. The unifying element in an interdisciplinary area study is not the common concern with an area or even the common concern with certain problems within that area. It is rather the identity of focus directed toward the same problems within the same area which gives unity to an interdisciplinary area study. In other words, representatives of different disciplines stand, as it were, on the same hill looking in the same direction at the same object and try to discern the same thing about this object, be it its nature, its movements, its influence upon other ob-

94

jects, or the influence to which it is subjected by other objects, and the like. These onlookers differ, however, in the kind of instruments they use in order to discern the common object of thèir intellectual curiosity. This is integrated area research.

Since the different scholars use different instruments on the same object, they are bound to see different qualities in that object. By communicating to each other what they have seen, the minds of all concerned correlate the results of the researches of the others with their own. This mutual communication is what is called "cross-fertilization."

Sixth, the different disciplines that are brought to bear upon an area problem are not equal with each other. If they were, true and full integration would be impossible. We have said that integrated research means that different disciplines want to know the same thing about the same object. But who determines what that same thing is going to be? Area research may center upon the economic structure of the Siamese village, and then it is economics which determines the common object of intellectual curiosity; and the other disciplines called in for co-operation, such as anthropology, geography, political science, must subordinate their own specific interests to the interests of economics. Or we are interested in the political structure of the Siamese village, and then it is political science which sets the theme and determines the outlook of the auxiliary sciences. In one word, interdisciplinary area research requires more "discipline" than disciplinary research; for it requires the subordination of the specific interests of certain disciplines to the dominant one. Integration requires a hierarchy of interests in which one interest has the function of integrating the others.

Seventh, underlying all area research must be the awareness that all the specific manifestations of a particular culture contain an element of universality, however undiscoverable or unprovable it may be in a particular instance. Area research, then, must take into account an element that transcends the limits of any particular area. More than that, it is this transcendent element which makes area research possible in the first place. For if we could not assume that, while investigating a foreign area, we should find not only things that are strange but also things that are familiar, we would not be

95

able even to try to understand a foreign area and would face it uncomprehendingly.

The element of universality, transcending any particular area and common to all, may be called human nature. However different its specific manifestations at different times and places, it is the same everywhere and at all times. Without assuming its identity in time and space, we could see in other cultures, past or present, nothing more than either a mass of incomprehensible facts or else a distorted image of our own culture. Thus every historian and area specialist must assume implicitly the identity of human nature in time and space in order to be able to understand at all, however loudly he may deny its existence. It is at this point that we come face to face with what is perhaps the most serious shortcoming of contemporary area studies.

Contemporary area studies assume that the key to the understanding of a foreign area lies in the investigation of the specific phenomena that make up that area. If we want to understand China we must study China; if we want to understand France we must study France. Yet might it not be said that, in order to understand China or France or any other area, it is first necessary to understand mankind, of which all areas are but particular manifestations? If I know something about human nature as such, I know something about Chinese and Frenchmen, for I know something about all men. It is true that this something I know about all men is general and liable to lead me astray if I try to explain through it the concreteness of a particular historical situation. Yet without such a conception of human nature, made articulate in a philosophy of man and society, a foreign area can be no more than a mysterious oddity, attractive or repulsive as the case may be, and at best to be understood in terms of one's own culture.

That this is not mere idle speculation everyday experience shows. Why is it that I am able to understand the Homeric heroes or Chaucer's pilgrims without having mastered the area research of ancient Troy and medieval England? Why is it that I am able to comprehend the domestic and foreign policies of contemporary Russia without being an area specialist in the Russian field? Why is it that I have a general understanding of contemporary China while I am virtually ignorant about China as an area? Why is it that the members of the British foreign service have been traditionally trained in the humanities and more particularly in the classics and then sent in succession to the four corners of the earth, showing frequently superb understanding of the areas in which they worked? The answer to these questions has already been given: if you know something about man as such you know something about all men. You know at least the contours of human nature which, when superimposed upon a concrete situation, may get blurred here and there and which always lack specific content and color. It is for area studies to provide an empirical check upon their correctness and that specific content and color. This, then, is a plea not for giving up area studies as at present executed and for reviving an exclusive humanistic approach, but rather for the recognition of the limitations of both. The future of area studies seems to lie in a combination of both approaches, with the emphasis upon one or the other according to the qualifications and preferences of the group undertaking such research.

A word might be said in passing about the lessons to be learned from the traditional classical studies which frequently have been referred to as the prototype of the area studies of our day. This they are not; for what distinguishes traditional classical studies and contemporary area studies is exactly the philosophical orientation in the former and lack of such orientation in the latter. The rationale underlying classical studies was no practical purpose or curiosity for its own sake or a special research interest, but the conviction that in the civilization of ancient Greece and Rome the nature of man in all its manifestations could be detected in its purest form, to be emulated by the generations to come. The error of that approach was its cultural absolutism which took classical civilization to be the norm by which all other civilizations were to be judged. The truth of classical studies, largely ignored by contemporary area studies, is to be found in their conviction, accepted as self-evident, that the study of any civilization requires an underlying conception of the nature of man which gives direction and form to the research to be undertaken.

Since what is wrong with area studies also handicaps international relations as an academic discipline, the remedies in both cases must be, *mutatis mutandis*, the same. We have seen that international relations has concerned itself indiscriminately with everything that is "international," that is, that transcends the boundaries of a particular nation. To establish an academic discipline with the adjective "international" as its focus is obviously no more possible than to center one on the adjective "national." Such attempts, on the national or international level, will lead either to the restoration, by dint of their own logic, of the traditional academic disciplines and consequently to the frustration of interdisciplinary integration, or else to the drowning of all discipline in a chaotic mass of unrelated data which will at best receive from the ever changing whims of public opinion a semblance of order and direction.

The need for a principle of order and a focus, narrower than the mere reference to things international and more germane to the things we want to know when we study international relations, could not have been lost on university administrations which were responsible for the organization of research and teaching in the field of international relations. The idea of the core, composed of what is considered to be the more important academic disciplines bearing upon international relations, has resulted from the recognition of that need. Yet it was a step in the wrong direction. The idea of the core fails to distinguish between the need for multidisciplinary knowledge, without which international relations cannot be understood, and the requirement of a principle of order or focus for intellectual curiosity, without which no academic discipline can exist. The idea of the core accepts the former while rejecting the latter.

An expert in international relations must of course know something about international law, international organization, international politics, international economics, international geography, diplomatic history. If he knows nothing more than that he possesses a collection of fragmentary knowledge taken from different disciplines; if he is able to integrate these fragments of knowledge into a new discipline called "international relations," as has already been pointed out, he does so by virtue of the integrative powers of his mind, not because of the training he has received. International relations, like area studies, must have a focus, and it cannot be law, politics, economics, geography, and what not at the same time. Not all that is important to know about international relations can have the same value as the integrating principle and focus of an academic discipline. International relations as an academic discipline, no less than area studies, requires a hierarchy of intellectual interests, one of which is predominant, providing the principle of integration, while the others are subsidiary, supplying the knowledge necessary for the satisfaction of the predominant interest.

What is the predominant interest of international relations as an academic discipline? Two different answers must be given to that question. The first is identical with the one we gave when we raised the same question with regard to area studies. That is to say, the possible predominant interests are as numerous as are the legitimate objects of intellectual curiosity. It is, then, as legitimate to put economics in the center of international relations as it is to put law or geography there and to subordinate other disciplines to the predominant economic, legal, or geographical interests. In this view as many "sciences" of international relations are possible as there exist predominant interests which correspond to legitimate objects of intellectual curiosity.

This answer to our question opens up three possibilities for academic organization. First, it is possible to deal with international relations, thus conceived, in the different established departments which are selected according to the predominant interest of the scholar and student. International economics would then be dealt with in the department of economics, which would request such aid from other departments as it needed. Second, special academic organizations can be established with one predominant interest as their focus. Thus one can visualize a department or institute of international economics which would group subsidiary disciplines around international economics as its center. Finally, a flexible program can be established, particularly useful for undergraduate instruction, to allow students to select within a department or committee of international relations a number of different combinations, which, however, all center upon one discipline which a student must master. It may be noted in passing that this last arrangement has been put into practice by some of the leading area institutes and schools of international relations.

The other answer to the question of what the predominant interest of international relations must be assumes that among a number of legitimate interests there is in a particular period of history one

99

which demands special attention. The educator must ask himself which among the many foci of international relations is most important for the student's interest to center upon, and the scholar must ask himself which among the many perspectives from which one can investigate international problems is most important from the theoretical and practical point of view. Today most institutions and students have turned to the study of international relations because of their interest in world politics. The primacy of politics over all other interests, in fact as well as in thought, in so far as the relations among nations and areas are concerned, needs only to be mentioned to be recognized. The recognition of this primacy of politics cannot but lead to the suggestion that, among the legitimate predominant interests upon which international relations as an academic discipline might be focused, international politics should take precedent over all others.

For the academic organization of the discipline of international relations this answer can mean two different things. It can mean the establishment of departments, committees, or schools which focus on international politics, subordinating other disciplines to it. Or it can mean that international relations is dealt with in this same way by that traditional academic discipline whose main subject matter is supposed to be the study of politics in all its manifestations, that is, the department of political science. The advisability of this solution will depend upon whether a department of political science actually puts the study of politics in the center of its endeavors or whether—as most of them do—it merely offers a disparate collection of courses whose common denominator is a vague and general relation to the activities of the state.

PART III

THE BURDEN OF AN

OBSOLESCENT TRADITION

W<small>E HAVE</small> pointed out that all great contributions to political thought have been a response to challenges arising from political reality. Their response was necessarily conditioned by an intellectual tradition which, in turn, was a response to the political reality of another day. To what extent is our political tradition adequate to the understanding of the contemporary political world? To what extent does it reflect the perennial truths about politics, and to what extent is it but the product of a particular historic configuration, doomed to obsolescence with the disappearance of the latter? In every historic period, political thought must answer these questions anew. The answers a historic period finds set the limits within which its political thought is to fulfil its creative function, forming a new intellectual tradition fated to be superseded again.

Contemporary political thought is unable to answer these questions; it is even unable to pose them. Its relativism prevents it from raising the perennial problem of the distinction between truth and opinion. In so far as it is consistent in its relativism it cannot even distinguish among different opinions, provided they are socially acceptable. Despairing of coming to terms with contemporary political reality, it retreats, as we have seen, into a methodological dogmatism which provides a respectable shelter from the risks of political controversy.

In the absence of such consistency and by virtue of its involvement in the political situation, political thought tends to identify uncritically a particular opinion, reflecting a particular political position and interest, with truth and thereby to transform theory into ideology. It finds its tools in an intellectual tradition which has been left behind by actual political developments and, thus being removed from political controversy, provides the canons of political orthodoxy to be interposed between the observer's mind and political reality. Outmoded political ideas tend to fill the gap left by the sterility of contemporary political thought. Thus the age lives in good measure upon the intellectual capital accumulated in the past, and the uncritical acceptance of that heritage, stifling the creative awareness of the present, has become a burden which impedes the growth not only of political thought but of political institutions as well.

On the plane of domestic politics, the great new fact with which political thought must come to terms is the diminution of the individual vis-à-vis the state and the concentrations of autonomous social power in the form of giant corporations, labor unions, and mass media of communication. The present age poses anew the problem of individual freedom, and it poses it in the novel configuration of a three-cornered contest between the state, the concentrations of autonomous social power, and the individual. How can the state be made strong enough to protect the individual against these concentrations of autonomous social forces, but not so strong as to be able to subvert the freedom of the individual? In other words, the administrative state raises an issue which cannot be understood, let alone solved, by the traditional juxtaposition between the state and the individual and the ritualistic manipulation of the traditional concepts of constitutional law.

The international scene has been in our time transformed by three great revolutions. The political revolution has destroyed the modern pluralistic state system, kept in being by a flexible balance of power, and replaced it with a bipolar world. The technological revolution has created the technical means both for the total destruction and the total unification of the world. The moral revolution has split the world into two hostile camps, divided not only by political interests but also by political philosophies and ways of life. Consequently, the intellectual tools which helped us in the past to understand and master the problems of international politics all need examination and adaptation to radically new conditions. Their unexamined use, as though this were still the world of their origin, not only impedes understanding but also, as will be shown, stands in the way of successful action.

We have tried elsewhere, both systematically and on the occasion of concrete political problems, to re-examine and reformulate the basic concepts of international politics. We have selected here five concepts whose uncritical use has persistently obscured thought and impeded action: freedom, political and economic, separation of powers, nationalism, neutrality and neutralism, and international law.

6 *Freedom*

During the Civil War, which was a war for freedom in a truer sense than most of the wars which have been so called, Abraham Lincoln laid bare the essentials of the dilemma which has baffled the philosophic understanding of freedom and which has made it appear that there was always something left to be desired in its political realization. On April 18, 1864, Lincoln gave a brief and unpretentious address to the crowd assembled at the Sanitary Fair in Baltimore.

"The world has never had a good definition of the word liberty," he said,

and the American people, just now, are much in want of one. We all declare for liberty; but in using the same *word* we do not all mean the same *thing*. With some the word liberty may mean for each man to do as he pleases with himself, and the product of his labor; while with others the same word may mean for some men to do as they please with other men, and the product of other men's labor. Here are two, not only different, but incompatible things, called by the same name—liberty. And it follows that each of the things is, by the respective parties, called by two different and incompatible names—liberty and tyranny.

The shepherd drives the wolf from the sheep's throat, for which the sheep thanks the shepherd as a *liberator*, while the wolf denounces him for the same act as the destroyer of liberty, especially as the sheep was a black one. Plainly the sheep and the wolf are not agreed upon a definition of the word liberty; and precisely the same difference prevails today among us human creatures, even in the North, and all professing to love liberty. Hence we behold the processes by which thousands are daily passing from under the yoke of bondage, hailed by some as the advance of liberty, and bewailed by others as the destruction of all liberty.

Political freedom, then, has two different and incompatible meanings according to whether we think of the holder or the subject of political power. Freedom for the holder of political power signifies the opportunity to exercise political domination; freedom for the subject means the absence of such domination. Not only are these two conceptions of freedom mutually exclusive in logic, but they are also incapable of coexisting in fact within any particular sphere of action. One can only be realized at the expense of the other, and the more there is of the one the less there is bound to be of the other.

The concept of freedom is contradictory as seen from the vantage point of the political master and his subject. It is also ambivalent in that most members of society are not simply one or the other, master or subject, but both at the same time. B is the master of C and also the subject of A, and C, in turn, is the master of D, and so on. Most men play a dual role with regard to political power, subjecting some to it and being subjected to it by others. When they claim freedom for themselves, what do they mean: their freedom to dominate others or their freedom from domination by others? Perhaps they mean one; perhaps they mean the other; perhaps they mean both. This ambivalence makes inevitably for continuous confusion, manifesting itself typically in ideologies which rationalize and justify the freedom to dominate in terms of the freedom from domination.

It follows that universal and absolute freedom is a contradiction in terms. In the political realm, the freedom of one is always paid for by the lack of freedom of somebody else. The political master can have his freedom only at the price of the freedom of those who are subject to him; the latter can be free only if the master is made to sacrifice his freedom as a master.

What applies to the freedom to exercise political power also reveals itself in the profession and application of the political truth which justifies and informs the exercise of political power. He who believes that he has a monopoly of truth in matters political is free to propound his "truth," which to him appears to be all the truth there is, and to act upon it only if the non-believers are not free to oppose their "truths" to his; for freedom for error to corrupt thought and action is incompatible with the freedom of *the* truth to prevail. On the other hand, the freedom of the many to compete in the market place for acceptance of their different truths requires the abrogation of the freedom of the one to impose his conception of truth upon all.

In any given society not everyone can be as free as everyone else. Every society must decide for itself who shall have what freedom. The kind of freedom a particular society is able to realize in a particular period of its history, then, depends upon the kind of political order under which it lives. The nature of that particular order, in turn, is determined by the fundamental values with which that society identifies itself and which it attempts to realize through the medium of politics. In short, the kind of liberty a society enjoys is determined by the kind of political justice it seeks. Liberty cannot be defined without justice, and it can only be realized by a particular political order informed by a particular sense of justice.

All attempts at realizing freedom have throughout history derived from one of two incompatible conceptions of justice: one, minoritarian; the other, equalitarian.

The minoritarian conception of justice assumes that only a minority, determined by birth, supernatural charisma, or qualifications of achievement, is capable of finding and understanding the truth about matters political and of acting successfully on it. The majority, not so endowed, is subject to the will of the minority, both for its own sake and for the sake of the whole commonwealth. From Plato and Aristotle to the modern justifications of aristocratic and totalitarian government, the denial of political freedom for the majority has derived from a conception of political justice which limits to a minority the ability and, hence, the right to enjoy political freedom.

This conception determines not only the over-all character of political society but also the specific nature of its institutions. It claims for these institutions the attribute of freedom, if not in good faith, at least in good logic. To what Lincoln experienced in the controversies over slavery we can add our experiences with totalitarian arguments.

Communist theory claims that the government monopoly of information and control over the mass media of communication means freedom of the press and the only freedom of the press there is, while what we call freedom of the press is but a sham. The absurdity of the argument does not lie in the claim itself but in the underlying assumption of a government monopoly of political truth, from which the claim follows with logical necessity. For since we have all the political truth there is, so the Communist argument runs, how can we allow freedom of expression to those who refuse to recognize the political truth and, hence, are by definition enemies of the truth, that is, criminals, saboteurs, or foreign agents? And what you in the West call freedom of the press is nothing but the license to sow confusion by propounding error as truth.

The decisive argument against the Communist idea of freedom

and against all political philosophies reserving political freedom to a minority, however defined, must come to terms with the philosophic assumption from which those political philosophies derive. That argument is two-pronged.

It opposes the monistic assumption of a monopoly of political truth vested in a minority with the pluralistic assumption that, while no member of society has a monopoly of political truth or can even be certain what action political truth requires in a given situation, all members of society as rational beings have access to a measure of political truth, however dimly seen. From this equalitarian political ontology and anthropology evolves an equalitarian conception of political justice which postulates equality of political rights and equal treatment of equal situations. Since no conception of political truth, or any political philosophy and program of action derived from it, is necessarily and demonstrably superior to any other, they must all have an equal chance to prevail, but none of them must be given an a priori chance to prevail once and for all. The mechanism through which this equal chance materializes is the periodical majority vote, which decides the issue temporarily either through popular elections or through the enactments of legislative assemblies.

Equalitarianism, then, attacks the minoritarian conception of political justice on the grounds that no minority can be politically so wise in comparison with the majority as to possess a monopoly of political wisdom. No minority can be trusted with absolute power on the assumption that it possesses absolute wisdom. When Cromwell appeals to the representatives of the Church of Scotland, "I beseech you, in the bowels of Christ, to think it possible you may be mistaken," he expresses in the religious sphere the equalitarian mood.

Yet equalitarianism not only refuses to accept the explicit minoritarian claim of infallibility but also rejects its implicit claim to incorruptibility. Here is the other prong of the equalitarian argument. The minoritarian claim to a monopoly of political freedom derives from the overt assumption of a monopoly of political wisdom and of necessity implies a monopoly of political goodness. For the minoritarian claim can be defended by the minority and accepted by the majority only on the assumption that the minority will not abuse its absolute power. The nature of man, as it reveals itself to introspection and through the evidence of history, militates against the correctness of that assumption. The inevitable corruptiveness of power is the political manifestation of the inevitability of sin. Equalitarianism attempts to limit the opportunities for the abuse of power by limiting the political freedom of the holders of power. Western constitutionalism is an elaborate device to subject the political freedom of the holders of political power to institutional limitations and legal controls.

The decisive safeguard, however, against the abuse of political power is the institution of periodical popular elections. The very fact that political power is subject to recall and can be taken for granted only for limited periods of time limits the duration of political power with mechanical sharpness. But it also limits the freedom with which political power can be used as long as it lasts. For since the holders of political power have a natural tendency to keep themselves in power by having themselves re-elected, they must use their political freedom in view of winning the ever impending elections. Thus the preferences of the electorate, real or fancied, are an ever present limitation on the freedom of the holders of political power to use that power as they would like to. The absolute ruler is free to govern as he sees fit, subject only to the limits of physical nature. The freedom of constitutional government is hemmed in not only by institutional devices and, in so far as it is democratic, by the mechanical limits of popular elections but also by the political dynamics of the democratic process. It is this contrast between the complete freedom of the absolute ruler to exercise the authority of government at his discretion and the limits within which constitutional government must operate which Theodore Roosevelt had in mind when he expressed the wish to be for twenty-four hours President, Congress, and Supreme Court at the same time.

The democratic processes, in order to be able to delimit the freedom of the rulers to govern, must themselves be free to bring the will of the majority to bear upon the personnel and policies of the government. The freedom of the government to control and replace the rulers and the limitations upon the rulers' freedom to govern are the two sides of the same coin, the latter being a function of the former. Without that freedom of the governed, democracy loses its substance; for it no longer provides the people with the freedom of choosing rulers and, through them, policies. A democracy that loses that freedom can survive only as the periodical plebiscitarian approval of the personnel and the policies of the government. This is the totalitarian type of democracy.

One would misunderstand the nature of democracy and of totalitarianism as well as their relationship were one to suggest that totalitarian elections are necessarily and always a sham and that they never reflect the true will of the people. They may well reflect that will, as elections in Nazi Germany and Fascist Italy undoubtedly did, expressing a consensus between the popular will and the government. Here lies the decisive difference between traditional autocracy and modern totalitarianism. Autocracy imposes its will upon an indifferent or hostile people; totalitarianism aims at, and may succeed in, governing with the consent of the governed.

However, what sets totalitarianism apart from genuine democracy is the manner in which the government attains the consent of the governed. Totalitarianism creates that consent through the monopolistic manipulation of the mass media of communication; the consent of the people does not set limits for the government but is a function of its unlimited freedom. In a genuine democracy, on the other hand, the consent of the governed is the temporary result of the interplay of antagonistic forces, competing freely with each other for popular support. The government enters this contest essentially as an equal; whatever advantages it may have by virtue of prestige, influence, and information do not substantially affect the principle of free competition. Thus a genuinely democratic government can never be certain whether it will survive the next election to be replaced by another which, in turn, must subject its personnel and policies to the popular judgment in still another election to come.

Genuine democracy must forever guard against the temptation to transform itself into an imperfect type and then to degenerate into totalitarianism. While democracy requires that the will of the people limit the freedom of the government, it also requires that the freedom of the popular will be limited. A popular will not so limited becomes the tyranny of the majority which destroys the freedom of political competition and thus uses the powers of the government to prevent a new majority from forming and to intrench itself permanently in the seat of power. There is only a small step from the destruction of the freedom of competition, that is, imperfect democracy, to the destruction of competition itself, that is, totalitarianism.

The freedom of political competition essential to democracy can be impaired in two different ways. The people are being deprived of their freedom of choosing among alternative policies by choosing among different candidates for office if the different candidates for office are not identified with different policies but compete for power as an end in itself, not as a means for a particular policy. The people may still be able to choose in terms of the personal qualities of the candidates, such as competence and trustworthiness; their choice has no meaning for the substance of the policies to be pursued. The people, if they do not vote for the person of a candidate as such, will then vote out of habit or not at all, and in the measure in which this happens democratic elections will have lost their ability to protect the freedom of the people by limiting the freedom of action of the government.

The other—and more insidious—threat to freedom of political competition stems from the tendency of all majorities to act upon the assumption that they are more—at best—than temporary approximations to political truth, that is, the repositories of all the political truth there is. They tend to think and act, as long as they last as majorities, as though their will provided the ultimate standard of thought and action and as though there were no higher law to limit their freedom. The majority, as long as it lasts, tends to become the absolute master, the tyrant, of the body politic, stifling in that body the vital spirit of questioning and initiative and evoking instead the submissiveness of conformity. Yet since there is no higher standard for thought and action than the will of the majority, in theory at least each successive majority may produce a new tyrant with a political truth of its own. One political orthodoxy may be succeeded by another, calling forth a new conformity, and the very relativism which is the philosophic mainspring of the supremacy of the majority will produce not only the tyranny of the majority but also a succession of tyrannies, all justified by the will of the majority.

While this is possible in theory, it is, however, not likely to occur for any length of time in practice. For the majority, by making itself the supreme arbiter of matters political, must at least implicitly deny to the minority the right to make itself the majority of tomorrow. Since the majority of today tends to claim a monopoly of political truth, it must also tend to claim a monopoly of political power, freezing the existing distribution of power. In one word, the majority of today tends to transform itself into a permanent majority and, by the same token, to reduce the minority of today to a permanent one.

This development not only reduces the minority to a permanent one but also deprives it of its democratic reason to exist. That reason is its ability, equal in principle to that of the majority, to have access to political truth and act upon it; hence its claim to compete freely for becoming the majority tomorrow. The assumption that the majority has a monopoly of political truth destroys the minority's political function and gives the respect for its existence an anachronistic quality. Since its continuing existence implicitly challenges the majority's monopolistic claims, is a living reminder of alternative rulers and policies, and may, by virtue of these attributes, become a political nuisance to the majority, the minority cannot for long survive the destruction of its philosophic justification and political function. With its destruction, democracy itself comes to an end. The unlimited freedom, that is, the tyranny, of the rulers corresponds to the unlimited lack of freedom of the ruled.

Thus decadent democracy goes through three stages before it transforms itself into its opposite: totalitarian tyranny. It starts out by emptying itself of part of its substance: it destroys the freedom of choosing policies by choosing men. Then it substitutes for the spirit of free political competition, which derives from a pluralistic conception of political truth, the monistic assumption that only the majority possesses that truth. Then it subjects the minority to restrictions which put it at a decisive disadvantage in the competition for intellectual influence and political power, thus transforming the majority into a permanent one, existing side by side with a permanent minority. The process of degeneration is consummated with the majority becoming the sole legitimate political organization, which combines the claim to a monopoly of political truth with a monopoly of political power.

Against these tendencies toward self-destruction, inherent in the dynamics of democracy, the institutions and the spirit of liberalism stand guard. Liberalism has erected two kinds of safeguards: one in the realm of philosophic principle, the other in the sphere of political action.

Liberalism holds certain truths to be self-evident, which no majority has the right to abrogate and from which, in turn, the legitimacy of majority rule derives. These truths, however formulated in a particular historic epoch, can be subsumed under the proposition that the individual—his integrity, happiness, and self-development—is the ultimate point of reference for the political order and, as such, owes nothing to any secular order or human institution.

It is on this absolute and transcendent foundation that the philosophy of genuine democracy rests, and it is within this immutable framework that the processes of genuine democracy take place. The pluralism of these processes is subordinated to, and oriented toward, those absolute and transcendent truths. It is this subordination and orientation that distinguishes the pluralism of the genuine type of democracy from the relativism of its corrupted types. For in the latter the will of the majority is the ultimate point of reference of the political order and the ultimate test of what is politically true. Whatever group gains the support of the majority for its point of view gains thereby also the attributes of political truth, and the content of political truth changes with every change in the majority. Out of this relativism which makes political truth a function of political power develops, as we have seen, first the tyranny, and then the totalitarianism, of the majority, unlimited as it is by an absolute, transcendent conception of political truth. Thus the relativism of majority rule, denying the existence of absolute, transcendent truth independent of the majority will, tends toward the immanent absolutism of a tyrannical or totalitarian majority, while the pluralism of genuine democracy assumes as its corollary the existence of such truth limiting the will of the majority.

As a matter of philosophic principle, the political order is oriented toward the individual; the political order is the means to the individual's end. Yet as a matter of political fact, as we have seen, it is the very earmark of politics that men use other men as means to their ends. That this cannot be otherwise is one of the paradoxes of the politics of liberalism; for political reality disavows, and does so continuously and drastically, the postulates of liberal philosophy. Liberalism believes in the truth of man's freedom, but it finds man everywhere a slave. Thus it adds another paradox—more shocking than the first for being the result of liberalism's own efforts—by creating political institutions which limit the freedom of some in order to preserve the freedom of others. Constitutional guaranties of civil rights and their legislative and judicial implementation are the liberal defenses of freedom of political competition. While the will of the majority decides how these guaranties are to be implemented, the existence of the guaranties themselves is not subject to that will. Quite to the contrary, these guaranties set the conditions under which the will of the majority is to be formed and exercised. They establish the framework of democratic legitimacy for the rule of the majority.

Yet the very need for these safeguards limiting the freedom of the majority points up the dilemma that liberalism faces. If the majority could be trusted with its power, the liberal safeguards would be unnecessary. Since it cannot be so trusted, its freedom must be curtailed for the very sake of freedom. The dilemma which concerned Lincoln in the individual relations between the wolf and the lamb reappears in the collective relations between majority and minority. It manifests itself here typically in the concrete terms of the antinomy between individual rights and some collective good, such as general welfare, administrative efficiency, national security. The liberal concern for individual rights may stand in the way of the maximization of such a collective good, and the greater the need for the full realization of a collective good appears to be, the greater is the temptation to sacrifice individual rights for its sake. Is individual freedom more important than national security, without which there will be no freedom at all? What benefits does a man draw from the Bill of Rights if, in the absence of measures of general welfare, it guarantees him the right to sleep under bridges and sell apples in the street?

This dilemma lies outside the purview of liberal philosophy, which inclined to identify itself in the nineteenth century with the individualistic prong of the dilemma and shifted in the twentieth to the other, collectivist, one. Thus the philosophy of liberalism can provide no intellectual tools with which to master this dilemma. The decline, in our time, of liberalism as theory and practice is the result.

Liberalism conceived of the problem of freedom in terms of a simple juxtaposition between society and the state. It saw the sole threat to individual freedom in the state, conceived either as an aristocratic minority or a democratic majority. Liberal policy, then, had a twofold aim: to erect a wall between the government and the people, behind which the citizens would be secure, and to confine the government behind that wall in as narrow a space as possible. The smaller the sphere of the state, the larger the sphere of individual freedom was bound to be.

However, the aspirations for power, and the struggle for power resulting from them, could not be so neatly confined; for these aspirations are not the exclusive property of any group but common to all men, ruler and ruled, oligarchs and democrats. The autonomous forces of society, left to themselves, engendered new accumulations of power as dangerous to the freedom of the individual as the power of the government had ever been. And while liberalism had assumed that the weakness of the government assured the freedom of the individual, it now became obvious that it also assured the unhindered growth of private power, destructive of individual freedom. Against these concentrations of private power, which derived primarily from economic controls, the state was called back from the corner in which it had been confined to do battle. The state, which had just been relegated to the inconspicuous and relatively innocuous role of a night watchman by a society fearful of its power, was now restored to power as the protector of individual rights. Thus the modern state bears a Janus head: one face that of a monster lusting for power over the individual, the other with the benevolent mien of the individual's defender against his fellows' infringements of his freedom.

The struggle for freedom in the modern state has thus become a three-cornered fight, and the old dilemma reappears in a new and intricate configuration. A new feudalism of giant concentrations of economic power in the form of corporations and labor unions vies with the old tyranny of the state for limiting the freedom of the individual, subjecting ever new spheres of formerly free individual action to ever more stringent restrictions. That new feudalism calls into being the "new despotism" of the administrative state, which, for the sake of individual freedom, superimposes its restrictions upon those of the concentrations of economic power. From the latter's vantage point, this is but the old tyranny in modern garb. Yet the mass of individual citizens welcomes the administrative state as the champion of freedom.

It is the measure of the inadequacy of the simple juxtapositions of nineteenth-century liberal philosophy and the measure of the inner contradictions and ambivalences of freedom as it actually operates in the modern state that both sides have a point. The administrative state can become a new despot to some and a new liberator to others, as majority rule can be both the nearest approximation to freedom in a mass society and a many-headed and, hence, unassailable destroyer of freedom.

7 *The New Despotism and the New Feudalism*

This precarious state of freedom in the modern age is most obvious in the economic sphere. It is the result of two factors: the denial of freedom from within the economic sphere itself through the accumulation of uncontrolled power in the hands of economic organizations, such as corporations and labor unions, and the denial of freedom in consequence of the intervention of the state in the economic sphere, in good measure in order to restore its freedom threatened from within. Thus the economic sphere has lost whatever autonomy it has had in the past: it is subject to political control as it, in turn, tries to control political decisions. We are in the presence of the revival of a truly political economy, and the major economic problems are political in nature.

This interconnectedness of the political and economic spheres is not peculiar to our age. Even in the heyday of nineteenth-century liberalism, the strict separation of the two spheres was in the nature of a political ideal rather than the reflection of observable reality. The monetary, tax, and tariff policies of the government had then, as they have now, a direct bearing upon the economic life—and so had the outlawry of the association of working men as criminal conspiracy. Yet the ideal of strict separation served the political purpose of protecting the economic forces from political control without impeding their influence in the political sphere.

What is peculiar to our age is not the interconnectedness of politics and economics but its positive philosophic justification and its all-persuasiveness. The state is no longer looked upon solely as the umpire who sees to it that the rules of the game are observed and who intervenes actively only if, as in the case of the railroads, the rules of the game favor one player to excess and thereby threaten to disrupt the game itself. In our age, aside from still being the umpire, the state has also become the most powerful player, who, in order to make sure of the outcome, in good measure rewrites the rules of the game as he goes along. No longer does the government or society at large rely exclusively upon the mechanisms of the market to insure that the game keeps going. Both deem it the continuing duty of the government to see to it that it does.

In the United States, the state pursues three main purposes in the economic sphere: observance of the rules of the game, maintenance of economic stability, and national defense.

The rules of the game are oriented toward the pluralistic objectives of American society. Thus they seek to prevent any sector of the economy from gaining absolute power vis-à-vis other sectors of the economy, competitors, or the individuals as such, by controlling and limiting its power. Regulatory commissions, legislation controlling and limiting the strong and supporting the weak, tariff and monetary policies serve this purpose.

While the state started to assume responsibility for the rules of the game in the last decades of the nineteenth century, it made itself responsible for economic stability in the 1930's. Economic stability, in this context, signifies the mitigation, if not the elimination in certain sectors, of the business cycle. Its main positive characteristics, as conceived by the government of the United States, are stability of employment, stability of the value of the dollar, and stability of agricultural prices. A plethora of legislative and administrative devices serves this purpose.

Since the end of the Second World War, technological research and industrial production have become to an ever increasing extent the backbone of military defense. The regular annual expenditure by the government of close to forty billion dollars on national defense, its decrease or increase from year to year, its shift from one sector of the economy to another, all exert a sometimes drastic influence upon the economic life of the nation. They have made the government the most important single customer for the products of the national economy. In addition, many tax and monetary policies and price and wage policies are determined by considerations of national defense.

With the government thus exerting an enormous controlling, limiting, and stimulating influence upon the economic life, the ability to influence the economic decisions of the government becomes an indispensable element in the competition for economic advantage. Economic competition manifests itself inevitably in competition for political influence. This political influence is exerted through two channels: control of, and pressure upon, government personnel.

The most effective political influence is exerted by the direct control of government personnel. The economic organization which has its representatives elected to the legislature or appointed to the relevant administrative and executive positions exerts its political influence as far as the political influence of its representatives reaches. In so far as the representatives of these economic organizations cannot decide the issue by themselves, the competition for political influence and, through it, economic advantage will be fought out within the collective bodies of the government by the representatives of different economic interests. While this relationship of direct control is typical in Europe, it is by no means unknown in the United States. State legislatures have been controlled by mining companies, public utilities, and railroads, and many individual members of Congress represent specific economic interests. Independent administrative agencies have come under the sway of the economic forces which they were intended to control. The large-scale interchange of top personnel between business and the executive branch of the government cannot help but influence, however subtly and intangibly, decisions of the government relevant to the economic sphere.

However, in the United States the most important political influence is exerted through the influence of pressure groups. The decision of the government agent—legislator, independent administrator, member of the executive branch—is here not a foregone conclusion by virtue of the economic control to which he is subject. His decision is in doubt, for he is still open to divergent economic pressures. The competition for determining the decisions of the government takes place not among the government agents themselves but between the government agent, on the one hand, and several economic pressure groups, on the other. Only after this competition among several pressure groups has been settled one way or another will the government agents compete with each other, provided the issue is still in doubt.

The political struggle, ostensibly fought for victory in periodical elections by political parties, reveals itself in good measure as a contest of economic forces for the control of government action. In consequence, the decision of the government, and more particularly of legislatures, ostensibly rendered "on the merits of the case," tends to reflect the weight of economic influence and, at worst, to give political sanction to decisions taken elsewhere. Legislators and administrators tend to transform themselves into ambassadors of economic forces, defending and promoting the interests of their mandatories in dealing with each other on behalf of them. The result is a new feudalism which, like that of the Middle Ages, diminishes the authority of the civil government and threatens it with extinction by parceling out its several functions among economic organizations to be appropriated and used as private property. And just like the feudalism of the Middle Ages, these new concentrations of private power tend to command the primary loyalties of the individual citizens who owe them their livelihood and security. In the end, the constitutionally established government tends to become, in the words of Chief Justice Marshall, a "solemn mockery," glossing over the loss of political vitality with the performance of political rituals.

If giant concentrations of economic power, in the form of corporations and labor unions, were thus to become laws unto themselves, deciding with finality the matters vital to them and using the government only for the purpose of ratifying these decisions, they would not only have drained the lifeblood from the body politic but also have destroyed the vital energies of the economic system. For the vitality of the American economic system has resided in its ability to renew itself on new technological opportunities, unfettered by the interests identified with an obsolescent technology. Seen from the vantage point of the individual enterprise, this is what we call freedom of competition. This freedom of competition has been a function of the rules of the economic game, as formulated and enforced by the state.

Yet the new feudalism, if it is not controlled and restrained, must inevitably tend to abrogate these rules of the game in order to assure the survival of the economic giants which, in turn, tend to take over the functions of the state. The consummation of this development, possible but not inevitable, would be a state of affairs in which for those giants the rule of life would not be freedom of competition, which might jeopardize their survival, but freedom from competition in order to secure their survival. The dynamics of the capitalistic system, especially in the United States, continually destroying and creating as life itself, would then give way to a gigantic system of vested interests in which the established giants would use the state to make themselves secure from competitive displacement, only to die the slow death of attrition.

It is the measure of the quandary which modern society faces in this problem that the most obvious cure raises issues as grave as the disease. That cure is a state strong enough to hold its own against the concentrations of private power. In good measure, such a state already exists. It is the state whose importance for the economic life of the nation we have discussed above. In so far as this state is able to act as an independent political force, controlling, restraining, and redirecting economic activities, it is indeed the strong state, capable of keeping the concentrations of private power in check. Yet such a state, by being strong enough for this task, cannot fail to be also strong enough to control, restrain, and redirect the economic activities of everybody. In other words, as the liberal tradition correctly assumes, a strong government, whatever else it may be able to accomplish, threatens the liberties of the individual, especially in the economic sphere.

Thus modern society is faced with a real dilemma: a government which is too weak to threaten the freedom of the individual is also too weak to hold its own against the new feudalism; and a government which is strong enough to keep the new feudalism in check in order to protect the freedom of the many is also strong enough to destroy the freedom of all. What, then, must it be: the new feudalism of private power or the new despotism of the public power? The problem thus posed cannot be solved by any simple formula which endeavors to restore the juxtaposition of society and state from which the philosophy of nineteenth-century liberalism evolved. Rather, the solution of the problem must start from the terms in which it poses itself in the twentieth century.

A fruitful approach to this dilemma is suggested by the principles underlying the constitutional devices, institutional arrangements, and political dynamics of the American system of government by which *The Federalist* successfully tried to combine, in the simple relations between society as a whole and the state, a strong government with a pluralistic society. The same combination, in the complex conditions of the contemporary, three-cornered contest, must rest upon the same foundation of the intricate interplay of multiple systems of checks and balances. These systems, if they work perfectly, limit on all levels of social interaction, private and governmental, the freedom of all for the sake of everybody's freedom. They do so in two different respects, through their internal structure and through their relations with each other. The classic analysis of these two functions is provided by Number 51 of *The Federalist*. As concerns the function of the internal structure of a particular system:

This policy of supplying by opposite and rival interests, the defect of better motives, might be traced through the whole system of human affairs, private as well as public. We see it particularly displayed in all the subordinate distributions of power; where the constant aim is, to divide and arrange the several offices in such a manner, as that each may be a check on the other; that the private interest of every individual, may be a sentinel over the public rights.

And for the relations among different systems:

It is of great importance in a republic, not only to guard the society against the oppression of its rulers; but to guard one part of the society against the injustice of the other part. Different interests necessarily exist in different classes of citizens. If a majority be united by a common interest, the rights of the minority will be insecure. There are but two methods of providing against this evil: The one by creating a will in the community independent of the majority, that is, of the society itself; the other by comprehending in the society so many separate descriptions of citizens, as will render an unjust combination of a majority of the whole very improbable, if not impracticable. . . . The second method will be exemplified in the federal republic of the United States. Whilst all authority in it will be derived from, and dependent on the society, the society itself will be broken into so many parts, interests, and classes of citizens, that the rights of individuals, or of the minority, will be in little danger from interested combinations of the majority. In a free government, the security of civil rights must be the same as that for religious rights. It consists in the one case in the multiplicity of interests, and in the other, in the multiplicity of sects. The degree of security in both cases will depend on the number of interests and sects. . . .

In the end, the freedom—economic and political—of the individual in the modern state is not the result of one specific constitutional device or institutional arrangement, although such a device or arrangement may well make freedom more secure. Freedom rather reposes upon the social order as a whole, the distribution of concrete values to which society is committed. It is not enough for society to recognize the inalienable right of the lambs to life, liberty, and the pursuit of happiness and to have on the statute books provisions against the activities of wolves detrimental to the lambs. The freedom of both the wolves and the lambs will in the end depend upon the values which society attributes, not in the abstract but in the carving out of concrete spheres of action, to the freedom of the wolves and the lambs. What is their due? How far can they be allowed to go? Since neither, and especially not the wolves, can be allowed to go as far as they would like and would be able to go, society must intervene, deciding the value it wishes to put upon their respective capabilities and interests and assigning to each a sphere and mode of action. That intervention may take the form of an explicit decision settling the issue once and for all. More likely and more typically, it will result from the interplay of the totality of social forces, opposing, checking, supporting each other, as the case may be, in ever changing configurations, forming an intricate web of horizontal and vertical connections. It is upon that complex and shifting ground that freedom rests in the modern world.

8 *Separation of Powers*[1]

In an illuminating analysis of its fundamental problems, Professor Gellhorn divides the history of administrative law into three periods, the first focusing its interest upon the constitutional divisions of power, the second searching for the appropriate boundaries of judicial review, and the third, in which we find ourselves at present, concentrating upon the procedures of administration itself.[2] Yet while addressing oneself to this latter task, one cannot but realize that the unfinished business of the preceding periods obstructs the adequate solution of the pressing problems of today.

The "pernicious abstractions" which after the Civil War superseded the great and simple truths of Marshall's Constitution are still impeding the recognition of specific problems of administrative law and their adequate solution. The delimitation of administrative powers under the rule of law is one such problem. Not only is it obscured by the philosophical and political struggle between the "planners" and the "traditionalists,"[3] but the main obstacle to its recognition and solution lies in a legal doctrine which, mistaking its legalistic abstractions for the Constitution, conceals the fundamental relations between statutory and administrative rules behind a veil of conceptualist distinctions and abstract theorems. Behind it and regardless of it, the realities of administrative and judicial practice deal with the realities of administrative problems in a realistic fashion; they may pay lip service to the theory, but they proceed as though it did not exist. It is the legal writers and the legislators who take the theory seriously and on the basis of it measure the administrative powers either too narrowly or too broadly but, lacking sound standards, not adequately.

[1] Legislation and judicial decisions have been covered through 1943. More recent legal material does not affect the theoretical conclusions of this chapter.

[2] Walter Gellhorn, *Federal Administrative Proceedings* (Baltimore: Johns Hopkins Press, 1941), p. 43.

[3] Hans J. Morgenthau, book review in *Columbia Law Review*, XLII (1941), 330.

We shall discuss here the theoretical problems raised by the rule-making functions of administrative agencies, in the light of both legal theory and administrative and judicial practice. We take as our point of departure the Fair Labor Standards Act, whose deficiencies, from the point of view of sound administrative theory, offer an illuminating illustration of the theoretical problems involved.

The main weakness from which the administration of the Fair Labor Standards Act suffers results from the division of functions between Congress and the administrator in regard to the coverage of the act. On the one hand, the statute in rather vague and general language circumscribes positively the coverage of the act. On the other hand, the administrator has the power to issue regulations interpreting, defining, and making definite certain general concepts determining the coverage of the statute. As a further complication, the act does not deal with these powers of the administrator in a uniform way; some derive from express delegation, others do not. According to legal doctrine, the former are considered to have the force of law while the latter are supposed to be only the private opinion of the administrator without any binding force. Primarily concerned with doing justice to the constitutional doctrine of the separation of powers, the act has failed to define clearly the boundaries between the domain of legislative enactment and the sphere of administrative rule-making. Thus it has come to pass that the administrator is, on the one hand, assuming powers which, under a sound division of functions, should be exercised by Congress, and that, on the other hand, powers that are necessary for the enforcement of the act and functionally belong to the administrator are vested neither in him nor in Congress nor anywhere else but are, in case of litigation, discharged by the courts. If there is no litigation they are actually discharged by the administrator, but, from the point of view of the theory, they are not discharged at all.

Congress, the administrator, most of the writers discussing the subject matter, and the courts pay their verbal respects to the classical doctrine that only Congress may make rules with the binding force of law, that the other departments of government are limited to applying and interpreting the legal rules created by Congress, and that, finally, Congress can delegate its rule-making powers to other branches of the government only by limiting the delegated powers to strictly defined subject matters and by subjecting them to definite standards. It follows that, on the one hand, any delegation of powers not satisfying these requirements is invalid and that, on the other hand, any rule created by non-legislative agencies without express congressional delegation is without binding effect.

The congressional deliberations preceding the enactment of the Fair Labor Standards Act took place in the shadow of the Supreme Court decisions in the Schechter[4] and Panama Refining Company[5] cases. These two decisions seemed to give new vigor to this time-honored doctrine, and hence Congress was fearful lest the Fair Labor Standards Act might suffer the fate of the National Industrial Recovery Act.[6] The attention of the members of the Senate and House committees on labor centered upon making the act safe from constitutional attack. Extreme care was therefore taken to delegate to the administrator strictly limited rule-making powers with regard to subject matter as well as standards. "This Act," stated Robert H. Jackson, then Assistant Attorney-General, in the congressional hearings, "combines everything, and is an attempt to take advantage of whatever theories may prevail on the Court at the time that the case is heard."[7]

The act, therefore, delegates comprehensive rule-making powers only in regard to the determination of minimum wages. Within this broad and comprehensive field the rule-making powers of the administrator are strictly circumscribed, apart from the general statutory standards, by the legislative determination of minimum and maximum wages as well as by the administrator's inability to change the industry committee's wage recommendation which he is permitted only to reject or accept *in toto*. He can accept a recommendation only under the condition that it is made in accordance with law and

[4] *A. L. A. Schechter Poultry Corp.* v. *United States, 295* U.S. 495 (1935).

[5] *Panama Refining Co.* v. *Ryan, 293* U.S. 388 (1935).

[6] The decisions seem not to have been interpreted correctly by Congress, for the issue at stake in these cases was not delegation, but alienation, of legislative powers; that is, Congress tried to confer on the President legislative powers without clear limitation of subject matter. Congress cannot divest itself of powers vested in it.

[7] *Joint Hearings before the Senate Committee on Education and Labor and the House Committee on Labor on S. 2475 and H. R. 2700, 75*th Cong., 1st sess. (1937), p. 54; 52 Stat. 1060 (1938), 29 U.S.C. § 202 (1940).

supported by the evidence adduced at the hearing; only in that he must determine whether the recommendation will carry out the legislative purposes does his administrative discretion enter the picture. The judicial character of the proceedings is furthermore emphasized by the provision for judicial review of the wage order. This whole quasi-judicial organization of a "sub-legislative, advisory"[8] institution of industry committees is due to the desire of Congress to meet all possible constitutional objections derived from the principles of due process and delegation of powers.

The act also delegates to the administrator the power to issue regulations and orders prescribing the reports to be made by employers subject to the act, and exempting learners, apprentices, and handicapped workers from the minimum wage provisions. In the remainder of the nineteen sections of the act, no coherent rule-making powers are delegated to the administrator. It is only in four isolated instances that the act empowers the administrator to define certain terms to be found in its provisions. Thus he may determine the reasonable cost of board, lodging, and other facilities; he may determine which industries are of a seasonal nature; he may define and delimit the terms "employed in a *bona fide* executive, administrative, professional, or local retailing capacity, or in the capacity of outside salesman"; and he may finally determine "the area of production" within the meaning of Section 13 (a) (10).

Following the popular conception of bureaucratic administration, one could have anticipated that the administrator would use to the limit the powers expressly conferred on him by Congress and take advantage of any opportunity to assume powers not expressly delegated but necessary for the administration of the act. Yet in a self-effacing fashion, which seems either to point to an administrative inferiority complex and give the lie to the popular conception of bureaucratic arrogance and tyranny or else to offer evidence of a super-Machiavellian hypocrisy, the administrator has accentuated and strengthened the legislative policy by emphasizing the narrowness of the delegated power, on the one hand, and, on the other, the legal impotence of his opinions in the broad domain where no expressly delegated powers exist.

[8] The apt characterization is taken from the Attorney General's Committee on Administrative Procedure, *Administration of the Fair Labor Standards Act of 1938, Wage and Hour Division*, I, 81.

The regulatory activities of the administrator under the Fair Labor Standards Act reflect most faithfully the constitutional doctrine according to which the administrative rule-making powers are dependent upon express statutory delegation. In harmony with this doctrine the administrator has issued regulations claiming the force of law only with respect to those matters which the act has expressly authorized him to regulate. The act deals, however, with a number of matters which are in need of further clarification and implementation, and, as regards the power to regulate them, the act is silent. Faced with the need for regulations, on the one hand, and the apparent lack of power to issue them, on the other, the administrator has resorted to a unique makeshift in publishing interpretative bulletins, which in the language of a legal brief or a learned legal paper explain the law to the public. The administrator is careful to point out in each bulletin (with the exception of No. 4) that the binding effect of these publications is exactly what the language suggests: the private opinion of the administrator.

The distinction between regulations and interpretative bulletins in the administration of the Fair Labor Standards Act corresponds closely to the distinction, developed by legal writers, between legislative and interpretative regulations. Whereas according to this theoretical distinction legislative regulations lay down the law and have the force and effect of law, deriving from a specific delegation of power and supported by statutory sanctions, interpretative regulations only construe the statute and have no more the force and effect of law than the interpretation of a private individual. The latter add nothing to the law as laid down by the statute; they merely guide subordinate administrative officers in the administration of the statute and, furthermore, inform the public of the way in which the administrative agency plans to administer the act. While the legislative regulation, if *intra vires*, must be applied by the courts, the interpretative regulation, being "only an extrinsic aid in deciphering the meaning of an ambiguous statute," may be refused judicial recognition. The theory, however, cannot overlook the fact that frequently interpretative regulations are given great weight by the courts. This fact is reconciled with the theory by the explanation that the interpretative regulations have such weight only if they construe the statute correctly and then it is actually the statute and not the regulation which the individual must obey.

It has been pointed out by those who adhere to this doctrine that on examination of administrative regulations it is frequently doubtful whether the administrative officer intended to issue a legislative or interpretative regulation, that the examination of the statutes does not always lead to unequivocal results, and that in theory and practice the two classes of administrative regulations are frequently confounded. These practical difficulties, however, seem to point to the main objection to which this doctrine exposes itself, namely, that the significance of the distinction between legislative and interpretative regulation does not lie in the one being legally binding and the other not, but is to be found in the degree of discretion allowed by the statute to the administrative officer, which discretion tends to be greater in the former than it is in the latter.

The distinction between legislation and interpretation is, under the American form of government, a matter of degree. Under a constitutional system where the acts of the legislator must meet constitutional requirements and are with respect to them subject to judicial review, one cannot legislate without interpreting the Constitution as construed by the courts. The considerations which guided Congress in formulating the Fair Labor Standards Act are a case in point. It is true that the discretion which the Constitution gives Congress with respect to ends, means, and procedure of legislation is so broad as to make the constitutional standards with which Congress as legislative body has to comply sometimes almost invisible. This is especially so in fields where the power of Congress to legislate is generally unquestioned. The traditional interpretation of the constitutional standards which delimit and define here the legislative powers of Congress has become so ingrained into the public mind that the very existence of these standards is only noticed in case of conflicting interpretations.

If Congress cannot legislate without interpreting the Constitution, an administrative officer cannot interpret an act of Congress without legislating. The traditional theory of interpretation starts with the assumption that sometimes the legislator has been unwilling or unable to say clearly what he wanted to say, that, therefore, the statute has been made "ambiguous," and that in a scientific procedure the correct, hidden "meaning" of the law can be detected. This scientific method of detection is called interpretation. This is, however, not the kind of interpretation courts and administrative agencies usually perform. Their interpretative function is not due to the ambiguity of the statute which is in need of clarification but to the abstractness of the statute which, being applied to a concrete factual situation, is in need of being made concrete. There exists, in other words, a gap between the abstract rule of the statute and the facts to which the rule is to be applied.

This gap judges and administrative officers are supposed to fill by creating, within the limits of the general, abstract rules of the statute, concrete, individualized rules directly applicable to the facts. There is nothing ambiguous in Section 13 (a) (3) of the Fair Labor Standards Act exempting from the minimum wage and maximum hours provisions of the act "any employee employed as a seaman . . ."; nor is there in the term "seaman" a hidden meaning which the professional skill of the lawyer is able to detect in about the same fashion in which the professional skill of the fisherman may detect the pearl hidden in the oyster. The meaning of the term "seaman" on the abstract and general level of the statutory enactment is perfectly clear. Everybody knows what a seaman is, that is to say, what the general characteristics of the abstract type "seaman" are. Yet difficulties arise when we apply the abstract definition and the general characteristics to a concrete situation. Is the ship's surgeon a seaman? And what about the cook, the purser, and the engineer; the pilot, stevedore, and longshoreman? Do the crew of a Mississippi steamer or the skeleton crew of a ship in port come under the exemption? These are questions to be answered by interpretation, that is, by specific, individualized rules applicable directly to the concrete situation.

It follows also from this example that interpretation cannot be a scientific procedure which reaches with logical necessity the one correct solution. The term "seaman" with respect to the enumerated concrete situations is obviously not capable of one determination only, to the exclusion of all others. It can be determined in different ways which are all equally legitimate from the point of view of science and logic. Which way one is to choose is then a matter of personal preference, not of logical necessity. This personal preference of the interpreter will be determined by pragmatic considerations of the values at stake and the interests to be protected, that is, with respect to statutory interpretation, by the policies and purposes of the act to be interpreted. The interpreter of the statute, when he makes his choice among those different logical possibilities, is therefore in search not of the one scientifically correct answer but of the answer which is best adapted to the policies and purposes of the act. Which interpretation meets this test is again a matter not of mere logical subsumption but of value judgments based upon the evaluation of those purposes and policies and of their relation to the term to be interpreted. Within the limits of those purposes and policies, on the one hand, and the abstract, general meaning of the term to be interpreted, on the other, the interpreter may choose the interpretation which in his judgment is most appropriate. How broad his discretion is depends upon the definiteness with which the act states its purposes and policies, as well as upon the strictness with which the act circumscribes the general, abstract meaning of the term.

What administrative agencies and courts do when they interpret a statutory provision such as Section 13 (a) (3) of the Fair Labor Standards Act is, therefore, not in essence but only in the degree of discretion which the interpreting official may exercise, different from what Congress is doing when it legislates under the Constitution, and from what the Supreme Court is doing when it interprets the Constitution. They all legislate by substituting specific, individualized rules for general and abstract rules[9] and by thus creating rules of law which would not exist had they not been created by them; they all interpret by remaining, while legislating, within the limits of abstract, general rules of law. He who interprets of necessity legislates, and he who legislates of necessity interprets.

With respect to the function they perform as legislators and interpreters, the only difference between the different rule-making bodies lies in the number of legislative choices which the rules to be interpreted allow them and, furthermore, in the degree of individualization and concreteness of the rules promulgated by them. At the top of the ladder, as far as broadness of discretion in rule-making and the abstractness and generality of the rules made are concerned, we find the courts interpreting the Constitution. Their discretion is lim-

[9] It should be noted that the terms "general," "abstract," "specific," and "individualized" are of course relative. What is specific and individualized with respect to the general welfare clause of the Constitution may be abstract and general with respect to an administrative regulation.

ited only by the logical limits of the constitutional concepts and the policies and purposes laid down therein. To the vastness of those logical limits and the vagueness of those policies and purposes corresponds the almost limitless broadness of this discretion. Since it is constitutional legislation with which the courts are here concerned, that is, the formulation of fundamental standards with which all official acts must comply, these rules are highly abstract and general.

The discretion of Congress, as a rule-making body, is only subject to the "great generalities" of the Constitution, as formulated by the courts. Hence, Congress is able to choose from among thousands of legislative means and ends, all equally legitimate under the logic, policies, and purposes of the constitutional principles, as formulated by the courts. Since it is the constitutional function of Congress to regulate the acts of groups of people rather than of individuals as such and to deal with typical situations rather than individual ones, its rules are naturally on a high level of abstractness and generality, though being inferior in this respect to the rules of the Constitution.

The discretion of the courts and administrative agencies, with respect to their rule-making functions under the laws of Congress, is limited not only by the logic, policies, and purposes of the Constitution, as formulated by the courts, but also by the logic, policies, and purposes of the statutes. Judge and administrator will find their choice of legislative means and ends to a greater or lesser extent limited by the statutory determination of those means and ends, and under extreme conditions their discretion may be narrowed down to a few alternatives or disappear completely. The increase in the concreteness and individualization of the rules on the statutory level, as over against the constitutional one, of necessity leads to a narrowing of the rule-making discretion on the next lower level, the level of administrative and judicial determination. This, the lowest level in the hierarchy of regulatory powers, is in direct contact with individuals as such whose behavior the government wants to determine, and with individual facts which the statute wishes to regulate. The rules created on this level attain, therefore, the highest degree of individualization and partake least of the abstract and general quality of constitutional and statutory rules.[10]

[10] The idea that the relation between administrative regulation and statute is in principle identical with the one between statute and Constitution has been well stated in *Boske* v. *Comingore,* 177 U.S. 459 (1899): "In determining whether the

These are, however, differences of degree, not of essence. The administrative officer or judge interpreting the term "seaman" within the meaning of the Fair Labor Standards Act performs exactly the same intellectual function as the member of Congress or the Supreme Court judge who interprets the term "interstate commerce" within the meaning of the Constitution. Both interpret the higher rule in order to find the limits of their discretion and both legislate within the limits of this discretion.

Since there is no functional distinction between legislation and interpretation, it is obvious that the distinction between legislative and interpretative regulations cannot be maintained on functional grounds. This is readily demonstrated by a comparison between several provisions of the Fair Labor Standards Act. The administrative determination of the term "seaman" within the meaning of Section 13 (a) (3) of the act is, according to the theory we are here discussing, an interpretative regulation since the act does not expressly delegate to the administrator the power to make this determination. On the other hand, Section 13 (a) (1) of the act provides

---

regulations promulgated by him are consistent with law, we must apply the rule of decision which controls when an act of Congress is assailed as not being within the powers conferred upon it by the Constitution; that is to say, a regulation adopted under Section 161 of the Revised Statutes should not be disregarded or annulled unless, in the judgment of the court, it is plainly and palpably inconsistent with law. Those who insist that such a regulation is invalid must make its invalidity so manifest that the court has no choice except to hold that the Secretary has exceeded his authority and employed means that are not at all appropriate to the end specified in the act of Congress" (at 470); accord *Pacific States Box and Basket Co.* v. *White*, 296 U.S. 176 (1935): "Every exertion of the police power, either by the legislature or by an administrative body, is an exercise of delegated power. Where it is by a statute, the legislature has acted under power delegated to it through the Constitution. Where the regulation is by an order of an administrative body, that body acts under a delegation from the legislature. The question of law may, of course, always be raised whether the legislature had power to delegate the authority exercised. . . . But where the regulation is within the scope of authority legally delegated, the presumption of the existence of facts justifying its specific exercise attaches alike to statutes, to municipal ordinances, and to orders of administrative bodies" (at 185); *State* ex rel. *Wis. Inspection Bureau* v. *Whitman*, 196 Wis. 472, 220 N.W. 929 (1928). It should be emphasized that the statements in the text do not deny the importance of the distinction between legislation and interpretation. What we oppose is only the tendency to erect those functions into conceptualist absolutes and to derive from them legal conclusions. This is the "jurisprudence of conceptions" which belongs to another day.

that the minimum wage and maximum hours provisions "shall not apply with respect to any employee employed in a bona fide executive, administrative, professional, or local retailing capacity . . . (as such terms are defined and delimited by regulations of the administrator)." Such regulations would be legislative in nature since the act delegates the power to make them expressly to the administrator and threatens non-compliance with legal sanctions. Yet no effort is needed to show that the "legislative" function the administrator is authorized to perform in the latter case is identical with the "interpretative" one he performs in the former. The limitations to which his discretion is subject are in both cases the same and so are the functions through which his discretion asserts itself.

If no functional difference corresponds to the distinction between legislative and interpretative regulations, how, then, is the distinction to be explained? The answer will be found in a political philosophy which attributes to the statutory enactments of the legislature a particular dignity not shared by the acts of any other branch of the government.

The doctrine of separation of powers, when in the seventeenth century it was cast in its modern mold, was at once confronted with a conflict between its political intention and a political fact. Its political intention was to destroy the absolute powers of the prince by dissolving those powers into three separate compartments of government, independent from each other and co-ordinated in complete equality. Had the doctrine of separation of powers stopped here, it would, as Hobbes[11] and Kant [12] recognized clearly, of necessity have led to the dissolution of the state itself. For even under a system of separation of powers the sovereign power, that is, the highest governmental power, must reside somewhere. Whenever the doctrine was faced with the test of political performance, it had to overcome this difficulty by destroying the mechanics of its system both from without and from within. It did so by adding to the three separate powers a fourth, the sovereign power, and by elevating one of the three separate powers over the others and making it representative of the sovereign. In the monarchy this fourth power, giving unity to the separate powers and at the same time neutralizing them, is the

[11] *De Cive* (Amsterdam, 1647), pp. xii, 5.

[12] *Rechtslehre* (Königsberg: Bey Nicolovius, 1797), pp. 45, 48.

monarch; in the democracies, such as the France of 1789 and the United States, it is the people, speaking through the constitution. The branch which is thus elevated over the others is in the monarchy, with the exception of England, the executive; in the democracies it is the legislature.

The latter emphasis is most outspoken in revolutionary France, of which Duguit, the great critic of the constitutional doctrine of the French Revolution, has said: "Ils déclarent les trois pouvoirs égaux et indépendants et ils subordonment au pouvoir législatif l'éxécutif et le judiciaire."[13] Similarly in England, modified, however, by the constitutional functions of the Crown, "[the] statute is the highest constitutional formulation of law, the means by which the supreme legislature, after the fullest deliberation, expresses its *final* will."[14] The same emphasis, even though mitigated by the institution of judicial review and the presidential veto, dominates the American legal system. Three factors have contributed to giving Congress as the legislative body a predominant position among the other powers of government.

Since the last decades of the sixteenth century it is the common possession of legal and political thought in the Western world that the statute (*Gesetz, loi, ley*), that is, the general and abstract rule of law addressed to the executive and judicial officers as such, is the successor of the *lex regia* of Roman, and of the *lex Dei* of canon law. Since the last centuries of the Roman Empire *lex* was understood as the authoritative expression of the will of the supreme power, either in the universe or in the state.[15] The general and abstract rule of law, which we call statute, even though not deriving directly from the sovereign power, is supposed to share in the dignity and the unique qualities which tradition attributes to the *lex* of Roman and canon law.[16]

Even though not a sovereign power itself, Congress, nevertheless, cannot fail to occupy in two respects a position markedly superior

[13] Léon Duguit, *La separation des pouvoirs et l'Assemblée nationale de 1789* (1893), p. 116.

[14] A. C. Allen, *Law in the Making* (Oxford: Clarendon Press, 1951), p. 489.

[15] See Ulpian, *Inst.* 12, § 6, pr. D. de const. princ. 1, 4.

[16] See Max Radin, "A Short Way with Statutes," *Harvard Law Review*, LVI (1942), 388, 391.

to the other branches of government. Congress is the only agency of the government through which the sovereign will of the people actually and directly expresses itself. In the Constitution and the institutions established directly under it, popular sovereignty manifests itself in a remote and frequently legalistic and theoretical rather than actual fashion. The popularly elected chief executive stands in a personally exalted but, with regard to concrete political action, vague and general relation to the sovereignty of the people. Only the members of Congress are the "representatives of the people," its agents sent by it to Washington in partial exercise of its sovereign powers. No branch of the government is physically closer to the seat of sovereignty.

The reputed superiority of the statutes is, however, most firmly grounded in the system of separation of powers as it functions under the constitutional form of government. Under this form the sovereign power of the people is supposed to have created the Constitution which guarantees that the co-ordinated executive, legislative, and judicial powers act only within the limits of the rule of law.[17] For the legislative branch and the judiciary, in so far as it interprets the Constitution, the rule of law is the Constitution itself; the same is true only within very narrow limits for the administrative and executive officers.[18] The great bulk of administrative, executive, and judicial acts, however, is subject to the rule of law as formulated in the statutes of Congress. In this view, it is the constitutional function of Congress and of Congress alone to make the rule of law; of the courts and of the courts alone to interpret it; of the executive and administrative branches and of them alone to apply it. Congress, by having, in seeming compliance with the doctrine of separation of powers, the monopoly of making general and abstract rules of law applicable to the great mass of public officials, appears in the eyes of the people as the lawmaker par excellence.

It is for this reason, and not only because of their closeness to the seat of the sovereign power, that the acts of Congress are considered superior to the acts of the other branches of the government. Above them there is only the Constitution, whereas theoretically beside them but actually beneath them are the judicial, executive, and

[17] See Mass. Const., Art. XXX (1780).

[18] See U.S. Const., Art. II.

administrative acts. The "will of Congress" as expressed in the statute is not, to be exact, the will of the sovereign, the people; yet it
comes closer to it than the expression of any other of the constituted
powers. Hence, the other branches of the government owe Congress
obedience. The judges may disregard executive or administrative
acts without much legalistic ado by declaring them "unreasonable,"
"clearly erroneous," or simply "not binding upon the courts." They
may disregard their own decisions by simply stating that the former
decision was wrong. Within the wide logical limits of the "great
generalities" of the Constitution they may move at will. Yet they
would not dare to disregard a statute because they think it is wrong,
that is, because they disagree with its purpose and policies; at least
they would not dare to say so. They will be most anxious to avoid
the impression that they would dare to infringe upon the legislative
monopoly of Congress and will invoke the voice of the sovereign
power itself, that is, the Constitution, in order to justify disregard
for a law of Congress.

Similarly an administrative officer may not be overanxious to prevent his acts from overlapping with the functions of other executive
or administrative officers. Yet he will be careful to show due respect
for the legal rules by which Congress and the courts have circumscribed the limits of his discretion. "Bureaucratic" rule-making seems
to be the farthest removed from the seat of sovereignty, that is, the
will of the people. It operates on the lowest level of abstractness and
generality and, therefore, seems to be the outgrowth of a government of men rather than of laws. And, finally and above all, it is a
novel and alien element within a system of separation of powers,
which knows only three branches of government, each of them performing an exclusive governmental function. Faithful to the doctrine that the rules of law emanating from Congress possess a peculiar dignity all their own and that Congress has the constitutional
monopoly to legislate, of which only Congress can deprive itself
through express delegation, the administrative officer will not dare
to "legislate" unless Congress has expressly told him to do so. It has
been said that "There is nothing sacred in Treasury regulations or
other rules," but there is something very sacred about an act of
Congress.

It is in this constitutional philosophy that we must see the real roots of the distinction between legislative and interpretative regulations and the basis of the conception that only the former can have binding legal effect. In its essence this doctrine is, as it were, the homage which the vice of administrative rule-making pays to the virtue of Congress' legislative exclusiveness. It derives from, and works with, abstract legalistic concepts which, developed three hundred years ago and now petrified into conceptual absolutes, are applied to problems of government entirely different from those which the seventeenth-century writers comprehended in those concepts. Its result is not sound legal theory but constitutional philosophy falsely applied, to wit: conceptualist superstition.

This doctrine has a basis neither in the actual administrative functions performed nor in sound legal theory; nor does it find support in the practice of administrative agencies and courts. Administrative agencies and courts pay their respects to the doctrine in words but do not respect it in deed. An examination of the practice of administrative agencies and courts in this respect will show that what those agencies say they do is not exactly what they actually do.

That the denial of binding legal effect, which is stereotyped in the interpretative bulletins of the administrator under the Fair Labor Standards Act, is of a mere verbal character becomes obvious from a close examination of the exact legal significance of the formula used by the administrator. The administrator in this formula makes three statements: first, that he will be guided by the interpretation in the performance of his administrative duties; second, that the interpretation is subject to judicial review; third, that the interpretation is subject to revision by the administrator himself.

The legal significance of the first statement can only be that the administrator, as far as he is concerned, will apply the statutory rules as interpreted by him, that is, that he will consider them as legally binding. He will apply them whenever his administrative duties obligate him to do so either within the Wage and Hour Division or with regard to employers and employees affected by the provisions of the act. This is exactly what any executive or administrative officer does who interprets an act of Congress with legally binding effect. The second statement likewise refers to the obvious; being subject to judicial review is not a distinctive quality of interpretative regulations devoid of binding legal effect but is, as a matter of principle, common to all acts of government as far as questions of law are concerned. The quality referred to in the third statement interpretative regulations likewise share with all governmental acts, with the exception of certain classes of judicial decisions. Hence, the analysis of the formula pretending to demonstrate the absence of legally binding force in interpretative regulations turns out to demonstrate the exact opposite, that is, the absence of a fundamental difference between interpretative regulations and other rules of law.

The artificial character of the distinction between legislative and interpretative regulations of which only the former would have legally binding effect becomes entirely obvious from an examination of judicial decisions. The courts, fearful of the extension of administrative power and preoccupied with the constitutional aspects of the matter, have concentrated their attack upon the constitutionality of the statutes and of the administrative procedure rather than upon the legality of the administrative regulation. Once the constitutionality of the statutory delegation of power and of the procedural safeguards with respect to the due process requirements was established, the courts have viewed with rather liberal eyes the actual extent of the delegated discretion and the actual use the administrative agencies make of their discretion in promulgating substantive rules and regulations.

The courts generally make no distinction between legislative and interpretative regulations, and in the few cases where a distinction is made, it has no practical importance; that is, the same rules apply regardless of the category to which the regulations are supposed to belong. In other words, for the question whether or not an administrative regulation is legally binding the distinction is irrelevant.

The courts start with the assumption that administrative regulations are not necessarily binding. They do not always state this assumption explicitly but often lay down the conditions under which administrative regulations are held binding, whereupon it follows by implication that in the absence of those conditions the regulations lack binding effect.

What, then, are the conditions, the professed and the actual ones, under which the courts hold administrative regulations legally binding? Logically, the first condition upon which the binding effect of an administrative regulation of necessity depends is the authority of the administrative agency to issue regulations at all. In other words the regulation must not be *ultra vires*. There must also be an objective possibility for administrative regulation which is not the case where the language of the statute does not lend itself to being made more concrete by such regulation since the statutory language is clear and not ambiguous. Once the regulatory power is established the use of the administrative discretion must meet the test of reasonableness and fairness from the point of view of the purposes and policies of the statute; in other words, there must not be an abuse of discretion. The regulation must, furthermore, satisfy mechanical standards with regard to the time of promulgation and the length of time it has been followed by the administrative agency: it must be contemporaneous with the statute from which its authority derives and represent uniform administrative practice over a long period of time. Finally, when during the existence of such administrative practice the authorizing statute is re-enacted without modification of the administrative practice, the regulation from which the latter derives is considered to have become part of the statute itself.

On the face of it, it appears as if the courts require administrative regulations to comply with a number of technical rules of an exceptional character before they recognize their legally binding effect. It can, however, be shown that these apparently special rules, with the exception of the last mentioned, are identical with the general requirements upon the fulfilment of which the judicial recognition of the binding effect of all legal rules, especially statutes, depends. The apparent difference between them is one of emphasis and formulation rather than of substance. While administrative regulations are declared to be binding only when they comply with certain conditions so that there is an implied presumption that normally they are not binding,[19] the presumption with regard to statutes is exactly converse.[20] Both statements, however, say in substance exactly the

---

[19] There is, however, a growing tendency to assimilate administrative regulations to statutes and to hold the former valid without any special qualification, the requirement of contemporaneous and long-continued construction either being entirely omitted or applied only in additional support of the already established validity of the regulation.

[20] *United States* v. *Carolene Products Co.,* 304 U.S. 144 (1938): "We proceed upon the rule often expressed in this court that an act of Congress is to be accepted as constitutional unless on examination it clearly appears to be in conflict with provisions of the Federal Constitution."

same, namely, that the validity of administrative regulations and statutes alike is subject to judicial review.

Under a system of judicial review of questions of law, all rules of law, regardless of the source from which they emanate (with the exception, of course, of the Constitution), are subject, under certain conditions, to approval by the courts. Since the courts have the last word in interpretation, nobody else's interpretation can be absolutely binding upon them. This holds true for statutes as well as executive orders and administrative regulations. Yet while the courts with reference to administrative regulations emphasize the conditions for their binding effect, with regard to statutes they stress the conditions under which binding effect is to be denied. This difference in emphasis stems from two considerations: first, the metaphysical deference for rules of law emanating from Congress and, second, the different degrees of discretion under which Congress and administrative agencies operate.

Administrative regulations, to be respected by the courts, must comply with certain specific conditions. Statutes, to be respected, need not satisfy any specific conditions; their descent from Congress is under normal conditions sufficient legitimation. For administrative regulations to be disregarded the negative proof that certain conditions are not present is sufficient; for statutes to be disregarded positive proof that certain conditions are present is necessary. In other words, when courts declare an administrative regulation valid, they pay first their respects to Congress and then qualified respects to the administrative agency. When they declare a statute valid, they pay their respects first to Congress and then to the Constitution. When, on the other hand, courts declare a statute unconstitutional, they offer their apologies to Congress, deploring their "painful duty"[21] and "irksome"[22] task, and bow before the Constitution. When courts find an administrative regulation devoid of binding effect, they offer apologies to nobody and bow before Congress.

The difference in emphasis is, further, due to the very wide degree of discretion Congress enjoys in its lawmaking activities as compared to the limitations which statutes usually impose upon sim-

[21] *McCulloch* v. *Maryland,* 4 Wheat. (U.S.) 316, 423 (1819).

[22] *Trustees of Dartmouth College* v. *Woodward,* 4 Wheat. (U.S.) 518, 625 (1819).

ilar activities of administrative bodies. Where the discretion is extremely wide the lawmaking body can in the usual course of events be presumed to remain within the limits of the discretion; the validity of the rule may normally be presumed and its lack of binding force considered the exception. Where the discretion is usually strictly confined within more or less narrow limits, transgression of these limitations is more likely, and validity will not be presumed but must be proved.

That the rules regarding *ultra vires* and abuse of discretion are identically applied to both statutes and administrative regulations is obvious.[23] The same is true with respect to the requirements of contemporaneous construction and long-continued uniform practice. The rule that a clear and unambiguous term cannot be subject to construction is a general principle of interpretation which is rarely applied to the construction of the Constitution by statute since most constitutional terms do not meet the requirements of the rule. It is, however, frequently used to limit the regulatory power of administrative agencies; for the statutes, being as a matter of principle more concrete and individualized than the Constitution, will often use concepts which are self-executing and not capable of further individualization or concreteness.

The only rule which the courts apply exclusively to administrative regulations is the so-called re-enactment rule.[24] It is indeed a deviation from the uniformity with which the courts otherwise approach statutes and regulations alike. The re-enactment rule owes its existence to two factors. On the one hand, there is the age-old desire of the courts to rationalize their rule-making activity by mechanical canons of interpretation which makes the judicial decision appear to be the result of an automatic device insuring objectivity and negating the possibility of judicial lawmaking. On the other hand, the re-enactment rule is another offering upon the altar of congressional supremacy and lawmaking exclusiveness. Contempo-

[23] Both standards will generally merge into the test of the constitutionality of the statute.

[24] It should, however, be noted that the re-enactment rule in England, where it originated, is a rule of statutory interpretation, to the effect that once the courts have given a statutory term or phrase a certain meaning, all subsequent statutes are supposed to use the term or phrase with this meaning.

raneous and long-continued administrative practice entitles the administrative regulation to great, yet not absolute, respect; the dignity of a binding rule of law can only come from Congress itself. Hence re-enactment, without change, of a statute construed by an administrative agency, or silent acquiescence by Congress in the administrative construction will give a contemporaneous and long-continued administrative regulation whatever it may still lack in legislative respectability.

The theoretical unsoundness of the re-enactment rule is commensurate with the confusion to which it has led in practical application. Dean Griswold has correctly pointed to the verbal character of the rule which is used by the courts to justify a result arrived at independently from the rule and which is not used at all when the courts disapprove of the result. In so far, the rule partakes of the general criticism which has been leveled against the fictitious character of the canons of interpretation.

More specifically, the rule overshoots the mark in a double sense when it endeavors not only to derive the binding force of administrative regulations from statutory re-enactment but also through this instrumentality to elevate administrative regulations to the level of the statute itself. By doing so, it gives, on the one hand, the administrative regulation more than it deserves and, on the other, it gives it less. Whatever binding force the administrative regulation possesses it receives from the statutory delegation, and it can have no binding force outside of it. Re-enactment cannot add to, nor can its absence detract from, this binding effect. If it exists it does so regardless of re-enactment; if it does not exist re-enactment cannot create it. There is only one way in which congressional re-enactment can convey to an administrative regulation the legal quality of the statute, that is, by incorporating the administrative rule into the statute and thus revoking implicitly the delegation and destroying the binding force of the administrative regulation *qua* administrative regulation altogether. To refer to an administrative regulation as possessing the legal quality of the statute is a contradiction in terms. An administrative regulation that obtains this quality, by this very fact, loses its character as administrative regulation. It is then no longer from administrative discretion created by statutory delegation but from congressional discretion created by constitutional delegation that it receives its binding force.[25]

Since no distinction as to binding effect can be drawn between legislative and interpretative regulations, and since, furthermore, legislative regulations originate in express delegation while interpretative regulations do not, the question arises whence the latter derive their legally binding force. In the case of the administrator under the Fair Labor Standards Act the problem is aggravated by the fact that it was the indubitable intent of Congress, expressed in legislative action before and after the passage of the act, to limit the rule-making powers of the administrator strictly to those matters expressly delegated to him for this purpose.

As Congress can only exercise those powers delegated by the Constitution, so an administrative officer can only exercise the powers delegated to him by statute. Yet as Congress holds delegated powers not expressly enumerated in the Constitution, so an administrative officer may have the authority to exercise delegated powers not expressly pointed out in the statute. In other words, the doctrine of implied powers, as developed in *McCulloch* v. *Maryland*[26] for Congress and the Constitution, applies a general principle applicable whenever general powers are delegated. Hence, there are implied powers vested in administrative agencies as there are implied powers vested in Congress, the extent of those powers generally being proportionate to the extent of expressly delegated powers and therefore usually larger in Congress than in the administrative agencies.

It should be noted from the outset that the doctrine of *McCulloch* v. *Maryland* does not take its point of departure from Article I, section 8 of the Constitution[27] but from "general reasoning." Since the Fair Labor Standards Act, in contrast to most acts conveying administrative powers, does not contain a clause analogous to this provision of the Constitution—here again note should be taken of the

[25] Otherwise there would be true delegation of delegated power and a violation of the basic constitutional principle that only Congress can exercise legislative functions directly under the Constitution.

[26] 4 Wheat. (U.S.) 316 (1819).

[27] "The Congress shall have power . . . to make all laws which shall be necessary and proper for carrying into execution the foregoing powers, and all other powers vested by this Constitution in the government of the United States, or in any department or officer thereof."

structural similarity between constitutional and statutory delegation —we are here only concerned with the propositions of this "general reasoning," the general principle contained therein, and its application to administrative law.

Chief Justice Marshall's argument sets forth the general proposition that the government of the United States is a government of enumerated powers and, hence, can exercise only the powers granted to it, and that with respect to the extent of these powers, the Constitution of the United States does not limit the powers of the federal government to those expressly granted; in other words, it does not require "that everything granted shall be expressly and minutely described;"[28] it does not exclude incidental or implied powers. Indeed, it cannot exclude them since, as a Constitution, it cannot "contain an accurate detail of all subdivisions of which its great powers will admit, and of all the means by which they may be carried into execution. . . . Its nature, therefore, requires that only its great outlines should be marked, its important objects designated, and the minor ingredients which compose those objects be deduced from the nature of the objects themselves. . . . In considering this question, then, we must never forget, that it is a constitution we are expounding."[29]

The general reasoning which led Chief Justice Marshall to these propositions grows out of the natural and necessary relationship between delegating and delegated authority which exists wherever powers are delegated within the framework of a system of legal rules. As far as the end of rule-making is concerned, the holder of delegated powers can have only the powers expressly delegated to him. With regard to the means appropriate to the end, he must have the power to put into effect the measures necessary for achieving the end, regardless of whether or not the delegating rule expressly intrusts him with such power; in so far, he has implied powers. Among the means at his disposal he may choose the one he deems most appropriate to achieving the end; in so far he has discretion. His im-

[28] *McCulloch* v. *Maryland,* 4 Wheat. (U.S.) 316, 406 (1819).

[29] *Ibid.,* at 407. Chief Justice Marshall continued by saying that a government which has the right to act "must according to the dictates of reason be allowed to select the means" and that a construction which would impede the exercise of expressly delegated powers by withholding a choice of means may only be adopted when "the words imperiously require it" (*ibid.,* at 408–9).

144

plied powers are delegated powers; for they are only an incident of the expressly enumerated powers which they serve as means to an end. Since the delegating authority must have intended the recipient of the delegation to perform the delegated functions effectively, it must have given him the means through which alone those functions can thus be discharged. The delegating authority, then, says in substance this: "I want you to achieve these ends (enumerated powers); you may do all that is necessary to achieve these ends (implied powers); among the means thus put at your disposal you may choose the one you deem most appropriate to the end (discretion)."

The implied powers being an incident of the enumerated ones and subordinated to them as means to an end, the extent of the former is to a high degree concomitant with the latter. The larger the powers conferred with regard to the ends, the larger the powers regularly to be implied as to means.[30] This correlation will be lessened or be entirely absent when the delegating rule, while conferring large enumerated powers, determines not only the end to be pursued but also the means to be employed and thus leaves little to implication. The same will be true when the nature of the end, though far-reaching, is such as to lend itself to easy realization, so that the power to be employed to this end need not be great.[31]

It was Chief Justice Marshall himself who in *Osborn* v. *The Bank of the United States*[32] recognized the general importance, beyond the relationship between Constitution and Congress, of the general reasoning of *McCulloch* v. *Maryland*. Whereas in the latter decision the Court discovered implied powers bestowed by the Constitution upon Congress, in *Osborn* v. *The Bank of the United States* the Court went one step further. Here the question arose whether a bank created by Congress, which performs some public functions as an agency of the federal government, whose principal business is, however, of a private nature, consisting of the usual banking operations, can be taxed by a state. The Court answered in the negative

[30] "It has been found, indeed, in the practical administration of the government, that a very large part, if not the largest part, of its functions have been performed in the exercise of powers thus implied." *Hepburn* v. *Griswold,* 8 Wall. (U.S.) 603, 613 (1869).

[31] The same distinction which is made in the text with regard to power applies to discretion.

[32] 9 Wheat. (U.S.) 738 (1824).

since the ordinary banking operations are a necessary means for the performance of the public function. The Court does here no longer deal directly with the relationship between the constitutionally determined ends and the means for achieving those ends, as left by constitutional implication to the determination of Congress (primary means). The performance of normal banking operations does not serve directly the constitutional end, but only indirectly by enabling the bank, the primary means, to function properly. In other words, the performance of normal banking operations is a means (secondary means) for a statutory end which, in turn, serves as a means (primary means) for the constitutional end. It is to the power of Congress to legislate with regard to these secondary means, subordinate to statutory ends, that the Supreme Court in the Osborn case and in the cases following it applies the doctrine of implied powers.

It is true that in these cases the powers with respect to secondary means were expressly conferred on the banking agencies by the statute. The question then arises whether those agencies would possess the same powers in the absence of express congressional delegation. Since without those powers the agencies were unable to perform the functions for which they were created by Congress, it seems to follow from the general premises of the doctrine of implied powers that they would enjoy those powers even in the absence of express congressional delegation.

It is in this sense that the Supreme Court answered the question in *Edward's Lessee* v. *Darby*.[33] Here the question arose whether commissioners under a North Carolina statute had the authority to have surveys made of certain reservations, located around salt licks and springs and not subject to the provisions of the act establishing land grants for soldiers. The statute authorized the commissioners to appoint surveyors for the more speedy and effective laying-off and surveying of the lands subject to such grants. With respect to the power of the commissioners to cause surveys of the reservations, the Court said:

We admit the statute does not give the authority to survey the reservations, in express terms, but do not admit that the authority may not, and does not, result by necessary implication from the duties they were ex-

[33] 12 Wheat. (U.S.) 206 (1827).

pressly required to perform, and from the general provisions of the statute. They were not expressly required by the statute to detemine what licks and springs were proper objects for reservation, and came within the provisions of the statute; but they were required to lay off and cause to be surveyed the lands granted to the officers and soldiers, subject to and so as not to interfere with these reservations. . . . It seems to result necessarily from these provisions, that the commissioners must first determine what were the proper subjects of reservation, and having determined that a given salt lick or spring came within the provisions of the law, the power and duty of laying off by survey the 640 acres reserved, and to be avoided, around the lick, seems necessarily and irresistibly to result to the commissioners, in all cases where they might deem it necessary to do so, in order to enable them to lay off the lands for the officers and soldiers, so as to avoid these reservations. . . . But more especially it was indispensable wherever the commissioners were about to lay off lands for the officers and soldiers, adjacent to a salt lick or spring, to have a survey made of the reservation, to give it figure and fixed locality; otherwise, the reservation being of quantity only, without boundary, one of two consequences must have resulted, namely, that it might lawfully be encroached upon on one side, and if on one, on any other side; or that, practically its uncertainty must have excluded a much larger quantity than was intended by law to be be reserved from the satisfaction of the claims of the officers and soldiers.[34]

The doctrine of implied powers with regard to executive departments was recognized by the Supreme Court in most sweeping terms in *United States* v. *Macdaniel*. Here the power of the Secretary of the Navy to pay a clerk of the department for services not authorized by law was in controversy. The Court said:

A practical knowledge of the action of any one of the great departments of the government, must convince every person that the head of a department, in the distribution of its duties and responsibilities, is often compelled to exercise his discretion. He is limited in the exercise of his powers by the law; but it does not follow that he must show a statutory provision for every thing he does. No government could be administered on such principles. To attempt to regulate by law the minute movements of every part of the complicated machinery of government, would evince a most unpardonable ignorance of the subject. Whilst the great outlines of its movements may be marked out, and limitations imposed on the exercise of its powers, there are numberless things which must be done, that can neither be anticipated nor defined, and which are essential to the proper action of the government. Hence, of necessity, usages have been established in every department of the government, which have become a kind of

[34] *Ibid.*, at 209.

common law, and regulate the rights and duties of those who act within their respective limits.[35]

The Supreme Court has thus far decided only a few cases in which the question as to the applicability of the doctrine of implied powers to administrative agencies was clearly put. In Mr. Justice Stone's dissenting opinion in *Arrow-Hart & Hegeman Electric Co. v. Federal Trade Commission*, the doctrine of implied powers is unmistakably applied to administrative agencies:

No more here, than there, should it be said that the purpose of the statute must be defeated because the law-makers did not attempt to provide with a meticulous precision how the Commission should proceed in every contingency that might arise. The dominating purpose of the statute is to restore to its original state the competition suppressed by the acquisition of the stock, and, just as we rejected a rigid literalism there in order to effect that purpose, and upheld an order which was but incidental, though necessary, to the effective exercise of the power specifically granted, so we should reject it now. . . . In this, as in most schemes for regulation by administrative bodies, there must be a balance between the general and the particular. When the courts are faced with interpretation of the particular, administration breaks down and the manifest purpose of the legislature is defeated unless it is recognized that, surrounding granted powers, there must be a penumbra which will give scope for practical operation. In carrying such schemes into operation the function of courts is constructive, not destructive, to make them, wherever reasonably possible, effective agencies for law enforcement and not to destroy them.[36]

The Supreme Court has come closest to applying the doctrine of *McCulloch* v. *Maryland* to administrative rule-making in *Phelps Dodge Corp.* v. *National Labor Relations Board*.[37] Section 10 (c) of the Nation Labor Relations Act authorizes the National Labor Relations Board "to take such affirmative action as will effectuate the policies of this Act." The Court proposes through Mr. Justice Frankfurter to pursue "the central clue to the Board's powers—effectuation of the policies of the act. . . ." By doing so the Court sets forth certain general standards by which the powers of administrative agencies are to be determined.

A statute expressive of such large public policy as that on which the National Labor Relations Board is based must be broadly phrased and necessarily carries with it the task of administrative application. There is an

[35] *United States* v. *Macdaniel,* 7 Pet. (U.S.) 1, 14 (1833).
[36] 291 U.S. 484, 606 (1934).   [37] 313 U.S. 177, 191 (1941).

area plainly covered by the language of the Act and an area no less plainly without it. But in the nature of things Congress could not catalogue all the devices and stratagems for circumventing the policies of the Act. Nor could it define the whole gamut of remedies to effectuate these policies in an infinite variety of specific situations. Congress met these difficulties by leaving the adaptations of means to end to the empiric process of administration. The exercise of the process was committed to the Board, subject to limited judicial review. Because the relation of remedy to policy is peculiarly a matter for administrative competence, courts must not enter the allowable area of the Board's discretion and must guard against the danger of sliding unconsciously from the narrow confines of law into the more spacious domain of policy. On the other hand, the power with which Congress invested the Board implies responsibility—the responsibility of exercising its judgment in employing the statutory powers. . . . All we are entitled to ask is that the statute speak through the Board where the statute does not speak for itself.[38]

Even though this reasoning proceeds technically in interpretation of Section 10 (c) of the National Labor Relations Act, its substance is of a general nature and capable of general application independently from the statutory provision which it purports to interpret. The standards by which the powers of the National Labor Relations Board under Section 10 (c) are to be defined, are the standards by which the powers of any administrative agency under any congressional enactment must be defined.

The issue came clearly into the open in *Cudahy Packing Co.* v. *Holland*. Here the administrator under the Fair Labor Standards Act claimed the authority to delegate his subpoena power to regional directors. This claim was founded upon express provisions of the act as well as upon the argument that the said authority was to be implied from the structure of the act and the nature of the duties imposed by the act upon the administrator. The Supreme Court, through Chief Justice Stone, refused to follow this argument for three reasons: first, the authority thus claimed would be without limitation with regard both to the addressees and the subject matter of the delegation; in other words, the administrator could delegate the subpoena power to any subordinate, and he could do so with regard to any other power he possesses; second, "unlimited authority of an administrative officer to delegate the exercise of the subpoena power is not lightly to be inferred. It is a power capable of

[38] *Ibid.*, at 194.

oppressive use, especially when it may be indiscriminately delegated and the subpoena is not returnable before a judicial officer;"[39] and third, the intent of Congress as revealed by the express grant of authority to delegate the subpoena power in other acts, and by the legislative history of the Fair Labor Standards Act itself, supports the view of the majority.

Nor can we assume, as the Government argues, that Congress is wholly without design in withholding the power in this case and granting it in others, or even if it had been that it is any part of the judicial function to restore to the Act what Congress has taken out of it. Even though Congress has under-estimated the burden which it has placed upon the Administrator, which is by no means clear, we think that the legislative record establishes that Congress has withheld from him authority to delegate the exercise of the subpoena power, and that this precludes our restoring it by construction.[40]

In a dissenting opinion, four justices, through Mr. Justice Douglas, pushed the doctrine of implied powers beyond the limits within which it had been recognized by *McCulloch* v. *Maryland, Osborn* v. *The Bank of the United States, Edward's Lessee* v. *Darby*, and *United States* v. *Macdaniel. McCulloch* v. *Maryland* recognized the authority of the Constitution to delegate by implication to Congress powers incidental to those expressly delegated. *Osborn* v. *The Bank of the United States, Edward's Lessee* v. *Darby*, and *United States* v. *Macdaniel* recognized the authority of Congress to delegate by implication to an administrative agency powers incidental to those expressly delegated. The dissenting opinion in *Cudahy Packing Co.* v. *Holland* recognizes the authority of Congress to delegate by implication to an administrative officer the power to subdelegate powers expressly delegated to him. The dissent establishes between the administrator and Congress a relation similar to the one which Chief Justice Marshall's opinions created between Congress and the Constitution; that is to say, the dissent accepts fully the doctrine of implied powers for administrative law. The parallelism between both opinions is not limited to the results; it reveals itself in the very line of reasoning by which Chief Justice Marshall's and Mr. Justice Doug-

[39] *Cudahy Packing Co.* v. *Holland,* 315 U.S. 357, 363 (1942).

[40] *Ibid.,* at 367.

las' opinions arrive at their conclusions.[41] Here and there, the importance of the functions expressly delegated is the basis of the argument. Next comes the assertion that without the implied powers claimed those functions cannot be effectively exercised. Finally, the argument derived from legislative practice and history is disposed of.[42]

The attempt to define the administrator's regulatory powers with regard to the coverage of the Fair Labor Standards Act by the doctrine of implied powers is marked by two problems peculiar to this act and not to be found in any of the decided cases.

In all cited cases, with the exception perhaps of *Edward's Lessee* v. *Darby*, the implied power was conceived as an incident of the expressly delegated power in terms of a means to an end. So in *McCulloch* v. *Maryland* the power of creating a corporation was considered a means for the effective carrying-out of the enumerated constitutional ends. In *Osborn* v. *The Bank of the United States* private banking operations were regarded as a means for carrying into effect the public functions of the bank. In *Phelps Dodge Corp.* v. *National Labor Relations Board* the powers of the board under consideration are clearly subordinate to the effectuation of the purposes of the act. The same holds true for the dissent in *Arrow-Hart and Hegeman Electric Co.* v. *Federal Trade Commission*. In *Cudahy Packing Corp.* v. *Holland*, finally, the authority to subdelegate the subpoena power is conceived as a means to put the law-enforcing functions of the administrator into effect.

The interpretation of the statutory terms limiting the coverage of the Fair Labor Standards Act cannot be conceived as a means for the accomplishing of the statutory ends as laid down in the minimum wage and maximum hour provisions. It is not so that the administrator has his choice among several means of which the determination of the coverage by interpretation of statutory terms is one. The relation between this interpretative activity and the legis-

[41] It must be noted that in Mr. Justice Douglas' opinion the argument concerning the existence of the administrator's implied powers is not separated from the argument dealing with the kind of power delegated to him by implication, that is, the power of subdelegation.

[42] Cf. *McCulloch* v. *Maryland,* 4 Wheat. (U.S.) 316, 422, 423, 427, 428, 430 (1819) (opinion of Marshall, C.J.) with *Cudahy Packing Co.* v. *Holland,* 315 U.S. 357, 368, 372, 373 (1942) (opinion of Douglas, J.).

lative purposes is one not of functional or teleological but of logical subordination. That is to say, it is logically impossible for the administrator to effectuate the policies and purposes of the act without limiting the coverage of the act by interpretation of the statutory terms. He may choose one among several interpretations, all equally remaining within the logical confines of the statutory term, but interpret he must. He has no choice between interpreting the statute or refraining from doing so. Interpretation is necessary for the effective discharge of the administrator's duties, not as a means to an end, but as a logical incident of the duties themselves.

This is so in a dual sense. The determination of minimum wages itself is to a certain extent dependent upon the coverage of the wage order; coverage is one of several factors which the administrator must take into consideration as a logically indispensable determinant of the rule-making process. Furthermore, the wage order as an enforcible rule, a command addressed to employer, employees, and public officials, is logically incomplete without making clear to whom it is addressed and to whom not. It is for those reasons that, regardless of the absence of express statutory delegation, the administrator could not help but issue interpretative bulletins determining the coverage of the act and that the courts have either accepted these interpretations as a matter of course or, when they have rejected them, they have done so for reasons which would invalidate any interpretation, whether or not issued under express delegation.

The conception of interpretative powers as the logical incident of the powers expressly conferred is also capable of meeting the problem of legislative practice and history. In this regard, too, the situation is different from the one in which the same problem presented itself in *Phelps Dodge Corp.* v. *Holland.* According to Chief Justice Marshall and Mr. Justice Douglas, the express grant of a certain power in one instance and the lack of such a grant in another is not, in the absence of a clear manifestation of the legislative intent, conclusive proof for the intention to withhold the power in the latter case. The legislative history of the Fair Labor Standards Act, however, shows clearly that the all-inclusive rule-making powers of the administrator, which the original bill envisaged, were finally limited to wage orders and the interpretation of a few scattered statutory terms and that Congress intended with this limitation to meet the constitutional objections which had led to the invalidation of the National Industrial Recovery Act. Neither were subsequent legislative attempts at giving the administrator general rule-making powers approved by Congress.

When, as in the case of the Fair Labor Standards Act, the legislative history shows unmistakably that the legislator did not expressly grant certain powers because he did not want to delegate them, the doctrine of implied powers is confronted with a serious obstacle. Powers which the legislator intends to withhold by refusing to grant them expressly, cannot be implied. When the silence of the statute cannot be interpreted as implied delegation but must be taken to mean refusal to delegate, considerations of rule-making convenience will not justify judicial and administrative officers in adding to the powers expressly granted. There seems to be nothing left but the appeal to the legislature.

Yet this conclusion is justified only when the withholding of powers limits the choice of means, making the performance of rule-making functions more difficult and, hence, is exclusively a matter of rule-making convenience. The conclusion has actually been drawn only with respect to such cases. When, however, the powers withheld are an essential element of the powers conferred so that without them these powers cannot be intelligently executed at all, the problem is no longer of legislative or administrative convenience with respect to rule-making but of the very existence of the expressly delegated regulatory powers. In such a case the presumption that it was the intent of Congress to grant effective regulatory powers must prevail over the legislative history which shows the congressional intent to withhold unconstitutional powers, this intent being mistakenly applied to incidental powers of doubtless constitutionality. Congress, when empowering the administrator to issue wage orders, cannot be presumed to have intentionally withheld powers without which the administrator cannot issue wage orders, that is to say, without which he cannot do what Congress wants him to do.

Once certain powers have been expressly delegated, the delegation of all incidental powers, essential for the execution of the former, must be presumed to have been intended, too. Congress may withhold powers for certain means, necessary for executing the expressly delegated powers, but not for all means or for essentials of the expressly delegated powers themselves. Congress cannot be presumed to have intended to confer no effective powers at all and thus to defeat its own legislative purpose.

What Congress actually intended to do was to grant those powers without which the purposes and policies of the act cannot be attained and to withhold those powers the delegation of which the Supreme Court was likely to consider unconstitutional. It is in the light of this intent that the act must be construed. The unconstitutionality of the delegation of powers essential from the point of view of the policies and purposes of the act would make the act itself unconstitutional. The mistaken congressional belief, however, about what is constitutional and what is not, is not able to defeat the policies and purposes of the act. Congress cannot by implication delegate unconstitutional powers which are of the essence of expressly delegated constitutional powers; here the unconstitutionality of the former is fatal to the constitutionality of the whole. Yet neither can Congress, mistakenly believing them to be unconstitutional, withhold powers, otherwise to be implied, which are of the essence of expressly delegated constitutional powers. As Lord Hobhouse said in *Salmon* v. *Duncombe:* "It is a very serious matter to hold that when the main object of a statute is clear it should be reduced to a nullity, by the draftsman's unskillfulness or ignorance of law."[43] In this case, the application by courts and administrative agencies of the presumption referred to above will protect the legislative purposes of Congress from being frustrated by the errors of its constitutional doctrine. By obliterating in actual performance the distinction between expressly delegated and not delegated but essential powers the administrator and the courts have done exactly that.

This is, however, not the last word. "For the question respecting the extent of the powers actually granted is perpetually arising, and will probably continue to arise as long as our system shall exist."[44]

[43] *Salmon* v. *Duncombe*, 11 App. Cas. 627, 634 (1886).

[44] *McCulloch* v. *Maryland*, 4 Wheat. 316, 405 (1819). *United States* v. *Bailey*, 9 Pet. (U.S.) 238 (1835), and *Caha* v. *United States*, 152 U.S. 211, 218 (1894) may also be quoted. The idea that the power to interpret is implied in the power to administer is also clearly expressed in *United States* ex rel. *Hall* v. *Payne*, 254 U.S. 343 (1920): "He [the Secretary of Labor] could not administer or apply the Act

Whenever there is an implied grant of power, there must be also an implied limitation of the power granted.

Looking at administrative law through the distorting lenses of a conceptualist theory of the Constitution, one has difficulty in admitting that the administrative function has developed into a co-ordinate fourth branch of the government which must be controlled directly by the Constitution and not by the "sterile refinements unrelated to affairs,"[45] by which the courts have connected verbally the exercise of the executive, judicial, and legislative functions with the constitutional text. It is only through such a direct confrontation of the problems of administrative law with the language and spirit of the Constitution that the administrative agencies can be made subject to the constitutional limitations upon which our system of government is founded, without losing the ability to fulfil their regulatory functions.[46] It is only through such an approach that administrative needs and constitutional abstractions can be built into a synthesis of concepts and principles, which will do for administrative law what the great decisions of Chief Justice Marshall's Supreme Court have done for the three traditional branches of the government.

We have endeavored to find in the administrative function itself a positive standard for determining the content of the powers of administrative agencies. Following the same approach, we will now search for a negative standard by which the scope of regulatory powers can be delimited.

Here again, the discrepancy between political philosophy and legal theory, on the one hand, and the actual solution of concrete

without construing it, and its construction involved the exercise of judgment and discretion"; cf. also *Marbury* v. *Madison,* 1 Cranch (U.S.) 137, 177 (1803): "Those who apply the rule to particular cases, must of necessity expound and interpret that rule."

45 Mr. Justice Frankfurter, concurring in *Graves* v. *New York* ex rel. *O'Keefe,* 306 U.S. 466, 488 (1939). Cf. also what Lord Bryce, *The American Commonwealth* (New York: Macmillan Co., 1912), p. 375, has to say about the same problem.

46 For the general aspects of this problem see Charles Howard McIlwain, "The Fundamental Law behind the Constitution of the United States," in *Constitutionalism and the Changing World* (New York: Macmillan Co., 1939), pp. 244 ff.; with respect to administrative law see A. A. Berle, "The Expansion of American Administrative Law," *Harvard Law Review,* XXX (1917), 430.

problems by the courts, on the other, is characteristic of the traditional point of view. We have seen how the traditional doctrine,
unwilling to admit that an administrative agency may have powers
not expressly delegated but implied, can nevertheless not fail to realize that administrative agencies actually perform functions of this
kind, and tries to reconcile theory and facts by a series of legalistic
distinctions and conceptualist doctrines.

With respect to the problem of implied limitations on regulatory
powers the situation is somewhat similar. On the constitutional level,
the reasoning takes as its point of departure the doctrine of the separation of powers and the principle that delegated powers cannot
be delegated, and arrives at the conclusion that the legislature cannot delegate rule-making powers to administrative agencies. In the
face of the obvious fact that such powers are actually delegated with
the approval of the courts, the principle is interpreted so as to refer
only to delegation unlimited as to subject matter and regulatory
policy. Since, however, the absence of a defined subject matter
would amount to a blanket delegation, nothing short of the surrender of the lawmaking function altogether could be considered unconstitutional. The practical importance of this requirement is,
therefore, extremely limited; it was found lacking only once, in
Schechter v. *United States.*[47] The requirement of a defined policy in
the form of a legislative standard has become practically obsolete
since standards of extreme vagueness have been considered to meet
the constitutional requirement. Hence, Elihu Root's much quoted
statement of 1916 holds even more true today: "Before these agencies the old doctrine prohibiting the delegation of legislative power
has virtually retired from the field and given up the fight."[48]

Another and seemingly more effective method of limiting the regulatory powers of administrative agencies is the extension of judicial
review under the due process clause. Yet judicial review, conceived
as trial *de novo*, does not solve the problem of limiting the administrative function but rather eliminates it by doing away with the co-
ordinate function altogether. It contributes nothing to the solution
of the problem with which we are here concerned but rather attempts to destroy the very conditions under which the problem
could arise at all.

[47] 295 U.S. 495 (1935), especially at 551.
[48] *Report of the American Bar Association,* XLI (1916), 368.

On the statutory level, the traditional canons of interpretation are applied to the language of the statute in order to ascertain whether the administrative agency has remained within the limits of the statutory standards or else has acted *ultra vires*. The courts have, however, not failed to recognize that there are cases of administrative rule-making which, even though remaining within the verbal limits of the statute, are nevertheless *ultra vires*. The courts have justified the invalidation of administrative rules of this kind by either straining the words of the statute as well as the canons of interpretation or by declaring the regulation arbitrary and unreasonable.

It is with the latter category of administrative regulations that we propose to deal. The test of reasonableness, where the term does not refer to standards well defined and clearly understood, is obviously less a standard by which the scope of administrative rule-making power can be delimited than the admission that such a standard cannot be found. The analysis of the cases invalidating administrative regulations which are not clearly in violation of the words of the statute will show that underlying these decisions is the inarticulate awareness of implied limitations which administrative regulations are not allowed to overstep. These limitations follow from the very nature of the administrative function and its relation to the legislative branch. It will furthermore be shown that these implied limitations upon regulatory powers in administrative law have their counterpart in the three traditional branches of the government.[49]

We take as our point of departure the Fair Labor Standards Act. This act, as pointed out before, constitutes a most serious and elaborate attempt to meet all possible constitutional requirements with

[49] The doctrine, preoccupied with the pseudo-problems of constitutional theology, has paid scant attention to the problem of implied powers and limitations in administrative law. Ernst Freund was, however, already aware of the existence of the problem and the unsatisfactory state of its solution; in *Standards of American Legislation* (Chicago: University of Chicago Press, 1917), p. 302, he stated: "The precise line of demarcation between matter to be determined by statute and matter to be left to regulation has not yet been satisfactorily settled"; see also Freund, "The Substitution of Rule for Discretion in Public Law," *American Political Science Review,* IX (1915), 666 and especially 676. See also James Hart, "The Exercise of Rule-Making Power," in *Studies on Administrative Management in the Government of the United States* (Washington, D.C.: Government Printing Office, 1937), p. 34: "Possibly the policy or standard need not be expressed in the delegation of rule-making power, if it may be implied with sufficient certainty and clarity."

respect to the scope of delegated regulatory powers and administrative procedure. Despite those unusual precautions, the act in practical operation has not avoided some of the difficulties which have befallen other administrative agencies. On the one hand, the act has refrained from delegating expressly to the administrator interpretative powers, believed to have been thus withheld, which are actually inherent in the administrative function. On the other hand, the act has delegated to the administrator apparently well-defined rule-making powers, the exercise of which has posed the problem of the scope of regulatory powers in administrative law.

One of the characteristic features of the regulations under the act is the tendency to circumscribe the categories of employees exempt from the operation of the act by rigid, mathematical formulas. It is with respect to the numerical standards of these regulations that the reported cases show an as yet uncertain and inarticulate awareness of implied limitations on regulatory powers. The courts do not limit to regulations under the Fair Labor Standards Act their opposition against abstract, rigid standards of a numerical nature. There is rather a general tendency to invalidate such standards whenever the statutory terms to be defined do not lend themselves to definitions of this kind but need for the adequate limitation of their content to be confronted with the facts of the individual case.

The courts have shown reluctance to follow the administrator in limiting the coverage of the statute by mathematical formulas and especially percentage rules, where the act itself uses terms such as "greater part," "substantial," "area," and the like. Technically, the argument of these decisions follows the familiar lines of statutory interpretation. The courts declare that it would be "unreasonable," "arbitrary," or "impossible" to define the statutory terms by rigid, mathematical formulas.

From the point of view of statutory interpretation it might, however, be argued that it is not outright impossible to define terms such as "area of production," "local retailing," "bona fide executive," and the like numerically and by percentages. If, for instance, Congress should have defined the constitutional term "interstate commerce" on the same percentage basis as the administrator under the Fair Labor Standards Act defines the identical statutory term, the courts would undoubtedly have approved of the statutory definition of the constitutional term. Why, then, are the courts hostile to similar definitions on the administrative level? The answer lies in the particular relationship between administrative regulation and congressional enactment. The clarification of this relationship, in turn, depends upon the answer to two questions: (1) What was the legislative policy under which the rule-making powers under consideration were delegated to the administrator? and (2) What function do the mathematical standards of these administrative regulations fulfil from the point of view of this legislative policy?

The delegation of regulatory powers to administrative agencies stems from "the inability of the legislature to formulate standards sufficiently definite for private guidance. This inability in turn may be due either to the inherent inapplicability of uniform standards to varying individual cases or to the temporary failure to discover such principles."[50] The outstanding example of the latter alternative is the delegation of rate-making powers to administrative agencies. In this case, administrative agencies, on the basis of technical and scientific knowledge that Congress does not possess, develop gradually, through the trial-and-error method not accessible to Congress, a definite or even rigid formula which will ultimately take the place of the legislative enactment and according to which future cases will uniformly be decided.

The specific rule-making powers[51] of the administrator under the Fair Labor Standards Act are obviously not of this kind. If Congress did not feel able to determine in the statute itself concepts such as "area of production," "bona fide executive," or "local retailing capacity," it was not because it did not possess the expert knowledge and experience which would be at the command of the administrator. No such knowledge and experience is needed for the understanding of the terms under consideration, and when Congress left the definition of these concepts to the administrator, it did not do so with the expectation that the particular technical competency of the administrator would enable him to do what Congress was unable to do.

[50] Ernst Freund, *Administrative Powers over Persons and Property* (Chicago: University of Chicago Press, 1928), p. 29.

[51] In contradistinction to the general powers relative to the determination of minimum wages.

The implied inability of Congress to define these terms is rather the result of the very nature of the terms which in the majority of cases are applicable to individual situations without further definition but which in a number of marginal cases are inherently incapable of abstract, uniform determination. In these marginal cases the determination must be made "upon all the facts shown in the record," "upon the facts in each particular case." Since, on the one hand, the nature of the terms to be defined makes abstract, uniform determination impossible and since, on the other hand, Congress is unable to give the individualized determination, on the basis of the particular case, which those terms require, Congress has delegated to the administrator the power to define these terms. For the administrative regulation, in contrast to the legislative enactment, is capable of flexibility in the light of changing circumstances and adaptable to the individual case, thus doing justice to these terms.

The administrator, when defining these terms in regulations of mathematical rigidity, has acted counter to the legislative policy under which he received these regulatory powers. If Congress had thought that formulas of mathematical precision could solve the problem of defining the terms under consideration, Congress could have written such formulas into the statute. For legislation in abstract, general, rigid terms is the province of congressional rule-making, while legislation in flexible, concrete terms is the proper field of administrative rule-making. By doing what Congress could have done but did not want to do, that is, to make abstract, general, inflexible regulations in mathematical terms, the administrator has neglected the implicit congressional mandate and overstepped the implied limitations to which the division of functions between Congress and administrative agencies subjects his regulatory powers. It is to this discrepancy between congressional intent and administrative regulation, between the proper delimitation of the spheres of congressional and administrative legislation and the actual extension of the latter, that the courts refer, when they declare regulations of this kind invalid as being "unreasonable" or "arbitrary."

This evaluation of the administrator's regulations is supported by the analysis of the functions which these mathematical standards are intended to fulfil according to the statements of the administrator himself. They lie exclusively in the realm of administrative convenience.

The foregoing discussion has led to four conclusions: (1) that administrative regulations of mathematical rigidity meet with wide disapproval by the courts; (2) that the functional relationship between statutory delegation and administrative regulation may require, in the latter, flexibility and adaptability to the particularities of the individual case; (3) that regulations of the rigid, general type owe their existence to considerations of administrative convenience; and (4) that there is a judicial trend against letting considerations of administrative convenience prevail over limitations which the statute, expressly or by implication, has placed upon administrative discretion.

These conclusions point toward the existence of implied limitations on regulatory powers in administrative law. These implied limitations have their roots in the same element to which the implied regulatory powers owe their existence, that is, the administrative function itself. In the same way in which the power to interpret is the logical by-product of the power to administer, the power to administer under an act of Congress precludes implicitly the power to do what Congress could have done but did not want to do. The administrative agency is, then, under a duty, the positive counterpart of this limitation, to execute the mandate of Congress whose explicit command must be read in the literal text of the statute and whose implicit injunctions must be sought in the particular purpose which Congress wishes to achieve through the delegation of regulatory powers. The administrative agency, in other words, must perform the particular administrative function, the performance of which is the implicit purpose of the delegation of regulatory powers.

How can this purpose be ascertained? The traditional answer, that it is the administrative function to "fill in the details"[52] of incomplete congressional legislation, has impeded rather than furthered the recognition of the problem and of its solution. This answer was correct when it was given, that is, when the traditional three branches of the government performed all governmental functions in relative separation and when, therefore, the assistance which the executive gave to the legislative branch in the performance of the latter's

[52] *Wayman v. Southard,* 10 Wheat. (U.S.) 1, 43 (1825).

functions could be explained correctly in the traditional terms of the separation of powers.

The problem today, in constitutional terms, lies in the development of a fourth branch of the government which, far from filling in mere details, has become quantitatively as well as qualitatively a co-ordinate partner of the three traditional branches. Quantitatively, administrative legislation exceeds by far enactments by Congress. Qualitatively, administrative regulations are genuine legislation, in many instances no more limited by statutory standards than congressional legislation is by constitutional standards. The attempt at limiting administrative regulative powers must therefore start with the recognition that a co-ordinate administrative function exists.

The second step toward a solution of our problem is the recognition of the source from which this co-ordinate administrative function derives. This source is congressional delegation, at the basis of which there may be one of two possible purposes. It is either that Congress does not wish to legislate even though it could and so for whatever reason, such as time-saving, political caution, and the like, delegates legislative powers to an administrative agency, or that Congress did not legislate because it could not have legislated without putting in jeopardy the very purposes for which the law was enacted and therefore delegated regulatory powers to administrative authorities. In the former type of delegation the administrative powers are limited only by the words of the statute, and expressed and implied limitations coincide. Hence, no particular problem with respect to implied limitations can arise. It is therefore with the latter category alone that we are concerned.

Here Congress may delegate regulatory powers for three kinds of reasons. It may do so in order to have the facts determined upon which the application of the law depends in an individual case. This is what is meant by "execution of the laws" in the traditional meaning of the term and is part of the traditional executive function. Second, Congress may delegate regulatory powers for the purpose of determining certain legislative standards, a determination which requires experimentation on the basis of scientific knowledge and technical skill; such trial-and-error method is beyond the reach of congressional action. Third, the purpose of congressional delegation may be to create flexible standards adaptable to the particular conditions of the individual case. Here again, Congress is incapable of discharging this particular function.

Under these three types of delegation the regulatory powers of the administrative agency are implicitly limited by the kind of administrative function it has to perform. One type of delegation allows only the exercise of regulatory powers of the executive type; the other, only the exercise of regulatory powers of an experimental nature; the third, only flexible administrative regulations. Consequently, under the executive type the administrative agency could not substitute its own standards for the statutory ones (which it would be allowed to do under the experimental and flexible types) without violating the implicit limitations which the statute prescribes. When only powers to regulate by trial and error are delegated, a regulation laying down at once a ready-made, definite standard which was at the disposal of Congress, without experimentation or the use of technical skill or scientific expertness, would again overstep the implied limits which the statute has marked out. Finally, under the flexible type a regulation which replaces the rigid standard of the statute by another rigid one, would, as we have seen, find itself outside the implied limitations imposed by the statute.

These three types of administrative regulation, violative of statutory standards, have this in common that they do what Congress could have done but did not want to do. The test according to which a doubtful case of violation must be determined is to be found in the administrative function which the regulations are supposed to fulfil in each particular case.[53] The nature of this function is revealed by the source of administrative power, that is, the statutory delegation.

We arrived at this conclusion by an empirical examination of a particular situation arising under the Fair Labor Standards Act and of the court decisions dealing with this situation and the problems underlying it. It can, however, be shown that these conclusions are only the special manifestation of a general principle of our constitutional system. In other words, the doctrine of implied limitations on

---

[53] Cf. Freund, *Administrative Powers over Persons and Property,* p. 91: "Delegated discretion is subject to unexpressed limitations which follow partly from the supremacy of the statute over its instrumentalities, and partly from the presumptive reservation of certain considerations for exclusive legislative control."

regulatory powers in administrative law is only the special application of a general doctrine of implied limitations in constitutional
law. In the same implicit way in which administrative powers are
limited by the functions which the statute delegates, the respective
powers of the federal and the state governments as well as the powers of the legislative, executive, and judicial branches of the federal
government in relation to each other are limited by the functions
which the federal constitution delegates to the federal government
and its three traditional branches. "Every positive direction contains
an implication against anything contrary to it, or which would frustrate or disappoint the purpose of that provision. The frame of the
government; the grant of legislative power itself; the organization
of the executive authority; the erection of the principal courts of
justice, create implied limitations . . . as strong as though a negative
was expressed in each instance."[54] According to Judge Cooley,
"There is no difficulty in saying that any such act, which under pretext of exercising such power is usurping another, is opposed to the
constitution and void."[55]

It follows by implication from the nature of the federal system
which protects the federal government as well as the several state
governments in their existence and in the proper discharge of their
functions, that neither government may tax agencies of the other.[56]

[54] *People* v. *Draper,* 15 N.Y. 532, 544 (1857).

[55] Thomas McIntyre Cooley, *A Treatise on the Constitutional Limitations* (8th
ed.; Boston: Little, Brown & Co., 1927), pp. 357–58; cf. *ibid.,* p. 355. See also
Judge Cooley in *People* v. *Salem,* 20 Mich. 452, 473 (1870): "It is conceded . . .
that there are certain limitations upon this power, not prescribed in express terms
by any constitutional provision, but inherent in the subject itself, which attend
its exercise under all circumstances and which are as inflexible and absolute in
their restraints as if directly imposed in the most positive of words." See Chief
Justice Marshall in *McCulloch* v. *Maryland,* 4 Wheat. (U.S.) 316, 407 (1819).
It was the intention of the Constitution that "the minor ingredients which compose those objects [of our political life] be deduced from the nature of the ob-
jects themselves." Cf. also *Knox* v. *Lee,* 12 Wall. (U.S.) 457 (1871); Thomas
McIntyre Cooley, *The General Principles of Constitutional Law in the United
States of America* (Boston: Little, Brown & Co., 1891), p. 100; Robert Kenneth
Carr, *The Supreme Court and Judicial Review* (New York: Farrar and Rinehart,
Inc., 1942), p. 96.

[56] W. W. Willoughby, *The Constitutional Law of the United States* (New
York: Baker, Voorhis & Co., 1910); Walter Farleigh Dodd, "Implied Powers and
Implied Limitations in Constitutional Law," *Yale Law Journal,* XXIX (1919),
140, 147.

It has even been suggested that the express limitations which the federal constitution imposes upon the states are relatively less important than the limitations derived from implication.[57] The constitutional principle of the supremacy of the federal government together with a grant of power to the federal government may impose an implied limitation upon the power of the states with regard to the matter delegated for regulation to the federal government. Whether such an implied limitation exists depends upon the nature of the power concerned. If the power granted to the federal government can be exercised only by one government within the same territory, such a limitation must be implied. As Chief Justice Marshall put it in *Sturges* v. *Crowninshield:* "Whenever . . . the nature of the power requires that it should be exercised exclusively by Congress, the subject is as completely taken from the state legislature as if they had been expressly forbidden to act on it."[58]

Turning from the relations between federal and state governments to the relations among the three traditional branches of the government, we find that the very principle of the separation of powers is an implied limitation upon the powers of the three branches in relation to each other. This limitation follows from the establishment by the Constitution of three branches of the government, each exercising a particular function of its own. It is from the nature of these functions that derive by implication the particular limitations by which the powers of the legislative, judicial, and executive branches of the government are circumscribed in their relation to each other.

The constitutional doctrine of implied limitations, manifesting itself as the doctrine of the "higher law" and in other natural law doctrines, was originally developed for the purpose of preventing a legislative absolutism which, unchecked, would encroach upon the liberties of the individual. Thus Judge Cooley wrote in the Preface to the second edition of his *Constitutional Limitations:* "In this sympathy and faith, he had written of jury trials and the other safeguards to personal liberty, of liberty of the press, and of vested rights; and he had also endeavored to point out that there are on all sides definite limitations which circumscribe the legislative authority,

---

[57] Dodd, *op. cit.*, pp. 138, 160.   [58] 4 Wheat. (U.S.) 122 (1819).

independent of the specific restrictions which the people impose by their State constitutions."[59]

Yet besides these implied limitations upon the legislative power, upon which attention has mainly been focused, there exist less spectacular ones, which, growing out of the legislative function itself, are similar in nature to, and fulfil a similar function as, implied limitations in administrative law. In the same way in which an act of Congress delegates administrative powers to an administrative agency, the Constitution delegates legislative powers to Congress; and in the same way in which, consequently, the administrative agency can perform no other but administrative functions, the legislative department can exercise no other but legislative authority. When Congress has only delegated the power to make flexible, concrete regulations, the administrative agency cannot make abstract, rigid ones which under the circumstances would be administrative regulations in form only but not in substance and would actually encroach upon the powers of Congress. Likewise, Congress cannot, in the form of a statute, make rules which are alien to the legislative function and belong actually to the judiciary. "The assumption of judicial power by the legislature in such a case is unconstitutional, because, though not expressly forbidden, it is nevertheless inconsistent with the provisions which have conferred upon another department the power the legislature is seeking to exercise."[60]

In *Schneiderman* v. *United States*,[61] for instance, the Supreme Court recognized the plenary powers of Congress over the jurisdiction of the federal courts. Once the power of the courts is established by act of Congress, the latter has, however, no power to "decree in the same breath that the judgment rendered shall have no conclusive effect. Limits it may place. But that is another matter from making an adjudication under Article III merely an advisory opinion or prima facie evidence of the fact or all the facts determined." This limitation upon the powers of Congress is implied from the very nature of the legislative and judicial functions and their relation to each other. On the same grounds, Congress could not, even if the Due Process Clause were omitted from the Consti-

---

[59] P. vii.   [60] *Ibid.*, p. 356.

[61] 63 S.Ct. 1355, 1357 (1943); cf. also *Gordon* v. *United States,* 117 U.S. 697 (1864); *In re Sanborn,* 148 U.S. 222 (1893).

tution, pass the property of·one citizen over to somebody else on the assumption that the latter was entitled to the property according to law.

Implied limitations, protecting the executive from encroachments by the legislative branch, are less obvious. This is so because the relation between the legislative and executive functions, with the latter charged with the execution of the acts of the former, makes for the subordination of the latter to the former. The inability of Congress to interfere with the removal power of the President offers, however, an example of implied limitations on the legislative power in its relations with the chief executive. In *Myers* v. *United States*[62] the Supreme Court declared the Tenure of Office Act of 1867 unconstitutional as interfering with a presidential power which by its nature is executive and not legislative. In other words, the investment of the chief executive with the general executive functions, with the power to execute the laws, and with the power to remove as an incident of the power to appoint, limits by implication the power of Congress in this matter.

Conversely, the executive branch is limited in its relations with Congress by the constitutional distribution of functions. Since the legislature makes the laws and the executive branch executes them, the latter's discretion is limited by the words and policies of congressional enactments. In applying the acts of Congress to concrete cases, the executive branch must interpret the terms of the statute and in so far may even be allowed to legislate. As noted before, express and implied limitations coincide here.

As regards implied limitations on the executive branch in its relations with the judiciary, one can quote decisions where the Supreme Court has refused to entertain appeals against decisions of a district judge, the execution of which depended upon the discretion of the Secretary of the Treasury.[63] Such decisions, not being the autonomous and, in the absence of appeal, final disposition of the issue, are not recognized as judicial ones against which an apeal to the Supreme Court would lie. The encroachment of the executive upon the judicial process deprives the latter of its judicial character.

[62] 272 U.S. 52 (1926), especially at 117, 161, 164.

[63] *United States* v. *Ferreira*, 13 How. (U.S.) 40 (1851); *Hayburn's Case*, 2 Dall. (U.S.) 408 (1792).

Finally, implied limitations upon the judiciary with regard to both the executive and legislative branches are at the foundation of the principle that the exercise of the discretionary powers of these two departments is not subject to judicial review. With regard to the executive branch, this principle was first laid down in *Marbury* v. *Madison*[64] relative to so-called political questions, and in *United States* v. *Eliason*[65] relative to executive rules and regulations. With respect to the legislative branch the principle is generally expressed in form of the requirement of judicial self-restraint or the prohibition of judicial legislation.

The investigation of implied regulatory powers and implied limitations on regulatory powers in administrative law has led to three conclusions whose importance reaches beyond the immediate purpose of this investigation:

1. The recognition of the administrative function as a co-ordinate fourth branch of the government is indispensable for a solution of the problems with which the spread of administrative law confronts our legal system, if we want this solution to do justice both to the need of administrative agencies for clearly defined and effective powers and to the necessity of keeping these powers within constitutional limits and under legal controls.

2. The traditional constitutional concepts and principles must be marshaled to this task by freeing their creative potentialities, dormant in the original meaning and functions, from the legalistic adulterations and conceptualist refinements by which a stagnant constitutional doctrine has endeavored to make them permanently subservient to a particular political philosophy.

3. From an examination of the court decisions relative to administrative law in the light of the original constitutional principles and concepts, certain general principles of administrative law, fulfilling the functions under 1, can be developed. Thus the decisions reveal clearly that the power to administer carries implicitly the power to interpret or, in other words, that administrative and interpretative powers are coextensive. That he who administers must interpret can be considered a recognized principle of administrative

64 1 Cranch (U.S.) 137 (1803).

65 16 Pet. (U.S.) 291 (1842).

law. The principle that the administrative power is implicitly limited by the delegated administrative function and that consequently administrative agencies cannot do what Congress could have done but did not want to do, is less clearly recognizable in the court decisions, but follows from the distribution of governmental powers on a functional basis, which is characteristic of the structure of American government.

9 _Nationalism_

The Western world faces in the universal triumph of nationalism some extraordinary paradoxes, pregnant with tragic irony. These paradoxes test its political imagination; they challenge its moral judgment; they put in jeopardy not only its own existence but the survival of civilized life on this planet. Yet it was not the enemy of the West and of civilization that gave the idea of nationalism to the world. That idea, together with Marxism, is the last great original contribution the West has made to the political thought and practice of the world. What has become a threat to civilization, the West has claimed as a condition of civilized life. What has become a source of political anarchy and oppression, the West has offered as the principle of political order and freedom. With what has become a mockery of political morality, the West set out to establish political justice throughout the world.

The idea of nationalism, both in its historic origins and in the political functions it has performed, is intimately connected with the idea of freedom and shares the latter's ambiguity. Nationalism as a political phenomenon must be understood as the aspiration for two freedoms, one collective, the other individual: the freedom of a nation from domination by another nation and the freedom of the individual to join the nation of his choice.

As the aspiration of a collectivity to be free, nationalism originated in the sixteenth and seventeenth centuries from the struggles of the territorial state against its two enemies, one—the feudal order —resisting it, as it were, from below; the other—the imperial power— from above. Both, defeated in the dynastic and religious wars of the age, proved to be incapable of exerting the functions of government in the territories claimed by the territorial princes who, in turn, were able to impose their rule upon the feudal lords and free themselves from the rule of the emperor. Thus the territorial state emerged in the political form of dynastic sovereignty, the monarch being the highest secular authority within his territory.

Dynastic sovereignty found its philosophic justification in its ability to defend the territory under its control against enemies from without and disorder from within. Bodin in the sixteenth century and Leibniz in the eighteenth justified the absolute monarchy in these terms. It remained unchallenged both in theory and practice as long as it met this test in actual performance. Yet when in 1791 the king of France appeared to be plotting with foreign monarchs against his country, the absolute monarchy failed the test as defender of the nation and its territory. First in practice and then in theory, the nation itself was called upon to defend its freedom. Thus nationalism as the collective expression of a nation's political identity was born.

That birth coincided with, and was really an integral part of, the triumph of individual liberty within France. The absolute monarchy was destroyed because it had betrayed the nation abroad and oppressed the individual at home. It left the stage of history as a defeated enemy of both individual and collective freedom. Individual freedom was taken as a precondition of national freedom, and the latter, in turn, was regarded as a mere extension of the former to the international scene. The political and legal principles, originally formulated to support and guarantee the freedom of the individual, were applied to the nation. The nation came to be regarded as a kind of collective personality with peculiar characteristics and inalienable rights of its own; and the typically liberal antithesis between individual freedom and feudalistic oppression was transferred to the nation where it was duplicated in the hostility between the national aspirations and the feudal state. The nation should be free from oppression, both from within and from without. Free nations had only one enemy, and he was common to all of them: the dynastic oppressor of their freedom, individual and collective. Political evil was, as it were, localized in the enemies of freedom.

Given these assumptions, there could be no enmity among free nations who were united in a solidarity of individual and collective self-interest against the enemies of anybody's freedom. The popular will should decide how and by whom the people were to be governed, and the determination of the state to which a people was to belong was part of this decision. Thus the principle of national

171

self-determination fulfils the postulates of both democracy and nationalism.

The practical political consequences of this new philosophy of nationalism, merging the ideas of individual and collective liberty, were immediate and striking. The Decree of Armed Propaganda of November 12, 1792, proclaimed: "The National Convention declares in the name of the French nation that it shall accord fraternity and aid to all peoples who want to recover their liberty, and charges the executive power with giving to the generals the orders necessary to bring aid to those peoples and to defend the citizens who are or might be persecuted for the cause of liberty." Napoleon conquered Europe in the name of this principle, destroying in the process more than two hundred dynastic sovereignties which were incapable of effective defense and disqualified from ruling in the name of their subjects.

In the struggle, dominating the better part of the nineteenth century, for the national unification of Germany and Italy and the national liberation of the Balkan nations from Turkish rule, the causes of national unity and freedom from oppression merged, for the liberal champions of nationalism as well as for their dynastic enemies. While the German liberals cried, "Through unity to liberty," Mazzini's flag of 1831 bore on one side the words "Unity and Independence," on the other "Liberty, Equality, Humanity." Metternich's policies, on the other hand, were opposed to the national movements as a manifestation of democratic tendencies. The foreign policy of Napoleon III, who favored the national movements because he saw, according to his foreign minister, "a real equilibrium only in the satisfied wishes of the nations of Europe," was ironically called "the diplomacy of universal suffrage."

The First World War seemed to confirm, rather than deny, the assumptions and expectations of nationalism; for was it not caused by the unfulfilled aspirations of the nationalities of the Austro-Hungarian Empire? Thus the Western alliance fought the war in the name of national self-determination, and Germany turned the same weapon against Russia. The result was a peace settlement that reflected to a very high degree the principle of national self-determination. Austria-Hungary and western Russia were dissolved into their national components, and the new frontiers of Germany followed in good measure the will of the populations concerned, which was either obvious, as in Alsace-Lorraine, or was determined by internationally supervised plebiscites, as in Silesia.

Yet that triumph of the principles of nationalism did not bring a viable order to central and eastern Europe. Nor did it bring justice to the populations concerned; it rather made the oppressors and oppressed exchange their roles. Thus what appeared at the time as the consummation of the expectations of nineteenth-century nation-alism—peace, order, and justice built on the satisfaction of national aspirations—turned into its first great moral and political crisis. That crisis revealed the insufficient, self-contradictory, and self-defeating nature of nationalism as the exclusive principle of international order and justice and its inevitable subordination in fact, and requisite subordination in theory, to an overriding political system.

Nationalism, taken by itself, is both in logic and experience a principle of disintegration and fragmentation, which is prevented from issuing in anarchy not by its own logic but by the political power which either puts a halt to its realization at a certain point, as did the peace settlement of 1919, or else uses it for its purposes up to a certain point, as did the unifiers of Germany and Italy in the nineteenth century. There are no inherent limits to the appli-cation of the principles of nationalism. If the peoples of Bulgaria, Greece, and Serbia could invoke these principles against Turkey, why could not the people of Macedonia invoke them against Bul-garia, Greece, and Serbia? If it was right for the Czechs and Slovaks to free themselves in the name of nationalism from Austrian rule, it could not be wrong for the Slovaks and Sudeten Germans to free themselves from Czech rule in the name of the selfsame principle. Poland, the very moment she had recovered her national identity from Austrian, German, and Russian rule, felt she had to defend it against the German, Ukrainian, and White Russian minorities within her borders, comprising one-third of her total population. Thus yesterday's oppressed cannot help becoming the oppressors of today because they are afraid lest they be again oppressed tomorrow. Hence, the process of national liberation must stop at some point, and that point is determined not by the logic of nationalism but by the configurations of interest and power between the rulers and the ruled and between competing nations.

This paradox of B invoking the principles of nationalism against A and denying them to C—both for the sake of his own survival—is accentuated by the practical impossibility of applying these principles consistently to mixed populations. The individual's rights to his property and pursuit of happiness become incompatible with his right to choose his government according to his national preferences when he is a member of a minority which is inextricably intermingled with the majority controlling the government. Not being able to enjoy both rights simultaneously, he must sacrifice one or the other. The treaties for the protection of minorities, to which Bulgaria, Montenegro, Romania, and Serbia were subjected in 1878 and Czechoslovakia, Poland, and Romania in 1919, tried to mitigate the dilemma by protecting certain minorities in the enjoyment of a free national life at least in certain fields, such as language, schools, religion.

However, such attempts were largely frustrated by the fact, which constitutes the second manifestation of the crisis of nationalism in the interwar period, that the conflicts between the new national states and their minorities were more intimately interwoven than ever before with the international conflicts among the new nation states and the great powers. This had always been the case within certain limits; Russia, for instance, had always supported the Balkan nations against Turkey and the Czechs and Serbs against Austria-Hungary. Yet as in the interwar period the new nation states competed with each other for power and were at the same time the pawns of the great powers in their struggle for hegemony, the national minorities became to an ever increasing extent, as it were, sub-pawns whose aspirations and grievances the contestants used to strengthen themselves and their friends and weaken their enemies.

All of central and eastern Europe from the Baltic to the Mediterranean became the stage for continuous interconnected and overlapping rivalries and conflicts: Poland versus Lithuania, Czechoslovakia versus Poland, Hungary versus Romania, Bulgaria versus Greece, Italy versus Yugoslavia, Germany versus Poland, and, overshadowing them all, the decline of France, the rise of Germany, the indecision of Britain, and the ever present threat of the Soviet Union. The instability which from 1878 to 1914 had been confined to the

Balkans, always threatening and in the end destroying the peace of Europe, now extended to all of central and eastern Europe, for the same causes and with the same results. As the fragmentation of the European part of the Turkish Empire into its national components brought forth the "Balkanization" of the Balkans, so did the fragmentation of the Austro-Hungarian and the western part of the Russian Empires lead to the Balkanization of that part of Europe. And while the First World War arose from the threat of Serb nationalism to Austria-Hungary, the Second World War became inevitable when Germany succeeded in using the German minority to destroy Czechoslovakia and was started on the pretext that the German minority needed protection against the government of Poland.

Nationalism, far from creating a juster and more viable international order, became the great disruptive and anarchical force of the interwar period. Into the severed members of the empires it shattered, nationalism poured the same passions which, first, as lust for power had created these empires and, then, as aspiration for freedom had destroyed them. The endemic disorder thus created cried out for a "new order," which only the strong could make and maintain. Germany and Russia, the new empire builders, saw their opportunity, and in a series of swift and effective strokes, starting in 1938 and ending in 1941, they seized the new nation states of central and eastern Europe, endeavoring to melt them down into new structures of empire.

It is another of the paradoxes of nationalism that its defeat on the eve of the Second World War was achieved in the name of the same principle which brought it victory in the aftermath of the First: national self-determination. Germany justified her use of the German minorities of Czechoslovakia and Poland for the destruction of these nation states with the same principle of national self-determination with which before the Czech, Slovak, and Polish nationalities had justified their attack upon, and destruction of, the Austro-Hungarian Empire. Yet while the words were the same, the passions behind them and the philosophy which roused and justified them were different not only in degree but in kind. The nationalism with which Nazi Germany and the Soviet Union set out to conquer the world has only the name in common with the nationalism of the nineteenth century and the first three decades of the twentieth.

The libertarian goals of the older nationalism were the rightful possession of all nations who wanted to be free; the world had room for as many nationalisms as there were nations that wanted to establish or preserve a state of their own. The international conflicts growing out of this nationalism were of two kinds: conflicts between a nationality and an alien master and conflicts between different nations over the delimitation of their respective boundaries. The issue at stake was either the application of the principles of nationalism or else their interpretation.

The new nationalism has only one thing in common with the old: the nation is the ultimate point of reference for political loyalties and actions. But here the similarity ends. For the old nationalism, the nation is the ultimate goal of political action, the end point of the political development beyond which there are other nationalisms with similar and equally justifiable goals. For the new nationalism, the nation is but the starting point of a universal mission whose ultimate goal reaches to the confines of the political world. While the old nationalism seeks one nation in one state and nothing else, the new one claims for one nation and one state the right to impose its own values and standards of action upon all the other nations.

The new nationalism is in truth a political religion, a nationalistic universalism which identifies the standards and goals of a particular nation with the principles that govern the universe. The few remaining nations of the first rank no longer oppose each other within a framework of shared beliefs and common values which impose effective limitations upon the means and ends of their policies. Rather they oppose each other now as the standard-bearers of moral systems, each of them of national origin and each of them claiming to provide universal moral standards which all the other nations ought to accept. The moral code of one nation flings the challenge of its universal claim into the face of another, which reciprocates in kind.

This transformation of nationalism was foreshadowed by the Napoleonic Wars and the First World War. The Napoleonic Wars were fought in the name of particular principles claiming universal validity: here the principles of the French Revolution, there the principle of legitimacy. For the West, the First World War transformed itself with the intervention of the United States into a crusade "to make the world safe for democracy." "It is our inestimable privilege," said Woodrow Wilson in his Fourth of July speech of 1918, "to concert with men out of every nation who shall make not only the liberties of America secure but the liberties of every other people as well." A few months after the democratic crusade had got under way, in October, 1917, the foundations were laid in Russia for another moral and political structure that, while accepted by only a fraction of humanity, also claimed to provide the common roof under which all humankind would eventually live together in justice and in peace.

This well-nigh universal commitment to the principles of nationalism revealed a profound difference between the attitude of the Western democracies and that of their totalitarian enemies. That difference was to have far-reaching moral and political consequences. The West had come to see in the principles of nationalism the revelation of universal truth to be lived up to regardless of political consequences. Totalitarianism looked at those principles as political tools to be used if their use promised results, to be discarded otherwise. Hitler did not hesitate to sacrifice the Germans of northern Italy for the friendship of Mussolini by transferring the majority of them to Germany. The nationalities policy of the Soviet Union, while committed in theory to national autonomy, has been at the service of the political and economic interests of the central government which, as the instrument of "democratic centralism," has manipulated, controlled, and destroyed their national life without regard to principles of any kind.

Yet when totalitarianism turned the principles of nationalism against the West, the West stood morally and intellectually disarmed. The totalitarian arguments being its own, it could not answer them. The West had welcomed the victory of national self-determination in the aftermath of the First World War on moral and political grounds, and it found itself now incapable, when Hitler used the German minority for the destruction of Czechoslovakia, of defending its interests against its principles. It even lent a helping hand to its defeat and congratulated itself upon its moral consistency. "Self-determination, the professed principle of the Treaty of Versailles, has been invoked by Herr Hitler against its written text, and his appeal has been allowed," wrote the London *Times* on September 28, 1938, commenting upon the Munich settlement.

The Second World War and the Cold War following it have both qualitatively and quantitatively magnified the paradoxes of nationalism which the interwar period had brought to the fore, and they have added a new one which has made nationalism altogether obsolete as a principle of political organization. The new fact that has created that new paradox is the feasibility of all-out atomic war.

The justification of the nation state, as of all political organization, is its ability to perform the functions for the sake of which political organization exists. The most elementary of these functions is the common defense of the life of the citizens and of the values of the civilization in which they live. A political organization which is no longer able to defend these values and even puts them in jeopardy must yield, either through peaceful transformation or violent destruction, to one capable of that defense. Thus, under the impact of the invention of gunpowder and of the first industrial revolution, the feudal order had to yield to the dynastic and the nation state. Under the technological conditions of the pre-atomic age, the stronger nation states could, as it were, erect a wall behind which their citizens could live secure and the weak nation states were similarly protected by the operation of the balance of power which added the resources of the strong to those of the weak. Thus under normal conditions no nation state was able to make more than marginal inroads upon the life and civilization of its neighbors.

The feasibility of all-out atomic war has completely destroyed this protective function of the nation state. No nation state is capable of protecting its citizens and its civilization against an all-out atomic attack. It safety rests solely in preventing such an attack from taking place. While in the pre-atomic age a nation state could count upon its physical ability to defend itself, in the atomic age it must rely upon its psychological ability to deter those who are physically able to destroy it. The prospective enemy must be induced to refrain from attacking; once he attacks, the victim is doomed.

This psychological mechanism of deterrence operates only on the condition that the prospective atomic aggressor is clearly identified beforehand, that is, that no more than two nations are capable of waging all-out atomic war; for it is only on this condition that deterrence operates with automatic certainty. Today, the Soviet Union knows that if it should attack the United States with atomic weapons, the United States would destroy it, and vice versa; that certainty deters both. Yet the time is close at hand when other nations will have the weapons with which to wage all-out atomic war. When that time has come, nations will have lost even the preventive capacity of psychological deterrence, which they still possess today. For the United States, if then attacked with atomic weapons, will no longer be able to identify the aggressor with certainty and, hence, deter the prospective aggressor with the certainty of retaliation. When this historic moment comes—as it surely must if the present trend is not reversed—the nation state will connote not life and civilization but anarchy and universal destruction.

It is in the shadow of this grim reality and grimmer prospect that the inherent paradoxes of nationalism have taken on a novel urgency, threatening to overwhelm the remnants of international order. Balkanization, demoralization, and barbarization on a world-wide scale are the result.

The age which has seen the nation state become obsolete witnesses the emergence of a multitude of new states fashioned from the fragments of the colonial empires. The number of sovereign states has approximately doubled since the First World War. Many of these new states would not have been viable political, military, and economic entities even in the heyday of the nation state, deficient as they are in the essential prerequisites of nationhood. They could not have fed, administered, and defended themselves then, nor can they now. The disorder and threats to peace which the dissolution, first, of the Turkish and, then, of the Austro-Hungarian and western part of the Russian Empires brought in its wake is being spread, in the name of nationalism, to ever wider areas of Africa and Asia. In our age, even the infinitely stronger nation states of Europe are no longer viable political, military, and economic entities, but must submit either to the support or the conquest of the two remaining nations of the first rank, which are significantly not nation states in the traditional sense but continental states. The tragedy of Hungary and the collapse of the British and French intervention in Egypt in November, 1956, have demonstrated in different ways both the continuing emotional strength of national aspirations and the political and military weakness of the nation state. Is it then reasonable to expect that these new nations, some of them so artificial as to be even lacking the ethnic and historic foundations of nationhood, will be able to create a viable order among themselves and with their more powerful neighbors?

Only two alternatives appear to be in store for them, perhaps one following the other: Balkanization and a new colonialism. The rivalries which have beset the successor states to the European empires have already appeared among them. Some of the former colonies would like to have colonies of their own. The natural resources of some continue to make them attractive as colonies for stronger nations who need these resources. Their weakness, necessitating continuous support from stronger nations, predestines them as pawns in the power struggles of the latter. Their attractiveness, coupled with weakness, is thus a standing invitation to conquest, conquest by one or the other of them or else from the outside. In any event, the disorder which is taking the place of the old order of empire is likely to call forth, as it did before in Europe, a new order which will be again an order of empire.

It is ironic—and perhaps inevitable—that the great nations of the West should actively promote and support this Balkanization of much of the world, and it is equally ironic—and certainly not inevitable—that they should applaud it. For while they may have no choice but to give up their empires, they cannot afford to look with indifference, let alone with satisfaction, upon the prospect that disorder and violence, exploited by communism, will spread over ever wider areas of the globe. Here we encounter on a world-wide scale and in the form of anticolonialism that moral perversion which made Great Britain congratulate herself upon having helped Hitler to destroy Czechoslovakia in the name of nationalism.

There was a time when the Western world looked upon empire as a respectable and even a noble thing. The libertarian standards and aspirations of the West itself gave empire a bad name. It was Jeremy Bentham who as far back as 1793 wrote a pamphlet with the title, "Emancipate Your Colonies." And the United States, ever mindful of its colonial origins, has throughout its history felt an emotional attachment to national and anticolonial movements, even though, if there were logic in such historic analogies, its sympathies ought to be today not with the Algerians but with the French *colons*, with the British planters and not with the Malayans.

With characteristic philosophic consistency and lack of political judgment, the West has applied the democratic principles of freedom and equality to the international scene, transforming them in the process from concrete political goals into abstract moral postulates. Yet wherever democracy has succeeded within the nation state, it was imbedded in a structured social order from which it received its vital strength and to which, in turn, it imparted form and direction.

It is this Western dedication to national freedom, not as a concrete political goal but as an eternal verity, which has made the West morally and politically helpless in the face of the anticolonial onslaught of the age. When Japan swept through Asia, carrying the banner of anticolonialism before her, the new colonialism supplanted the old with such immediacy and undisguised exploitation and oppression as to provide a ready target for the West's anticolonial indignation. The anticolonialism of the Soviet Union, Communist China, and the indigenous peoples of Africa and Asia is different and has had a different effect upon the moral consciousness of the West.

While it is for all of them a tool at the service of concrete political goals, used and discarded especially by the Soviet Union and Communist China as the occasion requires, its immediate goal appears to be national liberation and nothing more. What disorders will follow liberation and what new colonialism will follow the disorders is a matter for long-term concern, not for immediate political calculation. Furthermore, the colonialism which the Soviet Union has practiced in Europe since the end of the Second World War is geographically far removed from Africa and Asia, protected from immediate recognition by the "salt-water fallacy" which requires that a colony, to be recognized as such, be separated from the colonial power by some ocean. Finally, in Africa and Asia, as in the European resistance during the Second World War, communism fights in the forefront of nationalism, making for the time being little of the fact that its nationalism serves the interests of China or the Soviet Union. Thus in a strange and disquieting transformation, nationalism, the moral principle of the West, becomes the most potent weapon in the arsenal of its enemies; and disarmed before the triumph of its own ideal, the West applauds its own destruction.

This confrontation of nationalism as an absolute moral principle with nationalism as a tool of political power is novel only in its worldwide dimensions and world-shaking results. The contrast itself, and the moral and political dilemma it presents, is as old as nationalism itself. The ideologues of the French Revolution, the Frankfort Parliament of 1848, Mazzini, and Wilson provided the ideas and the moral fervor; Napoleon, Cavour, Bismarck, and Clemenceau fashioned the political and military tools of victory, harnessing the libertarian impulses of nationalism to the purposes of power, leaving the ideologues behind approving or disillusioned but in any event in impotence. Yet nationalism, from the French Revolution to the peace settlement of 1919—however bent to, and distorted by, the purposes of power—never completely lost sight of the individual and his freedom of choice. When, in violation of this principle, Bismarck expelled in 1885 thirty thousand Poles who were not German citizens, the principle still had sufficient strength to induce the Reichstag to register its protest. During that period, nationalism retained its essential democratic orientation. The ideal of "one nation, one state" was implemented by the principle of national self-determination which postulated the primacy of individual choice over the political interests of governments. As a matter of principle, frontiers were to be determined by the will of the people not by considerations of political and military expediency.

This order of priority has been reversed since the Second World War. Not only do the interests of the state now take precedence over the will of the people, but the people themselves—their life, liberty, and pursuit of happiness—count for nothing if they appear to stand in the way of the interests of the state. No longer are national minorities to be protected against the state; it is now the state which must be protected against the minorities. The gulf that separates international treaties for the protection of national minorities from the deportation and extermination of national minorities and whole nations also separates the old libertarian nationalism from the totalitarian nationalism of the age. By whatever causes one may explain this transformation—the political and military use which great powers made of small nations and national minorities in the interwar period and during the Second World War; nationalistic universalism taking the place of the pluralistic nationalism of the nineteenth century—its barbarous consequences deny all that nationalism once stood for.

How different that world is from the world our fathers thought they lived in! Nationalism, they thought, meant of necessity freedom, civilization, and justice; we know now that it can also mean slavery, barbarism, and death. Nationalism, they thought, would bring of necessity peace and order to the relations among nations; we know now that it has brought us disorder and war and threatens us with universal destruction. When the exepriences from which that knowledge derives had still to be made, a very wise liberal voiced his disillusionment and implied the remedy. "It may be said," wrote John Morley in 1874,

that the very fate of these aspirations has had a blighting effect on public enthusiasm and the capacity of feeling it. Not only have most of them now been fulfilled, and so passed from aspiration to actuality, but the results of their fulfilment have been so disappointing as to make us wonder whether it is really worth while to pray, when to have our prayers granted carries the world so very slight a way forward. The Austrian is no longer in Italy; the Pope has ceased to be master in Rome; the patriots of Hungary are now in possession of their rights, and have become friends of their old oppressors; the negro slave has been transformed into an American citizen. At home, again, the gods have listened to our vows. Parliament has been reformed, and the long-desired mechanical security provided for the voter's freedom. We no longer aspire after all these things, you may say because our hopes have been realised and our dreams have come true. It is possible that the comparatively prosaic results before our eyes at the end of all have thrown a chill over our political imagination.

"Political imagination" is indeed the key word. If the West cannot think of something better than nationalism, it may well lose the opportunity to think at all. It has been its moral virtue and besetting political sin to look at nationalism as though it were a self-sufficient political principle and could bring freedom, justice, order, and peace simply by being consistently applied. In truth, no political principle carries within itself such a force for good. What good and what evil it will work depends not only upon its own nature but also upon the configurations of interest and power in which and for the sake of which it is called upon to act.

The West has consistently tended to misunderstand the subtle and complex relationships between these configurations and political principles. Thereby, it has blunted its political will, its political judgment, and its political imagination. It has failed to see that political principles, such as nationalism, must direct, rechannel, even transform these configurations but that they cannot replace them. Yet when their work is done, they must themselves be replaced.

Nationalism has had its day. It was the political principle appropriate to the post-feudal and pre-atomic age. For the technology of the steam engine, it was indeed in good measure a force for progress. In the atomic age, it must make way for a political principle of larger dimensions, in tune with the world-wide configurations of interest and power of the age.

10 *Neutrality and Neutralism*

The President of the United States, at his press conference of June 6, 1956, had this to say about neutrality and neutralism:

If you are waging peace, you can't be too particular sometimes about the special attitudes that different countries take. We were a young country once, and our whole policy for the first hundred years was, or more, 150, we were neutral. We constantly asserted we were neutral in the wars of the world and wars in Europe and antagonisms.

Now, today there are certain nations that say they are neutral. This doesn't necessarily mean what it is so often interpreted to mean, neutral as between right and wrong or decency and indecency.

They are using the term "neutral" with respect to attachment to military alliances. And may I point out that I cannot see that that is always to the disadvantage of such a country as ours. . . .

So let us not translate this meaning of the word "neutral" as between contending military forces, even though the conflict is latent, and neutral as between right and wrong.[1]

On June 7 the White House issued the following official statement, intended to clarify the President's remarks:

Questions have been presented to the White House concerning the exact meaning of expressions in the President's press conference yesterday defending the right of certain nations to a neutral position. He particularly referred to neutrality as a refusal to take sides in any military line-up of world powers.

It is obvious that in some countries of the world there are certain ideological, geographical or other reasons making military alliances impractical. Such nations may declare themselves to be neutral, hoping thus to secure the support of world opinion against attack from any quarter. Neutrality does not mean either disarmament or immunity from attack. We have had historical examples of this kind of neutrality for many decades.

The President believes in the principle of collective security whereby the nations associate themselves together for each other's protection. This is the modern and enlightened way of obtaining security. . . . The President does believe that there are special conditions which justify political neutrality but that no nation has the right to be indifferent to the fate of an-

[1] *New York Times,* June 7, 1956, p. 10.

other, or, as he put it, to be "neutral as between right and wrong or decency and indecency."[2]

The very same day on which the President of the United States sought to clarify the American attitude toward neutrality and neutralism, the Foreign Minister of France shed light upon the Russian position:

When we insisted on the importance of reunification as the symbol of European balance, Monsieur Khrushchev declared that he preferred 20,-000,000 Germans with him to 70,000,000 against him, even neutralized. That does not mean he is against a neutral Germany but that he is against a Germany neutralized against him.[3]

On June 9, 1956, the Secretary of State of the United States, in the address which the President had heralded as "a definite attempt to bring this thing down to its realities, to its specifics, so we can all understand it," defined neutrality as the pretense "that a nation can best gain safety for itself by being indifferent to the fate of others. This has increasingly become an obsolete conception and, except under very exceptional circumstances, it is an immoral and short-sighted conception."[4] Queried at his press conference of June 12, 1956, about the relationship between his statement and that of the President, the Secretary of State affirmed three times "that there is no difference whatever between the President and myself on this subject." Asked about the "very exceptional circumstances" which would not render neutrality obsolete, he replied: "Well, the outstanding example of neutrality is, of course, Switzerland. Switzerland has declined to join the United Nations because it recognizes that the United Nations Charter is incompatible with strict neutrality."[5]

On July 4, 1956, the Vice-President of the United States gave an address at Manila, which is reported to have been prepared at the White House for use by the President who could not present it in person by reason of illness. In this address the Vice-President made the following statement about neutralism:

[2] *New York Times,* June 8, 1956, p. 2.

[3] *Christian Science Monitor* (Boston), June 9, 1956, p. 2.

[4] *New York Times,* June 10, 1956, p. 24.

[5] *Ibid.,* June 13, 1956, p. 4.

We have heard recently a great deal of discussion of the attitude that goes by the name of neutralism. Let us see how it bears on the problem of independence. I would feel that generally a nation that rejects the principles of collective security because it feels its independence will be compromised by association with other powers is not reading rightly the trends of modern history. It has far more to gain by standing together with free nations than by remaining aloof.

But there may be other reasons for neutralism. Many nations have the same principles which we share in common, and they are prepared to defend them. Yet they feel that their own internal problems compel them to abstain, at least for the moment, from mutual-security pacts and associations. They wish to devote all their energies to building their own political and economic systems. Or they may feel that they are too geographically exposed to risk provoking Communist colonial imperialism.

We in the United States can understand the attitudes of such powers. For over a century we tried to avoid being identified with any of the warring powers *blocs* of Europe. But we learned from hard experience that policies which worked well in the nineteenth century were completely inadequate in the twentieth. In 1917, we were forced to enter a terrific world war. Again in 1941, we were plunged into the blood bath of the Second World War.

Finally we learned our lesson. Together with most of the other nations of the world, we joined in a world organization designed to promote justice and insure peace. In addition, we joined regional alliances permitted under the charter of the United Nations. We found that the world is too small today for effective isolation....

But there is still another brand of neutralism that makes no moral distinction between the Communist world and the free world. With this viewpoint, we have no sympathy. How can we feel toward those who treat alike nations that believe in God and honor, religion and morality, and nations that boast of atheism and the rule of force and terror alone?

How can anyone treat as equals those who believe in the dignity of man and the basic rights of all men, and those who treat their subjects as mere machines? Is democracy to be equated with dictatorship? Is freedom the same as tyranny? ...

I know there are those who feel that friendly neutrality toward the Kremlin and Peiping may spare them. But you know the proverb: He who sups with the devil, must have a long spoon. The Communists have been ruthless toward the people of the nations that they have engulfed. They have no memory of former favors, no kindness toward those who tried to be friendly. They are cold and calculating masters. Those who feel that they can outmaneuver them are taking a fearful risk.[6]

[6] *Ibid.*, July 4, 1956, p. 2.

The Prime Minister of India took exception to Messrs. Nixon's and Dulles' statements at his press conference of July 7, 1956.

"I submit for consideration that Mr. Nixon and Mr. Dulles are saying something that is opposed to the democratic way of life," Mr. Nehru declared. "The very basis of democracy," he said, "is tolerance for differing points of view. . . ." He made clear his dislike of the term "neutralism" which, he said, connoted war and which in peacetime had no real validity.

"India's policy could better be explained as one of non-involvement in either the Soviet or Western bloc, of eschewing war and seeking peaceful settlements to all international problems and of concentrating mainly on internal Indian development," he said.[7]

The Prime Minister of Laos went one better by declaring: "Our country has no intention of joining any *bloc,* even the neutralist *bloc.* . . . Neutrality is more neutral than neutralism."[8]

Confronted with these contradictory statements which are but recent examples of a veritable Babel of tongues, the layman will be forgiven when he is confused. Yet the professional observer of foreign policy must search for the reasons which are responsible for these contradictions, and he will find them in certain legal and political trends which have come to dominate the international scene since the end of the First World War. Three such trends are relevant for our investigation: the legal commitment to collective security, the helplessness of an ever increasing number of nations faced with the threat of all-out war within a bipolar system of world politics, and the identification of international conflicts with irreconcilable philosophic and moral positions.

In order to understand the changes brought about by these factors, it is first necessary to visualize the legal and political situation which existed before these factors appeared on the international scene. That legal situation is encompassed by the status of neutrality as defined by international law. The political situation is determined by the desire of certain nations, for reasons of expediency, to keep out of certain wars.

Neutrality as a status of international law results from the desire of a nation not to be involved in a war waged by other nations. Therefore, neutrality is essentially a negative status depending upon

[7] *Ibid.,* July 7, 1956, p. 1.

[8] *Economist* (London), CLXXX (Sept. 22, 1956), p. 968.

the existence of definite relations between two nations, which the law calls war. Where there is no war in the legal sense of the term there can be no neutrality. Hence, the development of neutrality as a legal status depends upon the possibility of differentiating clearly between peace and war as two distinct situations defined by international law.

But neutrality is also a negative status in that the complex of rights and obligations which constitute the legal status of neutrality is determined less by the neutral, who desires to keep out of war and thereby retain the greatest possible freedom of action, than by the belligerents, who want to prevent the neutral from joining the other side and assure themselves of his support. In the struggle between war and neutrality for the delimitation of their respective spheres, war is the stronger contestant.

Neutrality and war are complementary concepts; the more there is of the one, the less there is of the other. The rights and obligations flowing from the status of neutrality are the result of a balance between the interests of the belligerents and the interests of the neutrals. The former seek to win the war by maximizing their advantages and minimizing those of the enemy. The latter seek to keep out of the war without renouncing those activities which they consider essential for the pursuit of their national interests. As long as these antagonistic interests are held in balance, international law safeguards the legal status of the neutrals.

Neutrality implies two fundamental obligations on the part of the neutral: abstention from interference with the military activities of the belligerents and impartiality toward them in their position as belligerents. The particular duties these two fundamental obligations impose on the neutral cannot be deduced from the abstract concepts of "abstention" and "impartiality." They depend exclusively upon the kind of warfare being waged. For the extent to which the neutral has to abstain from interference is determined by the extent of the military activities of the belligerents. If the scope of warfare is limited, the domain into which the neutral may extend his activities without risking involvement in the war will be vast. For example, because wars were conducted mainly by hired soldiers with the bulk of the population not actively participating in them, it was not regarded until the end of the eighteenth century as a violation of the duties of neutrality to assist belligerents with man-power. When, however, the whole population capable of bearing arms participated actively in the war, that is, with the introduction of universal military service, such assistance became incompatible with the legal status of neutrality.

The same interrelationship between the development of warfare and the rules of neutrality applies to the implements of war the neutral is allowed to supply to the belligerents. As long as but a small fraction of the economic resources of the belligerents was used for military purposes, the neutrals were free to give the belligerents all possible material aid. With the mobilization of the total material resources of the belligerents, the rules of neutrality were bound to change again. Material aid by non-belligerents now became as de-cisive an intervention in war as the assistance with manpower had been since the beginning of the nineteenth century, and therefore became incompatible with the status of a neutral.

Not only the content of the rules of neutrality but also the very possibility of remaining neutral depends upon the military-political situation in which the neutral finds himself. The neutral pursues a double aim: to keep out of war and to pursue his national interests with regard to the belligerents and other nations. The interest of the belligerents, on the other hand, is only one: to win the war. In the pursuit of his interests, the neutral may be faced with a dual dilem-ma: his aim to keep out of war may conflict either with his other aim to pursue his national interests vis-à-vis other nations or with the belligerents' aim to win the war.

The dilemma of the belligerents presents itself in much simpler terms. The belligerents look at the existence, the interests, and the "rights" of neutrals only from one angle: in what way are they likely to influence the outcome of the war? The position and in-terests of the neutrals may be respected as far as the belligerents believe this respect not to affect their mutual position in the war. But should a belligerent come to believe that the violation of the position or interests of the neutral would be detrimental to the enemy or advantageous to himself, he will not hesitate to violate them. He will only refrain from doing so if the disadvantages result-ing from such violation are likely to outweigh the advantages. In other words, neutrals owe their status as neutrals to considerations of political expediency on the part of the belligerents, not to the latter's respect for legal principles. And the desire of a nation to remain neutral counts for considerably less than objective conditions over which it has no control and, more particularly, the interests of the belligerents.

Hence, geographic isolation which puts the neutral's territory beyond the reach of military operations has always been—as the history of Great Britain, the Scandinavian countries, and the United States shows—the most reliable protection of neutral status. In the absence of such protection, a nation can eliminate a motive from the belligerents for violating its neutrality by pursuing, with regard to their conflicts, a policy of abstention and impartiality and by making it at the same time too costly for them to gain advantages at the expense of its neutral status. To that end, the neutral must make his armed forces a serious factor in the military calculations of the belligerents. He must secure the support of other powerful neutrals or of one of the belligerents or of both of them in defense of his neutrality against violation by either. There exists, then, an intimate relationship between the politico-legal status of neutrality and the balance of power.

The period between the Treaty of Westphalia and the First World War was the classical period of the balance of power in Europe. To the relative stability of the state system—the period of the Napoleonic Wars is the main exception—corresponded the relative security of the status of the neutrals. Wars were localized; the economic rights of neutrals were violated only in minor instances, their political status remained by and large intact. The First World War marks, as general wars have always done, the wholesale violation of the economic rights of all neutrals and the destruction of the political status of two of them, Belgium and Greece. The other nations which succeeded in remaining neutral owed the preservation of their neutrality either to the geographic factor—as did the non-European and Scandinavian countries as well as Spain—or to military-political considerations of expediency—as did the Netherlands and Switzerland.[9]

[9] On this point and those immediately following see Hans J. Morgenthau, "The Resurrection of Neutrality," *American Political Science Review*, XXXIII (1939), 473 ff.

With the end of the First World War began a new chapter in the history of neutrality. Collective security challenged neutrality as a legal status. The radical transformation which the state system underwent weakened the political foundations of neutrality.

Neutrality as a legal concept assumes the legality of war as an instrument of national policy as well as the right of any nation to intervene or not to intervene in a war on one side or the other as it sees fit. Collective security, on the contrary, derives logically from the distinction between lawful and unlawful war and stipulates the legal duty for all nations to join the nation waging lawful war. Collective security requires partiality leading to intervention; neutrality requires impartiality and abstention. Under collective security, the need for assistance of a victim of aggression determines action; under neutrality, action is determined by the interests of the individual nations.

It is obvious, then, that neutrality and collective security are mutually exclusive. Collective security, implying the universalization of war by virtue of an abstract legal principle, and neutrality, seeking the localization of war for reasons of expediency, cannot coexist. As it is with war, so it is with collective security in relation to neutrality: the more there is of the one, the less there is bound to be of the other. Had the Covenant of the League of Nations and the Charter of the United Nations established a full-fledged, working system of collective security, neutrality would indeed, as has been claimed, have been outlawed and become politically inoperative. In point of fact, neither the Covenant nor the Charter went so far. They embraced the ideal of collective security and left gaping holes in its legal fabric. Conversely, they did not kill neutrality but rather sentenced it to die, staying indefinitely the execution of the sentence.

The loophole through which both legal instruments have allowed neutrality to escape from execution by collective security is the non-automatic nature of enforcement measures. For in so far as a nation has the legal right to decide for itself whether and to what degree it shall participate in measures of collective security, it has also the legal right to substitute for the principle of collective security any other guide for action more consonant with its national interest, such as the principle of neutrality.

First of all, Articles 12 and 15 of the Covenant of the League of Nations, by allowing explicitly resort to war under certain circumstances, recognized by implication also the right to remain neutral with regard to such a war. Furthermore, the Covenant explicitly recognized the right to neutrality with regard to collective military measures, Article 16, paragraph 2, making such measures dependent upon a mere recommendation by the Council of the League. This discretionary nature of military measures, explicit in the text of the Covenant, was extended to all collective security measures to be taken under the Covenant through the interpretative resolutions passed by the Assembly of the League in 1921. These interpretative resolutions shifted the locus of decision from the Council to the individual member states and reduced the Council to a co-ordinating agency for the measures taken by the member states through the exercise of their own discretion.

Chapter VII of the Charter of the United Nations, comprising Articles 39 to 51, is the counterpart of Article 16 of the Covenant. These provisions take a decisive step beyond the Covenant in that they establish the complete authority of the Security Council over measures of collective security. Nothing in this system of collective security seems to be left to the discretion of the member states. And there appears to be no loophole through which the member states could escape from collective security into neutrality. Yet while indeed the Charter of the United Nations leaves no room for neutrality on condition that its system of collective security operates as intended, its very operation is contingent upon two conditions which restore the discretion of the member states and, through it, neutrality as a legal status.

One of these conditions is laid down in Article 43 of the Charter which makes collective military action dependent upon agreements to be concluded between the member states and the Security Council concerning "the numbers and types of forces, their degree of readiness and general location, and the nature of the facilities and assistance to be provided." While Article 43 provides that these agreements "shall be negotiated as soon as possible on the initiative of the Security Council," none has been negotiated. In the absence of such agreements, the provisions of the Charter concerning collective military measures remain a dead letter and the member states remain free to decide for themselves whether and to what extent they are to participate in such measures. Their discretion in this respect encompasses their right to remain neutral. This discretion is implicitly recognized by Article 106 of the Charter which provides that in the absence of the special agreements envisaged by Article 43 the great powers shall consult with one another and with other member states about collective military measures to be taken.

The other condition which goes to the very heart of the collective security system of the Charter is Article 27, paragraph 3, stipulating that "decisions of the Security Council . . . shall be made by an affirmative vote of seven members including the concurring votes of the permanent members." This provision for a great power veto eliminates from the outset any possibility of applying the collective security measures of the Charter against a permanent member of the Security Council. With the great powers thus beyond the reach of such measures, it remains for the individual nations to decide on the basis of expediency whether and to what extent they want to take measures against a great power. In other words, they have the right to remain neutral.

The Security Council is then capable of applying collective security measures only against nations of the second or third rank, that is, those which are not among its permanent members. This, however, is not likely to happen as long as the great powers are pitted against each other in fierce, interconnected, and world-encompassing competitions for power. Under such circumstances, collective security measures executed against any nation of the second or third rank are bound to affect the respective power positions of some or all of the great powers, and those who stand to lose through the application of such measures will use their discretion to interpose a veto against them. The result for the member states is again freedom of action, which includes neutrality.

This interpretation of the Charter is borne out by the legal situation which arose when the United Nations instituted in 1950 collective security measures against North Korea and Communist China. The Security Council was able to discharge its functions only so long as the Soviet Union, because of its temporary absence, was unable to veto the collective security measures the other members had agreed upon. With the return of the Soviet Union to the Security Council, the General Assembly was called upon to carry the burden of organizing the collective action of the United Nations. The functions of the General Assembly with regard to measures of collective security are limited by Articles 10 and 18 of the Charter to making recommendations to the member states by a two-thirds majority. Thus again the freedom of action of the member states and, with it, the right to remain neutral are preserved. This legal situation has not been affected by the "Uniting for Peace" resolution of November, 1950, seeking to strengthen the General Assembly as the principal agency for the co-ordination of collective measures.

This legal compatibility of neutrality with collective security, as conceived by the Covenant and the Charter, was demonstrated by the manner in which the legal provisions were put to the test of actual performance in terms of military measures. The attack of North Korea against South Korea on June 25, 1950, joined by Communist China in November of the same year, was a clear-cut case of aggression. Collective security would have required that all members of the United Nations come to the aid of South Korea as the victim of that aggression. In view of the nature and the military consequences of the aggression, this aid, to be effective, could only have taken the form of the dispatch of armed forces to the battle-front. Yet of the sixty members of the United Nations, only sixteen sent armed forces of any kind. The others—among them nations with military capabilities, such as Argentina, Brazil, Czechoslovakia, India, Mexico, Poland—remained neutral in that they abstained from active participation in the war on either side.

The survival of neutrality under the aegis of collective security is also attested to by the fact that by no means all wars which have occurred during that period became general wars, as they should have if no nation had remained neutral with regard to it. The very incidence of local wars, such as the Chaco War, the Italo-Ethiopian War, the Sino-Japanese War, the Russo-Finnish War, the Israeli-Arab War, demonstrate the incidence of neutrality. In the autumn of 1956 the government of the United States declared that it did not intend to participate in a war which might break out between some users of the Suez Canal and Egypt, that is, it intended to remain neutral. And even during so general a war as the Second World

War, some nations remained neutral, and their neutrality was universally respected.[10]

What has made neutrality problematical in the contemporary world is not so much the new international law of collective security as a novel political and military situation. The rationale of neutrality has always been the desire to keep out of war without having to forsake one's national interests. The realization of this dual objective has always depended upon the operations of the balance of power. A nation of the second or third rank has a chance to preserve its neutrality vis-à-vis the great powers only if an approximately equal distribution of power among the latter deters all of them from violating it. The history of Belgian and Swiss neutrality bears out this relationship between neutrality and the balance of power. Switzerland, in particular, owed the preservation of her neutrality in the two world wars to the fortuitous conditions of the military balance of power, effectively supported, it is true, by the consistent Swiss policy of abstention.[11]

Neutrality, being a function of the balance of power, partakes of the latter's precarious and unstable nature. Thus when the Covenant of the League seemed to offer an automatic and, hence, reliable alternative to the balance of power, the small nations were among the most fervent supporters of collective security. Yet this support involved them in an insoluble contradiction. Collective security, if it could be made to work, provides the best hope for the avoidance of war. Yet it could not be made to work without the active support of all nations, big and small; in order to make collective security a success, those nations whose survival depends upon remaining neutral in case of war must cease being neutral in order to avoid war. Yet if collective security should fail to deter a prospective aggressor, the commitment to collective security would expose the nations of the second and third rank to the very risks which their support of collective security was intended to avoid.

The small nations tried to reconcile these two positions by maxi-

[10] Cf. also Hans J. Morgenthau, *Politics among Nations* (2d ed.; New York: Alfred A. Knopf, 1954), pp. 274 ff., 388 ff.

[11] On Swiss neutrality see Hans J. Morgenthau, "The End of Switzerland's Differential Neutrality," *American Journal of International Law*, XXXII (1938), 558 ff.

mizing the protective effects of collective security for themselves and at the same time minimizing their own commitments to it. Thus in 1920 and 1921, the Scandinavian countries suggested that certain nations which, by fully participating in the measures provided for by Article 16 of the Covenant, would be exposed to grave dangers on account of their geographic and economic situation, be exempted from the rigorous application of this article. The same countries were in 1935–36 among the strongest supporters of League of Nations sanctions against Italy, the main burden of which, for military and geographic reasons, would have had to be borne by others.

The failure of these sanctions ended the League experiment in collective security. The collective security of the League was the institutional manifestation of Anglo-French military and political supremacy in Europe. It was under the umbrella of that supremacy that the small European nations sought, and believed to have found, protection. The overwhelming military power with which Great Britain and France emerged from the First World War signified the end of the European balance of power on which the neutrality of the small European nations had rested. Its heritage was taken over by the collective security of the League of Nations. Membership in the League seemed to guarantee those nations military protection superior to that which the balance of power would have afforded them. When Italy succeeded in defying the collective security of the League, she also demonstrated at the very least the unreliability, if not the disappearance, of Anglo-French supremacy in Europe. The small nations found themselves again face to face with a number of great powers of comparable strength, competing for power and openly following the counsels of expediency. The restoration of the balance of power called forth the traditional reaction of the small nations: neutrality.

After withdrawal from the League had been seriously discussed in some of the small European nations, Belgium, Denmark, Finland, Norway, Sweden, the Netherlands, Spain, and Switzerland, in a number of joint and several declarations, canceled for all practical purposes the obligations under Article 16 of the Covenant. While the League of Nations took formal cognizance of the restoration of the neutrality of Switzerland only, there can be no doubt that what the so-called traditional European neutrals had declared for themselves held equally true, regardless of legal theories and pretenses, for all nations, big and small: they would act in the face of war according to their interests as they saw them, to intervene or to remain neutral as they saw fit.

Thus the small European nations fell back upon the traditional safeguards of neutrality: rearmament and isolation. They tried to buttress the latter by regional understandings, such as the Scandinavian Rules of Neutrality of May 27, 1938, and the Convention of the Baltic States of November 18, 1938. They debated, but did not act upon, the idea of a "Third Europe," an organization of all nations who wanted to stay out of the approaching Second World War. This idea called for collective action on the part of the members of the organization for the purpose of preventing the outbreak of such a war and, if it should break out, of protecting their neutrality. The feasibility of this proposal depended upon two nonexistent conditions: a community of interests transcending the mere negative desire to stay out of the next general war and a concentration of power comparable to that which might threaten the neutrality of a member nation.

The members of the League, thus returning from the world of collective security to that of the balance of power, did not return to the same world they had left in 1919. The distribution of power that existed on the eve of the Second World War was not identical with the one that existed at the end of the First. It showed three tendencies which decisively impaired the protection which neutrality used to afford.

While in 1919 the distribution of power favored Great Britain and France, inducing the small European nations to seek their protection within a system of collective security, on the eve of the Second World War military and political power had almost as decisively shifted to the Axis powers. They had come to occupy a quasi-hegemonic position in central Europe. Furthermore, the fate of Austria and Czechoslovakia had shown that Great Britain and France could no longer be counted upon, even if they were still able, to take military risks in defense of the neutral status of small nations. Thus each of the three courses of action available to the traditional neutrals appeared equally unsatisfactory. They could follow the shift of power and join the Axis, thereby not only giving up their neutrality but also risking the loss of their national identity; they could join Great Britain and France, thereby running mortal risks without gaining additional protection; they could retreat in the impartial and abstemious isolation befitting a neutral, thereby running the same mortal risks but with the outside chance of being spared destruction and conquest.

Second, the technology of warfare had progressed to a point at which the protection of geographic location was largely eliminated. Furthermore, these technological developments greatly widened the gap separating the powers of the first rank from the others. Lacking the industrial basis for a modern war machine, the traditional neutrals had lost the military means with which to deter aggression by great powers.

Finally, the rise of totalitarian imperialism, already foreshadowed in the international policies of the Soviet Union in the twenties, added a new dimension to international politics, hostile to neutrality. To nations that consider themselves the repositories of universal truths which it is their historic mission to bring to the rest of humanity, the impartial aloofness of the neutrals becomes intolerable indifference, if not treason. In the contest between truth and falsehood, good and evil, neutrality appears to the crusading nations tantamount to passive hostility to be fought by all means fair or foul. What point can there be in the traditional impartiality and abstention of the neutral when subversion becomes one of the foremost weapons in the arsenal of nations, when races, classes, and parties fight on the domestic political plane the battle of nations?

The political and military developments following the Second World War have accentuated these tendencies, destructive of neutrality. The disparity of strength between the great powers and the other nations has developed into a bipolar political system in which there are only two nations of the first rank, separated by a gulf of unprecedented dimensions from all the other nations. The increase in the destructiveness of modern weapons needs but to be mentioned in order to show the utter impossibility for any nation not possessing them to deter another nation from their use.

These developments have been aggravated by the political context within which they have occurred: the Cold War. The political relationship called the Cold War signifies the absence of peace between the two blocs in that there has been no moral and legal agreement upon their relationships and, more particularly, upon the boundaries between them. Rather these political relationships are the result of the provisional *de facto* settlement established at the end of the Second World War primarily on military grounds. It is characteristic of the Cold War that both sides refuse to consider this settlement as either permanent or legitimate and try to change it in their favor by all means short of war. Thus psychological warfare, intervening directly in the domestic affairs of other nations through subversion, propaganda, and foreign aid, has become a major undertaking of the active contenders.

The effects of these developments upon neutrality as a viable legal and political status are of course beyond doubt. General war is bound to wipe out the distinction between belligerents and neutrals. Before the atomic fall-out and bacteriological contamination all men and nations, big and small, neutrals and belligerents, are equal. The Cold War has made many nations of the second and third rank the main bone of contention. Under these conditions they have no chance to remain neutral either in a "cold" or "hot" war since it is their fate, decided by others, to belong to one or the other bloc.

However, the effects of these developments in terms of policy have been both contradictory and ambivalent. Two periods have followed each other, not dissimilar to those that followed the First World War: one characterized by the virtual disappearance of neutrality as the objective of policy; the other, by attempts at its revival. Yet during the first period some nations gave the appearance of holding both positions at the same time, wanting simultaneously to be neutral and not to be neutral, to reap the benefits both of neutrality and of association with a great power. While both objectives cannot be attained simultaneously, the former is not attainable at all. Out of this conflict between desire and reality rises the first type of neutralism: the impotent striving for neutrality.

This period covers roughly the first decade following the Second World War. It was characterized by the tendency of the bipolar system to transform itself into a two-bloc system. That is to say, the two centers of first-rate power remaining in the world exerted an irresistible attraction upon most of the other nations to the point of complete identification with one or the other of these superpowers. The result was what might be called "bipolar collective security." Most nations of the world, instead of banding all together for mutual protection as the ideal of collective security would have required, huddled around one or the other of the superpowers, expecting and receiving their protection. Only a few nations, of which India is the outstanding example, were able during that period to resist that attraction of the two superpowers and to decline alignment with either side.

This development resulted from the drastic decline in the viability of all nations except the two superpowers in consequence of the Second World War. During that period, none of the European nations found within itself the political, military, and economic resources for survival. Thus the nations of western Europe had to lean for support upon the United States, while the eastern European nations fell victim to Russian conquest.

To this general factor must be added a specific one which applies, in varying degrees, only to the nations outside the Soviet orbit. These nations found in the atomic monopoly of the United States the main protection against the threat of Soviet imperialism. The intensity of this type of identification with the United States varied with the intensity with which the Soviet threat was experienced by different nations at different times. It reached its peak in the period between the coup d'état in Czechoslovakia and the end of the Korean War, having its main impact in western Europe.

Those were the objective conditions under which most nations had to exist, and their policy of identifying themselves with one or the other of the superpowers followed inevitably from them. Yet these conditions and policies were not accepted enthusiastically or even willingly by most of these nations. Nations who but recently had either been great powers or had at least been able to choose their allies could hardly welcome the force of circumstances which left them no choice. Thus, while they had to accept for the time being the dire necessity of identifying themselves with one or the other superpower, they hoped to be again able to pursue an independent foreign policy.

That hope had to remain inarticulate in the members of the Soviet bloc. In the West it was articulated in different rationalizations whose uniform aim was to conceal the fact of dependence and to make it appear as though the nation concerned still had freedom of choice. Thus a nation might insist upon enjoying the prestige of a great power in terms of participation in international conferences, a position of eminence in international organizations, and the like. Or a nation, might engage in a public debate about alternative foreign policies, asserting its ability and, if need be, resolution to choose one of them. Or a nation might indulge in Anglophobia, Francophobia, or anti-Americanism, thus proving to itself and to others—primarily, however, to itself—its continuing independence.

These manifestations of escapism were politically irrelevant as long as the objective conditions of world politics made it impracticable to follow them up with actual policies. As such, they called for sympathy and understanding rather than for moral condemnation. They are of immediate political concern only in so far as they find opportunities for political action. For they reveal a state of mind longing for such an opportunity.

It is the characteristic of the second period in which we find ourselves at present that new developments have made it possible at least for some nations to translate into actual policy this desire to escape identification with one or the other of the two superpowers. In other words, neutrality is no longer a daydream expressing itself in neurotic symptoms but has again become the possible objective of rational policy. Consequently, neutralism has taken on a new significance as a foreign policy seeking avoidance of a consistent alignment with either bloc. The trend of the bipolar system to transform itself into a two-bloc system has been arrested and reversed. Centrifugal tendencies counteract the magnetic attraction which the two major power centers exerted during the first decade following the Second World War. Nations of the second and third rank tend to move toward the outer confines of the two spheres of influence dominated by the superpowers and not only look longingly beyond these confines but also have started to pursue policies without regard to the preferences of the superpowers. Four factors are in the main responsible for this new trend.

First, many of the nations who had to join one of the superpowers for sheer sake of survival have regained much of their economic strength and political stability. For them to remain within the orbit of one of these powers has again become in good measure a matter of expediency, of choice rather than of necessity. This is true in particular of West Germany and Japan. Only in the Soviet bloc, as the experience of Poland and Hungary has shown, necessity still reigns.

Second, the distribution of military power in the world has been drastically altered by the emergence of the Soviet Union as an atomic power comparable to the United States. The American monopoly of atomic weapons has been replaced by an atomic balance of power which amounts to an atomic stalemate. With the American and Russian stockpiles canceling each other out, American atomic power has lost its protective function for the allies of the United States. While there is today, as has been pointed out above, no safety from atomic destruction for any nation, the risk is increased almost to the point of certainty for nations which are closely allied with one or the other of the superpowers. Or, to put it the other way around, there may be a somewhat better chance for a nation not so allied to escape atomic destruction than for one that is.

Third, the need for American military protection appears to be further diminished by the "new look" of Russian foreign policy. The Soviet Union, minimizing the expansionist tendencies of communism and stressing instead the mutual benefits to be derived from cultural, economic, and technological exchanges as well as from disarmament, creates an additional incentive for the allies of the United States to minimize their military and political commitments.

Fourth, such commitments may well appear as a positive handicap in view of the Russian promise of such benefits. For in so far as the United States and the Soviet Union are willing to compete in terms of economic assistance, a nation may well expect to maximize such assistance by placing itself uncommitted between the two competitors. What more can such a nation hope for than to have the best of both worlds without belonging to either?

This type of neutralism which, as a matter of policy, seeks, at the very least, to minimize a nation's identification with either bloc and may aim at an uncommitted position between both, is in its economic aspects nothing but a matter of calculated self-interest. Its success will depend both upon the bargaining strength of the neutralist nations and the policies of the superpowers. Burma, Egypt, Finland, India, Indonesia, and Yugoslavia have followed this course with different degrees of success; others are likely to follow their example, their success again depending upon the distribution of power and the quality of the policies pursued.

This type of neutralism is similar in its political purpose to the attempt to revive neutrality on the eve of the Second World War. It is born of the recognition that to keep out of war is for all nations no longer merely a question of expediency but of survival. It is impossible not to be skeptical about its chances of success. Iceland might have increased her chances to escape atomic destruction by embarking upon a neutralist policy. But how many other nations are in a similarly favorable geographic position? And it may well be argued that salvation for all nations, big and small, lies in the prevention of an atomic war, not in staying neutral once it has broken out.

The prevention of such a war, however, depends upon the continuation of the atomic stalemate which, in turn, requires a maximum of military strength on either side. To the extent that a nation shifting from an allied into a neutral position decreases the military strength of one side, without a compensating decrease on the other, the atomic balance of power is altered to the advantage of the latter and the chance for the outbreak of an atomic war is thereby increased. By pursuing such a course, a nation may well in the short run increase its security, while it contributes to the destruction of the very foundations upon which its security ultimately rests.

This argument may not be good for all nations in all circumstances, as Ireland, Sweden, Spain, and Switzerland proved in the Second World War. Yet, as a matter of principle, the futility of neutrality under the conditions of modern warfare seems to be borne out by the fate which befell the small European nations which tried to stay out of the Second World War by pursuing a neutralist policy. Thus the paradox seems to be inescapable that under contemporary conditions a nation serves the purpose of neutrality, which is to stay out of war, by giving up neutrality in order to prevent war from breaking out.

These doubts about the political wisdom of a policy of neutrality apply also to what may be called the grand design of both the escapist and the political type of neutralism: the idea of a "third force." Such a third force, composed of all or some European nations or members of the so-called Asian-African bloc, has been visualized as being poised in independence between the two superpowers and forming a bridge between them, taking Britain's place as the "balancer" in the world balance of power, thereby mitigating international conflict and contributing to the preservation of peace. It was first forcibly and brilliantly expressed in 1946 by General de Gaulle. It has since then been broached time and again by spokesmen for both kinds of neutralism. It partakes, however, of their fatal weakness: it is incapable of realization in the contemporary world.

For such a third force to be an effective instrument of restraint in the world balance of power, its members must, first of all, have permanent vital interests in common which enable them to act in unison on the political scene. Yet there is nothing but anticolonialism which unites the members of the so-called Asian-African bloc, and the nations of western Europe are united by their common opposition to Soviet imperialism only. Some of these nations have been able to act in unison with regard to a specific political problem. They have proved incapable of common political action on a permanent basis. Cases in point are the political impotence and military disintegration of NATO, the failure of all attempts at the political unification of Europe, the political emptiness of the Declaration of Bandung of April, 1955, and the political inconclusiveness of the meeting of Nasser, Nehru, and Tito in July, 1956. Yet even if such permanent common interests existed, they could not be supported by the power necessary to transform them into common policies.[12]

The third typical manifestation of neutralism is of an entirely different kind. It is not primarily concerned with the political and military struggle between East and West, but rather with the identification of that struggle with irreconcilably hostile philosophic and moral positions. It refuses to see the East-West struggle in terms of a struggle between right and wrong, good and evil and, hence, to be drawn into a "crusade" to extirpate evil on either side. In other words, when it comes to passing moral judgments upon either of the hostile political philosophies, social systems, and the policies pursued by them, a nation which is neutralist in this sense at the very

---

[12] The best analysis of this and the following type of neutralism is R. A. Scalapino, "Neutralism in Asia," *American Political Science Review,* XLVIII (1954), 49 ff.

least refuses to let its moral judgment influence its political attitudes and decisions.

This type of neutralism can, but does not need to, coincide with the desire, characteristic of the other two types, to keep out of, or leave, a military bloc. While a nation which espouses the latter types is likely also to be in sympathy with the former—India is a case in point—the reverse is not necessarily true. Quite to the contrary, the refusal to identify political and military judgments with moral ones, to subordinate the former to the latter, and to transform the political and military struggle into a world-wide crusade is indeed the prevailing governmental and popular attitude on this side of the Iron Curtain, even among the staunchest allies of the United States. This important fact is being obscured only by the vociferous and prominent criticism to which moral neutralism is from time to time exposed.

This criticism revives on the level of practical politics the controversy between utopianism and realism which has been one of the great issues of Western political philosophy since Machiavelli and which some of us thought had been settled once and for all, at least on that level of practical politics. This criticism takes the utopian side in assuming that the actions of nations toward each other must be judged by abstract moral principles, while realism sees in the national interest the standard by which such action must be judged. In the former view, a nation whose foreign policy does not reflect the ideal of international solidarity in terms of collective security is subject to moral reprobation, and so is a nation from whose foreign policy implacable hostility to the Communist philosophy and way of life is absent.

This criticism is untenable both on moral and political grounds. We have dealt with the philosophic merits of this position elsewhere[13] and limit ourselves here to four observations specifically relevant to the issue under discussion.

First, nations like to invoke abstract moral principles in justification of their position and in condemnation of those of their adversaries, but they act, as they must, in view of their interests as they see them. No nation has risked its existence or even its interests for the ideal of collective security, but all nations have, as has been

[13] Cf. Morgenthau, *Politics among Nations,* pp. 3 ff., and pp. 75 ff. above.

shown above, been guided in their support of measures of collective security by their respective interests. Some nations have at times talked as though they were willing to risk everything for the sake of wiping communism off the face of the earth, but during four decades of Communist rule there has been no nation actually willing to take such a risk for its moral convictions.

The invocation of abstract moral principles in foreign policy, then, performs the typical function of a political ideology, masking with the veil of morality the true nature of the interests and policies pursued. What this criticism of neutralism conceals is an immature approach to foreign policy which some of us hoped we had outgrown. We are impatient and disappointed with other nations who dare look at the world from the vantage point of their interests and not ours. Yet since we like to think that what we stand for is what all good men must stand for and that what we are doing is what the moral law requires of all men, we are shocked and morally outraged at the spectacle of nations who stand for different ideals and act in different ways. In a mature, realistic view of foreign policy which assumes the paramountcy of the national interest, this is as it must be. Given their different positions in the world and their different interests, there is nothing surprising in, say, India's not speaking and acting like the United States. It would indeed be surprising if it were otherwise.

Second, this criticism of moral neutralism is also politically immature in its assumption that a nation is necessarily the stronger and the more successful in foreign policy the more nations support it without qualification. This assumption may or may not be correct. It had at least the appearance of correctness as long as the bipolar system of world politics seemed to move inextricably toward a two-bloc system. A case could then have been made for a policy of maximizing membership in one's own bloc and minimizing that of the other. However, a case could even then have been made, and must now be made emphatically when the trend toward a two-bloc system is being reversed, in favor of the proposition that uncommitted nations, by virtue of their being uncommitted, are able to perform a vital function for the individual nations as well as for the community of nations as channels of communication, sources of information, and mediators.

Third, the critical approach to moral neutralism is morally and politically unconvincing when it makes foreign policy the test of anticommunism. How does this test account for the following facts: Communist Yugoslavia has been both neutralist internationally and anti-Stalinist domestically; pro-Russian Egypt and neutralist India have suppressed their Communist parties with unsurpassed fierceness; non-neutralist France and Italy harbor powerful and unmolested Communist parties? Is India to be condemned on moral grounds for combining a neutralist foreign policy with an anti-Communist domestic policy, and is France worthy of moral praise for combining a non-neutralist foreign policy with toleration of domestic communism? And how is one to fashion a sensible foreign policy guided by such moral judgments? Must one treat all these nations as equally unreliable partners and prospective enemies, since none of them is consistently anti-Communist in its policies? And must one overlook the fact that to be anti-Communist means in terms of foreign policy to be anti-Russian and anti-Chinese, an attitude which, in view of their respective interests, some nations can afford to take without limitation, others only up to a certain point, and others not at all? Must we condemn a nation of the latter type for not being able to do what we think it ought to do, thus doing our part in making sure that if such a nation should take sides it will not take ours? There must be something essentially wrong with a moral philosophy which finds itself caught in such absurdities.

What is essentially wrong with it—and this is the fourth observation we wish to offer—is the confusion between the sphere of private moral judgment and the realm of public action. Every man has the right and the duty to judge others, as he must himself, by a moral yardstick. Yet for him to act toward others as he judges them would be intellectually impertinent, morally repugnant, and impractical; for such action would leave out of account the limitations of moral judgment, the moral imperfection of human action, and the consequences, liable to be destructive of moral values, of action guided by nothing but an abstract moral judgment.

What is true of individuals applies by the same token to nations. There is something intellectually, morally, and politically preposterous in a nation's meting out with divine assurance moral praise and blame among the nations of the world. Such a nation is oblivious of the corruption to which moral judgment on matters political is particularly prone. It is also oblivious of the narrow limits within which nations, by virtue of the conditions under which they must live, are able to comply with abstract moral standards. Finally, and most importantly, it is oblivious of the responsibility for its own interests and survival, a responsibility which nobody else will discharge if it does not. The moral commitment to anticommunism as the standard by which to judge the foreign policy of nations is likely to have supremely immoral consequences. For the anti-Communist crusade as an instrument of foreign policy is likely to destroy all nations, Communist and anti-Communist alike.

11 *International Law*

If an event in the physical world contradicts scientific forecasts and thus challenges the assumptions on which the forecasts have been based, it is the natural reaction of scientific inquiry to re-examine the assumptions and attempt to reconcile scientific theory and empirical facts. The social sciences do not always react in that way. They have an inveterate tendency to stick to their assumptions and to suffer constant defeat from experience rather than to change their assumptions in the light of contradicting facts. This resistance to change is uppermost in the history of international law. None of the schemes and devices by which great humanitarians and shrewd politicians endeavored to reorganize the relations between states on the basis of law has stood the trial of history. Instead of asking whether the devices were adequate to the problems which they were supposed to solve, it was the general attitude of the internationalists to take the appropriateness of the devices for granted and to blame the facts for the failure. When the facts behave otherwise than we have predicted, they seem to say, too bad for the facts. Not unlike the sorcerers of primitive ages, they attempt to exorcise social evils by the indefatigable repetition of magic formulas. As the League of Nations was a failure, let us have another League. As the first and second peace conferences of the Hague did not succeed, let us have a third one. As arbitration never settled a political conflict which otherwise would have led to war, let us have more arbitration for the prevention of war. As the last disarmament conference was a waste of intellect and time, why not convoke another disarmament conference?

It is a strange paradox that the lay public has observed a much more skeptical and realistic, therefore scientific, attitude toward international law than the science of international law itself. The laymen were much quicker to recognize the gap between the rules of international law as represented by science, and the rules of international law as they exist in actual experience. The collapse, on the eve of the Second World War, of the hopes which the interwar period had placed on international law altogether destroyed public confidence in a science which, unmoved by what experience may show, invariably follows its preconceived pattern.[1] This breakdown implied the practical refutation of the ideas which had determined the development of international law since the last decades of the nineteenth century. Hence, the science of international law has since been confronted with the alternative of maintaining the traditional pattern of assumptions, concepts, and devices in spite of the teachings of history, or of revising this pattern and trying to reconcile the science of international law and its subject matter, that is, the rules of international law as they are actually applied. It ought to be obvious that only the latter way leads to theoretically correct and practically useful results. Yet that re-examination and revision has to overcome the methodological assumptions with which the traditional science of international law starts. These assumptions are embodied in the positivist doctrine of law.

Positivist philosophy restricts the object of scientific knowledge to matters than can be verified by observation and thus excludes from its domain all matters of an a priori, metaphysical nature. Legal positivism transfers this delimitation into the legal sphere. The legal positivist delimits the subject matter of his research in a dual way. On the one hand, he proposes to deal exclusively with matters legal, and for this purpose strictly separates the legal sphere from ethics and mores as well as psychology and sociology. Hence, his legalism. On the other hand, he restricts his attention within the legal sphere to the legal rules enacted by the state and excludes all law whose existence cannot be traced to the statute books or the decisions of the courts. Hence, his statist monism. This "positive" law the positivist accepts as it is, without passing judgment upon its ethical value or questioning its practical appropriateness. Hence, his agnosticism. The positivist cherishes the belief that the "positive" law is a logically coherent system which virtually contains, and through a mere process of logical deduction will actually produce, all rules necessary for the decision of all possible cases. Hence, his system worship and dogmatic conceptualism.

[1] Professor Quincy Wright could report in 1930 (*Research in International Law since the War* [Washington, D.C.: Carnegie Endowment for International Peace, 1930], p. 25): "Of the twenty jurists with whom the writer has corresponded, only two betrayed a note of pessimism at the prospects, and that in both cases was qualified."

The historic importance of the positivist school of jurisprudence for the science of law was fourfold. First, positivism accepted the breakdown of the great metaphysical systems of the eighteenth and the early nineteenth centuries and the resulting decadence of metaphysical jurisprudence as an established fact. It endeavored to save the scientific character of jurisprudence by eliminating from it all metaphysical elements, thus separating it from the discredited doctrines of natural law. In the second place, positivism recognized that the subject matter of jurisprudence was the law and nothing but the law, and that neither non-legal subjects nor non-legal considerations could have any place in it. Furthermore, legal positivism learned from the positivist movement in philosophy and the natural sciences that scientific objectivity is dependent upon an object intelligible in experience, and a method aimed at knowledge, not at evaluation. Finally, the great legal codifications of the European continental countries and the Anglo-American statutory law found in positivism a technique of interpretation and presentation. This technique fulfilled its purpose satisfactorily as long as the social and political philosophy of the statutes, either directly expressed by them or indirectly derived from them by way of logical deduction, was sufficient to meet the economic and social needs as well as the political demands and ethical requirements of a given society at a given historical moment.

To be sure, this correspondence between the statutes and the standards of society has never existed completely; even under static conditions there will always be a marginal sphere where the mere logical subsumption of a given case under statutory law would violate the standards of society. In order to satisfy the positivist assumptions of the logical completeness of the legal order and at the same time meet the standards of society, these standards had first to be read into the statutes from which they then appeared to have been derived by a mere logical process. Through the back door of pseudo-logical interpretation the outlawed company of natural law and extra-legal value judgments re-entered the legal system. This kind of pseudo-logical legerdemain became the predominant interpretative technique of legal positivism in the period of its decadence. In the last decades of the nineteenth century the standards of society departed farther and farther from the economic, social, political, and ethical assumptions from which the systems of statutory law had started.[2] Hence, the positivists were compelled to resort to a series of pseudo-logical makeshifts in order to maintain the fiction of legal self-sufficiency, on which positivist jurisprudence had founded its theoretical system.

From three sides this fiction was, and still is, under attack. From one side, sociological and realist jurisprudence, inspired partly and indirectly by the original sociological positivism of Comte, does away with the artificial barriers by which positivism has separated the legal sphere from the whole domain of the social sciences to which it actually belongs. Thus it destroys the positivist assumptions together with the positivist conclusions. From another side, the neo-positivism of Kelsen's pure theory of law maintains the basic assumptions of positivism but undertakes to achieve the positivist ends by purifying the legal science from all material, non-legal elements, thus eliminating the subject matter of positivist crypto-metaphysics.

Several schools of revived natural law, as well as the politico-ideological power of totalitarianism, joined in this dual scientific attack. Totalitarianism ostracized positivist jurisprudence as a manifestation of liberal decadence in Germany and Italy, where the domination of legal thought by positivism has been at times almost undisputed and where positivism has exerted its most far-reaching and fertile influence on the development of the legal science. Deprived of its traditional strongholds by political suppression and undermined by scientific criticism, positivism lost its dominant influence in modern legal thought.

In international law, unlike the other branches of legal science, positivism is still a determining influence. Ever since the turn of the century, internationalists have started with positivist assumptions, have followed the positivist method, and have professed adherence to the principles of positivism. Neither the opposition of natural law, nor Kelsen's neopositivist criticism, nor, finally, the rather implicit criticism of legal sociologists has been able to affect the predominance of positivist thought over the science of international law.[3] The

[2] An excellent analysis of this development is to be found in Julien Bonnecase's history of the French "École de l'Exégèse," *La pensée juridique française de 1804 à l'heure présente* (Bordeaux: Delmas, 1933), Vol. I.

[3] H. Lauterpacht, in *Private Law Sources and Analogies of International Law* (London: Longmans, Green & Co., 1927), p. 27, n. 5, and p. 58, n. 7; L. Oppen-

International Court of Justice still follows the time-honored pseudo-logical method of traditional positivism which prevailed in the domestic courts at the turn of the century. The annals of this highest international tribunal record no instance of a lawyer, like Brandeis in *Muller* v. *Oregon*,[4] daring to break through the network of positivist formulas, nor of any majority opinion which would not have clung, on a very high level of technical perfection, to the traditional pattern of positivist argumentation. When Judge Hudson looks for a realistic decision with respect to international law, he has to turn to the Court of Appeals of the State of New York.[5] Compared to municipal law, international law is in a retarded stage of scientific development.

The collapse of the international law of Geneva, when for the first time its fictions were confronted with the stark reality, meant of necessity the breakdown of the science which had been its ideological reflection. The post–World War I science of international law shared the short-lived and delusive splendor of its political master, and then shared with him the final detection of their common sham existence as well as the resulting disrepute. The helplessness of the science of international law in the face of those dangers, its very unawareness of them, its sincere self-deception as to its scientific character, are perhaps the gravest indictments which can be brought against the scientific value of the positivist doctrine of international

---

heim and H. Lauterpacht, *International Law* (8th ed.; London: Longmans, Green & Co., 1955), I, 106 ff., defends the opinion that positivism no longer dominates the science of international law but has been replaced by a new doctrine of moderate natural law. It is difficult to share this opinion. Natural law and the science of international law have in common only that they overstep the limits of experience. However, one would do injustice to the great metaphysical systems of natural law by identifying them with the science of international law. Whereas Suárez and Grotius were fully aware of the aprioristic, metaphysical character of their propositions and had good philosophical reasons for adhering to them, the positivist science of international law helplessly confuses reality and imagination, wish and fact, because it does no longer possess the scientific means of distinguishing between them.

4 208 U.S. 412 (1908). An excellent appraisal of the theoretical importance of this case is to be found in Felix Frankfurter, "Hours of Labor and Realism in Constitutional Law," *Harvard Law Review*, XXIX (1916), 353.

5 See the reference to Cardozo's opinion in *Techt* v. *Hughes*, 229 N.Y. 222, 241 (1920) in Manley O. Hudson, "International Law in the Twentieth Century," *Cornell Law Quarterly*, X (1925), 435, n. 75.

law. The failure of the post–World War I science of international law is not due to accidental circumstances; it grows out of the very assumptions and methods which have led legal positivism to defeat in the domestic field. Yet, in the international field the disastrous consequences of the genuine weakness of the positivist doctrine are magnified by the absence of the conditions which in the domestic domain made legal positivism at least a temporary and apparent success.

Legal positivism starts with the assumption that its subject matter is to be found exclusively in the written law of the state. Only the rules of law, and all the rules of law which statutes and court decisions present as such, are the material with which the positivist doctrine has to deal. The criterion of the existence, that is, the validity of a legal rule, is, then, its incorporation into the written law of the state. This criterion for the validity of legal rules means, if transferred to the international field, that the only valid rules of international law are those that are revealed by the decisions of courts and international treaties duly ratified and not formally revoked. Yet this concept is at once confronted with two problems for which the positivist doctrine of international law has no solution. On the one hand, all rules embodied in written documents are not valid international law, and, on the other hand, there are valid rules of international law other than the rules embodied in written documents. The positivist formula as applied to international law is at once too narrow and too broad.

The science of international law has not developed a criterion to distinguish, in an objective way, between *seemingly* and *actually* valid rules of international law. "One can assert that nine-tenths of the traditional doctrines of international law are not actual international law," said Professor Georg Jellinek as far back as 1905.[6] Declared Professor Oppenheim a few years later:

It is also indispensable that the science should free itself from the tyranny of phrases. As things are, there is scarcely a doctrine of the law of nations which is wholly free from the tyranny of phrases. . . . Any one who is in touch with the application of international law in diplomatic practice hears from statesmen every day the complaint that books put forth fanciful doctrines instead of the actual rules of law. Now it is often not difficult to push the irrelevant to one side and to extract what is legally essential from

[6] *System der subjektiven öffentlichen Rechte* (Tübingen, 1905), p. 321.

the waste of phrase-ridden discourse. But there are entire areas in which the tyranny of phrases so turns the head that rules which absolutely never were rules of law are represented as such.[7]

"On no subject of human interest, except theology," said John Chipman Gray at about the same time, "has there been so much loose writing and nebulous speculations as on international law."[8]

If these statements were true in the first decade of the century, the development of the post–World War I science of international law only added to their significance. The Covenant of the League of Nations, for instance, was a duly ratified document which was never repealed. But was it ever valid international law as a whole? If not, which provisions never had the quality of valid legal rules and which ones lost this quality in the course of the gradual collapse of the institution of Geneva? No treatise of the law of nations offers any general criterion to answer these questions, nor do the concrete answers given with reference to the actual validity of Article 16 of the Covenant reveal any such underlying objective criterion. The absolute denial of any validity, the assertion of a so-called *de facto* revision, and the defense of full validity, are advanced side by side. Similar problems arose with respect to the Briand-Kellogg Pact and the peace treaties of 1919, as well as to other political treaties, such as the Pact of the Little Entente, alliance treaties, the concepts of aggression, independence, intervention, government, and so forth. These provisions are embodied in written documents which were duly ratified and never invalidated. Have they ever been valid law from the beginning, and what has become of them in the years of their violation? Are they still valid? If they are not, what destroyed their validity? These are questions which the interpreter of domestic statutes, subject to a rational process of validation and invalidation, is not likely to be asked, and hence the positivist doctrine of international law, following the pattern of domestic positivism, has nothing with which to answer them.[9]

[7] L. Oppenheim, *The Future of International Law* (Oxford: Clarendon Press, 1921; first in German, 1911), pp. 58, 59; see also L. Oppenheim, "The Science of International Law," *American Journal of International Law,* II (1908), 315, 334.

[8] *The Nature and Sources of the Law* (New York: Macmillan Co., 1921; 1st ed., 1909), p. 127.

[9] This absence of any scientific test for the validity of the rules of international law is responsible for the perplexity into which some of the foremost representa-

The basic assumption of legal positivism that its exclusive subject matter is the written law of the state leads legal science not only to the inclusion of alleged legal rules which no longer have or never have had legal validity, but also to the exclusion of undoubtedly valid rules of law. Positivist jurisprudence, starting with the axiom of legal self-sufficiency, separates the law from the other normative spheres, that is, ethics and mores, on the one hand, and from the social sphere, comprehending the psychological, political, and economic fields, on the other hand. By doing so, positivism severs the actual relations between the law and the other branches of the normative and social sphere. It proceeds on the assumption that the law, as it really is, can be understood without the normative and social context in which it actually stands. From the application of this assumption to international law there results a threefold delimitation of legal research, contrary to the exigencies of reality, and hence a threefold misconception of what international law really is.

1. The normative sphere, comprehending the totality of rules governing a given society, is one whole with regard to the basic precepts it contains. Although there may be in a given society particular legal rules which contradict particular ethical rules or mores, and vice versa, the main bulk of basic ideals to be realized, of ends to be achieved, and of interests to be protected, is generally the same in the different branches of a given normative order. Law, ethics, and

---

tives of the international law of Geneva fell in the interwar period. Professor Georges Scelle, who had founded a whole system of "positive" international law upon "international solidarity," "international federalism," and like "social facts," in 1937 arrived at the conclusion that there is no such thing as international law at all. "Il n'y a plus en Europe de droit des gens," he wrote in the *Journal des nations*, No. 1665 (Feb. 28 and Mar. 1, 1937). "Il n'y a plus des traités." "The conclusion seems unescapable," said Professor Alfred Zimmern ("The Decline of International Standards," *International Affairs*, XVII [1938], 12), "that positive international law, so called, has no claim to the name of law." (See also Alfred Zimmern, *The League of Nations and the Rule of Law, 1918–1935* [London: Macmillan & Co., 1936], p. 94.) These scholars, who never cared for such "abstract" problems as criteria of the validity of a rule of law, fell from one error into the other. First, they accepted the assumed validity of post–World War I international law without question; then, since it had become obvious that the main bulk of this so-called international law never was valid law at all, they identified this product of their imagination with the main bulk of pre–World War I international law, which today is as valid as it has ever been, and declared that international law simply does not exist.

mores support each other in the pursuit of these aims. Legal rules refer to ethics and mores for the determination of their meaning and vice versa. The guiding influence, however, as to the ideals, ends, and interests to be pursued by the norms under which a given society lives, emanates from the ethical sphere. From it law and mores receive the fundamental distinctions between the good and the bad, the ends to be advanced and the ends to be opposed, the interests to be protected and the interests to be repudiated. At the foundation of any legal system there lies a body of principles which incorporate the guiding ideas of justice and order to be expounded by the rules of law. The intelligibility of any legal system depends upon the recognition of such a set of fundamental principles which constitute the ethical substance of the legal system and shed their illuminating light upon each particular rule of law.

This recognition is relatively easy in the domestic field where the constitution codifies the main bulk of those fundamental principles and a highly integrated public opinion provides supplementary moral guidance. The task is much more difficult with respect to international law. Here no such integrated body of principles exists separate from the rules of law. Some of those principles may be only partly expressed in these rules; others may not be expressed at all and hence have to be detected, in a dangerously uncertain procedure, in the general moral ideas underlying the international law of a certain time, a certain civilization, or even a certain nation. Yet the successful search for these principles is as essential for the scientific understanding of international law as for the understanding of any legal system.

Legal positivism is unable to grant this recognition; for at its basis there is the hostility to all matters metaphysical, that is, those which cannot be ascertained by actual observation. Since non-legal rules have generally entered the horizon of the positivist jurist as metaphysical rules of natural law, the positivist is inclined to identify natural law and ethics as such and to repudiate both as metaphysics. However, to exclude a priori a certain subject matter from scientific research by calling it metaphysical, instead of examining actual experience, is to blind one's self to a preconceived idea originating not in experience but in mere reasoning and thus to do violence to the facts. Hence, the positivist concept of the normative sphere itself reveals a metaphysical attitude, a kind of negative metaphysics which plainly contradicts the very assumptions of a positive science.

Yet positivism has never been quite able to live up to its legalistic and antimetaphysical assumptions. The very nature of its subject matter has compelled it time and again to violate its own assumptions and make use of fundamental principles not revealed by "positive" law. In order to give at least apparent satisfaction to these assumptions, positivism dares to make use of such principles only under the disguise of positivist concepts, and therefore develops a fictitious method which tries by pseudo-logical arguments to derive from "positive," that is, written rules of international law something that those rules do not contain. The interminable and quite sterile discussions on the foundation of the binding force of international law are evidence of this word-juggling, since this is a problem which, as defined in the positivist terms of mutual consent and the like, is contradictory in itself, and hence insoluble within the framework of positivism. The foundation of the binding force of "positive" law can logically be found, not in this "positive" law itself, but only outside it. Another example is the problem of sovereignty as defined and solved by positivism. Here again a fundamental principle which, by its very nature, cannot be derived from "positive" law, but from which "positive" law itself rather derives its meaning, is to be dealt with as if it were a rule of "positive" international law. It is because of these helpless attempts to reconcile its legalistic assumptions with actual legal experience that the positivist doctrine of international law is bound to misrepresent the reality of international law and fail to do justice to its actual content.

2. The rules of international law need to be interpreted not only in the light of the ideals and ethico-legal principles on which they are based but also within the sociological context of economic interests, social tensions, and aspirations for power, which are the motivating forces in the international field and which give rise to the factual situations to be regulated by international law. The correctness of this postulate for the interpretation of municipal law is today self-evident. Nobody would try to interpret social legislation without reference to the conflicting social interests to be evaluated and the social relations to be settled. Nobody would endeavor to grasp the

legal meaning of economic legislation without making economic interests and conflicts part of the reasoning. Even where the reference to the underlying economic and social forces and relations is not always explicit, as in the field of contracts, the sociological context is nevertheless always referred to by implication. It is only because of the highly typical and familiar character of the factual situations and their social and economic significance, which are completely and adequately expressed in the legal rules, that the mere reference to those legal rules implies the consideration of the social and economic factors basic to them.

It was, historically, the most disastrous error of positivism to misunderstand completely this implicit reference to the sociological context which every legal rule contains. This error can be traced to the tradition of the pandectists, who had in the Roman law the classical model of a highly typified legal system which expressed with perfect appropriateness the fundamental interests and relationships arising from the social activities of men. So perfectly was this sociological context represented in the abstractions of the Roman law that the pandectists were only too prone to forget its very existence and to deal with those abstractions as though they were independent logical entities. So did the positivists, both in the municipal and international fields.

This methodological error was of minor importance when the legal concepts were true abstractions from the interests and relations which they were supposed to regulate. When, however, those legal rules were applied to interests and relations to which some of them referred only partly, others not at all, that methodological error was bound to have a disastrous influence upon the scientific value of positivist jurisprudence. In the domestic field, it became instrumental in distorting legal reality and creating that positivist conceptualism with which a decadent legal science attempted to adapt the old legal rules to new economic and social needs while, at the same time, maintaining the fictitious assumption that the written law already contained logically all the rules necessary for the solution of those new problems. Thus juridical pseudo-logic became the artificial makeshift by which a static law could be reconciled with a dynamic social reality.

In the international field, the methodological error of neglecting the sociological context of international law led to even worse consequences. In the domestic field, the correspondence between legal concepts and sociological context was at least a temporary fact, and within this limit the neglect of the sociological context and the assumption of the self-sufficiency of the written law could be justified. In the most important branches of international law this correspondence has never, and could never have, existed. The sociological relationships underlying those branches of international law are characterized by their individual, atypical nature. A political situation in the international field is not likely to repeat itself exactly since the variety of factors of which it is composed makes for an indefinite number of possible combinations. Hence, only a strictly individualized rule of law will be adequate to it. International law provides partly for such individualized rules by restricting the application of a rule to one individual case and leaving the regulation of similar future cases to new legislative efforts. Peace treaties are instances of such individualized rules of international law.

In part, however, international law does maintain the form of the general, typical rule of law and depends on the interpretation of the rule to provide the flexible meaning which the ever changing sociological context requires. All political treaties which are intent upon establishing permanent rights and duties between the contracting parties are of this kind. The same generally and typically worded text may imply quite different rules, according to the political function which it is supposed to fulfil. Thus one is able, for instance, to distinguish three different periods in the history of the treaties of Locarno. Those three periods are characterized by three significant changes in the normative content of the rules, resulting from changes in the political context, although the wording of the rules remained unchanged. The Covenant of the League of Nations as a whole as well as particular provisions, for instance Article 16, were subjected to similar modifications as a result of factual sociological developments and not of legislative changes.

The same phenomenon occurs not only in temporary succession but also under contemporaneous yet different sociological conditions. The identical text of an arbitration treaty or non-aggression pact may have quite different legal meanings, according to the political situation existing between different contracting parties. Even one and the same legal rule, as, for instance, Article 16 of the Covenant, lends itself to different interpretations with respect to nations living under different political conditions.

The positivist doctrine of international law has ignored this particular relationship between the rules of international law and their sociological context. Positivism transplanted schematically the highly refined positivist method of formalist and conceptualist interpretation of municipal law into the domain of international law. This method developed under, and was justified by, the specific domestic conditions of a temporarily stabilized society where there was little tension between law and sociological context but almost complete rationalization and representation of the sociological context within the concepts of positive law. Schematically applied to a law and a society of a distinctly different nature, this method was bound to produce entirely inadequate results. Where the experience of international law showed that an individual situation required an individual interpretation of the legal rule, the positivist method could not fail to disregard all individual aspects of the factual situation and concentrate upon the general wording of the legal rule which, by virtue of its logical self-sufficiency, was supposed to contain all elements necessary for its understanding; and to this the sociological context could contribute nothing. An arbitration treaty which submitted all conflicts between the contracting parties to international tribunals was a legal document that revealed its legal significance through its text, i.e., another step toward the establishment of an international order based upon respect for law. Whether the treaty was concluded between Switzerland and Uruguay, or Denmark, Sweden, and Norway, or Great Britain and France, or Germany and Poland in 1925, 1935, or 1939—these were "political" considerations, irrelevant and lying beyond the scope of positivist interpretation.

3. The positivist doctrine, by recognizing as international law only the rules enforced by states, excludes from the domain of international law all rules whose validity cannot be traced to written official documents. On the other hand, the positivist doctrine cannot deny that such rules, such as many rules of general international law, actually exist. Confronted with the embarrassing dilemma of violating its own statist assumptions or of disregarding an obvious

part of legal experience, the positivist doctrine has taken refuge in a concept which has become a veritable panacea for its theoretical troubles. We are referring to the concept of customary law, which has served for the traditional doctrine of international law as a kind of collective designation for all the rules of international law the origin of which cannot directly be traced to written sources. I have pointed to the insurmountable theoretical difficulties of explaining the existence of a so-called customary law elsewhere,[10] and this is not the place to resume the discussion. It is sufficient to state that the reconciliation which the positivist doctrine is able to establish between its monist, legalistic assumptions and the existence of a so-called customary law is merely apparent. In order to save these assumptions as well as those facts, it resorts to a series of fictions, like tacit consent, recognition, judicial admission, and so forth, which indirectly endeavor to attribute the existence of the so-called customary rules of international law to the legislative will of states.

The fundamental weakness of the positivist doctrine of international law lies in its inadequacy to understand international law as it really is. Unfaithful to its own assumptions, it contains at the same time more and less than the actual rules of international law, which it furthermore submits to subjective evaluation in the light of ethical and political principles of assumedly universal, yet doubtful, validity. A truly scientific theory of international law must avoid these mistakes in order to come closer to reality. It seems to be a logical choice to call such a theory by the name of realist. There are, however, two objections to this choice. On the one hand, the increasing disrepute of the traditional doctrine of international law has led many practitioners of this doctrine to demonstrate their closeness to the reality of international law by calling themselves "realists."[11] This misuse has deprived the term of its distinctive character. On the other hand, realism has become a collective designation for several

10 *La réalité des normes* (Paris: Alcan, 1934), p. 89.

11 See, for instance, Erich Kaufmann, *Recueil des Cours de l'Académie de la Haye,* LIV (1935), 319, 320; Georges Scelle, *ibid.,* XLVI (1933), 691; Alfred Verdross, *ibid.,* XXX (1929), 277; Louis Le Fur, in *Revue de Droit International,* XVII (1936), 7—authors who have certainly not very much in common besides the claim of being "realists." Cf. also Roscoe Pound, *An Introduction to the Philosophy of Law* (New Haven: Yale University Press, 1937), p. 145, according to whom A. V. Lundstedt calls Pound, Kelsen, and Duguit "realists"!

tendencies in modern jurisprudence, all aiming at replacing, by different means, the fictitious legalism of traditional jurisprudence with a conception nearer to the realities of the law. All these tendencies have this in common: they do not regard the legal rules as definitely determined by their legislative or judicial formulation but search for the psychological, social, political, and economic forces which determine the actual content and operation of legal rules and which, in turn, are determined by them. In other words, their scientific goal is to formulate uniform functional relationships between those forces and the legal rules. Hence, "realist" jurisprudence is, in truth, "functional" jurisprudence.

The legacy which positivism has left to the science of international law consists in the task of comprehending the international law of a given time as standing in a dual functional relationship with the social forces of this time. On the one hand, international law is the function of the civilization in which it originates, that is, of the regulative ideas laid down in the ethics and mores of this civilization, of the political, economic, and general social forces prevailing in it, and, finally, of the specific psychological factors manifesting themselves in the individuals determining it. On the other hand, international law is a social mechanism working toward certain ends within this same civilization which, in turn, becomes a function of this same international law. By systematizing the rules of a given international law in terms of this dual functional relationship between rules and social forces, the functional theory will achieve a real scientific understanding of the legal rules which positivism even at its best was able to describe and systematize only according to superficial legalistic criteria.

Six important consequences for a functional theory of international law can be drawn from this recognition of the functional relationship between social forces and international law.

I. A functional theory of international law must start with the recognition of the particularly intimate nature of this relationship. In the domestic field, legal rules can be imposed by the group which holds the monopoly of organized physical force, that is, the officials of the state. The international sphere is characterized by the absence of such a group. International law owes its existence to identical or complementary interests of nations, backed by power as a last resort or, where such identical interests do not exist, to a balance of power which prevents a nation from breaking these rules of international law. Where there is neither community of interests nor balance of power, there is no international law. Whereas domestic law may originate in the arbitrary will of the lawmaking agencies of the state, international law is usually the result of objective social forces. When, in the international field, an arbitrary lawmaking power tries to impose rules supported neither by common interests nor by a balance of power, these rules never become valid law or gain only ephemeral existence and scant efficacy; the history of some of the rules embodied in the Treaty of Versailles and the Covenant of the League of Nations provides a striking example.

It is also due to this intimate relationship between social forces and legal rules that in the international field fundamental changes of the social forces and, hence, of the legal rules follow each other at frequent intervals and in an abrupt, often violent manner. In the domestic field the regulative social force dominating all others is the state. It has developed not only an overwhelming power apparatus but also highly refined mechanisms of legislative and judicial readjustment, which lead the social forces into certain channels without disrupting the legal and social continuity. The state selects in authoritative decisions the social forces to be recognized by the law. It decides to what extent the existing legal rules shall yield to changing conditions, to what extent they shall resist them, and in what ways they shall try to transform them. In the international field the authoritative decision is replaced by the free interplay of political and military forces. This makes a gradual readjustment of the law to changing social conditions extremely difficult. Any fundamental change of the social forces underlying a system of international law of necessity creates in the prospective beneficiaries of the change the desire to bring about a corresponding change of the legal rules, whereas the beneficiaries of the legal status quo will resist any change of the old order. Here a competitive contest for power will determine the victorious social forces, and the change of the existing legal order will be decided, not through a legal procedure provided for by this same legal order, but through a conflagration of conflicting social forces which challenge the legal order as a whole.

Where such a conflict between social forces and the rules of law exists, the character and function of the whole legal order undergo a transformation. We have proposed to call this relationship by the name of "tension" and have dealt with its legal consequences elsewhere.[12]

II. This recognition of the peculiar relationship between social forces and rules of international law provides the clue for restating, in functional terms, the criteria for the validity of international law. A rule of international law does not, as positivism was prone to believe, receive its validity from its enactment into a legal instrument, such as an international treaty. There are rules of international law which are valid although not enacted in such legal instruments, and there are rules of international law which are not valid although enacted in such instruments. Enactment, therefore, is no objective criterion for the alleged validity of a rule of international law. A rule, be it legal, moral, or conventional, is valid when its violation is likely to be followed by an unfavorable reaction, that is, a sanction against its violator. An alleged rule, the violation of which is not followed by such a sanction, is a mere idea, a wish, a suggestion, but not a valid rule. An alleged rule of international law against the violation of which no state reacts, or is likely to react, is proved, by this very absence of probable reaction, not to be a valid rule of international law. The gradual invalidation of the territorial provisions of the Treaty of Versailles and of most articles of the Covenant of the League of Nations, by violation and non-intervention of sanctions against these violations, provides experimental proof of the correctness of this concept of validity.

How, then, are we to know beforehand when such sanctions are likely to intervene on behalf of a violated norm and when not, and, hence, how can the science of international law determine which norms are valid and which are not? The consideration of the functional factor will give the answer.

1. The commonest and simplest test for the validity of an alleged rule of international law is this: nation A has, in the past, requested

---

[12] On the theory of international "tensions" see Hans J. Morgenthau, *La notion du "politique" et la théorie des différends internationaux* (Paris: Sirey, 1933), pp. 37 ff. This theory has been discussed in detail by Jean Ray, in *Annales sociologiques,* Ser. C, No. 1 (1935), pp. 163 ff. Cf. also Hans J. Morgenthau, *Politics among Nations* (2d ed.; New York: Alfred A. Knopf, 1954), pp. 404 ff.

nation B to perform certain actions corresponding to the rule, and nation B, in turn, has requested nation A to perform certain actions corresponding to the same or another rule. Where these identical or complementary interests in the mutual observance of these rules did not suffice to guarantee the actual observance, both nations were willing to enforce compliance with the rule by protest, reprisal, or military action. Where there was, in the past, a recognized identical or complementary interest in a certain action on the part of two or more nations, together with the willingness to enforce this action, there exists the likelihood that the same sanctions for the sake of the same interests will also be performed in the future. Respect for the status of diplomatic representatives has been, in the past, an interest recognized and guaranteed with sanctions by all nations; therefore, the forecast is justified that nations will follow the same course of action in the future.

The enactment of rules corresponding to such interests in international treaties may indicate the permanent nature of those interests, but this is an assumption which needs support from the facts and which can be disproved by them. Another indication of the permanence of such interests is their sublimation into moral principles, which pretend universal validity and endeavor to give certain interests of exceptional importance a justification superior to that which they could derive from the law.

2. The situation, however, is not always so simple. Three possible situations present themselves for examination.

a) Identical or complementary interests survive the willingness to enforce the actions corresponding to them. The provisions of the treaties of Locarno were the function of identical and complementary interests of the contracting parties. When Germany violated these treaties by remilitarizing the Rhineland, the interests of the signatories in the demilitarization survived their willingness to enforce an attitude corresponding to their interests, and thus the respective rules of international law lost their validity.

b) The willingness to enforce certain actions corresponding to identical or complementary interests survives the interests themselves. From the outset the provisions of the Treaty of Versailles establishing the German-Polish frontier did not correspond to the interests of either nation. These provisions were observed for a period of twenty years because there existed a balance of power between both nations and their respective allies, which prevented either of them from violating the law.

c) The interests and the willingness to enforce the actions corresponding to them disappear altogether. In this category belong the Franco-Russian alliance, the Pact of the Little Entente, the political provisions of the Covenant of the League of Nations, and numerous provisions of the peace treaties of 1919.

What does the analysis of these cases show with regard to the validity of international law? In the cases (*a*) and (*c*) the rules of international law become invalid according to the functional concept of validity because no longer does there exist a likelihood of sanctions being performed, should those rules be violated. In case (*b*) the validity of the rules depends upon a balance of power, which may be stable for a certain time and then suddenly become unstable. All cases have this in common: they make forecasts as to the likelihood of sanctions extremely uncertain. The enactment of the rules in international treaties is here of no avail and, as our examples have shown, is rather misleading. Their conformity with moral principles is scarcely more illuminating because of the difficulty mentioned above of ascertaining the exact content of such principles.

Where the functional relationship between social forces and international law is in a state of transition from (1) to one of the situations under (2) the development may stop at an intermediate point between (1), on the one hand, and (2*a*) and (*c*), on the other; proceed to (2*b*); or, finally, come to an end at (2*a*) or (*c*). Here, the validity of the respective rules of international law is, so to speak, in suspense and may be either maintained or destroyed. With respect to such rules the science of international law becomes a system of guesses, enjoying a greater or lesser chance of being proved true according to the factual development of the functional relationship between the social forces and the rules of international law.

III. It follows from this analysis that there exist two obviously different types of international law, one founded upon permanent and stable interests, the other based upon the temporary and fluctuating interests of nations. This differentiation is not only of fundamental importance for the understanding of the validity of international law; it leads to still more far-reaching consequences as to the subject matter, the methods, and the scientific character of the science of international law. One might even say that it leads to the recognition of two different sciences of international law which deal with different subject matters and require different methods of research and systematization.

The main bulk of the concepts and principles of international law has been derived from municipal civil law. These concepts and principles have been developed within a legal system characterized by the extraordinary stability of the interests underlying it. Hence, its application is, of necessity, restricted to legal systems based upon equally stable interests. In the international field such stable interests exist, for instance, with respect to diplomatic privileges, territorial jurisdiction, extradition, wide fields of maritime law, arbitral procedure, and so forth. This is the classical field of traditional international law as it has gradually developed in the practice of nations since the sixteenth century. We propose to call these rules nonpolitical international law, originating in the permanent interests of nations to put their normal relations upon a stable basis by providing for predictable and enforcible conduct with respect to these relations.

But there is another type of international law which expresses, in terms of rights and duties, temporary interests ever given to change. In this category belong political agreements, especially treaties of alliance and their modern substitutes, which, under the legalistic disguise of treaties of general arbitration, consultation, or friendship, frequently pursue aims at least preparatory to close political ties. The traditional science of international law treats both types of international law alike, applying to both the concepts and methods developed in municipal civil law. By doing so, it cannot but draw a completely distorted picture of those rules which belong in the category of political international law. Under such treatment, their validity appears to be firmly established, whereas it is actually always precarious; the interests which they are supposed to serve appear to be permanent and definite, whereas they are actually exposed to continuous change and tend to be uncertain; and consequently, the rights and duties established by them appear to be clearly determined, whereas they are actually subject to the most contradictory interpretations.

This writer knows of only one monograph dealing with political international law as an independent subject matter requiring concepts and methods of its own: Rafael Erich's *Alliances and Alliance Treaties*.[13] He is aware of only one systematic treatise clearly stating the functional relationship between the political rules of international law and the underlying social factors: Charles de Visscher's *Theory and Practice in Public International Law*.[14] Only one judicial opinion clearly points to the practical consequences of this relationship: Judge Anzilotti's dissenting opinion in the Austro-German Customs Union case.[15] It remains for a functional theory of international law to develop systematically concepts and methods capable of conveying the legal characteristics, as well as the functional dependence on political factors, of political international law.

IV. As we have seen, there exist functional relationships not only between the law and the non-normative social forces, but also between the law and the other branches of the normative sphere, that is, ethics and mores. The latter are threefold with regard to the validity and the content of the rules of law.

As has been shown elsewhere,[16] the validity of any legal system reposes upon a fundamental norm which itself cannot be of a legal nature but belongs of necessity to the domain of ethics and mores. Thus, the validity of the legal system of the United States reposes, on the one hand, upon an ethical rule enjoining the President, the members of Congress and of the Supreme Court to obey the Constitution, and, on the other hand, upon the mores keeping alive among the citizens the respect for the Constitution. When one or the other of these ethical foundations is lacking, the validity of the Constitution and of the legal system founded upon it is in a precari-

[13] In German, Helsingfors, 1907.

[14] Princeton: Princeton University Press, 1957.

[15] As to the defectiveness of the majority decision from the functional standpoint, see Hudson, "The World Court and the Austro-German Customs Régime," *American Bar Association Journal*, XVII (1931), 793: "In our national courts, a refusal to take account of the social and political conditions to which law must be applied, has produced some of the sharpest criticism of our legal systems. . . . An international court might similarly build a law in disregard of the political factors which condition its application, but it would almost certainly lack both the appearance and the substance of reality."

[16] *La réalité des normes*, pp. 76 ff., 174 ff., 216 ff.

ous state. When both are lacking, the Constitution, and with it the whole legal system, have ceased to exist as a living legal order even though they may not have been formally invalidated.

Not only does the validity of the legal system as a whole repose upon ethics and mores, but the validity of individual legal rules also stands frequently in a particular functional relationship with ethics and mores. The validity of one and the same precept, for instance, "Thou shall not kill," may repose upon the likelihood that against its violation there will intervene sanctions pertaining to the domains of ethics and mores as well as of law. Many provisions of the Constitution, of civil and criminal law, belong to this category and, therefore, are at the same time legal rules, ethical rules, and rules of the mores. It is obvious that this double or triple guaranty has an important bearing upon the observance and validity of a given precept. When such a multiple guaranty exists, that is, when ethics, mores, and law co-operate to realize a certain order of things, there is a much greater likelihood that this order will be realized than when the law alone seeks it.

It has already been pointed out that legal rules receive their precepts partly from ethics and mores. The meaning of these precepts requires explanation in the light of these other rules from which it is derived. The Constitution itself, for instance, does not reveal what "due process of law" or "freedom of contract" is; it is only by reference to the ethics and mores of a certain period of constitutional history that the meaning of these constitutional concepts can be determined. The moral order gives the law the standards on the basis of which its agents and subjects can distinguish between right and wrong. Implicit in any legal order is a system of moral standards according to which the law distinguishes between actions which it approves, actions which it disapproves, and actions with regard to which it is indifferent. These moral standards guide the judicial and executive agents of the law in interpreting and applying it. They relate the legal order directly to the moral convictions of the individual. It is from the conformity of those moral standards with these moral convictions that the particular legal rules receive their concrete meaning for the individual and their normative function for society.

The recognition, for international law, of these three fundamental relationships, calls for the discussion of a series of problems which the traditional science of international law does not even care to pose. What is, for instance, the empirical nature of the dual relationship between international law, on the one hand, and ethics and mores on the other? Are there ethics and mores of a truly international nature, or do we call by the name of "international" ethics and mores the precepts of which have been developed under the determining influence of the individual nations and are applied to international affairs in the interest of these nations? Which rules of international law belong at the same time to ethics and mores and so have a greater chance of being observed? The content of which rules of international law can be determined only by reference to ethics and mores, and to what kind of ethics and mores do these rules refer?

V. It follows from the preceding discussion that no branch of the traditional science of international law is more in need of reform than the doctrine of interpretation. The traditional doctrine has limited its efforts to transferring schematically the time-honored common and Roman law principles of interpretation to the international field. It has discussed the problem whether the wording of a treaty or the intentions of the parties shall be the main source of interpretation; it has gone deeply into the question whether preparatory materials may be used for purposes of interpretation; and it has advanced a great variety of so-called rules of construction. Yet it has completely overlooked the fact that, because of the peculiar relationship between social forces and rules of international law, the problem of interpretation in the international field shows unique aspects for which the traditional civil law technique of interpretation is utterly inadequate.

When in the domestic field the meaning of a contract is ascertained by the usual means of interpretation, the interpretative job is done. It is generally not too difficult to perform the same task with regard to an international treaty; but then the real problem of interpretation just begins. A contract of civil law generally uses standardized language whose legal meaning is definite or at least can be ascertained according to objective, universally recognized standards. On the other hand, the real meaning of an international treaty may be disguised with diplomatic language so that its wording is indicative only of what it does not mean. Under such circumstances, it is only from the social context that this treaty will receive its meaning. The political situation of the parties and their intentions with respect to this situation have to be ascertained in view of the subject matter of the treaty, for the time of the conclusion of the treaty as well as for the time of interpretation; for, as we have seen, the legal meaning of an international treaty is ever subject to change. From this analysis one may then conclude, in a laborious and always highly uncertain manner, what might be the probable objective of the treaty and the legal meaning of the particular stipulations serving this purpose.

What, for instance, does the term "independence" in an international treaty mean? Its meaning may coincide with the accepted meaning of the term, it may be somewhat different, it may be the exact opposite, or it may have no legal meaning at all. The rules of construction will not answer that question. It is only from the background of the social context and of the function the treaty is supposed to fulfil within it that a scientific interpretation can hope, at least within certain limits, to receive a satisfactory answer. The answer will, for instance, vary according to whether the nation to which the term applies is a colonial, semicolonial, or non-colonial country; whether the treaty is concluded between two nations of equal or different political power; whether or not, in the last case, the more powerful nation has imperialistic intentions with respect to the other party; whether the treaty is of a bilateral nature, pursuing a specific political aim, or is supported by the consensus of a great number of nations for the sake of a general purpose common to all of them.

VI. To fulfil its task, a functional theory of international law must take another step beyond positivism. Positivism assumed that it was more scientific than any previous attempt at understanding. Positivist science was supposed to be free from all metaphysical elements, not asking how things ought to be and what their "real" essence might be, but seeking only uniform relations between things verifiable in experience. "Je ne propose rien, je ne suppose rien, j'expose," was Comte's credo. But just as Comte ended in the metaphysics of his "religion of humanity," so legal positivism was not satisfied with knowing what the law actually was and how it worked. It was only too eager to remodel the world of the law after idealistic assumptions whose universal validity the respective authors took for granted. This tend-

233

ency, variously strong in the different branches of municipal law, is uppermost in the positivist doctrine of international law. The science of international law, completely absorbed by practical problems of what the rules of international law should be, paid almost no attention to the psychological and sociological laws governing the actions of men in the international sphere or to the possible legal rules growing out of such actions. Whoever would dare embark upon such research would be called "impractical," and the results of his studies, if ever mentioned at all, would be qualified as "worthless." Grandiose legalistic schemes purporting to solve the ills of the world replaced the less spectacular, painstaking search for the actual laws and the facts underlying them. This presumptuous enterprise has contributed nothing to the improvement of international relations, let alone the knowledge of what these international relations actually are. It has only shown the utter futility of all attempts to reform human conditions on the basis of idealistic assumptions without knowing the laws under which these conditions stand. As William Graham Sumner put it:

In this view, the worst vice in political discussions is that dogmatism which takes its stand on "great principles" or assumptions, instead of standing on an exact examination of things as they are and human nature as it is. . . . The social sciences are, as yet, the stronghold of all this pernicious dogmatism; and nowhere does it do more harm than in politics. The whole method of abstract speculation on political topics is vicious. It is popular because it is easy; it is easier to imagine a new world than to learn to know this one; it is easier to embark on speculations based on a few broad assumptions than it is to study the history of states and institutions; it is easier to catch up a popular dogma than it is to analyze it to see whether it is true or not. All this leads to confusion, to the admission of phrases and platitudes, to much disputing but little gain in the prosperity of nations.[17]

"The eagerness for premature practical application," to express the same thought in the words of Vilfredo Pareto, ". . . is ever obstructing the progress of science, along with a mania for preaching to people as to what they ought to do—an exceedingly bootless occupation—instead of finding out what they actually do."[18]

[17] *The Challenge of Facts and Other Essays* (New Haven: Yale University Press, 1914), pp. 245–46.

[18] *The Mind and Society* (New York: Harcourt, Brace & Co., 1935), II, 185.

Why, then, is it that the field within which the social sciences are able to work successfully is much narrower than the corresponding field of the natural sciences? It is again Sumner who knows the answer to this question. "The reason is because the elements of any sort of problem which we do not know so far surpass in number and importance those which we do know that our solutions have far greater chance to be wrong than to be right."[19] Thus the problem which the science of international law has to solve is clearly posed. The natural sciences had to discover the laws governing nature before they could hope to dominate the forces of nature, to prevent the dangers emanating from them, and to use them for human goals. In the same way, the social sciences cannot hope to master the forces of society unless they know the laws which govern the social relations of men. In the natural sciences, the discovery of the infinitesimal calculus by Newton and Leibniz was bound to precede modern technical inventions. The millennial attempts at constructing the airplane could not succeed as long as Carnot had not established his purely theoretical propositions on thermodynamics. Were it not for the theoretical efforts of Faraday, who himself did not invent anything of practical value, there would not be today any of the multiple uses of electricity for practical purposes. Had not Maxwell and Hertz, without any practical objective, carried out certain "abstruse and remote" calculations in the field of magnetism and electricity, Marconi could never have invented the radio.

The science of international law and the social sciences in general are still awaiting their Newton, their Leibniz, their Faraday, their Carnot, their Maxwell, and their Hertz. In all likelihood, they are waiting in vain.[20] In any event, to expect the contemporary lawyer to be an "engineer" or "technician" of the law means to expect Edison before Faraday, Wright before Carnot, Marconi before Maxwell and Hertz. And this is certainly a futile expectation.

[19] *Op. cit.*, p. 219.

[20] For the reasons, see *Scientific Man vs. Power Politics* (Chicago: University of Chicago Press, 1946).

DILEMMAS

OF POLITICAL

ACTION

The Autonomy of Political Action

POLITICAL action is beset by three dilemmas. One threatens its autonomy by substituting for its own proper rules those appropriate to other spheres of action. The other threatens its integrity by corrupting its rules in the service of alien ends. The third dilemma threatens failure through the mistaken choice of means and ends. The first dilemma, one might say, is intellectual in nature, while the second is a moral one; the third dilemma raises the issue of practical statecraft. In view of the theoretical compass of this book, we shall concern ourselves here only with the first two of these dilemmas.

The first dilemma, which raises the issue of the autonomy of the political sphere, grows from a general quality of our culture: the tendency to escape from the facts of political life, which bear the indelible and ubiquitous mark of the aspirations and the struggle for power. The escapist from politics seeks refuge in a realm of thought and action that allows him to think and act as though the facts of political life either did not exist at all or, at the very least, could be discarded by an act of will. The escapist from politics lacks respect for the existential qualities of political life. He refuses to acknowledge that the facts of politics are the children of necessity, not the bastards of some psychological or sociological aberration.

Yet the facts of politics are no more misconstrued and disregarded with impunity than are the facts of physics. Both take vengeance on their violators. The vengeance of the facts of physics is stark, swift, and unequivocal; but that of the facts of politics is often circuitous and ambiguous and may be recognized only by reflective hindsight. Violate the law of gravity, and the consequences will be clear for all to see. Violate the rules of the balance of power, and the consequences are likely to be obscure, at least to the contemporaries. The observance of the laws of nature is vouchsafed by man's instinct for self-preservation. The violation of the rules of politics does not as simply call forth their observance because the human mind does not as instinctively connect the untoward consequences with the violation of the rules.

The mind of Western man, in particular, doubts the very existence of those rules and their ineluctability. In consequence, confronted with a crisis in his political affairs, he tends to search not for the principles of right political action but for non-political substitutes. He tends to think about politics in non-political, e.g., moralistic, legalistic, militaristic, or economic, terms. He finds himself ever more deeply involved in the self-created dilemma between the requirements of right political action and his non-political preconceptions of what politics is all about, and, as long as these preconceptions persist, each political failure calls forth yet another non-political remedy only to join its predecessors in failure.

12 *The Escape from Power*

This refusal of our civilization to recognize the facts of political life is nowhere more strikingly formulated than in the first sentence of the first chapter of Rousseau's *Social Contract:* "Man is born free, but everywhere he is in chains." This statement expresses a persistent conviction of Western political thought, and its correctness has not often been questioned. It is, however, one of the most erroneous and distorting statements one can make about the facts of political life. The historian Émile Faguet has very well pointed to the logical weakness of this statement by explaining through the same kind of argument the nature of cows. "All cows," he said, "are born carnivorous, and everywhere they live on herbs." The absurdity of the statement as applied to cows is obvious. The absurdity of the same type of reasoning as applied to humans is less obvious, but not less real; for it is impossible to distinguish empirically between the status in which a man is born and the status in which he lives.

Yet this erroneous statement has had very important consequences for the understanding of the realities of political life; for it has made it appear that the normal and natural state of man is freedom and that his living in chains, his living in political servitude, is only an accident, something that can be remedied and abolished by a political mechanism or a legislative device or a social reform or an economic artifact.

Any realistic conception of politics must start with an assumption which is the exact opposite of Rousseau's. It must assume that man is born and lives in chains. He is the object of political domination, and the fact that points to his freedom is not an empirical fact, is not a condition of his existence, but is a condition of his moral life. In other words, freedom is a condition not of his empirical existence but of his moral existence. Man lives in chains, but everywhere he wants to be free. He revolts against the empirical fact of political domination, and he wants to escape those chains which bind him in servitude.

This is, however, not the whole story; for man living in chains not only wants to be free but also wants to be master. In other words, man's aspiration for power is not an accident of history; it is not a temporary deviation from a normal state of freedom; it is an all-permeating fact which is of the very essence of human existence. So we find, when we look at the facts of political life as they really are, that man lives in chains, but everywhere he wants to be a master.

This conception of man as a political being differs indeed fundamentally from the optimistic and superficial philosophy by which, in imitation of Rousseau and others, the nineteenth and twentieth centuries have conceived political life. They tried to escape the recognition of political domination and of the aspiration for power as ubiquitous facts by four fundamental devices: scientism, the dual moral standard, perfectionism, and totalitarianism. Most, if not all, of these devices are children of the nineteenth century. One of them, perfectionism, has an older history, but the other three have their roots, if not their flowering, in the intellectual movements of the nineteenth century.

What is scientism? It is the belief that the problems of social life are in essence similar to the problems of physical nature and that, in the same way in which one can understand the laws of nature and, by using this knowledge, dominate nature and harness it to one's own ends, one can understand the facts of society and, through this knowledge, create a gigantic social mechanism which is at the command of the scientific master.

However, three basic distinctions between the social and the physical world defeat this scientist conception of society. First of all, in the natural world we deal primarily with typical situations and typical phenomena as such. In the social world we deal primarily with individual events and individual phenomena as such. Furthermore, the social scientist is not a detached observer of social events as the natural scientist is a detached observer of the phenomena of nature. A physicist or chemist who investigates the qualities of uranium does so regardless of the religious, moral, political, social, or economic stake he may have in the result of his investigations. The political scientist or economist who investigates, say, a labor problem is of necessity determined in his outlook and in his methods and in the results at which he arrives by his personal involvement in the problem. Finally, the natural sciences deal with lifeless matter, and even where they deal with human beings or living matter they deal with them as some sort of mechanism. They do not deal with man as a rational being or a moral person. On the other hand, the social scientist deals with human beings as such, with the particularly human quality of human beings which is their rational and moral character. It is for these three reasons that the analogy between the natural and the social sciences falls to the ground.

Furthermore, scientism holds to the belief that political conflicts and political problems can be solved scientifically in the same way in which the problems of nature can be solved scientifically. The existence of political problems, of political conflict, of war, and of revolution, is assumed to be primarily the result of lack of knowledge, of lack of skill in the handling of social and political situations. Here, we are again in the presence of the idea, which we found underlying the first sentence of the first chapter of Rousseau's *Social Contract*, that the political phenomenon is a kind of accident, a kind of temporary deviation from the rule of reason which ought to dominate the life of man.

Actually, political problems grow out of certain conflicts of interests, certain basic antagonisms which no amount of knowledge can eliminate as such. Knowledge and political skill may solve these problems peacefully, but there is no scientific device that can solve the problems of war, of labor, of freedom, of authority in the same way in which the problem of, say, the air-cooled engine has been solved.

The problem of the air-cooled engine was solved when the scientists dealing with it found the formula by virtue of which the air-cooled engine could be constructed, and, once the formula was found, the natural scientists could, as it were, forget about the problem of the air-cooled engine and direct their attention to other problems. Political problems are not of this kind; they cannot be solved by the invention of a mechanical formula which will allow mankind to forget about them and turn its attention toward a not-yet-solved political problem. Being projections of human nature into society, they cannot be solved at all. They can only be restated, manipulated, and transformed, and each epoch has to come to terms with them anew.

The ideal of scientism as applied to politics is the disappearance of politics altogether. Scientism assumes that the abolition of politics can and will usher in an ideal state of society. The political philosophy of Marxism, for instance, is inspired by the belief, typical of scientism, that political domination and war are the outgrowth of a single cause, in this case of a particular economic system, and that with the disappearance of that system war and political domination will of themselves disappear. The main idea of scientism is clearly recognizable here: one needs only to use the right formula, to apply the right mechanical device, and the political domination of man by man and the violent clashes of human collectivities will disappear as temporary aberrations from the rule of co-operation and of reason.

The second attempt at escaping from the facts of political life we find in the idea of the dual standard of morality. This idea assumes that politics cannot perhaps be eliminated completely from human life but that it can be, as it were, quarantined. It can be relegated to a certain corner where certain bad principles of ethics apply, whereas the great majority of mankind will continue to live according to the good rules of ethics. In other words, there exists a dual standard of morality, one applicable to the political sphere and to the politicians, and another applicable to the rest of mankind. It is this dual standard of morality that was strikingly formulated by the greatest Italian statesman of modern times, Cavour, when he said: "If we had done for ourselves what we have done for Italy, what scoundrels we would have been."

But political domination and the lust for power cannot be limited to a particular segment of humanity which, because of its profession, is unable to comply with the generally applicable, respectable rules of ethics. This lust for power and this fact of political domination are universal experiences of mankind. In politics, it is true, they find their most extreme, violent, and brutal manifestations, but they are to be found wherever men live together in social groups, and that is everywhere. They are everywhere, hidden behind ideologies, disguised by the conventions of the good society. Hence, the idea of the dual standard of morality is another form of escapism from the brutal facts of political life and the ubiquitous lust for power.

The third type of escapism from these facts is perfectionism. Perfectionism recognizes the facts of political life as they exist. The perfectionist, however, believes that, by a sheer act of will on the part of the individual either through social reform or education or moral exhortation, man can be changed and can be made to abandon the evils of politics and the lust for power out of which those evils grow. The political philosophy of Woodrow Wilson provides the classical example of perfectionist escapism. Political domination and power politics with all the liabilities they impose on man, with all the evils they create, are the outgrowth of certain wicked political systems, such as autocracy or monarchy. Once democracy, brought to all countries of the earth either by force of arms or preferably by education and exhortation, has been universally accepted, the evils of politics will have been made an end to, and reason will rule over domestic and international society.

The contemporary advocacy of world government contains an element of perfectionist escapism. Actually, even if it were possible to establish world government tomorrow, the facts of political life would still be with us. The same problems growing out of the lust for power, the same conflicts resulting from the competition for power, the same mastery of one man over the other, and the revolt of the others against the mastery of one, the same basic fact that man is born in chains and everywhere wants to be master—these would still remain the elemental experiences of political life, even if world government were established.

The technological conditions and potentialities of the age have indeed made world government a rational necessity, but they have not made it a panacea for the evils and liabilities of politics. World government as such cannot resolve, for instance, the conflict between the Soviet Union and the United States by peaceful means. Regardless of constitutional changes on the international scene, this problem will continue to exist as it exists today, and, hence, the question of war or peace will continue to demand an answer. The answer to this question, under present world conditions, does not lie in world government but in facing squarely concrete problems which, if they are not solved peacefully, could lead to war—concrete problems such as American security as against Russian security, the unification of Germany, peace in the Middle East.

These problems are not to be solved by world government, any more than the problem of slavery was solved by the establishment of the government of the United States. A civil war, which after all is also a war, against the established government had to be fought in order to solve at least superficially the problem of slavery. Since the political problem was not solved when the government was established, it continued to pose itself, demanding a solution, and the lack of a solution led to the same disastrous results it would have led to if the government had not existed. The same would be true of world government. If the political problems separating the Soviet Union from the United States cannot be solved peacefully on their own terms, that is, by political means, world government would not save the world from the next war. The next war would, then, be a civil instead of a world war, and it would be only a matter of terminology whether Western civilization would perish in the course of the one instead of the other.

Western civilization has resorted during the past one hundred and fifty years to many other perfectionist devices in order to escape the facts of political life. For instance, men like Proudhon, Cobden, and Bright saw in free trade the one mechanism, the one political and economic reform, that would enable man to escape the fate that has been with him from the beginning of history. In its nature the escapism of free trade is not different from the escapism of world government or of the United Nations or of disarmament or of other mechanical devices whereby since the First World War men have tried to escape the combination of modern technology and the lust for power, which threatens to engulf and destroy them.

The fourth type of escapism we call totalitarianism, meaning by totalitarianism not merely the particular historic phenomenon which occurred in the twenties and thirties in Italy and in the thirties in Germany and after 1917 in Russia but a state of mind which is the exact opposite of perfectionism. Whereas perfectionism creates an abstract ideal to which it tries to elevate political life through force or exhortation or reform, totalitarianism, that is, the totalitarian state of mind, identifies the ideal with the facts of political life. What is, is good because it is, and power is to the totalitarian not only a fact of social life with which one must come to terms but also the ultimate standard for judging human affairs and the ideal source of all human values. He says "Yes" to his lust for power, and he recognizes no transcendent standard, no spiritual concept which might tame and restrain the lust for power by confronting it with an ideal alien and hostile to political domination.

So the gap between the political ideal and political reality, which perfectionism tries to resolve in favor of the ideal by elevating political reality to the level of the ideal, totalitarianism also tries to eliminate but by the opposite procedure, that is, by tearing the ideal down to the level of the brutal facts of political life. The excesses of power politics, the barbarities and evil propensities of the Bolshevist and Nazi regimes are foreordained in this identification of the realities of political life with the ideal of human life as such.

The totalitarian state of mind is a universal phenomenon. In its Fascist manifestation, it has lost its empires but won many souls. The Western democracies have widely accepted the Fascist standards without knowing it.

They, too, tend to equate and identify political success with moral superiority, thus seeking to eliminate the gap between the moral ideal and the facts of political life. They, too, try to resolve the tension between the two in favor of the political facts. This is perhaps the most dangerous manifestation of political escapism; for, while here the political facts as facts are recognized, their moral significance is obscured. Power is glorified as the source of all material and moral good, and those transcendent concepts by which power must be tamed, restrained, and transformed are denied an independent existence.

13 *The Moral Dilemma of Political Action*

On the plane of political action, the most common escape, especially in the United States, from the autonomy of politics has taken the form of moralism, that is, the substitution of what is popularly believed to be moral principles for the rules of politics. In the domestic sphere, the opportunities for the consistent substitution of moralism for politics are limited; for here failure, swift and obvious, is the punishment for violating the political rules. The situation is different in the international sphere; for success and failure in foreign policy are ambiguous terms, and the causal nexus between them and the actions seemingly leading up to them is often hard to establish. Since it is not always obvious what constitutes failure and what is responsible for it, false doctrines and practices have here a good chance to survive failure. Thus it is not by accident that foreign policy has provided the main opportunity for the moralistic attack upon the autonomy of the political sphere.

Dominant elements in Western culture, and American culture in particular, have consistently misunderstood the nature of foreign policy, and they have done so in the name of morality. In the process, our culture has deformed its understanding of morality and corrupted its moral judgment as well. It has imagined that the tension between foreign policy and morality, given in immediate experience, could easily be made to disappear in one of two ways. Either there could be a kind of reconciliation, a compromise by which foreign policy would be made moral, at least up to the point of non-violence and harmonious co-operation, and the moral law would be adapted to the exigencies of politics; perhaps there might even be two different kinds of moral law, one for man as such and as citizen of his nation and one for the relations among nations. Or else men would have a choice between power politics, morally bad, and another kind of foreign policy not tainted with the lust for power. In any event, there was presumed to be a way out of the dilemma with which the demands of foreign policy appear to confront the moral conscience.

246

The truth is that there is no way out. The moral dilemma of foreign policy is but a special and—it is true—particularly flagrant case of the moral dilemma which faces man on all levels of social action. Man cannot help sinning when he acts in relation to his fellow men; he may be able to minimize that sinfulness of social action, but he cannot escape it. For no social action can be completely free of the taint of egotism which, as selfishness, pride, or self-deception, seeks for the actor more than is his due. What is true of all social action is particularly true of political action and, within the latter, of foreign policy. For man's aspiration for power over other men, which is of the very essence of politics, implies the denial of what is the very core of Judeo-Christian morality—respect for man as an end in himself. The power relation is the very denial of that respect; for it seeks to use man as means to the end of another man. This denial is particularly flagrant in foreign policy; for the civilizing influences of law, morality, and mores are less effective here than they are on the domestic political scene.

How was it possible for our culture to misunderstand this moral dilemma of foreign policy and, turning its gaze from it, try to smooth and gloss over the conflict, thus doing justice neither to the responsibilities of foreign policy nor to the majesty of the moral law? This escape from both power politics and true morality stems in the main from three factors: man's ambivalent relationship to power and morality, the illusions of nineteenth-century liberalism, and the misunderstanding of the American experience.

The objective position of man on the political scene is always and of necessity ambivalent. While he seeks power over others, others seek power over him. His intellectual and moral attitudes toward power reflect this ambivalence of his objective position. While he takes the power drives of others for what they are or worse, he will close his eyes to his own aspirations for power, which appear to him as something different and nobler—justified by necessity and ethics —than they actually are. Thus ideological concealments, rationalizations, and justifications of necessity blind us both to the ubiquity and the moral deficiency of the aspiration for power. As John Adams put it:

Power always thinks it has a great soul and vast views beyond the comprehension of the weak and that it is doing God's service when it is violating all His laws. Our passions, ambitions, avarice, love and resentment, etc., possess so much metaphysical subtlety and so much overpowering eloquence that they insinuate themselves into the understanding and the conscience and convert both to their party.

Two historic experiences strengthened this ideological misunderstanding and depreciation of power. One was the experience of the Victorian age, as interpreted by liberal philosophy; the other, the experience of the first century of American history, as interpreted by a humanitarian, pacifist philosophy. To both, the struggle for power, especially on the international scene, appeared as the passing product of an ephemeral historic configuration. The liberals identified power politics with the rule of the aristocracy, a historic accident bound to disappear with the disappearance of autocratic government and its manifestations, such as trade barriers and colonialism.

The American experience seemed to provide experimental proof for the assumption that nations have a choice between power politics and a foreign policy not tainted by the lust for power. The Founding Fathers decided that the United States could not afford to get involved in the power politics of the European nations. Yet, to quote Washington, "The toils of European ambition, rivalship, interest, humor, or caprice," with which the United States should have nothing to do, were the only manifestations of power politics before the eyes of America. Abstention from European power politics could, therefore, be taken to mean abstention from power politics as such. This aloofness from European power politics remained a political fact at least until the end of the nineteenth century, if not until the intervention of the United States in the First World War in 1917. While in fact this isolation was the result of a complicated interplay of political and military forces, it was interpreted primarily, if not exclusively, as the result of a deliberate choice. The United States had turned her back on power politics and was applying to her foreign relations the same humanitarian principles of human betterment and peaceful competition which had worked so well at home and had made her both unique and great as a nation among nations.

The experiences of two world wars and of the aftermath of the Second have disabused many of us of these illusions. We have learned that we cannot escape the temptation and liabilities of power politics by an act of will. We must learn to live with them and still remain civilized; that is, we must make the best of them. Yet even at best, we cannot afford to forget that they are ever with us. These historic experiences have reawakened both our understanding of politics and our moral sensibilities. We have begun to resurrect from the rubble of false philosophies which did not stand the test of experience the great perennial truths about politics and morality of which Western civilization is the record. In this task political thinkers and theologians have joined. And it reveals as much about the nature of religious thought as about politics that many of the most important modern insights about politics have come from the pens of theologians.

Yet the illusions of the past are still with us. In *Speaking Frankly*, the account of his tenure as Secretary of State, Mr. James F. Byrnes reports an episode which occurred at the Paris Peace Conference in 1946:

After a heated session in Paris one afternoon, Chip Bohlen [then adviser to the American delegation] remained behind talking to a member of the Soviet delegation. The Soviet representative said it was impossible for him to understand the Americans. They had a reputation for being good traders and yet Secretary Byrnes for two days had been making speeches about principles—talking, he said, like a professor.

"Why doesn't he stop this talk about principles, and get down to business and start trading?" the Soviet representative asked Chip in all sincerity.

Chip attempted most unsuccessfully to explain that there were some questions which, in the opinion of Americans, involved principle and could not be settled by bargaining.[1]

This episode is significant not only for the pathetically honest lack of understanding between East and West that it reveals but more particularly for the light it sheds upon two diametrically opposed conceptions of foreign policy. On the one side, there is the political realist, the Machiavellian bargainer, who conceives of foreign policy exclusively in terms of power and for whom the end of power justifies all—or almost all—means employed; on the other side, there is the moralist, "talking like a professor"—or should one rather say "like a preacher"?—whose ability to bargain is strictly circumscribed, both in width and in depth, by his insistence upon principles which must be reflected in the bargain but cannot be made its object.

[1] (New York: Harper & Bros., 1947), pp. 280–81.

It is as tempting as it would be false to conceive of the opposition between these two schools of foreign policy as yet another example of the struggle between good and evil, between a noble and benevolent philosophy and practice of politics and a base and nefarious one. Such juxtapositions are tempting, for they fit quite naturally into the black-white pattern in which the struggle between East and West presents itself to the popular mind. Yet they are false just the same. They are false not only because any black-white pattern, conceived in moral and intellectual terms, is by definition inadequate to do justice to a political situation in which on either side good and evil, wisdom and error, are inextricably blended and intertwined. They are false also, and primarily, because what in Mr. Byrnes's episode is presented by implication as a typical expression of Russian realism, or Bolshevist lack of principle, or Soviet amoralism, can in fact look back on a respectable ancestry in the Western practice of foreign policy.

That member of the Soviet delegation, if he had known it and if he had dared to, might well have reminded Mr. Bohlen of Richelieu and Mazarin, of Cromwell and the two Pitts, of Hamilton and Jefferson the statesman, of Castlereagh and Canning, of Cavour, Disraeli, and Bismarck. And Mr. Bohlen, in turn, might have summoned to Mr. Byrnes's defense the shades of Fox and Burke, of Madison and Jefferson the philosopher, of Gladstone and Wilson. If they had felt in need of living witnesses, the Russian might have cited Winston Churchill; the American, Cordell Hull. In one word, then, what stood between the United States and the Soviet representatives in Paris in 1946 was the issue of moral principles versus the reason of state—the issue which Machiavelli had raised into the full consciousness of the Western world and which since then has never ceased to trouble its conscience and to transform into problems those acts of politics which in pre-Machiavellian times had been performed as a matter of course.

It is one of the glories of the political tradition of the English-speaking peoples, unrivaled in any other civilization, that their political theory, as their law, has in the main been developed not in comprehensive systematic efforts but in a series of debates concerned with the practical merits of limited, concrete issues. Three factors have fortuitously co-operated in making the political theory of the

English tongue a succession of "cases" debated in the forum of public opinion: an empirical bent of mind, aiming at immediate practical results rather than theoretical consistency; the ability to see in the concrete issue the particular instance of a general proposition rather than empirical proof for a priori abstractions; and, finally, the institution of public debate which is supposed to determine the decision in view of the rational merits of the case. Thus it has come about that while the issue of reason of state versus moral principles has on the Continent been fought out in the philosophic polemics of the Machiavellians and the anti-Machiavellians, leaving the issue in the end where they found it, in the English-speaking world the issue was always settled, at least for the moment; for, rising as it did from a concrete situation which demanded a decision, it had to be decided one way or the other. That decision, it is true, was, like the decision of the judge, only provisional and decided the issue only within the narrow confines of the situation within which it had arisen. It never purported to offer an abstract proposition settling the issue once and for all. It lacked in generality what it possessed in definiteness.

Thus it follows from the way the English-speaking peoples think in political matters that their political thought must be distilled from the debates through which the political issues of the day were settled. The problem that confronts us here has troubled the thought and life of the Anglo-American world before. To understand its nature and to assess its bearing upon the political issues of our day, the debates on great issues of the past can give us guidance. The problem has perhaps nowhere been stated with greater elemental simplicity, undiluted by side issues and undisguised by ideological rationalizations, than in the debate between Disraeli and Gladstone on the occasion of the "Bulgarian Atrocities." Disraeli made the case for the national interest in his speech in the House of Lords of July 18, 1878, on his return from the Congress of Berlin:

But I must make this observation to your lordships. We have a substantial interest in the East; it is a commanding interest, and its behest must be obeyed. But the interest of France in Egypt, and her interest in Syria, are, as she acknowledges, sentimental and traditionary interests; and, although I respect them, and although I wish to see in Lebanon and Egypt the influence of France fairly and justly maintained, and although her officers and ours in that part of the world—and especially in Egypt—are acting together with confidence and trust, we must remember that our connection with the East is not merely an affair of sentiment and tradition, but that we have urgent and substantial and enormous interests which we must guard and keep. Therefore, when we find that the progress of Russia is a progress which, whatever my be the intentions of Russia, necessarily in that part of the world produces such a state of disorganisation and want of confidence in the Porte, it comes to this—that if we do not interfere in vindication of our own interests, that part of Asia must become the victim of anarchy, and ultimately become part of the possessions of Russia.

. . . We do not, my lords, wish to enter into any unnecessary responsibility; but there is one responsibility from which we certainly shrink; we shrink from the responsibility of handing to our successors a weakened or a diminished Empire. Our opinion is, that the course we have taken will arrest the great evils which are destroying Asia Minor and the equally rich countries beyond. We see in the present state of affairs the Porte losing its influence over its subjects; we see a certainty, in our opinion, of increasing anarchy, of the dissolution of all those ties which, though feeble, yet still exist and which have kept society together in those countries. We see the inevitable result of such a state of things, and we cannot blame Russia for availing herself of it. But, yielding to Russia what she has obtained, we say to her—"Thus far, and no farther." Asia is large enough for both of us. There is no reason for these constant wars, or fears of wars, between Russia and England. Before the circumstances which led to the recent disastrous war, when none of those events which we have seen agitating the world had occurred, and when we were speaking in "another place" of the conduct of Russia in Central Asia, I vindicated that conduct, which I thought was unjustly attacked, and I said then—what I repeat now—there is room enough for Russia and England in Asia.

But the room that we require we must secure. We have, therefore, entered into an alliance—a defensive alliance—with Turkey, to guard her against any further attack from Russia.

The case for the other side was clearly stated in Gladstone's pamphlet, *Bulgarian Horrors and Russia in Turkestan*, which, in 1876, touched off the controversy:

My hope, therefore, is twofold. First, that, through the energetic attitude of the people of England, their Government may be led to declare distinctly, that it is for purposes of humanity alone that we have a fleet in Turkish waters. Secondly, that that fleet will be so distributed as to enable its force to be most promptly and efficiently applied, in case of need, on Turkish soil, in concert with the other Powers, for the defence of innocent lives, and to prevent the repetition of those recent scenes, at which hell itself might almost blush.

For it must not be forgotten that the last utterance on this subject was from the Prime Minister, and was to the effect that our fleet was in the

East for the support of British interests. I object to this constant system of appeal to our selfish leanings. It sets up false lights; it hides the true; it disturbs the world. Who has lifted a finger against British interests? Who has spoken a word? If the declaration be anything beyond mere idle brag it means that our fleet is waiting for the dissolution of the Turkish Empire, to have the first and the strongest hand in the seizure of the spoils. If this be the meaning, it is pure mischief: and if we want to form a just judgment upon it, we have only to put a parallel case. What should we say, if Russia had assembled an army on the Pruth, or Austria on the Danube, and Prince Gortschakoff or Count Andrassy were to announce that it was so gathered, and so posted for the defence of Russian, or of Austrian interests respectively?

Perhaps, in these unusual circumstances, before describing what it is that we should seek and should desire, it may be well to consider what we should carefully eschew. In the channel, which we have to navigate, with or without our Government, there are plenty of false lights set up for us, which lead to certain shipwreck. The matter has become too painfully real for us to be scared at present by the standing hobgoblin of Russia. Many a time has it done good service on the stage: it is at present out of repair, and unavailable. It is now too late to argue, as was argued some time back by a very clever and highly enlightened evening journal, that it might be quite proper that twelve or thirteen millions of Christians in Turkey should remain unhappy, rather than that (such was the alternative hardily presented) two hundred millions of men in India should be deprived of the benefits of British rule, and thirty millions more in the United Kingdom made uncomfortable by the apprehension of such a catastrophe.

This very juxtaposition of "power" politics and "moral" politics is fundamentally mistaken. It derives from the assumption that the principles of morality have the same substantive quality as, say, the principles of politics, economics, or law. This assumption leads logically to the conclusion that it is both possible and desirable to replace the principles of politics with those of morality. In truth, this substitution is possible only at the price of political failure and, hence, is neither possible nor desirable on rational grounds.

Morality is not just another branch of human activity, co-ordinate to the substantive branches, such as politics or economics. Quite to the contrary, it is superimposed upon them, limiting the choice of ends and means and delineating the legitimate sphere of a particular branch of action altogether. This later function is particularly vital for the political sphere. For the political actor is peculiarly tempted to blind himself to the limits of his power and thereby to overstep the boundaries of both prudence and morality.

It is not ignorance or misjudgment, that is, intellectual errors, against which the Greek tragedians and biblical prophets warn the powerful of the world but *hubris* and pride. The self-esteem engendered by power, which equates power and virtue, in the process loses all sense of moral and political proportion. Indeed, it is from the moral delusions and corruptions, the poisonous fruits of power, that these intellectual errors receive the strength to lead nations to disaster as though it were truth and not error that led them. The moral corruption of power blinds nations to the distinction between truth and error. Dazzled by the pride of power, they take truth for error, and vice versa, and make ready with unsuspecting confidence to jump into the abyss as if it were the consummation of their dreams.

A nation emerges victorious from a war, and in the exaltation of its supreme power it rejects as unacceptable, if not as outright offensive, the idea that it won the victory because it had better trained and better fed troops, more and better arms, and superior leadership. Providence, either as a personal divinity or as the objective logic of the historic process, has given victory to the nation which deserved it by virtue of its moral superiority. That alleged moral superiority is then taken to be a permanent quality which not only explains past victories but also justifies the national claim to be the lawgiver and arbiter of mankind.

A nation, thus supernaturally endowed, not only has the ability but believes that it has a sacred duty to reform the world in the image of its own supposed superiority. It can and must promote or forestall revolution or reform, as the case may be. It must contain other nations, advance itself, and never retreat. There is nothing it cannot do. What is more, there is nothing it ought not to do. It must and can bring salvation to all the world. By the standards of this national moral delusion, humanity naturally divides into two groups: one all black and the other all white. By definition those who are for you are good, and those who are against you are wicked.

Only future generations will be able to understand fully to what extent in our atomic policy the self-destructive tendencies of power have been at work; how the use of the atomic bomb and our emphasis upon its monopolistic possession and decisive importance have called into existence the very forces that nullify that advantage and turn it against us; how that possession has tempted us from miscalculation to miscalculation, overrating our own and underrating the power of other nations; how the emphasis on secrecy, assuming the permanency of that monopolistic possession, has done more than anything else to destroy the advantage it was intended to preserve; and how, finally, the awareness of such tremendous power has nourished a sense of mission which assumes in its holder an exclusive moral worth and duty of a magnitude commensurate with so much power.[2]

[2] It might be pointed out that this passage was written in 1950.

14 *The Military Displacement of Politics*

The autonomy of the political sphere is endangered not only by the misunderstanding of the nature and role of morality but also by the imperialism of other spheres of substantive action, of which in our culture the economic and military are the most important ones. The economic attack upon the political sphere dominated the nineteenth and the first decades of the twentieth centuries. Marxism and liberalism are its outstanding manifestations. When the experience of totalitarianism seemed to have proved conclusively that politics is not a derivation of economics but has an autonomous realm of its own, the Second World War and its aftermath raised the issue of the autonomy of politics again. This time, it was the military which infringed upon it.

The fundamental error behind all the individual blunders committed toward the end of the Second World War, and immediately afterward, was the neglect of Karl von Clausewitz' dictum that war is the continuation of policy by other means. The peaceful and warlike means by which a nation pursues its interests form a continuous process in which, though one means may replace the other, the ends remain the same. We also failed to recognize that foreign policy itself is a continuum beginning with the birth of a state and ending only with its death; isolationists and interventionists alike tended to believe that the "normal" thing for a state was to have no foreign policy at all. What separated the interventionists from the isolationists was the belief that certain crises might require, at least temporarily, an active foreign policy. But even the interventionists felt that after solving the given crisis one could try to return to a position of detachment, though developing and supporting in the meantime international institutions designed to meet the next crisis if and when it should arise. Foreign policy was thus regarded as something like a policeman's night stick, to be used only when it was necessary to bring a disturber of the peace to reason; war, in turn, was like the policeman's gun, to be used only *in extremis* to rid the world of a criminal. But here the analogy ends: the policeman always carries his gun with him, but we threw ours away twice after it had done the job.

War, we could see, did have a necessary connection with what preceded it—that is, with the criminal aggression that provoked it—but it had no organic relation with what followed it. Its purpose was only to eliminate a disturbance by eliminating the disturber; once that was done, the world would presumably settle back into normalcy and order. War, then, was a mere technical operation to be performed according to the rules of military art—a feat of military engineering like building a dam or flattening a mountain. To allow considerations of political expediency to interfere with military operations was unwise from the military point of view and might well be considered an immoral subversion of one self-sufficient department of human action for the sake of another. (It might be added in passing that economic specialists—for instance, administrators of foreign aid—have shown a very similar reluctance, for similar reasons, to let political considerations "violate" the autonomy of economic operations.)

This quality of American thinking emerges clearly from the contrast between the non-political American approach to war and the continuous and generally fruitless insistence of Churchill and his subordinates on the political significance of military action. The British and the Russians knew from long experience that wars are not fought just to bring about the unconditional surrender of the enemy; wars are means to political ends, and military victory, if it is to bear political fruits, must be shaped to those ends.

American military leaders were aware of this difference in outlook, both on the battlefield and afterward. In April, 1945, when the British wanted Patton's army to liberate as much of Czechoslovakia as possible, and Prague in particular, for the sake of the political advantages to be gained thereby, General Marshall passed the suggestion on to General Eisenhower with this comment: "Personally, and aside from all logistic, tactical, or strategical implications, I would be loath to hazard American lives for purely political reasons." Marshall had nothing to worry about in this respect, for Eisenhower replied the next day: "I shall not attempt any move I deem militarily unwise merely to gain a political advantage unless I receive specific order from the Combined Chiefs of Staff." The matter rested there despite repeated and urgent appeals from Churchill and the British chiefs of staff. Similar decisions were made on other occasions. General Bradley in his memoirs has this to say of the British insistence that the Americans take Berlin before the Russians: "As soldiers we looked naïvely on this British inclination to complicate the war with political foresight and non-military objectives."

This concentration on military objectives to the neglect of political considerations has one virtue: it is apt to win wars quickly, cheaply, and thoroughly. Yet such victories may be short-lived, and an enormous political and military price may have to be paid for them later. To win a war without regard for the political consequences of the victory may create political problems as serious as, or worse than, those that the victory was intended to settle; but such a victory leaves a country at least in a position to learn and to try to settle political problems by peaceful means.

Have we learned these lessons? On the face of it, it seems we have. Certainly we have been almost obsessed with the need to fashion our postwar policies so as to avoid the mistakes we and others made during the Second World War. We have learned that a power vacuum will exert a well-nigh irresistible attraction on a great dynamic nation in its vicinity. We have learned that in order to confine such a nation within the limits necessary to our own security it is not enough to show good will and reasonableness and to embody virtuous intentions in legal instruments. We have learned that the balance of power, far from being just an arbitrary device of reactionary diplomats and Machiavellian scholars, is the very law of life for independent units dealing with other independent units—domestic or international—that want to preserve their independence. Independent power, in order to be kept in check, must be met by independent power of approximately equal strength. In the effort to apply these lessons, we have embarked upon a long-range policy of "containment" and rearmament.

We have also learned that an imperialist power confronted with a coalition of powers of varying strength will attempt to eliminate the weaker members one after the other, until the most powerful member is left in the end outmaneuvered and alone. We have therefore developed an intricate system of alliances in the Western Hemisphere, Europe, and Asia, which, whatever the differences of legal language and institutional device, all amount to a declaration that we shall defend the territorial integrity of the members of these alliances as we would our own. We call this system of alliances "collective security" and have put it into operation by defending the Republic of South Korea against aggression by North Korea.

In these ways, we have obviously learned from history. Why, then, are we as uncertain as ever about the success of our policies and still beset by doubts about the course we have been taking in recent years? Have we still missed one of the important lessons of recent history, or have we misunderstood what it seemed to teach us? The answer is not completely reassuring. Though we have learned the lessons of recent history, chapter and verse, though we have memorized them and have never tired of reciting and applying them whenever faced with a problem which seemed to be similar to one of those that we failed to solve during the Second World War, yet we have failed to see that behind the specific lessons of history learned from specific blunders there stands *the* lesson of history, of *all* history, which alone gives meaning to the lessons to be derived from any particular period.

All political action is an attempt to influence human behavior; hence, all political action must be aware of the complexities and ambiguities of the human factor and must itself be ambiguous and complex—and in the right way. The political actor, conscious of history, must be aware of the malleability of the human will; yet he must also be aware of the limits of suasion and of the need for objective barriers to the human will. While he is making use of suasion, he must not be oblivious to the role of power, and vice versa, and of each he must have just the right quantity and quality, neither too much nor too little, neither too early nor too late, neither too strong nor too weak.

He must choose the right admixture, not only in terms of human nature, permanent as such but with the relations of its elements ever changing, but also in terms of the changing historical circumstances under which those elements of human nature confront each other in the form of collectivities called nations. How much suasion and power and what kind is available on my side at a particular moment in history, and how much of it and what kind is likely to be available tomorrow? How much and what kind of susceptibility to suasion and power is present on the other side at a particular moment of history, and how much and what kind is likely to be present tomorrow? And how much and what kind of suasion and power is the other side able to bring to bear upon me and others today and tomorrow? Such are the questions posed by the ever changing social environment.

When, during the closing years of the past war, we thought that Stalin was a somewhat gruff old gentleman who could be charmed into co-operation, we relied on suasion to a greater extent than the teachings of history justified. We think we have learned our lesson from this failure of a policy of suasion pure and simple. Now we seem to have forsworn suasion altogether and seem to rely exclusively upon force as a deterrent to the ambitions of the Soviet Union. We seem to forget that force as the instrument of a foreign policy aiming at the peaceful settlement of international conflicts must be a means to the end of foreign policy, not an end in itself. Force supplements suasion but does not replace it. Mr. Acheson, as Secretary of State, recognized this relation between suasion and force in the abstract when he proclaimed repeatedly that the objective of our foreign policy was the creation of situations of strength from which to negotiate a peaceful settlement with the Soviet Union. In practice, however, our foreign policy, preoccupied as it is with rearmament, seems to have lost sight of this objective. Consequently, it has not faced up squarely to the all-important question of timing: when shall we consider ourselves strong enough in relation to the Soviet Union to be able to negotiate from strength? A positive answer is being postponed to an ever more indefinite future. Trying to learn from history, we have set out on an armament race that must lead to war if it is not subordinated to the professed objective of a negotiated settlement. Here again we have learned but half the lesson and have replaced one error with another.[1]

Most often political blunders consist in this overemphasis of one element in a situation at the expense of others. The twenties and thirties saw the underestimation by the Western world of the uses of power toward moral and legal ends. The Second World War saw but a seeming interruption of that trend, for power was used then in an effort to restore conditions of harmony and "normalcy" under

[1] This chapter was, in the main, written in 1950.

which we could again rely on law and morality and, as it were, forget about power. We seemed at the time to have learned a lesson from our prewar relations with the Axis Powers: we had neglected power; now we would use it without limit until those who had compelled us to do so were forced to surrender their own power unconditionally. With that task accomplished, we would be able to return to the other extreme and build a new world, without power politics, on the foundations of law and morality.

Consistent with this point of view, we treated our wartime allies, including the Soviet Union, with that same disregard of considerations of power which had characterized our behavior toward everybody in the interwar period. Yet the same experience that had forced us into power politics against Hitler was to be repeated in our dealings with the Soviet Union. And here, too, we seem to have learned our lesson now. Having shown good will, we now "get tough." Since one cannot deal with the Soviet Union by legal contract and without regard for the realities of power, we will now use in dealing with her the instruments of power alone, without concern for legal stipulations to be agreed upon through mutual suasion. Just as the only alternative to appeasement of Germany, Japan, or Italy without power had been war, so the alternative to appeasement of the Soviet Union is another kind of war.

We also learned from the experiences of the thirties what a blunder isolationism was, which would let one fight only in defense of one's own country but not in defense of allies. But in learning that lesson we are by way of falling into the opposite error: having realized the error of fighting for nobody but one's self, we are now willing to fight for anybody threatened by the common enemy. Collective security, after all, is as abstract and non-political a principle of action as isolationism, equally impervious to the complexity of all political issues which must be decided not according to abstract principles but by the calculation of opposing interests and powers.

We intervened in Korea because the principle of collective security required it, thus seemingly avoiding the mistake Great Britain and France had made when they refused to defend Ethiopia in 1935–36 and Czechoslovakia in 1938. Actually, as pointed out before,[2] we made exactly the same mistake, only in a different way. In 1950, as

[2] See above, pp. 76 ff.

in 1935 and 1938, the issue might better have been decided in terms of the interests involved and the power available as against the interests and power of other nations. Instead, it was resolved in all three instances, either positively or negatively, in the abstract terms of collective security, a principle which could be applied against a major power only at the risk of world war. By substituting an abstract principle of law for the calculation of the concrete conditions of interests and power, we involved ourselves in a war that, in view of these relations of interests and power, we could neither win nor lose. Such are the results of a foreign policy that tries to avoid the mistakes of the past without understanding the principles that should have governed the actions of the past.

We realized what had been wrong with our policies, but in supplying what had been lacking we threw overboard what was no less essential than what we were trying to supply. Thus the very correction of past blunders created new ones. We had seen that diplomacy without power was not enough, so we added power and forgot about diplomacy. We had seen that a nation must stop aggression before it reaches her own shores, and we concluded that we had now to stop all aggression regardless of how our own interests and power were affected. We learned the specific lessons of the last two decades, but in the process we came to neglect the broad lesson of history: that political success depends upon the simultaneous or alternative use of different means at different times and the moderate use of all of them at all times.

Man is never able to look at history with the same objectivity as at inanimate nature. The moral limitation upon his understanding of history is pride: pride in his intellect, pride in his goodness, pride in the collectivity with which he identifies himself as against other collectivities.

Pride in intellect shows itself in the persistence with which ideas once adopted are applied time and again, regardless of the fact that they have been discredited by experience. A general whose strategy brought victory in one war finds in success an additional reason for using the same methods in the next war. He did it once, and he is going to do it again. What General MacArthur was able to do to the Japanese in the Second World War he must be able to do to the Chinese in the Korean War.

Even if a certain strategy has been unsuccessful, there is a strong tendency to try it out again, especially if the general sluggishness of the human mind encourages it. The Maginot line was a disastrous failure in the Second World War. But man is almost irresistibly attracted by the image of a wall behind which he will be safe from the enemy. Since the Maginot line was a failure, as was the Chinese Great Wall before it, why not build a bigger and better Maginot line? Or perhaps a bigger and better general will do what General Gamelin was unable to do with the Maginot line in 1940. The most subtle perversion of the lessons of history is that which appears to heed the experiences of the past and discard its faulty methods, while continuing nonetheless to think in terms of the past. To build a line of static fortifications parallel to the Rhine was certainly a mistake that we shall not emulate. Instead, we shall create a western European army that will defend Europe at the Elbe, at the Rhine, or wherever else it may be. We seem to have learned a lesson from history; but, in view of the novel requirements of global strategy and the numerical superiority of the Russian land armies, have we really?

Pride in intellect is joined by pride in virtue. All individuals and collectivities like to see their conflicts with others not in terms of interest and power determined by circumstances but in terms of moral values determined by abstract principles. When our policies fail, as they did in relation to the Soviet Union after the Second World War, the explanation cannot lie in our having miscalculated our interests and power in relation to the interests and power of the other side. Our failure must be the result of the wickedness of the other side, which took advantage of our guileless trust. We trusted once and were deceived; from now on we shall be on our guard and see the enemy for what he is. Yalta then becomes a symbol, not of the legal ratification of errors of political and military judgment, but of a moral deception that the wicked perpetrated upon the good.

While such one-sidedness, which impairs historical judgment and thus our ability to learn from history, seems inevitable in even the greatest of historians, there are specific manifestations of it that, as great statesmen have shown, can be controlled by moral discipline. One such manifestation is the habit of overestimating one's own power and underestimatng the other side's. The history of the relations between the Western world and the Soviet Union since 1917 could be written in terms of the underestimation of Russian power. From the Allied intervention in the Russian civil war through the debates on the implementation of the Franco-Russian alliance of 1935, the Russian offer of support to Czechoslovakia in 1938, the Anglo-French military mission to Moscow in 1939, the German attack upon the Soviet Union in 1941, the first atomic explosion in Russia in 1949, up to the very present, we have always underestimated the power of the Soviet Union. We have done so because we are inflexibly opposed on moral grounds to both communism and Russian imperialism. Thus our moral sentiment stands in the way of a correct appraisal of the realities of power. To separate our pride in our own moral superiority from our historical judgment, which might lead us to recognize the political and military superiority of the Soviet Union in certain respects, requires an effort at moral detachment which few are willing to make. It is easier and more satisfactory to conclude that political and military superiority necessarily go hand in hand with moral superiority. Yet the monopoly of the atomic bomb may have been, but was not of necessity, concomitant with a monopoly in virtue. Here again moral pride stands between our judgment and historical experience.

The classic example of this kind of pride, and of its disastrous political and military consequences, is Hitler's. Since Bismarck, it had been the basic axiom of German strategy that Germany could not win a two-front war. However, it was exactly such a war that she deliberately embarked upon both in 1914 and 1941. Hitler himself was resolved not to make this blunder, but he could not help making it, for he believed firmly that it was Germany's "mission" to triumph over her enemies. Holding such a faith, he was led to assume that Germany had already won the war against the West when she had not yet done so, and could therefore safely invade the Soviet Union.

If we find it so difficult to learn from history, the fault is not with history but with the pride and the intellectual limitations of men. History, in the words of Thucydides, is philosophy learned from examples. Those who are morally and intellectually inferior to its teachings, history leads to disaster. Those who are philosophers in the moral and intellectual sense, it teaches.

Of this ability to learn from history that the autonomy of the political sphere must be protected against encroachments of the military, Sir Winston Churchill provides the greatest contemporary example. Its literary manifestation is *Triumph and Tragedy*.[3] The range of this book is narrow in every respect—in subject matter, in style, and in purpose. It covers the period from the invasion of Normandy in June, 1944, to the Potsdam Conference of July, 1945. Its theme is, in the words of the author, "How the Great Democracies Triumphed, and So Were Able To Resume the Follies Which Had So Nearly Cost Them Their Life." Its central problem is simple: military strategy and its relation to foreign policy.

The style is of the same classic simplicity as the problem. As the problem raises a perennial issue of statecraft, so the mode of thought which the author brings to bear upon the problem moves within the perennial categories of political thought. Sir Winston Churchill's mind is not that of an intellectual who loves to think and know for the sake of thinking and knowledge. His is the intellect of a man of action who relives in thought past action and what preceded and followed it. Sir Winston thinks with a purpose which transcends thought. His purpose as a thinker is that of the man of action and, hence, is intensely personal; it is so in three different respects.

Its most personal purpose is to enable the author to relive in reminiscence his part in the drama of history, enjoying its victories, mourning its defeats. Yet this process of recollecting and reflective reliving is also one of simplification, of seeing, and of making others see, perhaps for the first time, the essence of one's action and its purpose, aside from what is but pretense and byplay. The first purpose, then, is autobiographical in the strict, classic sense of the term.

The second purpose is autobiographical in what one might call the political sense. It is to justify the author as past actor on the political scene. It is to prove that the author was right when he did what he did and when he gave advice that was not heeded. When the author must admit that he was wrong in action or advice, he at least evokes the sympathetic companionship of the reader, who learns to his satisfaction that the great and the powerful share in the human fallibility of all. Thus the author assigns himself the place in history which he deems his due or, at the very least, helps future historians to assign it to him.

Finally, the book teaches a lesson. By contrasting the mistakes of

[3] Boston: Houghton Mifflin Co., 1953.

the past with the principles of right action, the author calls our attention, by implication, to opportunities in the more recent past and in the future of making the same mistakes by neglecting the same principles. It is this contribution to political wisdom which makes this book important, particularly for us and at this time. What, then, transforms this autobiographical account of history into a source of political wisdom? With this question we approach the secret of Sir Winston's greatness.

That secret cannot be explained in this space, if it can be explained at all; it can only be adumbrated. It seems to lie in the conjuncture of three qualities, one intellectual, one practical, and one moral. These qualities are the intellectual grasp of statesmanship, the ability to act according to the requirements of statesmanship, and the subordination of all other considerations to these requirements. Others are as wise as Sir Winston; others again are as effective in action; and others still have dedicated themselves as single-mindedly to a purpose. Yet nobody alive combines to such a degree intellectual excellence with ability in action and dedication to a cause.

What John Stuart Mill said of Bentham applies also to Churchill: "The field of [his] labours was like the space between two parallel lines; narrow to excess in one direction, in another it reached to infinity." The field of Sir Winston's labors, of his interests, and of his understanding is narrow. Yet one is also struck with the enormity of the purposeful intellectual and moral force that sweeps through the narrow confines of his cause: to remember the past in order to learn how to act aright in matters political and military.

The outstanding quality of that intellectual force is the ability to see a problem in its true proportions, by not allowing the involvement of will and emotion to interfere with understanding. What is required of the statesman is, first of all, to see clearly: himself, the enemy, and then himself again as the enemy sees him. To see clearly means to see without passions, without the passion of pride, of hatred, and of contempt. The statesman must master the paradox of wanting passionately to win over an enemy to whom he feels passionately superior, and of having to view his relations with the enemy with the detachment and objectivity of the scholar. This book provides proof of the extent to which Sir Winston has mastered this paradox. His most spectacular failures are his support of "unconditional surrender" and his inability to reconcile Great Britain's moral and legal commitment to the independence of Poland with the political and military realities which the Russian conquest of eastern Europe had created.

The moral counterpart of the intellectual ability of mastering this paradox of passion and understanding is humility toward one's self and generosity toward others. As such, this moral attitude is not only a moral virtue in itself but one of the conditions for political success as well. The extent to which this book reveals these qualities is another measure of Sir Winston's greatness as a statesman. He deplores President Truman's decision to withdraw the American troops, on the eve of the Potsdam Conference, to the zonal borders agreed upon at Quebec and Yalta, a step against which he had repeatedly warned; and there is no doubt in his mind now, as there was none then, that he was right and Truman wrong. Yet he enumerates all the mitigating circumstances which can be cited in explanation and support of Mr. Truman's decision and adds: "Those who are only wise after the event should hold their peace." And, while he bends every effort to forestall Stalin's designs, with what understanding does he speak of Russian interests, and with what respect does he pay tribute to Stalin's qualities!

If the cause to which Sir Winston brings these qualities were less challenging intellectually, less demanding morally, and less vital for all of us, we would think less of Sir Winston's greatness. As it is, upon our ability to learn Sir Winston's lessons the survival of the West may well depend. That, then, completes Sir Winston's greatness: that he brings a great intellectual and moral force successfully to bear upon the greatest of all contemporary causes.

What are the lessons we can learn from Sir Winston's book? The relationships between political and military policy being its main theme, this book is a study in contrasts, the contrast between British and American policies, between Churchill's and Roosevelt's strategy and statecraft. That contrast can be defined in two fundamental and interrelated propositions. For Sir Winston, the war was a military means to a political end, and the influence of the political end upon the military means was to increase with the speed with which the armies of the Allies were approaching military victory. For the United States, the war was essentially a self-sufficient technical operation to be performed as quickly, as cheaply, and as thoroughly as the technical rules of warfare would allow. The political issue with which Sir Winston's strategy and statecraft were primarily concerned during the last year of the Second World War was no longer German and Japanese imperialism but the imperialism of the Soviet Union. For the American government, the approaching defeat of German and Japanese imperialism signified the elimination of the major political problem that faced the Western world, and what remained could safely be left to mutual good will, especially toward the Soviet Union, and to the United Nations.

In one word, Sir Winston's was a historic concept of the war, while the American was apocalyptic. Sir Winston viewed the war as part of a historic continuum, as a product of historic forces not in essence different from those that had preceded it and were likely to follow it, subject to historic laws, which are of the timeless essence of politics itself and for whose disregard a nation must pay a heavy price. Our government looked at the war as the catastrophic interruption of a normalcy which the victorious conclusion of the war would almost automatically restore. For us the war was like a thunderstorm darkening a peaceful scene; its passing would by itself restore peace. For Sir Winston the war—in its causes, manifestations, and consequences—was, as it were, part of the natural environment of nations, and its consequences would be determined by the policies carried on during the war.

In Sir Winston's thought and argument, as revealed in this book, one concern took precedence over all others: to meet the Russians as much to the east as possible. Whenever a military decision had to be made, small or great, Sir Winston hammered on this concern to the point of obnoxiousness. During the Italian campaign, he was obsessed with the opportunity to occupy Vienna before the Russians and urged that the invasion of southern France be sacrificed to the exploitation of this opportunity. After the Allied armies had crossed the Rhine, he urged striking directly at Berlin rather than southward, in order not to leave Berlin to the Russians. It was for similar reasons that he advised occupying as much as possible of Czechoslovakia, and more particularly Prague, and keeping what had been occupied. And when the war in Europe had ended with the surrender of Germany, he continued to view military operations in the light of their political consequences: he urged an over-all settlement with the Soviet Union while the armies of the United States were still intact and in Europe.

Sir Winston was defeated on every major issue. The only important exception was Greece, where he was able to act on his own, subordinating military to political considerations. When Greece was about to be conquered by communism and, through it, by Russian imperialism, he sent British forces to Greece to defeat that very underground army which had just been successfully fighting the Axis. It was argued then, as it is being argued now, that his advice was militarily unsound. However, this is not the point which Sir Winston's book raises. Sir Winston's concern—and ours—is not with the military soundness of this particular action or that but with the political quality of thinking which led to military action, however sound or unsound it might have been in its own military terms. It is the contrast between his own thinking and that of his American counterparts, and the political superiority of his to theirs, which is the main revelation of the book.

It would be as comforting as it would be false if one were to conclude that the main lesson of Sir Winston's book has been learned. Looking at Asia, the Middle East, and Europe—let alone at Washington—one cannot escape the conclusion that it has not been learned. Everywhere the requisite primacy of foreign policy over military policy is at best tenuous or ineffectual, if it exists at all. This book, then, is not only a repository of perennial wisdom; it also carries a very timely warning.

15 *The Disparagement of Diplomacy*

The traditional methods of diplomacy have been under continuous attack since the First World War and have to a considerable extent been discarded in practice since the end of the Second World War. Three main arguments have been directed against them. First, they have been held responsible for the political catastrophes which have befallen mankind in the last four decades or so; methods that appear to have been so unsuccessful must be replaced by better ones. Second, traditional diplomacy has been held to run counter to the principles of democracy, and from the assumption that democracy makes for peace—and autocracy, for war —it has been concluded that diplomacy must be "open," that is, exposed to public scrutiny in all its processes. Finally, the traditional diplomatic practices with their seemingly useless and wasteful formalities, horse-trading, and compromises have seemed to violate moral principles with which democratic nations have felt themselves identified; in other words, the age-old conflict between political realism and idealism has been transferred to the sphere of diplomacy.

These arguments against traditional diplomacy arise from the basic philosophic position, prevalent in our time, that political practices are the result of subjective preferences, to be changed at will. In truth, however, the traditional methods of diplomacy have not been invented by stupid and evil or, for that matter, wise and good men —even though they have certainly been used and abused by such men—but have grown ineluctably from the objective nature of things political. In their essence, they are the reflections of that objective nature, to be disregarded only at the risk of political failure. Whenever two autonomous social entities, anxious to maintain their autonomy, engage in political relations with each other, they cannot but resort to what we call the traditional methods of diplomacy. And it does not matter in this respect whether these diplomatic relations are carried on between two members of a family, two businessmen, two baseball clubs, two political parties, or two sovereign nations. On all levels of such relations, secrecy of negotiation—to mention only the most prominent and controversial aspect—is not an arbitrary procedural device to be used or dispensed with at will but grows from the objective nature of negotiations. No negotiations of any kind—be they for the contraction of a marriage, the sale of a piece of property, a deal for baseball players, or an international treaty—can be carried out in public without defeating their very purpose: the transformation of conflicting or inchoate interests into a common purpose of the contracting parties.

The specific arguments against the traditional methods of diplomacy are as untenable as is the basic philosophic position from which they stem. If it is true that the traditional practices of diplomacy constitute the method by which the business of foreign policy must be transacted, the failure of a particular foreign policy or of a whole era to bring peace and order to the world cannot be attributed to these practices per se but, at worst, to their incorrect use. This logical deduction is borne out by the experiences of recent history. For the disorganization of international society since the First World War has indeed been concomitant with the neglect, misunderstanding, and abuse of the traditional practices of diplomacy. While it would be far-fetched to suggest that the decline of diplomacy is responsible for the catastrophes that have befallen the world in recent times, it cannot be doubted that that decline has contributed to international disorder, being itself an outgrowth of a deep-seated disorder in the intellectual sphere.

Both the arguments—that democracy means peace and that diplomacy is immoral and therefore undemocratic—have grown from an intellectual attitude hostile to the very idea of foreign policy as an independent sphere of thought and action. They assume that the kind of foreign policy a nation pursues is determined by the kind of domestic institutions it possesses and the kind of political philosophy to which it adheres. All of recorded history militates against that assumption. The national interest of great powers and, in good measure, the methods by which it is to be secured are impervious to ideological or institutional changes. As far back as April 30, 1823, George Canning warned that "the general acquisition of free institutions is not necessarily a security for general peace." Our experience of total wars, waged by democracies for democratic tenets, gives substance to that warning.

The argument that diplomacy is particularly immoral and, hence, incompatible with democratic government similarly assumes that one can escape from the moral dilemmas of foreign policy by forswearing foreign policy itself. At the bottom of this argument there is a dual illusion: the illusion of the moral superiority of domestic politics over foreign policy and the illusion of the possibility of escaping foreign policy altogether. Both philosophic analysis and historic experience show that the moral problems that foreign policy raises are but a peculiar—and particularly drastic—manifestation of the moral problem of politics as such. Taking a wider view, one can even say that the moral problem of politics is but a peculiar instance of the moral problem which man encounters whenever he acts with reference to his fellow men. What distinguishes in this respect foreign policy from domestic politics and from the human situation in general is not the substance of the problem, which is identical on all levels of human interaction, but the social conditions under which the problem arises on the international plane.

There is, then, no way to escape the moral problem of politics, domestic or international; we can only endeavor to smooth down its sharp edges and to mitigate its practical consequences by changing not its substance but the social environment within which it is bound to arise in one form or another. It is not by accident that those who have tried to do more have taken a negative attitude toward foreign policy; for in the traditional methods of diplomacy they could not help seeing the outward manifestations of the political risks and moral liabilities of foreign policy itself. Opposition to the traditional methods of diplomacy is everywhere intimately connected with either an isolationist or universalistic attitude toward international relations. Both consider the traditional methods of diplomacy at best superfluous and at worst pernicious, for they so regard foreign policy itself. In the isolationist view, a country can afford to dispense with an active foreign policy and, hence, with diplomacy. In the universalistic view, foreign policy, carried on through diplomatic methods by sovereign nations, belongs to a dying age and is a stumbling block to the establishment of a more peaceful and orderly organization of the world.

This thought reveals itself in the recent attempts to set up the procedures of the United Nations as an alternative to the traditional methods of diplomacy. Here again, we are in the presence of the assumption that nations have a choice between the traditional methods of diplomacy and some other way of dealing with each other, a way that somehow leads to freedom from the risks and liabilities of foreign policy. In truth, of course, the procedures of the United Nations, as they have emerged in the practice of the organization, do not differ in substance from the traditional practices of diplomacy. What distinguishes the former from the latter is nothing but the social setting and the legal requirements which influence the way in which the traditional business of diplomacy is carried on within the agencies of the United Nations. The United Nations and traditional diplomacy are not mutually exclusive alternatives between which nations must choose. Rather, they supplement each other, serving identical purposes and partaking of the same qualities and characteristics. The secretary-general of the United Nations, in his *Annual Report on the Work of the Organization for July 1, 1954 through June 15, 1955,* has called attention to this relationship in these words:

We have only begun to make use of the real possibilities of the United Nations as the most representative instrument for the relaxation of tensions, for the lessening of distrust and misunderstanding, and for the discovery and delineation of new areas of common ground and interest. . . . Conference diplomacy may usefully be supplemented by more quiet diplomacy within the United Nations, whether directly between representatives of Member Governments or in contacts between the Secretary-General and Member Governments. The obligations of the Charter, the environment of institutions dedicated to seeking out the common ground among the national interests of Member States, the wide representation from all continents and cultures, the presence of the Secretariat established as a principal organ of the United Nations for the purpose of upholding and serving the international interest—all these can provide help not to be found elsewhere, if they are rightly applied and used.

Within the framework of the Charter there are many possibilities, as yet largely unexplored, for variation of practices. . . . It is my hope that solid progress can be made in the coming years in developing new forms of contact, new methods of deliberation and new techniques of reconciliation. With only slight adjustments, discussions of major issues of a kind that have occurred outside the United Nations could often be fitted into its framework, thus at the same time adding to the strength of the world organization and drawing strength from it.

With these considerations we are entering into the positive task of ascertaining the functions of traditional diplomacy and its permanent value. A nation, existing as it does as an equal among other nations, can deal with the outside world in one of three different ways. It can deny the importance of the other nations for itself and its own importance for them and retreat into the impotence of isolation. Or it can deny the equality of the other nations and try to impose its own will upon them by force of arms. In either case, at least in its pure, extreme realization, a nation can afford to dispense with diplomacy. Or a nation can want to pursue its interests in active contact and on the basis of equality with other nations, assuming the universality of that desire. In that case it cannot do without the constant redefinition and adjustment of its interests for the purpose of accommodating the interests of other nations.

Conflict of interests—actual, seeming, or potential—is the overriding fact of international society, as it is one of the overriding facts of all societies, even those most highly integrated and centralized. Diplomacy in all its diverse historic and social manifestations is the technique of accommodating such conflicting interests. That technique proceeds in two stages: the ascertainment of the facts of conflict and the formulation of the terms of settlement.

Nation A pursues certain interests and so does nation B, and the interests of A and B are on the face of them in conflict. Both nations want to settle this conflict peacefully. How can they go about it? They have to define their respective interests and ascertain the point of conflict. That investigation may lead them to one of three possible conclusions.

If what A wants and finds vital to itself B cannot cede without endangering its vital interests or its very existence, because of the intrinsic importance of the territory, frontier, port, or air base at issue, diplomatic accommodation is impossible. When Francis I of France was asked why he always made war against Charles V of Austria, he is reported to have answered: "Because we both want the same thing: Italy." As long as both kings wanted Italy badly enough, they could either go to war over it or else leave the issue unsettled, hoping for future developments to deflect the energies of both sides toward less contentious objectives. Often in history nations have indeed avoided war over their vital interests by allowing time to take the sting out of their conflicts. Yet in such cases it is to the restraint of warlike passions and the renunciation of quick and radical solutions rather than to the practices of diplomacy that the credit for the preservation of peace must go.

Nation A may again pursue an objective vital to itself which nation B could cede only at the price of a vital interest of its own. Yet, in contrast to the type of conflict just discussed, the importance of the objective to both sides is here not intrinsic to the objective itself but rather the result of a peculiar configuration of interests which are subject to manipulation. For instance, the Soviet Union has a vital interest in preventing a united Germany from joining the Western alliance, and the United States has a similarly vital interest in preventing such a Germany from being absorbed by the Soviet bloc. Taken by themselves, these positions are obviously incompatible and, as the history of East-West negotiations has thus far shown, not subject to diplomatic accommodation. Yet one can well imagine, without committing one's self to its practical feasibility in the immediate future, an over-all European or world-wide settlement of which a German settlement would form an organic part, satisfactory to the interests of both sides which could not be reconciled to the unification of Germany considered in isolation. In situations such as this, it is the task of diplomacy to redefine the seemingly incompatible, vital interests of the nations concerned in order to make them compatible.

This task of diplomacy is, as it were, strategic in nature and truly creative, not often attempted and rarely successful. It yields in practical importance to that function with which diplomacy is typically associated in the popular mind: the function of bargaining issuing in a compromise. In conflicts to which this function applies, nation A seeks an objective which nation B either is willing to grant only in part or refuses to grant at all without compensation. Conflicts of this kind concern non-vital interests of which nations are willing to dispose by way of negotiations. The technique of diplomacy consists here in ascertaining the interests of both sides and in allocating the objective at issue in view of these interests and of the power available for their support.

The same diplomatic technique serves not only the peaceful settlement of conflicts among nations but also the delineation and codification of common interests. In this respect it performs its classic function for the negotiation of treaties serving a common purpose of the contracting parties. Called upon to settle a conflict between two nations, diplomacy must create out of the conflicting interests a community of interests, a compromise, which cannot satisfy all parties completely but with which no party will be completely dissatisfied. When the representatives of two nations meet to negotiate a treaty, say, of commerce or alliance, they must discover and make precise an already existing community of interests. This community of interests, before it is crystallized in legal stipulations, is amorphous and inchoate, obscured and distorted by seeming and real conflicts. It is the task of diplomacy to define the area of that pre-existing community of interests and to express it in terms sufficiently precise to serve as a reliable foundation for future action. It need only be mentioned in passing that this function of diplomacy is identical with that of contractual negotiations on all levels of social interaction.

It must be obvious from what has been said thus far that the traditional methods of diplomacy are of vital importance to a nation that seeks to pursue its interests successfully and peaceably. A nation that is unwilling or unable to use diplomacy for that end is of necessity compelled either to forsake its interests or to pursue them by war. As pointed out before, nations have always had a choice among three alternatives: diplomacy, war, renunciation. Which one of these alternatives a nation chose in a concrete situation was a matter of rational calculation; none of them was excluded a priori on rational grounds.

Modern technology, especially in the form of all-out atomic war, has destroyed this rational equality among diplomacy, war, and renunciation and has greatly enhanced the importance of diplomacy. In view of that technology, there is no longer safety in renunciation or in victory in war. From the beginning of history to the Second World War the risks inherent in these three choices were commensurate with the advantages to be expected. Nations would miscalculate and suffer unexpected losses; but it was never rationally foreordained that they could not win. War, in particular, was a rational means to a rational end; victory would justify the risks and losses incurred, and the consequences of defeat were not from the outset out of all proportion to the gains to be expected from victory.

The possibility of all-out atomic war has destroyed these rational relationships. When universal destruction is the result of victory and defeat alike, war itself is no longer a matter of rational choice but becomes an instrument of suicidal despair. The pursuit of a nation's interests short of all-out atomic war, then, becomes a matter of self-preservation. Even on the assumption—at present a moot one—that limited wars can and will still be safely waged, the risk of such a limited war developing into an all-out atomic one will always be present. Hence, the imperative of the avoidance of all-out atomic war gives, at the very least, unprecedented urgency to the pursuit of a nation's interests by peaceful means. Such peaceful pursuit, as we know, spells diplomacy. Neither diplomacy nor all-out atomic war is today one among several rational choices available to a nation. As all-out atomic war is tantamount to suicide, so successful diplomacy provides the only certain chance for survival. A nation which under present conditions is either unwilling or unable to take full advantage of the traditional methods of diplomacy condemns itself either to the slow death of attrition or the sudden death of atomic destruction.

The vital importance that the traditional methods of diplomacy receive from the possibility of all-out atomic war is underlined by the more specific political developments which may well mark the end of the first postwar decade as the beginning of a new era in international relations. The first decade following the Second World War was characterized on the international scene by three basic political phenomena: the bipolarity of international politics, the tendency of this bipolar political system to transform itself into a two-bloc system, and the policy of containment. These three basic facts combined in minimizing the traditional methods of diplomacy, both as a matter of fact and in terms of the objective opportunities available.

During that decade, effective power for purposes of foreign policy was concentrated in Washington and Moscow, and these two power poles tended to attract like magnets most of the other centers of power. Whatever they might have preferred had they been free to choose, Great Britain and France, Poland and China had to lean upon one or the other of the superpowers for political, military, and economic support. Such countries could not have remained neutral, let alone have changed sides, in the East-West conflict, short of a domestic revolution of radical dimensions. In such a situation, rigid in its alignments and inflexible in either side's conception of the interests involved, the main task of both sides is not to make and receive concessions but, at the very least, to hold the line and, at the very best, to advance it unilaterally. Since the balance of power made the latter alternative unfeasible short of a general war, both sides were of necessity reduced to a policy of containment which for all practical purposes forsook advancement at the expense of the other side while at the same time preventing the other side from advancing.

Such a situation of "cold war" offered little opportunity for the use of diplomatic methods either within the two power blocs or between them. The inner coherence of the two blocs resulted primarily from the ineluctable necessity which made their members seek shelter under the roof of one or the other of the superpowers. During that period, the discrepancy of strength between the two superpowers, on the one hand, and their respective allies, on the other, was so obviously extreme and the consequences for those who would dare step out of line so obviously dire that there was very little need for diplomacy to crystallize so obvious a community of interests.

The relations between the two blocs were no less clearly defined by the objective situation. The essence of the policy of containment was military rather than political. It consisted in the main in the warning, supported by actual preparedness, that a step taken by the other side beyond the line of military demarcation of 1945 would of necessity lead to a general war.

The services diplomacy was able to perform for this policy of containment were hardly different from those diplomacy has traditionally performed for the conduct of real war. It could announce the conditions for the settlement of the Cold War and use such and similar announcements for purposes of psychological warfare. The very modalities of the Cold War, then, inevitably transformed diplomacy into a mere auxiliary of a war waged against the enemy, not for the purpose of accommodating conflicting interests, but for the triumph, however verbal, of one nation over the other. Thus it is not by accident that during the first decade following the Second

World War the traditional methods of diplomacy virtually ceased to operate in the relations between East and West and that the moves carried on under the labels and with the personnel of diplomacy at the many East-West conferences and within the United Nations served purposes not only far removed from but often diametrically opposed to those of traditional diplomacy.

This period of postwar history has come to a close. It is being replaced by an era marked by greater flexibility within the two power blocs—a tendency toward the loosening of their inner coherence if not toward their dissolution—and, consequently, by greater flexibility in the relationship between the two power blocs as well. To meet the problems of this new era the methods of the Cold War are inadequate. As the conditions of the Cold War led necessarily to the disuse and misuse of the practices of diplomacy, so the new era of international relations with equal necessity calls for the restoration of these practices.

Four facts are in the main responsible for this change in international relations: the decrease in the dependence of the powers of second rank upon the superpowers; the impending rise of Germany and Japan to great-power status; the impending dispersion of atomic power among a multitude of nations, some of which, by virtue of their possession of atomic power, will gain or regain the status of great powers; finally, the spread and sharpening of the colonial revolutions in Asia, Africa, and Latin America.

Viewed from the vantage point of the United States, each of these new facts requires the vigorous application of the traditional practices of diplomacy. Since neither the American atomic monopoly nor extreme dependence upon American support can any longer be relied upon to secure the coherence of the Western alliance, the United States must again resort to the time-honored diplomatic method of fashioning a legally and politically viable community of interests out of the one that exists objectively in an inchoate and ill-defined form. Germany and Japan, no longer the object of the victor's dispositions, must be persuaded by the same methods to see in association with the West the best chance for pursuing their interests. It is hardly necessary to emphasize that a similar approach to the colonial revolutions has been long overdue.

Thus the situation that confronts the United States at the moment of this writing poses the perennial problem of diplomacy with renewed urgency. The objections to the use of diplomacy are without merit. Its indispensability for a successful and peaceful foreign policy grows from the very nature of things political. The possibility of all-out atomic war has made its successful use the condition of survival. The new era of international relations has made its restoration of vital concern for the foreign policy of the United States.

16 _The Decline of Democratic Government_

Democratic government in the United States has declined by virtue of three basic misunderstandings: misunderstanding of the nature of politics, of the purposes of government in a revolutionary age, of the function of government in a democracy. These misunderstandings have corrupted our political judgment and perverted our actions with a subtle yet well-nigh irresistible logic.

Under the impact of nineteenth-century liberalism, Anglo-American society has been strongly influenced, and at times dominated, by a philosophy that denies politics a prominent and honorable place in the order of things. Politics as a conflict of interests decided through a struggle for power is here regarded as an ephemeral phenomenon, a kind of residue of either aristocratic or capitalistic society, for the time being to be pushed into a corner fenced off by constitutional safeguards and ultimately to be abolished altogether. The corollary to this conception of politics as a passing and inferior phase of social life is the erection of the private virtues as the sole standard by which the qualities of both private and public action and the qualifications of both private and public persons are to be judged. This philosophy necessarily destroys the tension between the private and the public sphere, between man per se and man as a citizen, which has been a perennial theme of Western political thought. For that philosophy, Aristotle's question of whether the virtue of a good man is identical with the virtue of a good citizen is meaningless, for here the virtue of a good man and of a good citizen are by definition identical.

This philosophy is translated into the folklore of American politics as the conviction that the main qualification for a political career is personal honesty. A politician may be wrongheaded in judgment, weak in decision, unsuccessful in action. "But don't you see how sincere he is," people will say. "He is at least an honest man." "He means well." The man in the street transfers the values he cherishes in his private life to the political stage and judges the actors by the same standards he applies to himself and his fellows in their private spheres.

The values of the Eisenhower administration, both in verbal expression and in the character of its most prominent members, conform to these popular standards, and its virtually unshakable popularity owes much to this identity of political standards. The President, with characteristic frankness and consistency, has time and again measured his public actions by the yardstick of private values and expressed his conviction that since he did not find these public actions wanting, when tested by the values of private life, they had passed the political test as well. He summarized his philosophy in his news conference of August 8, 1957, in these terms: "I, as you know, never employ threats. I never try to hold up clubs of any kind, I just say, 'this is what I believe to be best for the United States,' and I try to convince people by the logic of my position. If that is wrong politically, well then I suppose you will just have to say I am wrong, but that is my method, and that is what I try to do." The public sphere appears here as a mere extension of private life, devoid of those conflicts of interests to be settled by contests of power, by employing threats and holding up clubs—methods which are traditionally associated with politics—and subject to the same rational rules of conduct which are supposed to make the private sphere orderly, peaceful, and harmonious.

When the President was asked at his news conference of July 31, 1957, about the circumstances under which Mr. Gluck was appointed ambassador to Ceylon, he replied with indignation, ". . . in the first place, if anybody is ever recommended to me on the basis of any contribution he has ever made to any political party, that man will never be considered. I never heard it mentioned to me as a consideration, and I don't take it very kindly as suggesting I would be influenced by such things." Here again, the issue was seen in strictly private terms. The issue for the President hinged exclusively upon his personal knowledge of a campaign contribution, and since he had no such knowledge there was no issue. In this philosophy there is no room for the recognition of an objective conflict of interests to which the state of the conscience of any single individual may well be irrelevant.

It stands to reason that Mr. George Humphrey's philosophy of government is simply the application of the alleged principles of private business to the political sphere. And for Mr. Charles Wilson national defense was a problem of production and organization within the limits of sound finance as defined by Mr. Humphrey, completely divorced from any meaningful political context. Of the many of Mr. Wilson's statements showing a complete unawareness of this political context, none is perhaps more revealing than the one he made June 29, 1956, as a witness before the Senate Armed Services Subcommittee on Air Power:

> The Russian people, the ones that I have known through the years, have a great many qualities that Americans have. As a matter of fact, basically I think that the Russian people rather like Americans.
>
> It is too bad that we have got this conflict of ideology and that they have got a dictatorship on their hands. They wanted to get rid of the czar and they got something that is just as bad or worse, temporarily.
>
> It is very interesting. One of the troubles, they think of our type of free competitive society as the same thing they had under the czars, and of course it is not that thing at all. They have replaced in what you might call their point of hate.
>
> It is too bad they did away with the czars completely. If some of them were still left in one piece of Russia so they could hate the czars, they would not be hating our people so much.

A defense establishment which is intended to cope with an international situation thus conceived in terms of private emotions is likely to be different from one that seeks to defend the national interest in a world of conflicting interests and competing power.

Not only have the dominant members of the Eisenhower administration expressed themselves and acted in terms of a philosophy alien to politics, but many of them have also been selected in view of their excellence as private citizens, on the assumption that the qualities which go into the making of a good man and, more particularly, of a good businessman, go also into the making of a good statesman. Indeed, many selections have been excellent within the limits of the standards applied. Certainly, men like Eisenhower, Benson, Humphrey, and Wilson are superior in private excellence to many of their respective predecessors. But these excellent men have in all innocence done greater damage to the political life and the political interests of the nation than many of their less worthy predecessors; for they have brought to their public offices nothing but personal excellence, no understanding of political life, let alone ability to cope with the processes of politics.

The experience of this contrast between personal excellence and, more particularly, success in business and failure in politics is by no means limited to this administration nor even to this country. Look at the records of Baldwin and Chamberlain in Great Britain, of Cuno and Bruning in Germany! They were all good men, and how ruinous their governments were for their respective nations! In this country it is particularly illuminating to compare the virtually uniform political failure of the production geniuses with the spectacular political successes of the investment bankers. Why is it that the Knudsens and the Wilsons have failed and the Forrestals, the Lovetts, the Nitzes have succeeded? Because the excellence of the investment banker is, as it were, akin to that of the statesman while the excellence of the production genius is alien to it.

A good man who becomes an actor on the political scene without knowing anything about the rules of politics is like a good man who goes into business without knowing anything about it or who drives a car while being ignorant of driving. Yet while it is well recognized that society must protect itself against the latter, it feels no need for protection against the former. The virtuous political dilettante has for it even a well-nigh irresistible fascination. It is as though society were anxious to atone for the sacrifices of private virtue which the political sphere demands and to take out insurance against the moral risks of political action by identifying itself with political leaders who sacrifice the public good on the altar of their private virtue.

Society has learned to take the bad men in its stride and even to protect itself against those who know the rules of the political game only too well and use them to the detriment of society. Society will have to learn, if it wants to survive, that it needs protection also from the good men who are too good even to take note of the rules of the political game. And it must reconcile itself to the uncomfortable paradox that bad men who put their knowledge of those rules at the service of society are to be preferred to good men whose ignorance and moral selfishness put the very survival of society in jeopardy. In short, it must learn what Henry Taylor taught more than a century ago when he wrote in the *Statesman:* "It sometimes happens that he who would not hurt a fly will hurt a nation."

From the soil of this misunderstanding of what politics is all about two intellectual and political weeds have grown: utopian liberalism and utopian conservatism. This country has had its share of the former; it is now being taught the political lessons of the latter. Conservatism has become a modish word, which has been made to provide respectable cover for a multitude of intellectual and political sins. As the nihilists of the Left call themselves democratic, while disavowing with their very being the tenets of democracy, so the nihilists of the Right, who used in the twenties and thirties to proclaim their adherence to "true" democracy, now try to monopolize conservatism for themselves. Yet the iron test of the authenticity of a professed conservatism is its attitude to civil liberties, that is, restraints upon the powers of government on behalf of the individual. By this test, Hegel, at the beginning of the nineteenth century, could deny Haller the right to call himself conservative, and the German resistance to Nazism was as authentically conservative as McCarthyism, in spite of its claim, was not.

Authentic conservatism concerns either the philosophy and methods of politics or its purposes. The confusion between these two types is likely to do more damage to American politics in the long run than political nihilism, pretending to be conservative, has done. Conservatism of philosophy and method is indeed part and parcel of the American political tradition. *The Federalist* is its greatest literary monument, Alexander Hamilton is its greatest theoretician, John Quincy Adams and Abraham Lincoln are in different ways its greatest practitioners, and Woodrow Wilson is its greatest antithesis in theory and practice. That conservatism holds—as we saw the realist philosophy of international relations to hold—that the world, imperfect as it is from the rational point of view, is the result of forces inherent in human nature. To improve the world one must work with those forces, not against them. This being inherently a world of opposing interests and of conflict among them, moral principles can never be fully realized, but must at best be approximated through the ever temporary balancing of interests and the ever

285

precarious settlement of conflicts. Conservatism, then, sees in a system of checks and balances a universal principle for all pluralist societies. It appeals to historic precedent rather than abstract principles and aims at the realization of the lesser evil rather than of the absolute good.

A good case can be made, it seems to me, in favor of the proposition that this conservatism of philosophy and method presents political reality as it ought to be presented and deals with it as it ought to be dealt with. I have argued that case more than a decade ago in *Scientific Man vs. Power Politics*, when, I might say in passing, it was not fashionable but most unwelcome to argue the conservative side of political philosophy and method.

On the other hand, the conservative view of the purposes of politics endows the status quo with a special dignity and seeks to maintain and improve it. This conservatism lives in the best of all possible worlds, and, if it can conceive of a different world at all, it finds that world not in the future but in the past, a golden age to be restored. That conservatism has its natural political environment in Europe; it has no place in the American tradition of politics. Europe, in contrast to America, has known classes, determined by heredity or otherwise sharply and permanently defined in composition and social status, which have had a stake in defending the present status quo or restoring an actual or fictitious status quo of the past. But for the defense or restoration of what status quo could the American conservative fight? For private power, state's rights, the abolition of the income tax, exclusive male suffrage, nullification, slavery, or perhaps the British monarchy? The absurdity of this rhetorical question illustrates the absurdity of the conservative position in terms of purposes within the context of American politics.

The great issues of American politics concern neither the preservation of the present nor the restoration of the past but the creation, without reference to either, of the future. American politics does not defend the past and present against the future but one kind of future against another kind of future. While in philosophy and method conservatism is the most potent single influence in American politics, the purposes of our politics from the very beginning were unique and revolutionary, not only in the narrow political sense, but also in the more general terms of being oblivious to tradition. They have so remained throughout, only temporarily disfigured by periods which were dominated by a conservatism of purpose and, hence, in the context of American politics spelled stagnation. In other words, the point of reference of American politics has never been the present, and only in a historically inconsequential way has it been the past.

In the past, the United States could afford such intermittent periods of stagnation; for the world around it, relatively speaking, stagnated too, and, more importantly, when the United States moved forward again it set the pace for the world and in many respects left it behind. Today it is the world that moves ahead and the United States which is being left behind. All around us the world is in violent transformation. The political revolution has destroyed the state system, which for half a millennium had provided the political girders for Western civilization, and has brought to the fore two superpowers threatening each other and the world with destruction. At the same time it has dissolved the old order of empire into the anarchy of scores of feeble sovereignties, whose uncontrolled frictions may well provide the sparks for the ultimate conflagration. A succession of technological revolutions has virtually eliminated the elements of time and space from this globe and, by adding to the numerical superiority of the so-called backward peoples the social and military potential of modern industry, challenges Western civilization from still another quarter. Finally, the moral revolution of totalitarianism denies the basic values upon which Western civilization has been built and, as bolshevism, attracts millions of people throughout the world to its militant support.

How have we reacted to this triple challenge? We have reacted by a conservatism of stagnation, which is not only oblivious of the revolutionary dynamism of our national tradition but also self-defeating as a weapon in the international contest in which the nation is engaged. We have projected the antirevolutionary and conservative image of our national task and destiny onto the international scene, seeing in the political, technological, and moral ferment of the world but the evil effects of the cunning obstinacy of the doomed leaders of bolshevism. Unwilling to adjust the comforting and flattering picture we have formed of our national life to the national realities, we proceeded to adjust the international realities to that picture. Thus we are looking at a world which appears in need of improvement, adjustment, and reform, but not of radical, unheard-of change. The world cries out for transformations commensurate in their revolutionary novelty with the revolutions that threaten it; it cries out for political imagination, audacity, and the risky experiment. What we are offering it is nothing but stagnation, masquerading in the garb of a utopian conservatism. Faced with the moral and virtually certain danger that soon a great number of nations will have atomic weapons, we continue the old game of disarmament negotiations, which is no longer good even for purposes of propaganda. Our policies in Europe and Asia are stagnant; we continue unwilling either to change the status quo of which we disapprove or to recognize it. Latin America has become our forgotten back yard which we think we can take for granted. Asia, the Middle East, and Africa are for us primarily opportunities for the conclusion of military alliances and the expenditure of money for ill-defined purposes.

In consequence of underestimating the revolutionary tradition of our society and the revolutionary nature of the world with which we must come to terms, we have made underestimation of the Soviet Union a national habit of mind. All the evidence of the Russian capabilities, from General Guillaume's "Soviet Arms and Soviet Power," published in 1949 by the *Infantry Journal,* to our own intelligence reports, made no impression upon the official mind; for if it had, we would have had to discard a whole philosophy which we are mistaking for our way of life.

This retreat into a stagnant conservatism has been accompanied by a retreat from government itself. This is not surprising, since the conservative commitment to holding the line, to keeping things as they are in domestic and foreign policy, required less of an expenditure of energy and of ideas than dynamic and imaginative policies do. That this atrophy of government, inevitably resulting from the atrophy of its purposes, has been acutely aggravated by the lapse of leadership at the top is too obvious to require elaboration; but it might be pointed out that that lapse of leadership was, in turn, made possible and perhaps even temporarily tolerable by that decline in purpose.

When we speak of the atrophy of government, we obviously do

not refer to the quantity of institutions and their activities which go by the name of government; for there has been no decline of those. What we have in mind is a subtle quality which is vital to a democratic government: its quality as a teacher and leader. In its absence the government cannot govern in a truly democratic fashion, that is, with the freely given consent of the governed. Modern government—democratic or non-democratic—is not merely the formulation and execution of policies. It is also and necessarily the creation of public consent for the policies formulated and to be executed. In non-democratic societies this consent is created by the government's monopolistic manipulation of the mass media of communication. Democracies create it ideally through the free interplay of plural opinions and interests, out of which the consensus of the majority emerges.

From these different conceptions of consent two different attitudes toward secrecy and truth follow. A non-democratic government can afford to conceal and misrepresent because there are no autonomous social forces which could expose it to scrutiny and propose factual and political alternatives. Under certain conditions, it will even be compelled to conceal and misrepresent because it will have no other way to create consent for its policy. A democratic government, while having an obvious advantage in the contest of opinion, ideally at least cannot afford nor does it need to conceal and misrepresent. A responsible parliament and an alert public opinion force it to lay its cards on the table or at the very least check the government version of the truth against their own. And the assumption of democratic pluralism that neither the government nor anybody else has a monopoly of truth in matters political minimizes the temptation for the government to impose its version upon society by concealment and misrepresentation.

It is the measure of the decline of democratic government in the United States that the administration has—not on occasion but consistently—concealed from the people and its elected representatives information in both the most vital and the most trivial matters and misrepresented the truth known to it. While the administration was aware of the deterioration of American power in comparison with that of the Soviet Union, its most eminent spokesmen assured us time

289

and again that our strength vis-à-vis the Soviet Union was unimpaired if not actually increased. What we were told officially was, at best, but a hint of the actual state of affairs. To speak of very trivial things in passing, the American people have not been allowed to learn what present the king of Saudi Arabia gave the President on his visit in January, 1957.

Secrecy and misrepresentation, not as occasional aberrations but as a system of government, are in our case intimately related to the atrophy of government of which we have spoken earlier. The administration, philosophically and politically committed to stagnation and, hence, unable to lead and educate, has put appearance in the place of substance. Thus it is not by accident that the techniques of advertising have so thoroughly replaced the processes of free discussion in the relations between government and people. Judged by the standards of advertising, the result has been gratifying. The administration has been popular, and the people have been happy. Yet judged by the standards of the American destiny and survival, the result has been disquieting in the extreme. We witness the beginning of a crisis of confidence in the administration, and we must beware lest it turn into a crisis of confidence in the democratic processes themselves.

Before men want to be governed well, they want to be governed. Before they choose between good and bad policies, they want some policies to choose from. Regardless of the course they want the ship of state to take, they want to be sure that a strong hand is at the helm. The great revolutions of the modern age—from the French Revolution of 1789 through the two Russian revolutions of 1917 and the Fascist revolutions in Italy and Germany to the Chinese revolution of the forties—were carried forward by men who were dismayed, not only at being governed badly, but also and more importantly at not being governed enough. These revolutions owed their success to the determination and ability of their leaders to seize power, to hold it, and to use it to govern perhaps badly but firmly. The modern masses have risen in despair and fury not against some particular policy but against the weakness of government, reflected in spectacular failures.

Of the failures which are likely to be in store for us, we have had only a first and very partial glimpse. We are but at the beginning of our disillusions, frustrations, and tribulations. Faced with this crisis in its fortunes, as taxing as any it has experienced, the nation certainly stands in need of sound policies. What it needs more is a government that restores its sense of mission, that galvanizes its latent energies by giving them a purpose, that, in short, acts as the guardian of the nation's past and an earnest of its future. The nation has no such government now.

DILEMMAS

OF POLITICAL

ACTION

The Integrity of Political Action

As the autonomy of the political sphere must be protected from the encroachments of other spheres of action, so must its integrity be safeguarded against corruption from within. This conflict between integrity and corruption creates the classic dilemma of democratic politics. The democracy of ancient Greece fell victim to it, and we suffer from it, unwilling to face it and, if for no other reason, unable to cope with it. Stripped to their essentials, the two horns of the dilemma are the demands of right political action in terms of the action's justice and success and the demands of political power in terms of the actor's personal success, which depends in good measure upon the approval of a largely ignorant and emotional public. In one word, this is the dilemma between statesmanlike and demagogic action.

It is the essence of the dilemma that in a democracy it is at the very best difficult and hazardous to satisfy these two demands simultaneously and that, especially in the short run, it is frequently impossible to do so. The right political action—right in terms of the justice of ends and means and of the expediency of means—is likely to be unpopular and, hence, endanger the actor's political power, and the latter requires to be safeguarded by action which, while popular, is likely to be unsound. Furthermore, the soundness of a policy, in so far as it is revealed by its success, frequently becomes apparent only in the long run, while the demands of personal power must be satisfied in the short run. As Machiavelli put it:

> Here we have to note two things; first, that the people often, deceived by an illusive good, desire their own ruin, and, unless they are made sensible of the evil of the one and the benefit of the other course by some one in whom they have confidence, they will expose the republic to infinite peril and damage. And if it happens that the people have no confidence in any one, as sometimes will be the case when they have been deceived before by events or men, then it will inevitably lead to the ruin of the state. Dante says upon this point in his discourse "On Monarchy," that the people often shout, "Life to our death, and death to our life!" It is this want of confidence on the part of the people that causes good measures to be often rejected in republics. . . . If we consider now what is easy and what difficult to persuade a people to, we may make this distinction: either what you wish to persuade them to represents at first sight gain or loss, or it seems brave or cowardly. And if you propose to them anything that upon its face seems profitable and courageous, though there be really a loss concealed under it which may involve the ruin of the republic, the multitude will ever be most easily persuaded to it. But if the measure proposed seems doubtful and likely to cause loss, then it will be difficult to persuade the people to it, even though the benefit and welfare of the republic were concealed under it.[1]

The actor, having to strike a balance between two demands, none of which he is able to satisfy fully, is forced by the very logic of the democratic process, if he were not already by the propensities of his human nature, to yield to the demands of personal power more than to those of right political action. For if he were to act otherwise he would thereby jeopardize his very ability to act at all on the political stage: his personal power. Starting out with a compromise between the demands of sound policy and the demands of personal power, he is tempted to follow what appears in the short run to be the line of least resistance, by sacrificing more and more of the substance of sound policy to considerations of personal power. This process of corruption, particularly far advanced in foreign policy, puts into question the very survival of democratic government.

[1] *Discourses on Livy* i. 53.

17 *The Decline of the Democratic Process*

The crisis of American politics, domestic and international, and the prevailing unawareness of its gravity and of its very existence are rooted in two misunderstandings and misuses of American democracy. They affect the very essence of democratic government. One concerns the position and functions of the President; the other, the relationship between the requirements of sound policy and the will of the majority. The major weaknesses of American policies can be traced to one or the other or both of these misunderstandings and misuses.

Democratic government is government by popular choice—choice of men and, through it, choice of policy. A government that can keep itself in power regardless of the preferences of the people is not democratic at all; a government whose choice by the people does not also imply a choice of policy is but imperfectly so. It follows that a perfectly democratic system of government must be partisan government in the sense that those who have been elected to govern stand for one set of policies and those who have been rejected at the polls are committed to another set of policies. The candidates for office have been judged by the policies with which they are identified and by their ability to carry them through, and at the next elections they will again be judged by these criteria.

The government of the United States, as presently constituted on its highest level, is not perfectly democratic. The President was re-elected in 1956, not because he stood for specific policies which the electorate preferred to those of his opponent, but because he was committed only to general aspirations shared by all men of good will. It is exactly this lack of partisanship, this commitment to unexceptional generalities which imply no commitment to anything concrete in terms of policy, which made him into the incarnation of the nation's better self, the symbol of its nobler longings. Thus he was re-elected, not on the strength of particular foreign policies executed or proposed, but as a symbol of the nation's longing for peace, as the man who had brought peace to Korea and would preserve it elsewhere.

This popular image of the President reflects Mr. Eisenhower's own conception of the Presidency in theory and practice. Supported by an optimistic philosophy, unaware of man's propensities for evil and the tragic dilemmas of human existence, he has limited himself, by and large, to the enunciation of general principles, leaving the political task of their implementation to subordinates or to nobody in particular. His interest in factual information and day-by-day administration has been sporadic, and his intervention in the formation of policy has generally been reserved for crisis situations. Thus the President, by divorcing his person and his office from the partisanship of politics, has transformed the character of politics itself. Politics has lost its fanatical partisanship and bitter animosities, and the warming benevolence of a President who appears to be above politics envelops the nation as in a *union sacrée*.

It is the fatal weakness of Mr. Eisenhower's contribution to the substance of American foreign policy that it is informed by the same philosophy of abstention, conciliation, and pacification as is his domestic one. Conciliation and pacification as ends in themselves can, under certain circumstances, be virtues at home; they are, except under the rarest of circumstances, vices abroad. And one may well speculate whether the price the nation will have to pay in the long run even for its present domestic tranquillity in terms of moral stagnation, intellectual sterility, issues unrecognized, and problems unsolved will not turn out to be vastly excessive.

The price we must pay for international tranquillity as an end in itself is not a matter of speculation but of historic experience. Optimistic assumptions about human nature may be able to support for a while domestic policies carried on in a civilized Western society. They are bound to be disappointed on the international scene. For here conciliation and peace can hardly ever be ends in themselves but must be sought as the by-product of a political settlement which actually reconciles antagonistic interests and thereby deprives the parties concerned of the incentive to seek redress by force. At home and abroad, the President's philosophy spells avoidance of problems, abstention from action, tranquillity as an end in itself. Yet what can be tolerated in the short run at home—for here the agencies for thought and action other than the President continuously operate on behalf of the United States—becomes a mortal danger abroad. For if the United States does not reflect on the problems that concern it and does not try to solve them on its own terms, the enemies of the United States do so reflect and act. International peace and tranquillity achieved at the price of abstention from thought and action, then, are tantamount to retreat and surrender.

The new conception of the Presidency not only impairs the freedom of choice at democracy's decisive moment—the presidential elections—and leads to impotence in its application to foreign policy but it also impairs the day-by-day democratic processes by destroying the functions of the opposition. Historically, that destruction has manifested itself as the corruption of bipartisanship in foreign policy. Bipartisanship, as originally conceived at the end of the Second World War, carried the negative implication that a foreign policy ought not to be opposed by one party for the sole reason that the President and Secretary of State belonging to the other party were carrying it out. In positive terms, bipartisanship implied that the opposition party should support sound foreign policies and oppose unsound ones, regardless of the party affiliation of those carrying them out. Conceived in these terms, bipartisanship recognized the elemental fact that the consequences of foreign policy are not limited, as are those of many domestic ones, to a particular segment of the population identified with one or the other party, but affect the whole nation for generations to come. Bipartisanship drew from this fact the sound and indispensable conclusion that party strife for its own sake must stop at the point where the whole nation meets other nations in defense of its interests and its very existence.

However, bipartisanship, as originally conceived, never did imply that the opposition should not oppose when opposition appeared justified by the demerits of the foreign policy pursued. Nor did it imply that the opposition should forego what is not only its privilege but also its mission, whose fulfilment is indispensable for the proper functioning of the democratic process: to submit alternative policies for the administration to adopt or else for the people to support by changing the administration. An opposition that does not perform these two functions deprives the people in yet another way of that choice of policies essential to democracy.

This is indeed what the opposition was doing during Mr. Eisenhower's first term. It abdicated its mission, confounding bipartisanship with conformity. What did its titular head and its leaders in Congress contribute to public enlightenment, to the clarification of the issues, to intellectual and political pressure upon the administration? What the policy of the British Labour party was in successive international crises we know. But what was the policy of the Democratic party of the United States? The answer is simple and disquieting: there was no such policy. Nor is the picture that the mass media of communication present much more reassuring. A very few notable exceptions notwithstanding, the abdication of judgment and will of the political opposition was duplicated here. Everybody seemed to emulate the President's example and rise above politics, sharing in the nobility of his sentiments and general objectives. The result is national unity, paid for with the lifeblood of the democratic process. For this is not the unity of a people who, after weighing the alternatives, have decided what they want and how to get what they want. It is rather like a fog that makes us all brothers in blindness.

Yet among those whose duty it is to lead by criticizing and proposing—the public officials, politicians, correspondents, columnists, commentators, academicians—the failure is one of will rather than of judgment. Of those who keep silent or speak only by indirection so great as to confuse the ignorant and to be intelligible only to the informed, the great majority know the awful truth. Why is it that during Mr. Eisenhower's first term none of the policy-makers who express their misgivings and forebodings freely in private raised his voice in anguish or resigned in protest? And what of all the others who have to risk much less? They have all become the victims of the official conception of the Presidency, which allows only of whispered hints as some isolated deficiency here and there and must regard political attack and even frank debate, the very dynamics of democracy, as a sacrilege against the spirit of the nation, incarnate as it is in the person of the President.

The debilitating effect which a new conception of the Presidency and the corruption of bipartisanship reflecting it has had upon the foreign policy of the United States is, in turn, reflected and aggravated by a new conception of the office of the Secretary of State and a new method of gaining public and, more particularly, congressional support in the conduct of foreign policy.

Mr. Dulles' conception of his office in one respect curiously duplicates Mr. Eisenhower's conception of the Presidency: both conceive of their offices as being divorced from the day-by-day operations of policy formation and execution. What Gettysburg and Augusta are for the President, all the capitals of the world are for the Secretary of State: respectable escapes from the daily responsibilities of government. Here, however, the analogy ends. For while Mr. Dulles has shut himself off from the regular departmental channels of information and advice, he has kept a monopoly on major policy decisions and has taken an unprecedentedly large part in certain phases of their execution, so large a part as to keep him from his desk for about one-third of his tenure of office. The results have been unfortunate in four different respects.

The Secretary of State has been unable to perform adequately the very functions of policy formation which he considers his exclusive prerogative. Not even the wisest and most experienced of secretaries of state can afford to dispense with the information and advice of his subordinates; and the most traveled of secretaries of state can afford it even less. The great abilities and greater self-confidence of Mr. Dulles have not compensated for this deficiency. In consequence, Mr. Dulles has not had the time or the incentive, in terms of new knowledge and new ideas, to deal constructively with the drastic changes that have occurred in recent years on the international scene. This is one of the reasons why his tenure of office has been outstanding not for bold initiative and innovation in policy but rather for the virtually mechanical continuation of established routines long after they had served their purpose.

Mr. Dulles' assumption of the role of roving ambassador and ubiquitous negotiator has impaired the performance of his functions in yet another way. There is great wisdom, reflecting the nature of things, in the tradition that requires the head of the foreign office to stay at home and reflect and decide, and the ambassadors to go abroad and negotiate. This division of labor not only frees the head of the foreign office from preoccupation with details obstructing his over-all view of foreign relations but also protects him from involvement in the intrigues, indiscretions, and commitments inseparable from the routine of diplomacy. Mr. Dulles, by doing what ambassadors are supposed to do, has not been able to do the job only he could have done. Furthermore, he has wasted the prestige of his office on a multitude of minutiae, magnifying them far beyond their intrinsic importance. He owes his unpopularity abroad and the foreign mistrust of his word in good measure to that assumption of functions which no Secretary of State ought to assume.

The Secretary of State has also been unable to exert effective control over his department on behalf of his own policies. Mr. Dulles has sought to carry the formation of policy in his own head and leave the implementation of the policy through day-by-day administration and execution to subordinates. Yet in actual performance policy formation cannot be so neatly separated from implementation, and those who control the day-by-day operations of the Department uncontrolled by the Secretary become, by the very logic of their functions, makers of policy on their own. The permanent functional and frequent physical separation of the Secretary from the Department has transformed the top echelon of his subordinates into a sort of collective leadership performing the institutional functions of the Secretary without his permanent control and without his authority. Thus the undersecretary of state, the counselor, the legal adviser, certain deputy undersecretaries and assistant secretaries, severally or collectively, have been carrying out functions which only the Secretary should perform and can perform successfully.

Such a state of affairs is fraught with danger under the best of circumstances, that is, when the Secretary and his immediate subordinates see eye to eye on policy; for it is bound to result in misunderstandings, misinterpretations, disorganization, and the incoherence of policies. However, the circumstances under which Mr. Dulles' system has operated were never of the best. For reasons that shall be discussed in a moment, Mr. Dulles frequently appointed to key positions in his department men who were out of sympathy with his own policies. This being so, it is but natural that in the process of execution the Secretary's policies were often infused with the spirit of their opponents. The Secretary's policies were sometimes so completely perverted by his subordinates that deliberate sabotage provides the only plausible explanation.

The effects of this situation were clear to see in the Suez crisis of

November, 1956. The Department of State ceased to function as the instrument of a viable American foreign policy. It split into two factions, committed to radically different and mutually exclusive policies. One faction looked at the trend of American foreign policy with alarm and despair. The other faction welcomed that trend, being in good measure of its own making, with enthusiastic expectations. One day, one faction seemed to prevail; another day, the other, and there was nobody above them to mold out of the welter of opinion a foreign policy capable of execution and promising success.

These weaknesses were compounded by the revival of a propensity, which has at times exerted a strong influence upon the conduct of American foreign policy, to look at foreign policy with a lawyer's eye and to manipulate it with a lawyer's tools. It would certainly be preposterous to suggest that lawyers cannot make great statesmen and diplomatists; the pages of history are full of them. But those lawyers were transformed by their political experience into something more than lawyers; they were able to transcend the limits of their craft. It is the strength and weakness of Mr. Dulles that he has brought to his office a first-rate legal mind which excels in negotiations and in deft maneuver but fails in the constructive tasks of statesmanship. For the lawyer's mind is uncongenial to these tasks.

The lawyer sees reality dissolved into a sequence of isolated "cases," each to be dealt with on its "merits." Thus Great Britain and France committed "aggression" against Egypt and must not be allowed to get away with it. Little does it matter that this "case" has a history which antedates the invasion of Egypt and that it will make history long after the last British and French soldiers have left Egyptian territory. Let us first close this "case" by restoring the pre-invasion status quo, and we shall then turn to the next "case" if and when it arises. The subject matter with which the lawyer thus endeavors to deal being a continuum of which the particular "case" is an organic and inseparable element, the lawyer's method is singularly inadequate to deal with it. Its political manifestations are the conception of policy as the reaction to the initiative of others; improvisation, since before a "case" arises there is nothing to be done; aversion to long-range planning, since the scope of action is limited by the dimensions of the "case" and when the "case" is settled action must await another "case."

The lawyer is particularly averse to long-range planning that entails risks and requires daring because he has been conditioned in dealing with his clients—and is not the government just another client?—to chart a course that avoids trouble, minimizes risks, and is plainly calculable. He plans foreign policy as he would plan an estate. Examining a plan for action, he sets himself the task of finding its faults in terms of these criteria, and he cannot help finding them in any plan for international action. For such is the nature of foreign policy that success must be paid for with troubles, risks, and the threat of the unknown. To be fearful of that price means to do nothing, and the lawyer's caution becomes the paralysis of the statesman.

These deficiencies which have sapped the strength of American foreign policy are overshadowed in lasting importance by a dilemma which is, as it were, built into the constitutional and political system of the United States: how to reconcile the requirements of sound foreign policy with the requirement of popular and, more particularly, congressional support. The problem of how to reconcile these two factors which in the nature of things cannot be fully reconciled has bedeviled the conduct of American foreign policy since Washington's day. For, if American statesmen go too far in complying with the requirements of sound foreign policy, they are likely to lose the support of opinion at home; if they go too far in accommodating that opinion at the expense of what sound foreign policy requires, they risk jeopardizing the interests of the country and thus in the long run the support of opinion as well.

The task of the statesman, then, is twofold: to impress upon the people the requirements of sound foreign policy by telling them the facts of political life and what they require of the nation, and then to strike a compromise which leaves the essence of a sound foreign policy intact. It must be said, and it is being said with deep regret by one who expected great things in this regard from the co-operation between an immensely popular President and an experienced and skilful Secretary of State, that the Eisenhower administration has failed in both tasks. It is this failure which is in good measure responsible for the sterility of American foreign policy, for the dis-

asters which have befallen and threaten it, and for the popular ignorance of the bearing of these disasters upon the future of America
and of the world.

That the administration has failed to educate the people hardly
needs to be argued. Official statements have been consistently at
odds with the facts and their import for the interests and policies of
the United States. Let anyone make a compilation of the official
statements about the Suez Canal crisis and compare them with the
facts as reported by the same newspapers! Let anyone undertake a
history of world affairs since 1953, using only official statements and
forgetting everything else he knows, and what a mélange of fiction
and caricature we would get! In one word, the public relations expert has taken over from the statesman.

In the task of fashioning a compromise between the requirements
of foreign policy and the preferences of public opinion, the administration has likewise failed. The Secretary of State has been haunted
by the memory of his able and high-minded predecessor who failed
in this task because he failed to marshal public opinion in support of
sound policies and compounded his failure when in the end he even
embraced unsound ones without gaining popular support. Mr. Dulles
resolved not to repeat that failure. Instead of heeding Sir William
Harcourt's advice that "political heads of departments are necessary
to tell the civil service what the public will not stand," thus approaching the public with a sound and settled policy, he would first get
popular and, more particularly, congressional support at whatever
cost in policy commitments and then, with the home front secure,
face the nations of the world with the right policies. The plan was
ingenious but doomed to failure on two counts. Its success was pred-
icated upon the possibility of appeasing the opponents of American
foreign policy as it had developed since 1939, and that possibility
never existed. No concession could reconcile these men to the
active involvement of the United States in the affairs of the world,
to its risks, liabilities, opportunities, and rewards. They had to be
disarmed and neutralized, not appeased. Yet by trying to appease
them, Mr. Dulles destroyed the very instrument without which no
foreign policy could be successfully pursued, his own department,
and narrowed his freedom of action to such an extent as to foreclose
any fresh initiative, any creative response to novel situations.

The destruction of the Department of State proceeded in two stages: the elimination of most of the able and experienced members of its higher ranks and the appointment to key positions of men whose main qualification was sympathy with the philosophy and policies of the irrreconcilable opposition. Thus foreign aid was administered by a man who did not believe in foreign aid; the Refugee Act was administered by a man who did not believe in immigration; some key men in the Far Eastern Division do not believe in negotiations with Communist China; and the only visible qualification of one undersecretary of state for his eminent position was the Hoover name which evokes memories dear to the opposition. The purpose of these appointments was to commit the opposition to the support of the foreign policies of the administration. Actually they committed a powerful group within the Department to the support of opposition policies. The opposition, far from giving hostages to Mr. Dulles, imprisoned him in a cell of old ideas and old policies from which he could not move when momentous opportunities for fresh initiatives—the atomic stalemate, the new Soviet policies, the stirrings of Asia and Africa, the disintegration of the alliances, the rise of Germany and Japan—knocked at the door.

What of the remedy? What of the cure? The cure is as grand and simple as the disease is stark and simple.

It is for the President to reassert his historic role as both the initiator of policy and the awakener of public opinion. It is true that only a strong, wise, and shrewd President can marshal to the support of wise policies the strength and wisdom latent in that slumbering giant—American public opinion. Yet while it is true that great men have rarely been elected President of the United States, it is upon that greatness, which is the greatness of its people personified, that the United States, from Washington to Franklin D. Roosevelt, has had to rely in the conduct of its foreign affairs. It is upon that greatness that Western Civilization must rely for its survival.

Those words we addressed in 1949 to Mr. Eisenhower's predecessor. If they were true then they are true today. Will Mr. Eisenhower heed their truth? Will he ever know that it exists?

18 *The Corruption of Patriotism*

Of the surrender of sound principles of policy to the pressures of demagogic politics and the resulting corruption of the democratic processes, the security policies of the United States, culminating in the years 1953–55, provide an extreme example. It is possible to explain the security system of the President's Executive Order 10450 of April 27, 1953—which incidentally the Eisenhower administration inherited and perfected but did not create—psychologically as a reaction to the laxity preceding it; it is impossible to defend it on rational and empirical grounds. We are faced with the stark fact, which the scholar cannot evade, that well-meaning and otherwise intelligent men were joined by the great majority of the people in embracing a philosophy of security, which is in truth a mythology, and a policy of security, which is in truth a series of ritualistic performances requiring human sacrifices, both completely divorced from reality and reason.

A critical analysis of the security regulations, as applied to the Department of State, must answer four basic questions. What is to be secured? Against whom is it to be secured? By what means is it being secured? What is the cost of security in terms of other goals to which the nation is equally committed?

A security system, in so far as it concerns the Department of State, must protect the integrity and secrecy of foreign policy. It has to assure, first of all, that the foreign policy of the United States is not determined by persons who owe primary loyalty to a foreign power and, hence, put its interests above those of the United States. Or, to put it in positive terms, it has to assure that those who determine American foreign policy are loyal to the United States. If there had ever existed, as is widely but falsely believed, in the Department of State a pro-Communist clique who deliberately worked for the triumph of communism in China, a security system would have to prevent such a situation from repeating itself.

It must, however, be said that the very mechanics by which the foreign policy of the United States is conducted make it extremely unlikely that such a situation could ever arise. The formation of American foreign policy is characterized by a diffusion so extreme as to border on chaos. The determination of American foreign policy is subject to a multitude of influences, not only from within the Department of State, but also from a great number of executive agencies which are directly or indirectly concerned with the conduct of foreign policy. To them must be added the—often decisive— influence that both houses of Congress exert upon the conduct of American foreign policy. A multitude of people, typically organized in committees, on all levels of the governmental hierarchy are continuously called upon to analyze a certain political situation and to propose a policy dealing with it. Out of that welter of divergent opinions, certain basic propositions are slowly distilled which are submitted to the President for final approval. It is only when the President has spoken with the ultimate authority of his office, not infrequently choosing among alternative policies, that the foreign policy of the United States has been determined.

Given this diffuse process of policy formation, no one foreign agent, however highly placed, could deflect the foreign policy of the United States from its national course. For his advice favoring a foreign power would be counteracted by the multitude of loyal officials who also participate in the process of policy formation. For a foreign power to subvert the foreign policy of the United States, a network of agents is needed strategically located not only in the Department of State but also in the other governmental establishments, such as the White House and the National Security Council, which are directly concerned with the determination of American foreign policy. No foreign power was able to establish such a network when American public opinion was hardly aware of the problem of security and when security regulations were extremely lax. It is important in this context to remind ourselves that there is no evidence to suggest that any of the officials who were concerned with the conduct of American foreign policy and whose pro-Communist sympathies have been proven have been able, or have even attempted, to influence American foreign policy in favor of a foreign nation.

The classic activity of the foreign agent, at least in popular imagination, is indeed not the determination of policy but the transmission of secrets. The prototype of the foreign agent is the spy. Not only public opinion but all governments assume that espionage is an enterprise worthwhile for all. Hence, they embark upon espionage for themselves and endeavor to protect themselves against the espionage of others. However, this assumption, at least as it concerns foreign policy in contrast to military dispositions and planning, is open to radical doubt.

It stands, of course, to reason that genuine military secrets must be protected. The quality and quantity of weapons, the disposition of the armed forces, war plans, and codes fall into that category. In so far as the operations of the Department of State deal with such military secrets, they require protection on military grounds. Secret-service operations with which the Department of State concerns itself must be protected on similar grounds. The considerations of the problem of secrecy in the Department of State that follow, then, apply exclusively to foreign policy proper.

I was once told by an official of the Department of State that from his long experience he could remember only two documents the transmission of which would have been advantageous to a foreign power. From my own much more limited experience, I do not remember a single top-secret document, let alone any document of a lower security classification, the knowledge of which would have been advantageous to a foreign power. I would go so far as to say that if a foreign power would gain knowledge of all the classified documents I have seen or written, such knowledge might be advantageous to the United States rather than to that power, provided it would be advantageous to the United States to confound a foreign power as to the nature of our foreign policy and its future course. As concerns espionage with regard to foreign policy in general, it is hardly more than a racket, engaged in by shady characters frequently working both sides of the street. The typical information thus obtained is either phony, irrelevant, or public property.

That this cannot be otherwise, a consideration of foreign policy, especially as it must be practiced under present world conditions, will make obvious. The great lines of action which the foreign policies of the great powers are likely to take are predetermined by their respective national interests as they are rationally defined by the small group which ultimately decides upon the course of action. This has always been so and is so today. The Cold War has, however, imposed a peculiar rigidity upon the foreign policies of the great powers, which leaves very little room for maneuver in the implementation of their respective national interests. Given this situation, there can be hardly any secrets which rational analysis could not detect but which espionage would be able to uncover. In order to know what Chinese policy with regard to Korea or Formosa is likely to be, it is not necessary, and probably not even expedient, to pilfer the secret files of the foreign office in Peiping; it is only necessary to ask one's self what the national interest of China has been with regard to these two regions and what it is likely to be as interpreted by the present rulers of China. In order to know what the Soviet Union is up to with regard to Germany, and vice versa, it is not necessary, and will avail little, to have secret agents in the foreign offices of Bonn and Moscow. If rational analysis cannot answer our quest, nothing else will.

The security regulations, as applied to the Department of State, completely misunderstood the nature of foreign policy and the problem of security with regard to it. Executive Order 10450 distinguishes among different positions in view of their different relevance for security but leaves the actual determination of that relevance to the officers charged with the enforcement of the executive order [Sec. 3 (A) par. 2, (B) par. 1; Sec. 8 (A) 1]. In its application to the Department of State that distinction between different degrees of sensitivity disappeared. The security policy of the Department of State conceived of foreign policy as one vast operation, all elements of which, from the determination of policy to the washing of windows, are equally important in view of their bearing upon integrity and secrecy.

In truth, what needs protection from foreign subversion is not the whole process of foreign policy in all its ramifications but only those elements of it that, in the nature of things, are capable of being subverted, that is, that small area where decisions are actually made and which has access to military secrets and secret-service operations. Secrecy in foreign policy serves not so much the security of the United States in terms of concealment of its plans and operations as it protects its officials who must be free to express their opinions

without concern for the favorable or unfavorable reaction of out-
siders. If the officials who are engaged in the conduct of foreign
policy could not rely upon their official actions and expressions of
opinion being made in confidence, they would at the very least be
tempted to surrender their own professional judgment of the merits
of the case to outside pressures, domestic and foreign. In the absence
of secrecy, an official could not be expected to express his opinions
about the personnel and policies of a foreign government without
anticipating the reactions of that government. Nor could he be expected to express his opinions about the policies of his own government without regard for domestic political reactions.

The main purpose of secrecy, then, is the protection of the professional integrity of the Foreign Service and affiliated agencies. Security regulations which seek to protect that professional integrity
must obviously be different from those which seek to protect the
United States against the betrayal of official secrets. Security regulations which are completely unaware of the former function but
animated by an unrealistic assessment of the need for the performance of the latter are likely to fail in both. More will have to be said
on this point later on.

Against whom are the integrity and secrecy of American foreign
policy to be secured? How can we determine beforehand who is
likely to be disloyal if participation in the conduct of American foreign policy should be intrusted to him? How does, in one word, the
mark of Cain look, which is supposed to set the prospective traitor
apart from the mass of loyal citizens? Section 8 of Executive Order
10450 undertakes to answer that question. It enumerates close to one
hundred characteristics, any one of which excludes a man from government employment as a security risk, his employment being not
"clearly consistent with the national security." Yet that list of characteristics, according to the preamble of Section 8, is not intended
to be exhaustive but rather to establish general categories to which
the security officials may add other related ones.

These characteristics fall into three different categories:

1. Those which make a person unfit for government service on
obvious security grounds, such as "commission of any act of sabotage, espionage, treason, or sedition . . ." [Sec. 8 (A) 2].

2. Characteristics which make a person unfit for government

service in general, without any special reference to security, such as "An adjudication of insanity, or treatment for serious mental or neurological disorder without satisfactory evidence of cure" [Sec. 8 (A) 1. IV].

3. Characteristics the absence of which in the composite reveal a picture of the "normal" good American, who alone is worthy of government employment, such as "any criminal, infamous, dishonest, immoral, or notoriously disgraceful conduct, habitual use of intoxicants to excess, drug addiction, or sex perversion" [Sec. 8 (A) 1. III].[1]

Here is indeed the crux of the matter. What the security regulations are trying to do in the third category is to localize treason as an outstanding but surreptitious evil by making it a function of other outstanding but patent evils. In this philosophy a man who has deviated drastically in other respects from the moral standards of society is more likely to deviate from those moral standards by committing treason than one who has not so deviated. This assumption is illogical to begin with, and there is not a shred of empirical evidence to support it. Its illogical character stems from the very nature of treason which is an act of disloyalty committed by a person who, in view of his revealed qualities, appears to be deserving of trust. If it were possible to identify the prospective traitor by some outward quality, the commission of treason would by definition become impossible. That the assumption of a necessary relationship between general immorality and the particular immorality of treason also is untenable on empirical grounds can be shown by putting the following two questions to the empirical test: Are people who deviate in a particular respect from the moral standards of society more likely to commit treason than others, and are traitors as a type likely to be immoral in other respects as well?

In order to answer the first of these two questions, let us take the type of immorality which not only constitutes a particularly radical and repulsive violation of "normal" moral standards but by general consensus is also most obviously conducive to treason: sexual perversion. That the homosexual is peculiarly prone to commit crimes

---

[1] Some of these characteristics taken in isolation, such as drug addiction, disqualify a person for government service in general and, hence, belong to the second category.

under the threat of blackmail is hardly doubted by anyone who faces the problem for the first time. Yet neither the histories of diplomacy and of treason nor the recollections of practitioners of diplomacy, in so far as I could ascertain, contain an instance of a homosexual having committed an act of treason under the threat of blackmail.

Nor is there any such evidence with regard to a very mild "deviation," completely devoid in itself of any negative moral connotation: that of having relatives behind the Iron Curtain. That an official who has relatives living behind the Iron Curtain is particularly susceptible to committing treason under blackmail sounds on the face of it so plausible that it is virtually accepted as self-evident. But who knows of an official who has violated security regulations under such circumstances? Here again, what on the face of it looks like common sense reveals itself on closer examination as superstition which unchallenged repetition has vested with the plausibility of truth.

Executive Order 10450 assumes the existence of two easily discernible types of men, one likely to commit treason, the other not. The composite picture of the latter, which emerges from Executive Order 10450 and its application to the personnel of the Department of State, is the ideal type of a Babbitt with strong pseudopuritanical connotations. He is a person who is "normal" in every respect, that is, who conforms to certain requirements which a "good" American is supposed to possess. In their application to the Department of State, these requirements run the whole gamut of actions, associations, attitudes, and opinions with which a person might identify himself. It is significant for the concern with conformity rather than with security that much emphasis has been put upon conformity with a conservative ideal in the field of political opinion and attitudes and with a pseudopuritanical ideal in the sphere of sexual behavior. In the course of security investigations, officials of the State Department have been asked about their attitude toward Franklin D. Roosevelt, the New Deal, and the recognition of the Communist government of China. Investigators have also shown an almost obsessive curiosity about the pre- and extramarital sexual activities of public officials.

It stands to reason that this ideal of the "good" American is at odds in one or the other respect with the actual behavior of most men who have ever lived and are now living. Hardly an American statesman from Franklin and Washington to Dulles and Eisenhower has, and could have, lived up to it, and most of them would fail the test on multiple grounds. And it is not by accident that men of un-doubted loyalty and merit have been dismissed from the Foreign Service as security risks under Executive Order 10450. For that executive order makes virtually everybody a security risk and for two reasons. First of all, as already pointed out, few men will correspond in every respect to the ideal picture of the "good" American which is implicit in Executive Order 10450 and its application (and it may be doubted that those who do make desirable public servants). More importantly, few men will be so transparently good, approaching saintliness, that it can be said of them that their employment is "clearly consistent with the interests of the national security," which is the general standard repeated again and again by the executive order.

I am myself indifferent honest; but yet I could accuse me of such things, that it were better my mother had not borne me: I am very proud, re-vengeful, ambitious; with more offenses at my beck than I have thoughts to put them in, imagination to give them shape, or time to act them in. What should such fellows as I do crawling between earth and heaven? We are arrant knaves all; believe none of us.

These words of Hamlet all men can say of themselves and of each other. Even the best man's goodness is darkened at least by the shadow of a doubt, and thus he is a security risk within the meaning of Executive Order 10450.

The security regulations, as applied to the Department of State, operated essentially through three instrumentalities: security investigations, police supervision, and political pressure.

That a person be subjected to a security check before he is employed in a sensitive position by the Department of State is an obvious necessity. Yet in the eyes of the Department of State a man's loyalty is never settled once and for all (as actually it cannot be, in view of what we have said above). Since no man can ever be fully trusted, all men are forever suspect on grounds of security and, hence, are at all times subject to renewed security investigations. The case of Mr. John Paton Davies, Jr., who underwent nine security investigations, has gained nationwide attention; yet his case is but an extreme example of a fairly typical situation. Hundreds of officials of the Department of State have been subjected to multiple security investigations by different agencies, for different purposes, and on different grounds. A patently scurrilous denunciation can call forth a new security investigation, proceeding as though nothing at all were known of the individual's record as a private citizen and public official.

This multiplication of security investigations is institutionalized by the requirement that the personnel file of every official of the Department of State in whose personnel status a change, such as a new assignment or promotion, is contemplated be checked for security. In the course of such a check any old incident which has been satisfactorily explained in preceding security investigations can jeopardize the official's career and destroy his reputation. An official who has been suggested for a promotion by virtue of his professional competence (of which compliance with security regulations is obviously a part) may be suspended for months as a security risk because ten years ago, on the instigation of the government, he joined an organization infiltrated by Communists in order to combat their influence. Never mind that this incident was a matter of record from the very beginning, that It has been explained to the satisfaction of all concerned time and again; now it must be explained again and with it the whole life of the official, private and public, from the day of his birth to this, and it is he who must prove that the continuation of his employment is "clearly consistent with the interests of the national security," by collecting affidavits from public and private acquaintances testifying that they found nothing wrong with him. By requiring the official to disprove the suspicion of being a security risk, it eliminates for all practical purposes from the evidence to be weighed the positive record of his accomplishments. A man may have given outstanding service over a long period of time in the most sensitive positions. Let him have had dinner with somebody who is suspected of having once been a Communist, and he will be unable to prove that he is not a security risk.

The assumption that all men are really security risks and that this defect, shared by all men, can somehow be neutralized, if not eliminated, through the proper social arrangements cannot but give rise to a psychology which is indistinguishable from that of the police state. For given these two assumptions, eternal vigilance becomes the price of security. Treat everybody as though he were a traitor, and you will be safe from treason.

The Department of State acted upon these assumptions and established a system of supervision which in good part is supposed to operate covertly but of which everybody within the Department is—jokingly or indignantly—aware. The Bureau of Security of the Department of State employs, of course, a staff whose personnel and functions are officially known. Aside from this official staff, it employs a network of agents (both categories estimated to total more than a thousand) whose identity and functions are not supposed to be known. Individuals have been placed in the different functional and geographic units of the Department of State for the ostensible purpose of performing the substantive functions of these units, yet for the actual purpose of supervising and reporting on their colleagues. Delegations to international conferences are accompanied by individuals who perform similar functions, traditionally associated with a GPU or Gestapo. The Secretary of State himself has invested this system with the authority of his office by imposing, through Department Circular 95 of April 15, 1954, upon all officials of his Department the duty to be informers.

I am aware that no agency of the government can improve, or even maintain, its level of effectiveness unless it is receiving a stream of new ideas and constructive criticisms. I hope that the inspection operation will be the focal reception point of that stream. I have told Mr. McLeod that in his capacity as administrator of the inspection operation he should be available at any time to receive personally from any of our people the benefit of their thinking on improving operations and procedures or on other problems, official and personal.

In brief, I regard the internal inspection operation of the Department as one of its most important concerns. Its success will depend upon the cooperation and aid received generally from employees of the Department.

There have been persistent rumors, in the nature of things hard to verify, of tapped telephones, hidden microphones, steamed-open letters, and special rooms and devices for the grilling of suspects. But regardless of whether or not there is any evidence to support these rumors, the very fact that they could be spread and widely believed reveals a spirit vastly different from that which is supposed to prevail in an agency of a democratic government.

This emphasis upon the vital importance of investigation and supervision for purposes of security, institutionalized in a special bureau within the Department of State, inevitably led to a shift—lasting through most of Mr. Eisenhower's first term—of effective control over the operations of the Department from the Secretary and Undersecretary of State and the heads of the functional and geographic units to the Bureau of Security. This shift has occurred in all modern totalitarian states and has given rise to a phenomenon which has been aptly called the "dual state." It is characteristic of the "dual state" that in it, as a matter of law, the power of making decisions remains with the authorities charged by law with making them while, as a matter of fact, by virtue of their power over life and death, the agents of the secret police—co-ordinated to, but independent from, the official makers of decision—at the very least exert an effective veto over the decisions. Once the secret police has established itself firmly in an agency of the government, it will have less and less need for intervening drastically in day-by-day operations; for its omnipresence and reputed omnipotence will generally be sufficient for the constituted authorities to avoid any action which might displease the secret police.

The Bureau of Security in the Department of State, as originally constituted, was combined with, and hence had direct control over, four areas of operation: security, consular affairs, personnel, and inspection of United States missions abroad. While the administrator of the Bureau of Security has been deprived of direct responsibility for the two latter functions, it is generally believed that the first incumbent of the office retained effective control over personnel because the office of personnel continued to be administered in the spirit of, and in close co-operation with, the Bureau of Security. For the powers of the Bureau of Security by themselves are all-pervading in so far as the hiring, assignment, promotion, and firing of personnel are concerned.

The powers which the Bureau of Security assumed over the operations of the Department of State flowed only in part from its police functions as such. As in fully developed totalitarian systems the power of the secret police is in good measure the reflection of the political power of its head, a Himmler or a Beria, so did the power of the Bureau of Security over the Department of State reflect in good measure the political power of those whose political philosophy its leading officials represented, to whom they owed their positions and their primary loyalties as well. Those were not the President of the United States or the Secretary of State but certain members of Congress and, more particularly, of the Senate. The police system which was established in the Department of State was their secret police in a more profound sense than it was the secret police of the executive branch. It was through it that these members of Congress were kept informed about the—presumably secret—operations of the Department of State, and it was through it that they exerted a direct or indirect influence upon its operations. To an extent which changes with the ebbs and tides of political fortune, it was these members of Congress, and not the President or the Secretary of State, who determined the operations of the Department of State and its affiliated agencies.

The most spectacular instance of this extra-constitutional influence to have come to light thus far is provided by the International Information Administration. The report which the chief consultant to its director has published[2] leaves no doubt but that, at least from February through July, 1953, Senator McCarthy and his friends in Congress had taken over the functions which, according to the Constitution, the President and the Secretary of State are supposed to perform. These members of Congress determined the policies of the International Information Administration as concerns both personnel and substance. It was to them that the top officials of the agency reported; it was their approval which they had to seek; and it was their orders which they were supposed to execute. And when they finally incurred the displeasure of their congressional masters, they had to resign.

For these members of Congress, all men were suspect as traitors, but diplomats in particular were so. For they deviate in certain obvious respects from the ideal type of the "normal" good American: they know foreign languages, spend much of their lives abroad, have many contacts with foreigners, concern themselves professionally

[2] Martin Merson, *The Private Diary of a Public Servant* (New York: Macmillan Co., 1955).

316

with foreign countries—and they tend to be intellectuals, committing their brains rather than their passions to the conduct of foreign policy. Thus it is not by accident that an enterprise which started out to protect the integrity and secrecy of American foreign policy transformed itself, as we have seen, in an undertaking to assure conformity and ended in an attempt to make the United States safe from foreign policy as such. What began as a technical operation to improve the protection of the United States against subversion and espionage matured into an onslaught—"know-nothing" in its philosophy and isolationist in its implicit purpose—against the very existence of an active American foreign policy.

Obviously, to preserve the integrity and secrecy of foreign policy is only one among many objectives to which the United States is committed. A policy, however sound and successful in its own terms, must be evaluated in terms of the impact it has upon other national objectives, as important or even more important than its own. Such scrutiny is particularly required for a policy which is so unsound and unsuccessful as we believe the security policy of the Department of State to have been. What, then, has been the price in terms of equally or more important objectives we have had to pay for the security policy of the Department of State? That price is being paid primarily in three areas: the effectiveness of American foreign policy, the prestige of the United States abroad, and the security of the United States.

In the *New York Times* of January 17, 1954, five of the most distinguished older diplomatists of the United States, four of whom have been ambassadors and an equal number under or assistant secretaries of state, summarized the "sinister results" of the security policy of the Department of State in these words:

The conclusion has become inescapable, for instance, that a Foreign Service officer who reports on persons and events to the very best of his ability and who makes recommendations which at the time he conscientiously believes to be in the interest of the United States may subsequently find his loyalty and integrity challenged and may even be forced out of the service and discredited forever as a private citizen. A premium therefore has been put upon reporting and upon recommendations which are ambiguously stated or so cautiously set forth as to be deceiving.

When any such tendency begins its insidious work it is not long before accuracy and initiative have been sacrificed to acceptability and conform-

317

ity. The ultimate result is a threat to national security. In this connection the history of the Nazi and Fascist foreign services before the Second World War is pertinent.

The forces which are working for conformity from the outside are being reinforced by the present administrative set-up within the Department of State which subordinates normal personnel administration to considerations of security.

It is obvious, of course, that candidates for the Foreign Service should be carefully investigated before appointment and that their work should at all times be under the exacting scrutiny of their professional superiors. But when initial investigation attaches undue importance to such factors as even a temporary departure from conservative political and economic views, casual association with persons holding views not currently in fashion or subscription to a periodical labeled as "liberal"; when subsequent investigation is carried to the point of delaying a promotion list for a year and routine transfers from one post to another; when investigations of individual officers must be kept up-to-date to within ninety days; when an easy path has been opened to even the anonymous informer; and when the results of these investigations are evaluated not by persons experienced in the Foreign Service or even acquainted at firsthand with conditions abroad, but by persons of quite different experience, it is relevant to inquire whether we are not laying the foundations of a Foreign Service competent to serve a totalitarian government rather than the government of the United States as we have heretofore known it.

Fear is playing an important part in American life at the present time. As a result the self-confidence, the confidence in others, the sense of fair play and the instinct to protect the rights of the nonconformist are—temporarily, it is to be hoped—in abeyance. But it would be tragic if this fear, expressing itself in an exaggerated emphasis on security, should lead us to cripple the Foreign Service, our first line of national defense, at the very time when its effectiveness is essential to our filling the place which history has assigned to us.

For an impartial professional observer, the conclusion is inevitable that more than a year after this letter was written the Department of State was hardly competent to serve any government, totalitarian or otherwise. Not only the morale but also the professional competence and capacity for teamwork of its members had drastically declined. The Department of State which the Eisenhower administration inherited was, to say the least, a useful instrument of foreign policy. Its obvious administrative weaknesses were compensated for by the intellectual ability, technical competence, and devotion of most of its top and middle layer officials. Many of these officials have either been dismissed or have voluntarily resigned. Of the officials of this type with whom the American High Commission in Germany was staffed in 1953, not a single one was left two years later. They could not have been replaced even under the best possible circumstances with a new team of equal competence and experience. For no nation is rich enough in diplomatic talent, demanding a rare combination of extraordinary qualities of mind and character, to be able to afford taking one team out of the game and replacing it with another one equally good. What is possible in football cannot be done in diplomacy.

The United States could not have afforded the loss of its ablest diplomatists even under the best of circumstances. Yet the circumstances under which the United States had to make good this loss were far from being the best. A system that makes security the overriding consideration gives a golden opportunity for advancement to the incompetent, the time server, and the informer, who has never uttered a wrong thought and who has never associated with the wrong person. A system that not only does not require professional competence but actually suspects it cannot help using standards of selection congenial to that point of view. But it goes without saying that those standards are incompatible with the standards by which diplomatists ought to be selected.

Not only has there been deterioration at the top and in the middle layers of the departmental hierarchy, but there has also been starvation at the bottom. A system characterized by repeated security investigations, police supervision, and political pressure has depleted the lower ranks of the Foreign Service. Many younger officials have been dismissed as security risks, and many more have resigned of their own volition. What is worse is that such a system must act as a deterrent upon both application for employment and employment itself. The number of graduates of our institutions of higher learning who in 1954 or 1955 chose to make the Foreign Service their career was small as compared with that of three or four years earlier. The few who applied then may have been the bravest and the most desperate, but they could hardly have been the best; and those who were able to pass the security test and were actually hired were not necessarily the best of them, and even many of them resigned soon in disgust.

This decline in the quality and quantity of the personnel of the Department of State was matched by the decline in the quality of its operations. The premonitions of the five diplomatists which we have quoted above were fully borne out by events. Objective analytical reporting, the prime function of diplomacy, fell to a low ebb in the Foreign Service. Diplomatic reports were no longer as regularly read by the officials at the respective geographic desks in Washington as they were in times past; for they contained frequently nothing more than digests of the newspapers of the countries concerned, which the official in Washington can and does read himself. Heads of missions refused to allow the transmission to Washington of reports painting a picture of the local situation at variance either with reports of other agencies or with the estimate of the situation prevailing in Washington.

This abdication of independent judgment is, of course, the result of the fear that deviation from the "official line" might jeopardize one's chances for advancement, if not one's very livelihood and reputation. Yet this fear is more than the subjective anticipation of an evil which is largely imaginary, as is much of the fear of being "controversial," so prevalent in academic life. That fear is, indeed, the fruit of bitter experience. Officials were dismissed for having reported facts that they were not supposed to report and for having advocated policies that they were not supposed to advocate; and officials were subjected to still another security investigation on the complaint of a foreign government which did not approve of the policies they advocated.

Under the impact of all these influences, the Department of State probably did not become more immune to subversion and treason than it was before. A case could even be made for the proposition that an official whom the "dual state" constantly subjects to the moral stress of having to reconcile his own professional judgments and moral principles with those of the organization in which he works may become particularly prone to laxity and failure of judgment in matters of security. In any event, the Department of State ceased to be the eyes, ears, and brains of the foreign policy of the United States. Its eyes became blind; its ears, deaf; and its brains, dull. Yet a foreign policy that makes itself incapable of knowing the facts with which it must deal and of understanding the problems it must solve can rely for success upon nothing but the vagaries of luck.

It must, however, be said that this dark picture is brightened by a few light spots. Through luck, personal connections, or the inefficiency of the security system, there remained in the Department of State a few officials who did not yield to the pressures which incessantly bore upon them. Forsaken from above, spied upon from below, surrounded by all manner of opportunists and worse, they risked their careers, their positions, and their honor in maintaining for themselves and in defending in their subordinates the traditional standards of intellectual integrity, professional competence, and devotion to duty. If and when out of the ruins of today a new foreign service will be built, worthy of the traditions and the mission of America, the nation will owe a great debt to these brave, able, and devoted men who defended in obscurity and against great odds the pitiful remnants of a fine tradition.

This disintegration of the Foreign Service of the United States is better known abroad than it is at home. The governments and the public of foreign countries have seen with amazement officials, of whose competence and loyalty they have had tangible evidence, investigated, dismissed, or forced to resign as security risks. Continuous contacts with our representatives abroad provide them with unmistakable evidence of the diminution of their professional competence. In consequence, the influence the United States should be able to exert by virtue of its material strength and of the mission it has assumed for the free world has drastically declined. The word of the United States is no longer listened to with respect. What is worse, the very image of the United States as the champion of justice and freedom against totalitarian oppression has been obscured. If the United States owed its position in the world to nothing but its material power, such foreign reactions would be of little consequence. In truth, however, the United States has been able to command the sympathies of millions of people abroad, not because it has more atomic bombs than the Soviet Union, but because it was founded upon, and has tried to live up to, certain principles of government to which those millions of people are also committed. Seeing the last best hope of the free world forsake these principles and even seemingly be proud of a security system that the London *Economist* has called a "vicious stupidity,"[3] many of our friends abroad began to doubt whether there is much to choose between East and West.

This loosening of the bonds of sympathy that unite America to its friends abroad raises a specter more ominous still: the loosening of the bonds of loyalty which tie the citizens of the United States to their own government. The United States was founded upon loyalty, not to a king or piece of territory, but to an ideal of political justice. We pledge allegiance to a flag which is a symbol of "liberty and justice for all." Loyalty which attaches to a man or a territory may not be affected by injustice perpetrated by that man or within that territory. A nation which was built on a common belief in certain principles of justice, whose citizens have voluntarily come together from all over the world to share in the practice of those principles, which owes its very existence to a revolt against injustice—such a nation stands and falls, as a nation, with its loyalty to those principles.

The loyalty of its citizens presupposes the loyalty of its government, not as a matter of verbalization but of policy, to those principles of justice. The government of such a nation cannot help committing injustices by sacrificing some of the freedom and interests of individuals to a higher good. The government of such a nation will be forgiven sporadic injustices not justified by the achievement of such a higher good. The government of such a nation will embark upon a deliberate policy of injustice only at the risk of weakening the very foundation of loyalty which supports its voluntary acceptance by its citizens.

A citizen, unjustly accused of disloyalty, condemned and ostracized, may well be tempted to conclude that if he is to be treated as disloyal he may as well act the part.[4] To the government's severance of the ties which unite government and citizen, he might want to respond in kind. The man whom his government has cast into the

[3] Jan. 8, 1955, p. 110.

[4] This psychological process is strikingly revealed in this statement by the leader of a juvenile gang, reported in the *New York Times* of March 25, 1958, p. 26: " 'That's the way it starts,' Vincent says, 'I've seen it happen many times. The police blame you for something you didn't do. You get a record. They send you away. So, then, the kid comes back and he says, "Well, I'm going to do something and get a record of my own. At least then if I'm sent up it will be for something I did myself." ' "

outer darkness may make common cause with the forces of darkness. The alienation of the government from the principles upon which it was founded and, in consequence, from some of its citizens may well have brought in its wake the alienation of some citizens from the government. Thus a policy which sought to protect the government from disloyalty may well have corrupted, by dint of its own corruption, if not the actions so at least the minds of some of the citizens upon whose loyal services the government could otherwise have counted. A policy intended to protect the country from treason is likely to have actually increased if not the actuality so at least the risk of treason.

Such, then, is the price we were paying for Executive Order 10450, as applied to the Department of State. It is a high price to pay. Paid for what? For nothing.

19 *The Subversion of Foreign Policy*

The destruction of the Foreign Service of the United States, in order to take the wind out of the sails of the domestic opposition, is paralleled by the paralysis and the distortion of the foreign policy of the United States. The first two years of Mr. Eisenhower's foreign policy provide a case study of the corrupting effects that considerations of domestic politics can exert upon the conduct of foreign policy. An attempt to assess this period of American foreign policy must overcome three formidable obstacles. One, the nature of the standards of evaluation, is inherent in the nature of all foreign policy; the second, the conduct of foreign policy in view of popular preferences, is peculiar to democratic foreign policy; the third, the utter contrast between the presentation and the substance of foreign policy, seems to be inherent in the nature of Mr. Eisenhower's foreign policy.

What is the standard by which we judge the quality of foreign policy? Is it success? If so, then inevitably the incompetent heir will reap the fruits of his wise predecessor's labors and take credit for the results of what was actually somebody else's achievement. Conversely, the great statesman to whom it has fallen to dispose of the bankrupt estate of the preceding government must take the blame for a failure which is not his own. The verdicts of popular history are indeed permeated with misjudgments of this kind.

Yet, how do we determine success and failure in foreign policy? Surveying the centuries, history is able to assess the contribution of a particular move at a particular time to the ultimate success or failure of a nation's foreign policy. The contemporary observer is handicapped by his ignorance of the consequences of contemporary policies. Judged by success alone, Hitler's foreign policy, if viewed in the perspective of 1938–40, made Bismarck's look like a mere preparation for greater things to come. But how did it look but five years later? Who did not think in 1929 that the Briand-Kellogg Pact was a great success, and who did not think so of the Teheran, Yalta, and Potsdam agreements at the time of their conclusion? But who would think so now?

However, we do not object to the Briand-Kellogg Pact and the wartime agreements with the Soviet Union solely or even primarily for their lack of success. What we are critical of is the cause of their failure, that is, the wrong way of thinking about foreign policy which made the framers of these agreements expect success when failure could have been avoided only by fortuitous circumstances lying beyond the ken of their intentions and control. What makes foreign policy deserving of praise or blame is, then, not success or failure per se but a way of thinking about foreign policy which by virtue of its inherent qualities is likely to lead to success or failure. A foreign policy based upon correct thinking deserves to be called "good" even though it fails for reasons that have nothing to do with the quality of thought that went into it, and a foreign policy derived from wrong thinking must be called "bad" even though it succeeds in spite of the deficiences of the reasoning from which it stems.

What do we mean when we speak of correct thinking and the quality of reasoning on matters of foreign policy? We assume, as pointed out elsewhere in greater detail,[1] that there exists an objective rational standard by which the quality of political action can be judged. This assumption derives from the rational nature of man which the actor on the political scene cannot help bringing to bear upon his action to a greater or lesser degree. It is the degree of conformity between political action and rational requirements which determines the quality of the action. The active participant in politics as well as the detached observer of the political scene cannot but proceed on this assumption. For they would not be able to judge political action at all, beyond the crudest statements about success or failure, if they did not carry in their minds a picture of what a certain political action ought to have been. Actors and observers alike cannot help sharing in the assumption of the rationality of this picture; for otherwise they would have no common ground for correlating each other's thoughts and actions.

It is no argument to say that the rational requirements of foreign policy are difficult to ascertain and ambiguous in nature and that

[1] *Politics among Nations* (2d ed.; New York: Alfred A. Knopf, 1954), pp. 7–8.

their application to concrete problems is even more so. The fact remains that the assumption of the possibility of judging foreign policy rationally, in terms of the quality of reasoning underlying it, is the precondition for both the intellectual comprehension of foreign policy and for its objective evaluation.

This task of evaluation is even more complicated when foreign policy is carried on under the conditions of democratic control. Two factors make it so. First of all, a democratically conducted foreign policy, as pointed out in chapter 17, is of necessity a compromise between the rational requirements of good foreign policy and the emotional preferences of public opinion. If one wanted to overstate the case, one might say that a democratically conducted foreign policy is of necessity bad foreign policy. In any case, a foreign policy carried on under democratic control must fall short of the rational requirements of good foreign policy; for it must satisfy emotional preferences whose satisfaction is incompatible with meeting those requirements. It would, therefore, be unjust to judge a democratic foreign policy exclusively by its compliance with these requirements; such judgment must be qualified by the need, greater or lesser as the case may be but always present, to compromise with the emotional preferences of public opinion.

The ultimate judgment on a democratic foreign policy will then be composed of two specific judgments: one establishing the degree to which a foreign policy meets the rational requirements of good foreign policy, and the other assessing the need for compromise with public opinion and the degree to which foreign policy has met that need. Did it yield not enough and thus destroy the foundation of public opinion on which democratic foreign policy must operate? Or did it yield too much, deviating from rational requirements to such an extent as to condemn foreign policy to failure? It is answers to questions such as these which will determine the ultimate verdict. It is with them that we are here concerned.

The other factor complicating the evaluation of democratic foreign policy results from the one just discussed. Not only must democratic foreign policy make concessions to public opinion, but it must also present its foreign policy in terms acceptable to public opinion. That is to say, it must make it appear as though it responds to the emotional preferences of public opinion to a greater extent than it actually does. It must cover those of its rational elements that are least likely to find favor with public opinion with a veil of emotional pronouncements which are intended to conceal its true nature from the public eye. It is for the objective observer to distinguish between public pronouncements on foreign policy that reveal and those that conceal the true nature of the foreign policy actually pursued, by correlating pronouncement with action.

This is a very difficult task at best. It has been made even more difficult by the way United States foreign policy has been traditionally conducted and the particular way the Eisenhower administration has been conducting its foreign policy. The processes by which decisions on foreign policy are arrived at in the United States are chaotic in the extreme. The writer has endeavored elsewhere to analyze the constitutional and political factors that make them so.[2] It is a further peculiarity of the American system that this business of institutionalized chaos is carried on on the public stage. Given the importance of public opinion for the determination of foreign policy, this can hardly be otherwise; for that course of action which can mobilize public opinion in its support has gained a great advantage in the struggle for the ultimate determination of United States foreign policy. Thus it is possible, and has almost become customary, that on any pending question of foreign policy any member of the executive or legislative branches of the government, be it the Vice-President, the Secretary of State, the Chairman of the Joint Chiefs of Staff, the party leaders in Congress, or a ranking member of the foreign affairs committee of either house formulates his own foreign policy in public speech. Thus on United States over-all relations with the Soviet bloc as well as on more specific questions, such as American policies toward Communist China and the problems raised for American policy by the Indochina War, prominent members of the Eisenhower administration and of the Republican party in Congress have publicly advocated policies that did not become the policies of the United States. It was only from subsequent action, taken upon the responsibility of the President, that it was possible to determine in retrospect what the policy of the United States actually had been.

2 "The Conduct of Foreign Policy," in S. D. Bailey (ed.), *Aspects of American Government* (London: Hansard Society, 1950), pp. 99 ff.

To complicate matters still further, action taken on the responsibility of the President has sometimes belied the President's own words. For it is a peculiarity of the Eisenhower administration that it is the first democratic government whose relations with the public imitate on a large and institutionalized scale the techniques of public relations experts and commercial advertising. This is so with regard to form and content. Mr. Robert Montgomery, a movie actor, has the official title of White House adviser on radio and television. The President on television conveys the impression that he smiles and raises his voice or hand not on an impulse of his own but rather on somebody else's cue. The first cabinet meeting ever televised, in which the Secretary of State reported on the London Conference of 1954, conveyed the impression of a performance staged by experts and executed by amateurs. In the words of Mr. Alistair Cooke:

> The whole show had a relaxed, closed-door air, almost like a Cabinet meeting. In the lead part ... Mr. Dulles gave a naturalistic performance of great ease and articulateness. Mr. Henry Cabot Lodge made the most of a single-sentence tribute to the President for his peaceful atomic energy proposals. Cast as the unsleeping watchdog of the people's purse, Mr. Secretary of the Treasury Humphrey expressed with moving verisimilitude his concern that the Paris Agreement should not cost the American taxpayer one extra nickel. Mrs. Hobby conveyed an intelligent anxiety over the Saar.
>
> Only Secretary of Agriculture Ezra Benson, an artless man from the West, had to be prodded into his line by Mr. Dulles, who suggested after an anxious pause that some of them might now be wondering "how the Soviet Union is taking this." Mr. Benson was indeed wondering just that, and made an alert retrieve. It was the only missed cue in an otherwise flawless performance, surely an enviable record for any amateur dramatic company.[3]

The ascendancy of the public relations expert over the responsible political leader has also been marked in the substance of what the leaders of the Eisenhower administration have told the people about the foreign policy they are pursuing. Here, too, the methods of salesmanship have largely replaced the principles of responsible democratic leadership, and, in consequence, it has become a principle of government to impress the public favorably at any price, even that of truth, rather than to inform it. Spectacular announcements have

[3] *Manchester Guardian Weekly,* Oct. 28, 1954, p. 2.

been made carrying the impression of momentous decisions in foreign policy which turned out to be meaningless in view of the actual policies pursued. Five major announcements of this kind, creating a great deal of public comment and controversy but no policies even faintly reflecting them, were made during the first two years of the Eisenhower administration: liberation, the unleashing of Chiang Kai-shek, agonizing reappraisal, the "new look," and intervention in Indochina.

During the election campaign of 1952 and during the first months of its tenure of office, the spokesmen for the Eisenhower administration announced that the old policy of containment was to be replaced by a policy of liberation. Yet as the London *Economist* put it as early as August 30, 1952, "Unhappily 'liberation' applied to Eastern Europe—and Asia—means either the risk of war or it means nothing . . . . 'Liberation' entails no risk of war only when it means nothing." Yet the Eisenhower administration has shied away from the risk of war at least as much as did its predecessor. And when the East German revolt in June, 1953, and the Hungarian revolution of October, 1956, coming closer to success than anybody had dared to expect, put the policy of liberation to the test of actual performance, it became obvious that in actuality the policy of liberation was indistinguishable from the policy of containment.

In his State of the Union message of February 2, 1953, President Eisenhower declared, "In June, 1950, following the aggressive attack on the Republic of Korea, the United States Seventh Fleet was instructed both to prevent attack upon Formosa and also to insure that Formosa should not be used as a base of operations against the Chinese Communist mainland." In view of the Chinese intervention in the Korean War, the President declared that he was "issuing instructions that the Seventh Fleet no longer be employed to shield Communist China." This announcement implied a fundamental change in the Far Eastern policies of the United States from the preservation of the status quo to the active attempt to restore Chiang Kai-shek's rule on the Asiatic mainland. In actuality, no such change occurred. Quite to the contrary, the Eisenhower administration seems to have been at least as anxious as its predecessor to limit the military activities of Chiang Kai-shek to strictly defensive measures. By making this limitation part of agreements with Chiang Kai-shek negotiated at the end of 1954, the Eisenhower administration went even beyond the unilateral declaration of policy contained in President Truman's instructions to the Seventh Fleet of June, 1950.

On December 14, 1953, Secretary of State Dulles declared at the meeting of the North Atlantic Council, "If, however, the European Defense Community should not become effective, if France and Germany remain apart, so that they would again be potential enemies, then indeed there would be grave doubt whether Continental Europe could be made a place of safety. That would compel an agonizing reappraisal of basic United States policy."[4] This statement implied the threat that in certain contingencies the United States might lose its interest in the military defense of Europe and leave it to its fate. This threat called forth much comment and little anxiety in Europe and elsewhere. As an incentive for France to ratify the European Defense Community, it was ineffective. For in order to take this threat seriously one would have had to assume that the United States had committed itself to the defense of western Europe, not because it deemed its own defense dependent upon it, but because it happened to approve of the policies of certain European nations. Few observers were, and no responsible statesman was, willing to make so fantastic an assumption.

However, the most far-reaching and most widely commented upon announcement of this kind was the Secretary of State's speech of January 12, 1954, proclaiming the "new look" in American foreign policy as the result of "some basic policy decisions" which the President and the National Security Council had taken. Mr. Lester Pearson, then Canadian secretary of state for external affairs, thought as late as March 15, 1954, that this speech "may turn out to be one of the most important of our times." The present writer, on March 29, 1954, published an article in the *New Republic* interpreting and evaluating this speech as if it meant what it said. Yet Mr. Walter Lippmann could say on March 18 that "The official explanations of the new look have become so voluminous that it is almost a career in itself to keep up with them" and characterize it as "a case of excessive salesmanship," concluding that "there is no doubt that the words of the text convey the impression that something momentous and novel has been decided. But everything that has been said since then

[4] *New York Times,* Dec. 15, 1953.

by the Chiefs of Staff, notably by Admiral Carney, and no less so by Mr. Dulles himself, make it plain that there has been no radical change in our strategic policy."

On the same day, the *Manchester Guardian* summed it all up by saying, "The 'new look' in American military strategy is mainly old merchandise in a new package. There is really nothing new in relying on 'massive mobile retaliatory power' as the principal safeguard of peace—nothing new, that is, except the sales campaign by which the Administration is trying to persuade the American people that some small changes make the strategy of 1954 fundamentally sounder than the strategy of 1953." On March 19, the Senate Committee on Foreign Relations was the scene of the following dialogue between Senator Mansfield and Mr. Dulles, who for all practical purposes buried the "new look" under the cover of military secrecy:

SENATOR MANSFIELD: Do you consider this new policy a new policy?
SECRETARY DULLES: It certainly has new aspects.
SENATOR MANSFIELD: What are they?
SECRETARY DULLES: Well, I am sorry I cannot go into that here. All I can say to you, and you will have to take it on faith, is that a series of new decisions have been taken by the National Security Council and many have been involved, close, and difficult decisions, but there is today on the record a series of decisions which are largely derived from this basic philosophy which were not there a year and a half ago.

While the "new look" was the most spectacular and far-reaching of these announcements, the official declarations concerning the Indochina War were politically the most harmful; for these dealt not with general principles of United States policy but with a concrete situation which required action here and now. On March 25, 1954, the President declared at his news conference that the defense of Indochina was of "transcendent importance." On March 29, the Secretary of State announced: "Under the conditions of today, the imposition on South-East Asia of the political system of Communist Russia and its Chinese Communist ally, by whatever means, would be a grave threat to the whole free community. The United States feels that that possibility should not be passively accepted, but should be met by united action. This might have serious risks, but these risks are far less than would face us a few years from now if we dare not be resolute today." The President and the Secretary of State referred to Indochina as the cork in the bottle of Southeast Asia and as the first in a row of dominoes whose fall would necessarily cause the downfall of the others. Yet no action of any kind reflected even faintly the conception of policy which these words seemed to convey. It was, in the words of the *Economist* of August 21, 1954, this "spectacle of vociferous inaction" which led to "the worst diplomatic disaster in recent American history."

This "foreign policy by hoax" has served to confuse the American people. It has raised doubts in the minds of many about the reliability of public pronouncements on anything and has thus led to the beginnings of a crisis of confidence which endangers democratic government itself. It has raised similar doubts in the minds of friends and enemies alike. The allies of the United States have been fearful lest political action might conform to official utterance. The enemies of the United States must similarly doubt the reliability of official announcements of policy, and they might even doubt it on the wrong occasion when the peace of the world may well depend upon whether or not a warning by the government of the United States is to be believed. The government of a great nation may, or even must, bluff from time to time; but it can afford to bluff only within the framework of a consistent policy understood by all. However, when it erects bluff into a principle of foreign policy, it risks that it would not be believed even if it should. While the spokesmen for the Eisenhower administration have benefited from this "foreign policy by hoax" in that they were able to pose for a fleeting moment as the initiators of new and bold policies, their prestige at home and abroad has suffered in the long run, as has the foreign policy of the United States.

This conduct of foreign policy for the apparent primary purpose of gaining popularity at home results from a misunderstanding of the fundamental relations which must exist between democratic government and public opinion. It also results from a misunderstanding of the conditions which the constitutional and political system of the United States imposes upon these relationships. This misunderstanding the Eisenhower administration has inherited from its predecessor, but it has immensely aggravated it. That aggravation has created a constitutional and political crisis of the first order, which is no less real for being in good measure hidden from the public view by the personal prestige of the President.

The Eisenhower administration assumes correctly that democratic government must be responsive to public opinion, but it errs grievously in the manner in which it tries to bring that response about. Regarding public opinion as the ultimate arbiter of foreign policy, it tries first to ascertain what the preferences of public opinion are and then to comply with them. In the process of bringing its foreign policy into harmony with public opinion, it assumes—and there lies its error—that public opinion with regard to a certain foreign policy pre-exists that foreign policy itself, somewhat in the manner in which a rule of law pre-exists the action to be judged by it. In truth, public opinion is not a static thing to be ascertained and quantified by polls as legal precedents are by the science of law and as the data of nature are by the natural sciences. Rather it is a dynamic thing to be created and continuously re-created by that selfsame political leadership which also creates the foreign policy to be supported by public opinion.

If the executive branch cannot obtain the support of public opinion for a certain policy it would like to pursue, it is not because public opinion—"naturally," as it were—is opposed to this particular foreign policy but because the political leadership of the executive branch has not been effective and has been replaced by political leadership hostile to this foreign policy. In other words, the contest is really not between the foreign policy of the executive branch and public opinion but between the former and other political forces propounding a different foreign policy. The executive branch, by surrendering passively its own initiative to the verdict of public opinion, in truth surrenders to the political opposition which has taken hold of public opinion. In consequence, the executive branch condemns itself to executing the foreign policy of its opponents, which it cannot help doing but half-heartedly and ineffectually; for, knowing better than the opposition and, furthermore, bearing responsibility for the consequences of its acts, whatever it does in order to satisfy the opposition always falls short of the standards which the opposition has erected and the executive branch has accepted as its own. In consequence, the foreign policy of the executive branch will always stand condemned in the eyes of public opinion as having sought and achieved less than public opinion had a right to expect in view of the standards which the executive branch professes as its own.

Of this vicious circle in which the executive branch is caught because it misunderstands the nature of public opinion and, in consequence, surrenders initiative in foreign policy to the opposition, the China policy of the Eisenhower administration is the classic example. There can be no doubt that a majority of the leading officials who advised Mr. Eisenhower on foreign policy during the first years of his tenure of office were opposed to the policies which the President had been pursuing in the Far East. That majority was composed of two groups. By far the larger of these groups wanted to advance toward a more aggressive position, even at the risk of a limited war with Communist China; by far the smaller one would have liked to retreat into less exposed positions. The actual policy of the United States was able to maintain an intermediate position between those two extremes, which followed the line of least resistance by trying neither to advance nor to retreat but to maintain the status quo.

Yet a rational examination of the forces opposing each other in the Far East and their probable dynamics cannot but lead to the conclusion that a policy of the status quo was not likely to be tenable in the long run. Both the United States and Communist China would have to go forward or backward, but they were not likely to remain indefinitely where they were then. Why, then, was the policy of the United States based upon an assumption that cannot be supported by rational argument? The answer is to be found in the surrender, in reasoning if not in policy, to an opposition whose reasoning, contradictory in itself, does not provide the basis for a rational policy, but which has been able to mold public opinion by default of the executive branch.

Public opinion with regard to Communist China was dominated by two strong contradictory emotions: to make somehow good the defeat which the United States suffered through the defection of China to the Communist camp, and to do so without getting involved in a major war on the continent of Asia. The opposition presented a program designed to meet these two emotional preferences. It promised the overthrow of the Communist regime of China and the restoration of Chiang Kai-shek's rule through aerial bombard-

334

ment and a naval blockade, using Formosa as a springboard. Yet a careful reading of the minutes of the joint congressional committee investigating in 1951 the dismissal of General MacArthur can leave no doubt in the mind of the unbiased reader about the military and political emptiness of the Far Eastern policies of the opposition. For the opposition was not able to devise the policies the United States would have had to pursue short of all-out war if the Communist regime of China should have been able to withstand the limited measures of war proposed, if the conflict should not have been limited to China, and if the Chinese people should not have been waiting to be liberated from their Communist government. In one word, the program of the opposition served as an effective instrument for the demagogue to achieve an illusory reconciliation of policy with popular emotional preferences which cannot be reconciled in action. Hence, that program offered no basis for a rational policy which any responsible government would have been able to pursue.

Nevertheless, the Eisenhower administration, frightened like its predecessor by this specter of public opinion, at least appeared to have accepted the objectives and expectations of the opposition and thus allowed its own policies to be judged by the standards of the opposition. Judged by these standards, its policies could not help being found wanting. For, on the one hand, it was responsible enough not to embark upon military adventures; yet, on the other, it committed itself at least to the defense of Formosa, whose indispensability for the defense of the United States was accepted as a dogma by government and opposition alike. In consequence, the executive branch found itself continuously on the defensive, apologizing, as it were, for not living up to its own standards and feeling compelled from time to time to substitute for policy a momentous announcement or a grandiose gesture suggesting the imminence of forceful action. The executive branch had thus become the prisoner of the opposition. Too responsible to do what the opposition wanted it to do and prevented by its fear of public opinion from substituting a positive policy of its own for that of the opposition, the executive branch was reduced to having no positive policy at all, while trying to make it appear as though it were following in the footsteps of the opposition, however cautiously.

The Eisenhower administration was handicapped not only by its misunderstanding of public opinion, a misunderstanding it shares with its predecessor, but it added to that error one which is peculiarly its own: the misunderstanding of the nature of the "opposition" as it operates under the conditions of the American constitutional and political system. President Eisenhower's thinking on this matter was dominated by two basic assumptions: that of the two-party system in which the President's party supports the executive branch while the other party opposes it, and the assumption of the equality, in separation, of the executive and the legislative branch with regard to the conduct of foreign policy. Both assumptions are completely at odds with the constitutional principles and political practices of the American government. It can safely be said that diametrically opposite assumptions come closer to reflecting the actual facts of American political life.

On any controversial issue of United States foreign policy no Republican President can count upon the support of all members of his party. A Republican President, pursuing a rational foreign policy in a responsible manner, cannot help having at least a third of the Republican party in Congress against him, and on many a crucial issue he cannot count upon the support of even a bare majority. This seeming paradox is the result not of accident but of the political revolution which has transformed the American political scene in the last twenty-five years.

The general political and social outlook and the specific policies which this revolution has pushed to the fore are supported by a solid majority of the people but not by a majority of the Republican party in Congress. It follows that a Republican President, to be elected and to be re-elected, must identify himself with this outlook and these policies supported by the majority of the people. Yet he will have the support of his own party without major defections only between his nomination as a presidential candidate and his election, but neither before nor after. For the revolution which has transformed the political life of the United States has split the Republican party right down the middle. Its left wing has accepted, at least as inevitable, the results of that revolution, while its right wing lives in a prerevolutionary age, pursuing prerevolutionary policies with the fanaticism and irresponsibility of desperation.

The core of the opposition to a Republican President's foreign policies lies here, and it is against that opposition that the President must make his foreign policies prevail. A Republican President who thinks and operates in terms of party discipline and looks at the Republican party as his own and the Democratic party as the opposition confounds the American political system with the British and completely misreads the lines which divide both Congress and the people with regard to foreign policy. When it comes to foreign policy a Republican President has no party of his own to rely on, but must rely upon a bloc composed, at best, of the main bulk of the Democratic and a tenuous majority of the Republican party and, at worst, of a majority of the Democratic and a minority of the Republican party.

A Republican President who, like Mr. Eisenhower, conducts foreign policy with a view to maintaining the unity of his own party can do so only at the price of his own paralysis or of his own surrender. For political compromise is possible among groups that have certain basic assumptions in common and are at one in the desire to reconcile their formulation in a particular instance and to adjust their application for practical purposes. However, there can be no compromise with a group that denies the very assumptions of the foreign policy which the United States has pursued in the last decade and a half and regards the very principles of that foreign policy as an intellectual and moral aberration, if not close or tantamount to treason.

Misunderstanding what "opposition" means in American political life, the Eisenhower administration continuously and vainly tried to appease its real opposition which is within the Republican party, and it at the same time blessed, if not actively participated in, the attempts of that very opposition to stigmatize as the perpetrators and condoners of treason that very group within Congress and within the country which in terms of numbers and conviction provides the most solid support for the foreign policies the Eisenhower administration would have liked to pursue. This misunderstanding was symbolized in the paradoxical position of Senator Knowland who, as majority and minority leader in the Senate, had the official function to rally his party to the support of the President's foreign policies and who by conviction was the most outspoken critic of them. Even the most dexterous of politicians cannot at the same time be the chief spokesman for the executive branch and the leader of the opposition.

337

As the President has misjudged the meaning of "opposition" within the American political system, so has he misunderstood the relation the Constitution establishes between the President and Congress with regard to the conduct of foreign policy. Here again, the President has thought in terms of peaceful co-operation, while conflict is foreordained in the nature of things. The Constitution nowhere assigns the ultimate responsibility for the conduct of foreign policy to a particular office. It assigns certain functions to the President, others to Congress, and others still to the President and the Senate to be discharged in co-operation. Apart from these specific grants, the Constitution limits itself to an over-all distribution of powers between the President and Congress by vesting in the former the executive power and making him commander-in-chief of the armed forces and by vesting all legislative powers and the power of appropriations in Congress.

This silence of the Constitution as to where the ultimate responsibility for the conduct of American foreign policy rests is, in the words of Professor Corwin, "an invitation to struggle for the privilege of directing American foreign policy." This invitation has been accepted by all Presidents from Washington to Truman; for it could have been declined only at the price of surrendering the powers of the Presidency to a Congress which, in the nature of things, could not have discharged them. President Eisenhower was in large measure willing to pay that price, without, however, buying the peace with Congress he sought. Quite to the contrary, each surrender of executive powers to Congress called forth congressional demands for more, and, when the President retreated, he did not retreat into a prepared position from which to fight back but simply yielded to congressional pressure, waiting for renewed pressure to push him farther back. He resisted those pressures only when the issue of peace or war was directly at stake, not realizing that paralysis or surrender on other issues greatly complicated his task to defend his position against the advocates of war within his own administration and party.

It is at this point that the problem of the "opposition," discussed before, and the problem of the relations between the President and Congress merge. For when it is said that the President surrendered some of the prerogatives of his office in the conduct of foreign policy to Congress, the issue is oversimplified. It is not Congress as such, acting as a collective body by majority rule, which took over functions which by tradition and logic are the President's. It is to the opposition within his own party that the President surrendered them. While the more spectacular raids of the congressional opposition upon the executive preserve abated from 1955 onward, the impact which the opposition made upon both the substantive foreign policies and the personnel of the Eisenhower administration has been lasting and destructive of those very policies.

It stands to reason that a foreign policy which must be carried on under such conditions of domestic politics can leave little room for the initiative of even the greatest of statesmen. One might pause for a moment and imagine Sir Winston Churchill in his policies toward Egypt endeavoring to satisfy not only the military and political interests of Great Britain and the Egyptian aspirations for the evacuation of the Suez Canal Zone but also the opposition within his own party to that evacuation. Confronted with the choice between the national interest of Great Britain and considerations of domestic politics, he did not hesitate to choose the former. Yet the Eisenhower administration, confronted with similar choices, short of the ultimate choice between peace and war, invariably tended to choose the latter. In this it went far beyond those concessions which the requirements of democratic control and the peculiarities of the American constitutional and political system make inevitable.

Yet it is a tribute to President Eisenhower's innate good sense and a manifestation of the narrow limits within which objective circumstances confine initiative in foreign policy that the Eisenhower administration was by and large able, during the first years of its tenure of office, to continue the foreign policies of its predecessor, preserving its strong points, perpetuating and aggravating its weaknesses. It suffered its severest defeat on the plane of the imponderables of moral leadership and political prestige. And their drastic decline during the first two years of the Eisenhower administration can be directly traced to the ascendancy, during that very same period, of a kind of domestic politics that is incompatible not only with good foreign policy but with democratic government itself.

PART V

DILEMMAS

OF RESTORATION

The decline of Western political thought has called forth five typical reactions. These reactions are not only representative of the main streams of contemporary political thought, outside the methodological dogmatism and ideological rationalizations which do not face the problem of restoration at all but rather form an elaborate undertaking to avoid having to face it. But these five contemporary intellectual trends constitute also prototypes of reacting to a declining intellectual tradition. What can a man do who has become aware of such decline? He can corrupt the old ideas in order to make it appear as though they could explain the new facts; this is the case of Harold Laski. He can surrender himself to the facts as they are and gain from them whatever meaning they convey; this is the case of E. H. Carr. He can evoke the ideal of a past that never existed; this is the case of Bertrand de Jouvenel. He can seek both meaning and consolation in an imaginative interpretation of the facts, evoking the remembrance of religious experience; this is the case of Arnold Toynbee. He can search for the perennial truths of which the old ideas, the facts of experience, and the past are, as it were, intimations; this is the case of Walter Lippmann.

20 The Corruption of Liberal Thought: Harold Laski

The decline of the political philosophy of liberalism is due to the defects of its general philosophy, which contemporary developments have brought to the fore. What liberalism had to say about the nature of man, society, and politics is at odds with what we have experienced. More specifically, it has been unable to reconcile its original libertarian assumptions and postulates with its latter-day philosophy of the administrative and welfare state. Professor Laski, the most brilliant, erudite, and prolific exponent of the last stage of liberalism, exemplifies the philosophic insufficiency and political confusion of liberal thought. He also exemplifies the intellectual corruption that follows inevitably from an attempt to square the disparate elements of liberalism with each other and with the experiences of the age.

Liberty in the Modern State makes these points in ways quite unintended and unsuspected by its author. The book was first published in 1930; it was republished with a long, new introduction in 1937, then republished again in 1949.[1] The Introduction to this last edition was obviously completed in 1947 and incorporates substantial parts of that of 1937. Shockingly great is the distance between the Introduction and the main body of the book, which is a substantially unchanged reprint of the edition of 1930. That distance concerns philosophy and scholarship, quality of argument and of language, and, above all, intellectual responsibility. In the decline of a once great and exceptionally gifted mind, it demonstrates the initial weakness of the political philosophy of liberalism, the recent decomposition of that philosophy, and the reasons for the decline of liberty itself.

The only substantial deviations from the preceding editions occur in the Introduction, and philosophically they are less significant than the lack of change in the body of the book. The Introduction to the edition of 1937 started with a discussion of the crisis of capitalist

[1] New York: Viking Press, 1949.

democracy and of its inherent tendencies toward fascism, followed by a sympathetic and optimistic dissertation on the Soviet Union. This dissertation has been substantially retained in the 1949 edition, with only a few significant changes, to one of which we shall return. The other part has been replaced by a new discussion of the ills of capitalist democracy, arriving at the dual conclusion that "private ownership of the means of production is no longer compatible with democratic institutions" (p. 17) and that "the principle of national sovereignty has exhausted its usefulness" (p. 18).

When the body of this book first appeared in 1930 it was received with deserved praise. The nobility of its moral concern for the individual, the cogency of its argument, the sweep of its erudition are indeed impressive. Its strength, no less than its weakness, is in large measure that of John Stuart Mill, and this is high praise indeed. There is, it is true, already in the Laski of 1930 a certain sentimental verbosity and fuzziness in concepts which are happily absent in Mill. Yet the philosophic position of Laski is that of classic liberalism. Professors Hayek and Mises can hardly have found fault with it. In his own words, this is

the essence of [the] argument. I have taken the view that liberty means that there is no restraint upon those conditions which, in modern civilization, are the necessary guarantees of individual happiness. There is no liberty without freedom of speech. There is no liberty if special privilege restricts the franchise to a portion of the community. There is no liberty if a dominant opinion can control the social habits of the rest without persuading the latter that there are reasonable grounds for the control. For, as I have argued, since each man's experience is ultimately unique, he alone can fully appreciate its significance. . . .

But no man, of course, stands alone. He lives with others and in others. His liberty, therefore, is never absolute, since the conflict of experience means the imposition of certain ways of behavior upon all of us lest conflict destroy peace. That imposition, broadly speaking, is essential to liberty, since it makes for peace; and peace is the condition of continuity of liberty [p. 129].

The philosophic weakness of this position is to be found in the weakness of its five basic concepts: liberty, the individual, the individual good, the common good, the identification of the absolute and relative good.

The problem of liberty in relation to the state concerns, in the words of John Stuart Mill, "the nature and limits of the power which can be legitimately exercised by society over the individual." Its perennial theme is "the struggle between Liberty and Authority." A concept of liberty as broad and indefinite as that used by Laski carries within itself the possibility of conclusions destructive of the very antithesis which gives rise to the problem of liberty. This problem is intelligible only under the assumption that man ought to be free from political authority in certain respects and subject to it in others. The assumptions of totalitarianism, destroying the rights of the individual in the face of political authority, and the assumptions of anarchism, denying the claims of political authority, make it altogether impossible to speak of liberty in the political sense. It has often been noticed that a consistent liberalism leads to anarchism. Laski recognizes that connection, too, and approves of it.

The conception of the individual as a unique personality with experiences and judgments all his own may be valid in some systems of art, religion, or psychology, but it certainly is the very negation of political experience. However right the author may be in his strictures against the excesses of the idealistic theory of the state, political authority is founded upon a consensus of all or at least of the majority, that is, upon shared moral and political convictions which are the very negation of that uniqueness and privacy upon which Laski dwells. Such consensus may be the product of a common religion, a secular tradition, the national mores or it may be instilled in the reluctant citizens with fire and sword. Without it there can be no state and no government; for without it there can be no political authority accepted at least by the majority as legitimate, nor that voluntary obedience which the author so rightly stresses. Here again, the conclusion from the premise is anarchy.

Laski conceives of the individual good, which freedom must promote, as happiness, and of happiness as the satisfaction of individual desires. We are here not concerned with the question of whether such a conception of happiness is psychologically valid. Even if it were, it would still have to be admitted that it is a distinctive characteristic of civil society, as it is of individual morality, to approve of certain desires as good and to reject others as bad. As a philosophic conception, happiness has meaning only within the context of a system of selective values which define what happiness is in

345

the first place. In the absence of such a system, happiness will be defined by the accident of implicit valuations, that is, by the preferences of the author or of the group for which he pretends to speak.

Laski is, of course, not oblivious of the inevitability of conflict arising from the incompatibility of unique personalities and their valuations and desires, and he recognizes the consequent need for a mediating force. He finds that force in reason. However, reason in the abstract has nothing to say about the solution of social conflicts. It is only in the concrete, in a specific philosophic and social context, that reason can tell us which interests must be protected and which sacrificed. In other words, no rational solution of a social conflict, in theory or in practice, can dispense with a political philosophy which has developed a concept of the common good, or with an appraisal of the power of the social forces identified with the two sides of the conflict. Yet Laski's conception of the common good is identical with the sum total of the individual desires mediated by reason. That argument begs the question and leaves the problem where we encountered it.

These weaknesses of Laski's philosophic position are intimately connected with the last of the weaknesses that we have proposed to discuss. Political philosophy, to be fruitful, must make the Aristotelian distinction between what is ideally good and what is good under the circumstances. It is one thing to provide an ideal solution for the conflict between liberty and authority, a solution which might well be tantamount to anarchism. It is quite another thing to consider the problem of liberty in the context of what is attainable under the conditions of British society in 1930 or of American society in 1950. To confound both approaches, as Laski does, may lead, if the author is consistent, to the condemnation of all actually possible solutions in view of the unattainable ideal. If the author is inconsistent but is quite naturally moved by strong personal preferences, as Laski is, he will measure some political systems by the ideal, others by the attainable, and thus obtain the political conclusions that he prefers to obtain.

These defects, let us repeat it, are the defects of the intellectual tradition to which Laski belongs. The faults of the Introduction of 1937 and 1947 are all his own. To point all of them out and analyze them would require a book. Let us limit ourselves to four representative ones: one conceptual, one philosophic, and two factual.

On the very first page of the Introduction the conceptual foundation for any rational discussion of the problem of liberty disintegrates with the statement that "the future of liberty depends upon the realization of those four freedoms upon which President Roosevelt laid such eloquent emphasis. . . ." It is fanciful to suggest that the determination of "the nature and limits of the power which can be legitimately exercised by society over the individual" depends upon the realization of such vague and unattainable ideals as freedom from fear and freedom from want. Given this conceptual starting point, no demonstration is needed to show that these ideals, whatever they may mean, are not, and are not likely to be, realized and that, hence, liberty does not exist and is not likely to exist. There is nothing left for us to do but to bewail this sad state of affairs with sentimental rhetoric and to comment on it with the shopworn clichés of progressive journalism.

To turn to an example of philosophic analysis, it is obvious that the phenomenon of fascism has a profound bearing upon the problem of liberty in our time. What, then, is the purpose of fascism in this respect? "The purpose of fascism is to prevent the relations of production from coming into a natural harmony with the forces of production; for that prevention, and increasingly, the method of coercion is inescapable" (p. 30). Can anything be simpler, or more absurd? One must, then, I suppose, assume that the wave of pseudo-religious fanaticism with its worship of violence for its own sake, which swept through Germany long before the industrialists as a class, together with virtually all other social groups, jumped on the bandwagon of naziism, was just an ideological superstructure whirling in the air until it settled down upon its material foundations, discovered as a dialectic afterthought. To call this kind of reasoning by cliché Marxism would be an insult to the memory of Marx and Engels, Kautsky and Luxemburg, Lenin and Trotsky. Call it "Pravdaism" or "Browderism," if you wish.

But let us consider simple matters, matters of fact. On pages 20–21 we read: ". . . and it is still more true of the great corporations today than it was when General Negrier wrote of them nearly forty years ago that *'les sociétés financières estiment que les gouverne-*

ments ont le devoir de faire la guerre pour assurer leurs bénéfices' ['the corporations believe that it is the governments' duty to make war so that they may be assured of their profits']." The general, whoever he was, may plead ignorance, for he could not have been acquainted with the empirical studies of Robbins, Schumpeter, Staley, Sulzbach, Viner, and Winslow, which have exploded the Marxist myth of the warmongering capitalists. But what excuses does Laski have?

Laski finds little actual liberty in the Soviet Union but great promise for the future. On page 43 of the edition of 1937 he said: "In the classic sense of absolute liberalism freedom does not exist in the Soviet Union." This is, of course, true of the Soviet Union as of all other political systems past or present, and, hence, the statement is trivial. On page 27 of the edition of 1949 that passage reads as follows: "In the classic sense the Four Freedoms do not exist in the Soviet Union." The truth is that, while we can speak of classic liberalism in contrast to other types, there is no such thing as freedom from want or freedom from fear in the classic or in any other sense. There is freedom from want and freedom from fear, or there is not. Laski must have known that the Four Freedoms are not realized in the Soviet Union; yet his political preferences did not allow him to admit it. Thus he suggested that, while the Four Freedoms in the classic sense do not exist in the Soviet Union, they might well exist in some other sense.

How was such a descent from the comparative heights of 1930 possible? The answer to this question will shed light upon the decline of liberalism as theory and practice of government.

The rise of bolshevism and fascism in the Western world denied the very assumptions upon which the philosophy of nineteenth-century liberalism had been founded. The society of rational individuals, either developing their unique personalities and satisfying their desires in harmony or settling conflicts among them by the appeal to reason, revealed itself as a mirage engendered by the fleeting conditions of a unique historic constellation. Under different historic conditions, such as those of the interwar years, large segments of Western society showed none of the rational qualities of the liberal prototype. Instead, they sought a new consensus either in revealed religion or in the political religions of totalitarianism. In the face of this phenomenon, for the advent of which their political philosophy did not prepare them, the liberals either continue to reassert the laissez-faire principles of 1850 and thus, by standing still while society moves, become the spokesmen for the tories of the 1950's; or they embrace, sometimes without knowing it, one or the other of the totalitarian creeds. Laski, who cannot be a Fascist and can no longer be a liberal in the "classic" sense in which he was one in 1930, becomes a Marxist who tries to interpret the reality of Russian bolshevism in terms of the liberal philosophy. He tries to do for bolshevism what in the thirties so many of his countrymen tried to do for fascism, that is, to prove that totalitarianism is really a kind of advanced liberalism, disfigured by some blemishes of which time will take care.

Yet the Laski of 1930 at least intimated the impossibility of such a task. He showed then that absolute power, far from tending to limit and reform itself, has the innate tendency to increase its hold upon the individual and to become more oppressive as voluntary obedience wanes. He could have added, if his philosophy had not obscured the realities of politics, that this is particularly true of an absolute power which identifies its monopoly of power with a monopoly of truth, whose monopoly of the most effective weapons of warfare makes popular revolution impossible, and whose totalitarian control no private activity can escape. Here lies the real threat to liberty in our time. The Laski of 1930 could see at least part of that truth, the Laski of 1947 cannot. In this respect, it may be said, Professor Laski differs somewhat from the Bourbons of the Restoration. They are said to have learned nothing and to have forgotten nothing. Comparing the Laski of 1947 with the Laski of 1930 one cannot help concluding, with genuine sorrow, that he has learned little and forgotten a great deal.

21 The Surrender to the Immanence of Power: E. H. Carr

Of the four books which constitute Mr. Carr's major contribution to political thought, one, *The Twenty Years' Crisis*,[1] is primarily diagnostic and critical; the three others, *Conditions of Peace*,[2] *Nationalism and After*,[3] and *The Soviet Impact on the Western World*,[4] are intended to be primarily constructive and to offer a cure for the disease.

The foundation upon which the critical analysis of *The Twenty Years' Crisis* is built is the juxtaposition of utopianism and realism. In its period of immaturity, all science goes through a utopian stage "in which the element of wish or purpose is overwhelmingly strong, and the inclination to analyze facts and means weak or non-existent" (p. 8). That initial stage is succeeded by a period of realism which is able "to distinguish the analysis of what is from aspiration about what should be" (p. 13). Realism "places its emphasis on the acceptance of facts and on the analysis of their causes and consequences" (p. 14). The experiences of the interwar years revealed the weakness of the utopian approach to international politics and made its realistic analysis both possible and imperative. Yet a mature political science must combine utopian and realistic thought, purpose and analysis, ethics and politics.

According to Mr. Carr, "the exposure by realistic criticism of the hollowness of the utopian edifice is the most urgent task of the moment in international thought" (p. 113). "Clearly all popular postwar theories of international politics are reflections, seen in an America mirror, of nineteenth-century liberal thought" (p. 37). Mr. Carr finds the utopian element in the belief that "nineteenth century liberal democracy was based, not on a balance of forces peculiar to the economic development of the period and of the countries concerned, but on certain *a priori* rational principles which had only to be applied in other contexts to produce similar results" (p. 37).

[1] London: Macmillan & Co., 1940.   [3] New York: Macmillan Co., 1945.
[2] New York: Macmillan Co., 1942.   [4] New York: Macmillan Co., 1947.

This writer has no quarrel with Mr. Carr's detailed analysis, in the light of these assumptions, of the main modes of international thought and of the institutional devices which were carried from the domestic scene of the nineteenth century to the international scene of the twentieth. The League of Nations, harmony of interests, collective security, and identification of the national interest with the universal good are indeed classic examples of a utopian rationalism which erects limited experiences and interests into absolute principles and deduces from those principles solutions capable of universal application. "What matters is that these supposedly absolute and universal principles were not principles at all, but the unconscious reflections of national policy based on a particular interpretation of national interests at a particular time. . . . The bankruptcy of utopianism resides not in its failure to live up to its principles, but in the exposure of its inability to provide any absolute and disinterested standard for the conduct of international affairs" (p. 111).

Yet while Mr. Carr destroys the nineteenth-century legacy of political thought, he knows that realism is not enough. "Consistent realism excludes four things which appear to be essential ingredients of all effective political thinking: a finite goal, an emotional appeal, a right of moral judgment, and a ground for action" (p. 113). "Having demolished the current utopia with the weapons of realism, we still need to build a new utopia of our own, which will one day fall to the same weapons. The human will, will continue to seek an escape from the logical consequences of realism in the vision of an international order which, as soon as it crystallizes itself into concrete political form, becomes tainted with self-interest and hypocrisy, and must once more be attacked with the instruments of realism" (p. 118).

Thus Mr. Carr, the realist, sets out in search of a new utopia, and all his subsequent thinking becomes the Odyssey of a mind that has discovered the phenomenon of power and longs to transcend it. That search for principles which can give moral meaning, and set normative limits, to the struggle for power on the international scene brings Mr. Carr back to where he started from: to power itself.

That return to power takes on four different aspects in different periods of Mr. Carr's thinking: appeasement of Germany in *The*

Twenty Years' Crisis, the postulate of a strong collectivist state in *Conditions of Peace*, the sacrifice of the small nations to the great powers in *Nationalism and After*, fascination by the Soviet Union in *The Soviet Impact on the Western World*.

In *The Twenty Years' Crisis*, the last word of international morality is the demand for self-sacrifice. That demand is addressed particularly to the beneficiaries of the status quo. They must give up some of their advantages, not only to those who seek adjustments within the framework of the existing status quo, but also and primarily to those who challenge the existence and justice of that status quo itself. "The process of give-and-take must apply to challenges to the existing order. Those who profit most by that order can in the long run only hope to maintain it by making sufficient concessions to make it tolerable to those who profit by it least. And the responsibility for seeing that these changes take place as far as possible in an orderly way rests as much on the defenders as on the challengers" (p. 215). In consequence, "a successful foreign policy must oscillate between the apparently opposite poles of force and appeasement" (p. 284). The Munich settlement of 1938, then, becomes a modern paradigm of a successful foreign policy thus defined, and Neville Chamberlain, the prototype of a statesman combining the elements of realism and utopianism in his thought and action. "The element of power was present" in that settlement. "The element of morality was also present in the form of the common recognition by the powers . . . of a criterion applicable to the dispute: the principle of self-determination. . . . The change in itself was one which corresponded both to a change in the European equilibrium of forces and to accepted canons of international morality" (p. 282).

The Twenty Years' Crisis was in page proof when the Second World War broke out; *Conditions of Peace* was in the press when the attack on Pearl Harbor brought the United States into the war and Germany and Japan were at the summit of their power. *The Twenty Years' Crisis* attacked the application of the nineteenth-century philosophy of liberal democracy to international affairs; *Conditions of Peace* examines that philosophy in all its manifestations and finds it wanting. More determinedly and more seriously than even *The Twenty Years' Crisis*, *Conditions of Peace* is permeated with the conviction that the twentieth century is fundamentally different from the century that preceded it and that there could be a turning-back to the nineteenth-century modes of thought and action only at the risk of catastrophic failure. The democracies were satisfied to defend the domestic and international status quo with the outworn ideas and institutions of the nineteenth century. Thus it fell to bolshevism and fascism to offer the world a new political order. "Soviet Russia, soon to be followed by Fascist Italy and Nazi Germany, found in 'planned economy' the new twentieth-century concept which was to replace nineteenth-century liberalism; and having gained the initiative, these countries at length compelled the conservative Powers to follow slowly and reluctantly in their train" (p. xx). The idealists of the English-speaking world transform themselves into the reactionaries of the twentieth century, "carried away by the last expiring convulsions of a world revolution which set in 150 years ago" and putting themselves "in opposition to the new world revolution which first broke through the crust of the existing order in the Bolshevik revolution of 1917" (p. 7). Hitler, the Napoleon of the twentieth century, "has consummated the work, which Marx and Lenin had begun, of overthrowing the nineteenth-century capitalistic system . . . and in this sense his work, like that of Napoleon, cannot and will not be undone" (pp. 9–10).

The revolution of the twentieth century is directed against liberal democracy, national self-determination, and laissez faire economics. The revolutionary challenge to democracy and national self-determination must be met by redefinition and reinterpretation. The challege to nineteenth-century economics must be met by a planned economy. It is here that the foremost task of revolutionary renewal is to be found. Democratic forms and political rights have been rendered illusory by the overriding force of economic power. "Under existing democratic institutions, the will of the unorganised majority is impotent to assert itself against the domination of organised economic power. It has come to be widely believed today, and with much plausibility, that the attitudes and policies of political parties in most democratic countries are determined only in a minor degree by the opinions of the electorate which they purport to represent, and in a major degree by the vested interests which supply the bulk of the party funds. In other words, national policy on vital issues is really settled, as Marx alleged, not by a democratic counting of votes, but by the result of a perpetual struggle for power between rival economic interests . . ." (pp. 27–28). "Democracy must be redefined as a system of government based on political rights valid not merely against military, but against economic, power" (p. 23). To make planning possible, we must search for a "moral purpose powerful enough to generate self-sacrifice on the scale requisite to enable civilization to survive" (p. 119). Communism, like Christianity, has such a moral purpose. "The cooperation between the Western peoples and Soviet Russia in the war should help to resolve the antithesis, incidental rather than fundamental, between the secular ideals of Christianity and those of Communism" (p. 121). In both the domestic and the international spheres, the traditional emphasis upon rights and benefits must be replaced by stress on obligations and services.

These themes are more fully developed in *Nationalism and After*, published at the end of the Second World War, and in *The Soviet Impact on the Western World*, published in 1947, when the conflict between the Soviet Union and the Western world had reached unprecedented depths. Mr. Carr makes a convincing case for the assertion that twentieth-century nationalism differs profoundly from its nineteenth-century predecessor. This difference is the result of three factors: "the bringing of new social strata within the effective membership of the nation, the visible reunion of economic with political power, and the increase in the number of nations" (p. 18). "The combination of these factors has found expression in two world wars, or two installments of the same world war, in a single generation, and has imparted to them a peculiar quality of embittered exasperation for which it would be difficult to find a precedent in any war in history" (p. 27). "The failure to create an international community of nations on the basis of international treaties and international law marks the final bankruptcy of nationalism in the West" (p. 32).

Mr. Carr detects a retrogression of unbridled nationalism in certain tendencies which have become visible during the Second World War, such as the widespread collaboration with the German conqueror and the acceptance of a new, supranational order. The nation as the final unit of international organization has been made obsolete by modern military and economic developments. The self-sufficient nation can no longer assure to its members military security or economic well-being. National self-determination, in particular, applied without regard to such military and economic considerations, has become an anarchical force destructive of international order. The solution, according to Mr. Carr, lies in the separation of non-political from political authority. The nation may remain the center of certain types of non-political authority and loyalty. Politically, economically, and militarily the nation must yield to multinational units of which the *Grossraum* of Nazi Germany and the Soviet Union are the outstanding examples.

In *The Soviet Impact on the Western World*, the Soviet Union takes the place of the pioneer of the future. As Hitler was saluted as the Napoleon of the twentieth century in *Conditions of Peace*, so now Stalin appears to Mr. Carr as the Wilson of the Second World War. "The missionary role which had been filled in the first World War by American democracy and Woodrow Wilson had passed in the second World War to Soviet democracy and Marshal Stalin" (p. 3). What Mr. Carr calls "Soviet democracy" is, according to him, really an offshoot of Western democracy. In the West, political democracy and social democracy became antagonistic after the middle class had achieved its revolutionary objectives against the feudal order. The bourgeoisie of the West led political democracy to victory. The Russian proletariat achieved social democracy. "The challenge which Soviet democracy presents to the Western world is a challenge to complete the unfinished revolution" (p. 10). In consequence, Mr. Carr equates the Cromwellian, Jacobin, and Bolshevist dictatorships as instruments for achieving democracy. "There is, therefore, no essential incompatibility between democracy and dictatorship" (p. 11). Since in this view the Soviet Union has become the champion of democracy in the mid-twentieth century, it is not surprising to learn that "the cult of the 'common man' now fashionable in English-speaking countries is perhaps a first result of the impact of Soviet democracy" (p. 12). "The broad lines of Soviet policy may be dictated from the center. But the Soviet Union has never ignored the human element, or underestimated the extent to which the execution of any policy depends on the enthusiasm and initiative of the individual citizen; and it has shown itself as well aware as the western world of what Sir Ernest Barker has described as a main function of democracy—to 'enlist the effective thought of the whole community in the operation of discussion.' Here at any rate is a challenge of Soviet democracy to western political institutions about which western democrats will be well advised to ponder" (pp. 18–19). What is true of the cult of the common man and of public discussion is also true of planning: ". . . Lord Keynes' doctrines found such ready acceptance in Great Britain and elsewhere partly because the ground had already been prepared in the minds of his contemporaries by contemplation of the planned economy of the Soviet Union" (p. 34).

In international affairs the Soviet impact has been in the main twofold: the development of propaganda as a normal instrument of foreign policy and the emphasis upon the power factor as against its ideological disguises, practiced by the Western statesmen of the League of Nations period. Fundamentally, however, the Soviet impact on the Western world is moral. "The gravamen of the Marxist revolution is not that it has exposed the failures and shortcomings of western democracy, but that it has called in question the moral authority of the ideals and principles of western democracy by declaring them to be a reflexion of the interests of a privileged class" (p. 94). "The fate of the western world will turn on its ability to meet the Soviet challenge by a successful search for new forms of social and economic action in which what is valid in individualist and democratic tradition can be applied to the problems of mass civilization" (p. 113).

There can be no doubt that Mr. Carr's work constitutes a contribution to political thought of the first order. No contemporary thinker, with the exception of Reinhold Niebuhr, has seen more clearly and exposed with more acute brilliance the essential defects of Western political thought. Even in so monumental a failure as *The Soviet Impact on the Western World*—a failure because it confronts Soviet ideology with democratic practice—there is much critical analysis which Western thinkers might well ponder. Yet, as we have seen, it was Mr. Carr's purpose not only to give a critical analysis of the Western tradition of political thought but also to replace the old and obsolete with a new synthesis of realism and utopianism, theory and practice, ethics and politics; and the main bulk of Mr. Carr's work is dedicated to that purpose. In view of this purpose the over-all impression of Mr. Carr's work is one of failure. What are the reasons for the failure of a work undertaken with so singular an equipment of mind, learning, and honest purpose?

The fundamental reason is philosophic. Mr. Carr sets out to discover a new morality in the political world without a clear notion of what morality is. The philosophically untenable equation of utopia, theory, and morality, which is at the foundation of *The Twenty Years' Crisis*, leads of necessity to a relativistic, instrumentalist conception of morality. Morality, then, becomes "an escape from the logical consequences of realism, which, once it is achieved, must once more be attacked with instruments of realism" (*The Twenty Years' Crisis*, p. 118). In another contribution to the problem, "The Moral Foundations for World Order,"[5] Mr. Carr has nothing better to offer than a "compromise between morality and power," and throughout his work he relies heavily upon Niebuhr's *Moral Man and Immoral Society*, unaware that Mr. Niebuhr has long since given up the juxtaposition which the title indicates.

Consequently, Mr. Carr has no transcendent point of view from which to survey the political scene and to appraise the phenomenon of power. Thus the political moralist transforms himself into a utopian of power. Whoever holds seeming superiority of power becomes of necessity the repository of superior morality as well. Power thus corrupts, not only the actor on the political scene, but even the observer, unfortified by a transcendent standard of ethics. This is the lesson taught by the fate of the political romantics of whom the outstanding representatives are Adam Müller and Carl Schmitt. It is a dangerous thing to be a Machiavelli. It is a disastrous thing to be a Machiavelli without *virtù*.

[5] In *Foundations for World Order* (Denver: Social Science Foundation, University of Denver, 1948).

22 *The Evocation of the Past: Bertrand de Jouvenel*

Bertrand de Jouvenel undertakes to face the problem of power, indeed the central problem of our age, but in truth he does not face it at all. The intended confrontation becomes evasion and escape. It must be borne in mind that theoretical concern with power as a general phenomenon is peculiar to our age. Before Hobbes, no Western political thinker dealt systematically with power as a general phenomenon, and Hobbes himself remained an incident rather than the founder of a tradition. It was only in the historiography and philosophy of history of the nineteenth century that such a tradition was established, and the sociology and political science of the twentieth century have taken up the theme. Yet they have done so only halfheartedly, qualifying and distorting, obscuring and embellishing the reality of power as a general phenomenon. Of this modern tendency to face the problem of power but to face it, as it were, with a squinting eye, M. de Jouvenel's book, *On Power: Its Nature and the History of Its Growth*,[1] is an outstanding example. It is outstanding in its originality and brilliance, its force of argument, and the relevance of its diagnosis. It is also outstanding in the arbitrariness of its argumentation from history and in the partiality with which the central problem is posed and developed.

It is significant—and the significance of it will become fully apparent in the course of the discussion—that the book is not "on power" at all. According to the translator, "the word 'Power,' whenever it begins with a capital letter, denotes the central governmental authority in states or communities—*l'ensemble des éléments gouvernementaux* . . ." (p. xiii). In other words, the book is concerned only with a particular type of power, that is, governmental power, while implicitly assuming in the title and throughout the argument that there is no other power to be concerned about. This substitution of *pars pro toto* gives the book its peculiar focus. The book

[1] New York: Viking Press, 1949.

358

observes with striking clarity what is within that focus; it sees either not at all or only in dim, distorted outline what is outside the focus. But all the time, by means of a semantic equivocation, the illusion is created that the focus comprises not only Power, that is, government, but also power as such, that is, as a general social phenomenon. It requires a very attentive reader to keep in mind that in the terminology of the author Power is sometimes quite different from power, different as object of scientific analysis and different as object of moral evaluation.

The central theme of the book is the enormous power of the modern state. The modern state has become a "Minotaur," and the continuous increase in the power of the state for almost a thousand years is concomitant with the incessant advance of warfare toward total war. "Therefore the extension of Power, which means its ability to control ever more completely a nation's activities, is responsible for the extension of war" (p. 7). Democracy, in turn, is responsible for the extension of Power. "Democracy, then, in the centralizing, pattern-making, absolutist shape which we have given to it is, it is clear, the time of tyranny's incubation" (p. 11). It is the purpose of the book "to examine the reasons why, and the way in which, Power grows in society" (p. 13).

At the core of the author's argument lies the contrast between aristocratic and monarchical government, on the one hand, and democracy, on the other. The bad and dangerous effects of Power are connected with the latter; what is beneficial and harmless in Power derives from the former. The modern history of the Western world is generally conceived as a progression toward liberty and, in turn, toward limitation on government, liberty becoming greater and government growing weaker as we approach the twentieth century. According to the author, the exact opposite is true. "The idea that Power is of God buttressed, so it is said, a monarchy that was both arbitrary and unlimited right through the Dark Ages. . . . There is not a word of truth in all this. Let us remember . . . that Power in medieval times was shared . . . , limited . . . , and that, above all, it was not sovereign. . . . In fact, so far from having been a cause of greatness in Power, the conception of divine sovereignty was for many centuries the companion of its weakness" (p. 28).

"The consecrated king of the Middle Ages was a Power as tied down and as little arbitrary as we can conceive. He was simultaneously constrained by standing human law, i.e., custom, and by the Divine Law, and could hardly trust his own reading of his duty about anything. The court of peers was there to compel his respect for custom, and the Church took care that he continued as the assiduous viceregent of the heavenly king, whose instructions in their every point he must obey" (p. 30).

The common belief in the progressive liberation of the individual is an illusion. "The reason [for this illusion] is that there are in society, in addition to the state and the individual, social authorities as well, which also claim from the human being their due of obedience and services. And the diminution or disappearance of his obligations to a social authority may affect his life and stir his interest more than the aggravation of his obligations to the political authority" (p. 158).

A revolution, prepared by Marsilius of Padua and by the Reformation, was needed to substitute for the sovereignty of God the sovereignty of the people. With the weakening of the Church, God was transformed from an ally of the people against Power into an ally of Power against the people. With that transformation the absolute monarchy came into existence. Yet at the same time there arose the doctrine that Power is conferred by the people, thus barring the road to absolutism. That, according to the author, is "the great illusion" (p. 33). By quoting extensively from Hobbes, Spinoza, and Rousseau, the author reaches the conclusion that the unlimited character of Power is the inevitable result of popular sovereignty. "What a contrast is here," he exclaims by juxtaposing Spinoza and St. Augustine, "between a Power which is held to the execution of the divine law and one which, after subsuming every individual right, has become a law to itself!" (p. 35).

Popular sovereignty and divine sovereignty seem to be rather similar in their relation to Power. "Both allow a right of command which, though it is unlimited, is not inherent in the governors. The right belongs to a superior power—whether it be God or the people —which cannot by its nature exercise the right itself. Therefore they have to confer a mandate on a Power which can exercise it. Both state more or less explicitly that the mandatories will be tied by rules: in other words, Power's behaviour is subject to either the

Divine Will or the general will" (p. 39). Yet the holders of Power tend to usurp the sovereignty which in theory they exercise by delegation. "They will in the end give themselves out as resuming in their own persons the Divine Will or the general will, as the case may be; Louis XIV, for instance, claimed the rights of God, and Napoleon those of the people" (p. 39). Control of Power, either through the Church or through parliament, is bound to remain ineffective; for sovereignty, being "in essence one and indivisible" (p. 40), cannot be shared by two different sets of agents. Thus the monarchy wins over the Church at the end of the Middle Ages, as in our age either the executive or the legislature comes to dominate the people.

This despotism of our age, however, is likely to be more formidable than that of divine sovereignty for two reasons. Popular sovereignty dispenses with "the Divine Will, which shows itself to men under the forms of a Law Eternal, to command whatever he pleases" (p. 42). Further, popular sovereignty justifies itself primarily in terms of its origin, so that whatever the people want is good because they want it. Medieval Power is limited by the conception of its end, which must be just for Power to be legitimate. When the conception of the end of government reappears in the political thought of the nineteenth century, it is no longer connected with individuals as such but with the state as an organism, which has an existence of its own transcending that of its individual members and is an end in itself, to which the individuals are subservient. This is the heritage of Hegel. In it democracy takes on a new meaning. "In the sense of individualist social philosophy it is the rule of the Rights of Man; in a political philosophy divorced from social individualism it is the absolutism of a government which draws its title from the masses" (p. 47). Here, then, the end is no longer, as it was in the Middle Ages, justice in the sense that each individual must obtain his due. Justice, now, becomes a postulate of society, and to realize this end the limitless expansion of Power is justified.

Underlying this discussion is the conception that Power, that is, the state and its government, are not "the natural product of human sociability" (p. 99). They owe their existence to the instinct of domination, that is, the lust for power (with a small *p*). "The monarch is not in the least the creature of his people, set up to satisfy their wants. He is rather a parasitic and dominating growth which has detached itself from the dominating group of parasitic conquerors. But the need to establish his authority, to maintain it and keep it supplied, binds him to a course of conduct which profits the vast majority of his subjects. To suppose that majority rule functions only in democracy is a fantastic illusion. The king, who is but one solitary individual, stands far more in need of the general support of society than any other form of government. And, since it is human nature for habit to engender affection, the king, though acting at first only from concern for authority, comes to act with affection as well and in the end to be motivated by affection. The mystical principle of the *rex* has come again" (p. 106).

This duality and inner contradiction of Power is of its essence; it must be egoist and social at the same time. To prepare for Power which has rid itself of its egoism and has become completely virtuous is the worst of illusions; "it has become the fruitful cause of the great disturbances which desolate our age and threaten the very existence of civilization" (p. 117). "It is a noteworthy fact that all the greatest political mistakes stem from defective appraisals of the common good—mistakes from which egoism, had it been called into consultation, would have warned Power off" (p. 124). Similarly, it is not surprising that the philosopher constructing a simple and rigid system of thought finds himself in alliance with the tyrant who endeavors to translate such a system of thought into action. To accomplish what the philosopher demands, Power must grow to enormous dimensions, and Power grows in proportion to the moral sublimity and comprehensiveness of the utopian scheme.

The growth of Power manifests itself in history in three different respects: in the ever increasing quantity of human and material resources which Power marshals for its own purposes, especially for the purposes of war; in the ability of Power to make the laws, and any kind of them, instead of, as in the Middle Ages, being subject to an unchangeable set of rules of conduct; and in the leveling process by which all intermediate social authorities are eliminated. In this last capacity Power plays a revolutionary role. As the king destroys the feudal aristocracy, so the modern state undermines the capitalist authorities. In these revolutions, Power is always the ally of the common people. "The passion for absolutism is, inevitably, in conspiracy with the passion for equality" (p. 177).

"Where will it end? In the destruction of all other commands for the benefit of one alone—that of the state. In each man's absolute freedom from every family and social authority, a freedom the price of which is complete submission to the state. In the complete equality as between themselves of all citizens, paid for by their equal abasement before the power of their absolute master—the state. In the disappearance of every constraint which does not emanate from the state, and in the denial of every pre-eminence which is not approved by the state. In a word, it ends in the atomization of society, and in the rupture of every private tie linking man and man, whose only bond is now their common bondage to the state. The extremes of individualism and socialism meet: that was their predestined course" (p. 172). Yet this is not the end. "Conqueror though it is of the aristocracy which took shape in society, the state will in the end be dismembered by the statocracy which it itself has borne. The beneficiaries of the state leave it, taking with them a veritable dowry of wealth and authority, leaving the state impoverished and powerless. Then it becomes the turn of the state to break down these new social molecules, containing as they do the human energies which it needs. And so the process of the state's expansion starts all over again.

"Such is the spectacle which history presents to us. Now we see an aggressive state pulling down what other authorities have built up, now we see an omnipotent and distended state bursting like a ripe spore and releasing from its midst a new feudalism which robs it of its substance" (p. 176). And each popular revolution, undertaken in the name of liberty, is but a milestone in the growth of Power. "In the final analysis revolutions are made, not for man, but for Power" (p. 235).

Of this development, democracy is the prime example. "Conceived as the foundation of liberty, it paves the way for tyranny. Born for the purpose of standing as a bulwark against Power, it ends by providing Power with the finest soil it has ever had in which to spread itself over the social field" (p. 238). It amounts to "the substitution of the arbitrary will of a body or of a crowd for the arbitrary will of a monarch as the principle of rule" (p. 252). This development is particularly obvious in modern parliamentary institutions. "What had been a body for the protection of private citizens is now one for the advancement of the public interest, and has been clothed with the formidable power of legislation. . . . In the end, therefore, the principle of legality, intended as the absolute guarantee of each man's liberty, was to come to justify the absolute commission of that liberty to the discretion of a parliamentary aristocracy" (pp. 242–43).

Here again, monarchy gains by comparison. "The royal will was, and was known to be, that of a crowned head, his favourite, or his minister; it was in that respect as human and *personal* as that of anyone else. The will of democratic Power goes by the name of *general*. It crushes each individual beneath the weight of the sum of the individuals represented by it; it oppresses each private interest in the name of a general interest which is incarnate in itself. The democratic fiction confers on the rulers the authority of the whole. It is the whole that both wills and acts" (p. 257). "It comes to this: that the 'Power of the people,' so called, is in fact linked to the people only by an extremely slack umbilical cord—general elections; it is, to all intents and purposes, a 'Power over the people,' a Power which is all the greater for getting its authorization from this cord" (p. 280).

Ultimately, sovereignty passes "from parliament to the victorious machine, and elections are now no more than a plebiscite by which a whole people puts itself in the power of a small gang" (p. 275). The end is inevitably a totalitarianism which promises security and destroys liberty. Power, erecting the fragments of its knowledge into a dogma to bring happiness to mankind, transforms itself into a theocracy whose beneficence and, hence, whose authority have no limits. Thus totalitarian democracy unites, for the first time in Western civilization, the spiritual and temporal powers. "From not having known how to preserve, and from not knowing how to restore, the delicate and living harmony of a highly civilized society, we are returning to the form of cohesion which is that of the primitive tribe" (p. 377).

The great merit of this book lies in a penetrating and subtle analysis of the growth of governmental power in our time and of the pitfalls that modern mass democracy encounters. In this analysis the book is incomparably superior to anything that goes with us by the name of academic political philosophy. As a systematic philosophic system, however, it suffers from four major weaknesses, weaknesses so major as to vitiate its claim altogether to be a valid political philosophy.

We have already pointed to the semantic distortion resulting from the use of the term "Power" with a capital "P" as a synonym of government. This distortion, however, is but a symptom of the use of Power as a metaphysical abstraction which has an essence, a life, a behavior of its own. Thus we read for instance that "it is of Power's essence not to be weak" (p. 11). Power (with a small p) can obviously be conceived as a quality of a certain individual in his relations with another individual. In this sense we can say that A has power over B or that B fears the power of A. It is also possible to abstract from certain individuals as points of reference for power and refer to certain offices and a certain status regardless of the individuals connected with them. Thus we can say that the President of the United States, whoever he may be, has a certain kind of power with regard to the members of the cabinet, whoever they may be. It is also possible to attribute to such power certain qualities which it has in common with, or in which it differs from, power in general or certain other types of power.

What M. de Jouvenel does is bad metaphysics in that Hegelian tradition which has rendered useless so much of German social philosophy. The method of that metaphysics consists in endowing a metaphor, such as Power or Leviathan or Minotaur, or a legal abstraction, such as the government or the state, with certain qualities which are meaningful only when they are attributed to real persons. From the hypostatized qualities of such a metaphysical entity theoretical and practical conclusions are drawn, and the nature of the conclusions is limited only by the imagination of the author who has endowed the metaphysical entity with certain qualities in the first place.

Bad metaphysics leads of necessity to bad political philosophy. The metaphysics of Power distorts, if it does not blot out, the reality of power. What validity is there in the assertion that Power in the Middle Ages, that is, the authority of the prince, was limited and beneficial and that liberty flourished under it, without any con-

sideration of the power of the Church and of the feudal lords because they had only power and not Power? The test of the author's
assertion, which, as we have seen, is at the core of his philosophy,
can be provided, not by this kind of metaphysical juggling, but only
by raising the question: what was the status of the common man
vis-à-vis the public authorities, say, in the twelfth and eighteenth
centuries in comparison with what it is in the Western world today?
Is M. de Jouvenel prepared to defend the proposition that the
common man enjoyed greater freedom—moral, intellectual, social—
in those past centuries than he is enjoying today? To put that question is to answer it. It is a fundamental objection to the author's
philosophic method that it incapacitates him even to put that question in empirical terms.

M. de Jouvenel achieves the same result of the glorification of
medieval monarchy and of the damnation of modern democracy
by yet another, more common and also more vulgar device. He
rightly stresses the enormous increase in the power of the state in
our time and the concomitant threat to individual liberty. He contrasts with this sad state of affairs the constitutional principles and
arrangements of times past. The juxtaposition of the political practices of one society with the constitutional theory and law of another, however, is not philosophy but demagogy. By this device
Communist writers prove to their satisfaction that true democracy
exists only in the Soviet Union and that what the Western world
calls democracy is but a fraud. And there can indeed be no doubt
that the provisions of the Soviet constitution are more democratic
than the political practices of the United States. Is it any more convincing to tell us that the medieval state, in contrast to modern
democracy, was limited by the divine law without telling us to what
political uses that divine law was put? Or that in medieval times
Power, that is, the royal authority, was limited by the power of the
feudal barons without asking whose will regularly prevailed in case
of conflict, the king's or the barons'?

Finally, many of the author's strictures against modern democracy
are vitiated by his failure to distinguish between the general evils
which flow from the ubiquity of the lust for power and, hence, are
beyond remedy by human effort, and the specific evils which result
from concrete historic circumstances and, hence, are subject to correction by the processes of history, supported by conscious human

effort. All power, however spelled, negates the freedom of the individuals over whom it is exercised, and the concentrated, monopolistic power of the modern state is particularly dangerous to individual liberty. That danger does not stem from the innate metaphysical qualities of Power, nor from the disappearance of intermediate social authorities, nor from the enfeeblement of the belief in divine law as a limiting factor on government. Its causes are fivefold: intellectual, moral, political, economic, and technological.

The secularization of thought, as it manifests itself in the spirit of science, has given the modern mind an unprecedented confidence in its own efforts, unaided by supernatural powers and virtually unlimited by the obstacles of nature, a confidence which, under the conditions of modern technology, is transferred to the government as an agency of central planning. A mass civilization, under the impact of the scientific spirit and largely oblivious of the heritage of Western civilization and catering to the lowest instincts of the greatest number, is destroying in those responsible for government, that is, in all, the sense of moral discrimination which is the prerequisite of good government. The participation of the broad masses of the population in the political processes under democratic conditions has led to an unprecedented centralization of the processes of government. The modern conditions of economic activity have brought about an unprecedented centralization of economic power which, in turn, has called into being, as a corrective, the centralized powers of the state. This centralization is in good measure the result of the character of modern technology which, by giving the state a monopoly of the most destructive weapons of warfare, has made popular revolutions impossible. Of this phenomenon, which bears so heavily upon his central theme, the learned author has, strangely enough, nothing to say.

To call attention to and illuminate the evils of centralized power, in the face of the prevailing thoughtless optimism, is a great merit indeed. The modern state, by solving some problems, raises others which must be solved in turn. That the mechanical repetition of democratic incantations will not solve them is certain. It is no less certain that they will not be solved by a backward-looking romantic aristocratism which follows in the footpaths of Bonald, De Maistre, De Tocqueville, and Taine and shares in their brilliance and insights as well as in their aberrations.

23 The Rediscovery of Imagination and Religion: Arnold Toynbee

The reaction against philosophic relativism, methodological dogmatism, and positivist scientism has been most sweeping not in the field of political science but in that of history. Arnold Toynbee's work, by virtue of its very existence, is a frontal attack against the mood prevailing in all the social sciences. In *A Study of History* Mr. Toynbee tries to restore the claims of historic imagination and spirituality. Yet by doing so, he raises anew and more profoundly the dilemma of truth in matters political. He does so in three spheres: historiography, philosophy of history, and religion.

Mr. Toynbee's work poses anew, by implication, the problem of historiography. If what Mr. Toynbee is doing is a valid writing of history, then most of what is going by the name of academic history is, at worst, irrelevant or, at best, mere preparation. On the other hand, if the writing of history is a science with all that the word "science" connotes in terms of the use of documentary evidence and the renunciation of judgments of value, then certainly Mr. Toynbee is not a historian. This conflict between two conceptions of history is not likely to be resolved through methodological argument; for within that argument the philosophic assumption predetermines the conclusion. Method being a means to an end, achievement is the only valid test of method. What, then, is it that we expect history to achieve?

Burckhardt has told us that it is the purpose of history "to make us not clever for one day but wise forever." History imparts its wisdom by giving a meaningful account of the life and deeds of men who came before us. This account receives its meaning from the connection which the selective and appraising mind of the historian establishes between the data of history and the perennial concerns of man.

If this be the standard by which history must be judged, then Mr. Toynbee's contribution dwarfs scientific historiography, not in this or that of its manifestations, but as a category of historic thinking.

The great achievement of Mr. Toynbee as a historian lies in that very subjectivity which is the horror of scientific historiography. Mr. Toynbee has recovered the courage, which the scientific dogma had put to sleep, to ask from history questions which are meaningful for him and, through him as a man, for other men as well and to force history to answer him. Never mind that history may have no answer to some of the questions Mr. Toynbee asks, that the facts are sometimes arranged to produce the answers expected, and that not all the "facts" are facts in the scientific sense. Mr. Toynbee has awakened the historic imagination from its dogmatic slumber; he has communicated his own wonderment about the ways of man to his readers, and through innumerable flashes of insight, suggestive reinterpretations, and fertile hypotheses he has demonstrated by his own example the worth of historiography in the classic manner.

Compare with the richness and infectious dynamics of his historic imagination the unproblematic poverty of scientific historiography! The "science" of history leaves nothing to the imagination. What cannot be proved by the documents not only is not true but can have no meaning to be communicated by the historian. To have demonstrated, not through argument but through example, the richness of philosophic historiography, however problematical in detail, as against the self-impoverishment of "scientific" history, unproblematic in detail but a problem in its very conception of history, is the great merit of Mr. Toynbee's work. What in our time had become a mere historic recollection, Mr. Toynbee has again made a living reality: the creativeness of the historic imagination.

This historic imagination is not at the service of history, properly speaking. It is not Mr. Toynbee's purpose to give a coherent account of the historic process. His purpose is philosophic rather than historical. He searches for the laws which determine the rise and fall of civilizations.

On the face of it, such an undertaking appears to be sociological rather than philosophic. For it appears to require, not the philosophic assessment of the different civilizations from an over-all world view, but rather the empirical analysis of the morphology of civilizations, proceeding from empirically verifiable similarities to ever broadening generalizations. The main categories Mr. Toynbee employs, such as challenge and response, contacts in space and contacts in time, point to such a sociological intent. And in page after page the work reads like a gigantic collection of sociological essays and aphorisms, of illuminating similarities and analogies across the accustomed barriers of historic time, but loosely held together by the work's general plan. Still, the general plan is philosophic and could have been no other. For what Mr. Toynbee sets out to do is beyond the ken of empirical verification.

The possibility of all empirical verification resides in the shared perspective of all actual and potential observers. Astronomy as empirical science is possible because observers with the same perceptive and rational faculties look at the same object from the same planetary perspective. The deeper we move from the world of nature into the world of man as the subject and object of valuations, the more we find the objectivity of empirical science qualified by the ever narrowing limits of common perspective. For astronomy these limits are for all practical purposes irrelevant, since they coincide with the confines of the earth. In the sciences of man the rational core, common to all science, is diminished, obscured, and distorted by the inevitably partial perspective of the observer.

That impairment is minimized when both the object and the perspective of observation are identical with the confines of a particular civilization. A parochial civilization, looking at itself from the perspective of its own values, can achieve a high degree of empirical objectivity, given the limits of that perspective. Impairment is maximized when the perspectives of one civilization are applied to an object lying beyond its confines. For, in order to do justice to such an object, the observer would have to transcend the confines of his own civilization and apply to that object categories that transcend the confines of any particular civilization and, hence, are applicable to all. This, however, is an epistemological impossibility. It is this impossibility which Mr. Toynbee has endeavored to achieve.

The examination of but a few of Mr. Toynbee's basic concepts will show that it is impossible to verify them empirically but that they must be validated philosophically if they are to be validated at all. The very concept of civilization lacks empirical precision, once we leave behind the two extremes of primitivity and such generalizations as Western and Eastern civilization and share Mr. Toynbee's concern with the major historic civilizations. At what point can we say that a civilization is autonomous, that it is a derivative "offshoot" of another, or that it has no autonomy of its own, being a mere variety of a dominant one? Obviously American civilization is both distinct from, and similar to, British civilization. An Englishman might well try to comprehend American civilization in the terms of his own, or at best regard it as a mere "offshoot" of his own, while the American might assume its autonomy; for the Chinese observer, on the other hand, the differences between the two civilizations, obvious to both Englishman and American, might be hardly worth noting. From the point of view of imperial Rome, Roman civilization was the culmination of the civilization of Greece; for Hellenism it might very well have looked like Greek civilization in a state of decay; and Western Christian civilization has seen the civilization of Greece and Rome as a mere preparation for itself. Can one speak of one Chinese civilization as a continuum extending through the whole history of the Chinese state, or is it possible and necessary to speak of a number of civilizations following each other within the geographic and political space called China? Here again, the answer will differ according to the observer's perspective. There is no need to multiply examples in order to show that judgments about a civilization are mere reflections of the valuations of a particular one. It is not by accident that there has been a tendency for history to be written in terms of political or geographic units rather than of civilizations; for the former lend themselves more readily to empirical verification than do the latter.

What is true of the very concept of civilization applies also to the specific concepts referring to its alleged life cycle. What are the verifiable characteristics of the birth and death of a civilization, when does it flower, when break down and disintegrate? Did the Greek, Roman, and Jewish civilizations ever die or were they but transferred by political circumstances from one geographic locale to another? If we should assume that Greek civilization actually died, did it die through the degeneration of its inner life-substance, or was it killed, as it were, by military assassination, which in view of its own inner potentialities was a mere accident? If Western civilization should dissolve tomorrow into radioactive rubble, would it have died a "natural" death because of inner exhaustion or would it have committed suicide in an isolated act of intellectual and moral degeneracy, or would it have been killed by an atomic assassin? If Western civilization should be spared atomic destruction and if it should move into an age of material abundance, who is to prove scientifically that such a civilization would be inferior, or for that matter superior, to, say, the thirteenth or eighteenth or nineteenth centuries of Western civilization? The answers to all these questions obviously depend upon what we mean by civilization. To speak again of Western civilization only, there are those who see nothing but decay from the fifteenth century onward; there are others who see nothing but darkness before the fifteenth century and nothing but decay from the seventeenth century onward. For still others, Western civilization culminates at the turn of the nineteenth century, while there are those for whom all history preceding Marx is a mere prescientific preparation for the self-emancipation of man.

The concept of civilization and of its different stages, then, which we apply to other civilizations, cannot but be a function of the valuations of our own. The very simile of life and death has an objective, empirically verifiable meaning for biological units and is still susceptible of a high degree of empirical precision in the political sphere: a state or a party can be said to live and die. However, when we speak of the life and death of a nation as a cultural entity, we sacrifice, in a measure which will change with differing historic situations, empirical precision for a philosophic metaphor. That substitution of philosophic valuation for empirical science is bound to become total when we enter the realm of civilization, which as a concept is a kind of synthesis of the valuations of a member of a particular civilization. The appraisal of civilizations other than one's own is possible only through the erection of a partial world view into a philosophic system claiming universal validity. From Vico through Hegel and Comte to Marx, philosophy had the self-confidence to sit in judgment over all history and to assign to its different periods what appeared to be their rightful place. Our age has transferred its confidence from philosophy to science. Thus it must endeavor to prove scientifically what other ages have tried to demonstrate through philosophy.

This is the tragic paradox which Marx was still able to overcome by identifying philosophy and science, but before which Spengler and Toynbee could not but founder. For, unlike Marx, they have no philosophic system to fall back on which would lend their valuations at least an element of rational objectivity. In this respect Mr. Toynbee is philosophically more sophisticated than Spengler. He is aware of the dilemma without being able to overcome it. Spengler, with that Hegelian consistency which takes absurd conclusions in its stride as long as they follow logically from premises, forces the history of civilizations into the biological straitjacket and, again not unlike Hegel, finds in the apparent trends of the contemporary scene experimental proof for the pseudoscientific premise of biological necessity.

Mr. Toynbee, with an intention as sweeping as any of the system-builders before him, has too much common sense to sacrifice the evidence of history on the altar of logical consistency. He allows for human creativity to modify, if not stop altogether, the life cycle of all civilizations, and particularly of our own. Yet this concession to the unpredictability of history, which is a function of human freedom, confronts Mr. Toynbee with still another dilemma. If a civilization can escape its life cycle by an act of human will, if, in other words, it can refuse to die if it so wills and knows how to live for ever, what, then, is the cognitive value of the biological scheme? Is there a tendency in civilizations to die, which tendency can be reversed? Or were other civilizations bound to die while ours—faint echo of *Roma eterna*—might live for ever. Obviously, what Mr. Toynbee's concession to common sense has gained for history it has lost for philosophy.

It is a measure of Mr. Toynbee's philosophic sophistication that he not only allows human freedom to qualify, if not disrupt, the determinism of the biological life cycle but he is also aware of the need for standards of evaluation which transcend the empirical sequence of biological phases. He does not, and cannot, find these standards in philosophy; for our age has lost the rational boldness and self-reliance which still allowed a Comte and a Marx to build a philosophic system which pretended to explain the laws by which history proceeds. Instead Mr. Toynbee turns to religion. By doing so, Mr. Toynbee raises three issues: the meaning of the return to religion, the value for civilization of a return to religion, the ability of a civilization to return to religion by an act of will.

Mr. Toynbee's claim that only religion can save Western civilization coincides with a popular movement, especially strong in the United States, which also seeks in religion salvation from the evils and dangers of the times. Church membership is rising; prominent intellectuals are converted or return to the fold of their church; politicians justify themselves and their policies in religious terms; and the display of religious observances has begun to become standard practice for public men. Much of Mr. Toynbee's popularity in the United States can be attributed to the apparent convergence of his call for the renewal of religious faith with these popular tendencies. He is in danger of becoming the prophet of a new cult, a kind of Billy Graham of the eggheads.

This popularity is unjust to Mr. Toynbee's intent, but it illuminates the weakness of his achievement. Mr. Toynbee has no illusions about the impossibility of reviving a lost religious faith by joining or rejoining an established church. He calls not so much for a return to a particular established religion as for a revival of religious faith which might find confirmation in any established religion or a combination of elements of them. Mr. Toynbee's personal preference, if I understand him aright, seems to be a kind of intellectual and aesthetic eclecticism which open-mindedly accepts and receives all that is congenial in the different historic religions.

However, this stress upon a new syncretic religion tends to obscure a distinction which is vital for the understanding of the religious problem and, in turn, has strengthened the popular misunderstanding of Mr. Toynbee's position to which we have just referred. This confusion concerns the distinction between religion and religiosity. It can well be argued—and I would support the argument—that most of the failures of the modern age and many of its accomplishments stem from one single source: the lack of religiosity. Modern man, as he sees himself, has become a self-sufficient entity who knows what he sees and can do what he wills. He has lost the awareness of his dependence upon a will and a power which are beyond his understanding and control. To warn modern man against the irreligious self-glorification, which in a sense is his self-mutilation, for it deprives human experience of mystery, tragedy, and guilt, is one thing; to advocate a kind of religious eclecticism is quite another.

This distinction between religiosity and religion has a direct bearing upon the question which is central to Mr. Toynbee's concern and for the sake of which he has raised the issue of religion in the first place: What makes a civilization live and what will enable our civilization in particular to survive? Mr. Toynbee answers: Return to religion by reviving your religious faith. Yet this answer is open to serious doubt. The doubt arises not from metaphysical speculation but from the experience of history itself. Is there any historic evidence to show that religious ages are monopolistically or even especially productive of the values of civilization, as commonly understood? And is there not rather overwhelming historic evidence in support of the proposition that the weakening of religious faith coincides with the flowering of civilizations, as commonly understood?

We are using the term "commonly understood" on purpose; for here the observer's subjective preference, as pointed out above, is bound to color his judgment. If we assume that only religious civilization is worthy of the name, it cannot be hard to demonstrate that the flowering of civilization depends upon religious faith. Yet if we give to civilization its common secular meaning, it can hardly be open to doubt that from Plato to Kant, from Sophocles to Dostoevski, from Michelangelo to Rodin, the weakening of religious faith and the flowering of civilization not only coincide in time but also are organically interconnected. It is true that these great achievements of civilization owe their greatness to the religious experience of mystery, tragedy, and guilt. Yet it must further be allowed that the achievements of material civilization, in terms of rational control of nature and society, owe much, if not everything, to the modern denial of both religious faith and religiosity, which assumes the limitless powers of man and demonstrates them within self-chosen limits.

But even if it were true that the return to religious faith can save Western civilization, can a civilization recover its religious faith by an act of will? Here it is necessary, paradoxical as it may seem, to invoke the very spirit of religion against its most learned advocate. It requires nothing but an act of will to join a church and to perform its rituals. To have religious faith demands an act of grace, for which, however, man may well prepare himself through rational instruction. Religiosity, in turn, is the fruit of experience, more particularly of suffering, transformed into intellectual and moral awareness by mind and conscience.

The clarion calling a civilization to return to religion, en masse as it were, finds, and must find, its response in a eclectic idolatry, often blasphemous in man's self-identification with the deity, which popularizes the trappings of religion without reviving the dormant substance of its religiosity. To restore man to the fulness of his stature and thus give his civilization a new lease on life requires indeed the teaching of men like Mr. Toynbee. Yet their teaching must seek to illuminate a mysterious, tragic, and sinful experience common to all men in terms of a religiosity likewise common to all men. Neither a teacher nor a whole civilization can by an act of will create the symbolic and ritualistic expressions of religiosity thus restored; least of all can they create them out of the fragments of religions, whose decline has made the restoration of religiosity necessary in the first place. What religions will grow from this new religiosity man must leave to fate. He must be content to be ready, and to make others ready, to see the signs and to read them aright when they appear.

What Mr. Toynbee has been trying to do as a philosopher of history could no longer be done in an age which tries to reduce truth to science. What Mr. Toynbee has been trying to do as a herald of religious faith no man could have achieved in any age. One hundred years ago he might have been the last of the great philosophers of history. Four hundred years ago he might have been the last of the great scholastics—or mystics. Such achievements are not for this age. Yet Mr. Toynbee's Icarian effort does for our age what the great representative works of the mind have done for others. It both presents its spirit and attempts to transcend it in the search for the perennial truths by which all ages must be judged. His achievement belongs to all ages; his failure belongs to his own and, hence, is ours as well as his.

24 *The Revival of Objective Standards: Walter Lippmann*

"And where are the political theorists of democracy today?" Professor Alfred Cobban of University College, London, asks and answers this question in an important article, "The Decline of Political Theory," published in the *Political Science Quarterly* of September, 1953:

> Democracy, for lack of thought, has ceased to be a live political idea. . . .
> For the most part it has ceased to be discussed seriously and in relation to
> the concrete problems of practical politics. It has largely become a mean-
> ingless formula. Politicians, like the princes in the fairy tale condemned
> to the oracular utterances of frogs, seem scarcely able to open their
> mouths without some platitude flopping out, wet and flappy, and slightly
> repulsive, but is this political theory? If it is, no wonder that practical
> men prefer to ignore it. Coins can remain valid currency even when they
> are worn quite smooth. Political ideas need periodical recoining if they
> are to retain their value.

It is the great contribution, one is almost tempted to say the historic contribution, of Walter Lippmann's *The Public Philosophy*,[1] that it poses the fundamental problems of democracy again in terms relevant to the concrete political problems of the day. All great contributions to political theory, from the biblical prophets and Plato to Laski—and I grant that the span in both time and quality is considerable—have reflected not upon the theories of others, let alone upon theories about theories—an innocuous and, hence, popular academic pastime—but upon the concrete, burning, "controversial" political problems of their times. To do this requires a peculiar combination of detachment and absorption, a commitment both to a society and to a truth transcending it. It also requires a philosophy that is not merely the reflection of popular preferences but is grounded in a rational perception of the true order of things. Finally, it requires the moral courage to pit one's independent knowledge of what is true in matters political and of what needs to be done against what the crowd believes and wants. If these qualities

[1] Boston: Little, Brown & Co., 1955.

make the authentic political philosopher, Walter Lippmann has again proved that he is one.

The decisive experience which in this book has moved Mr. Lippmann's thinking on its course, is the derangement of the relationships which ought to exist in a democracy between the government and the people: "The people have acquired power which they are incapable of exercising, and the governments they elect have lost powers which they must recover if they are to govern. . . . Where mass opinion dominates the government, there is a morbid derangement of the true functions of power. The derangement brings about the enfeeblement, verging on paralysis, of the capacity to govern. This breakdown in the constitutional order is the cause of the precipitate and catastrophic decline of Western society" (pp. 14–15). More particularly, legislative assemblies have usurped the powers which rightfully belong to the executive branch and which they are unable to exercise properly. Representative government tends to become paralyzed government. The people, then, must choose between freedom and authority: "They will choose authority, which promises to be paternal, in preference to freedom which threatens to be fratricidal. . . . No ideal of freedom and of democracy will long be allowed to stand in the way of their being governed" (p. 61). In this fashion the very weakness of democracy as a viable political order has given birth to totalitarianism as an antidote.

Democracy which has thus perished and which is threatened today is of the Jacobin type. It equates good policy with the will of a legislative or popular majority and, hence, is forced to the conclusion that a proposition is good because it is popular. By making the will of the people its ultimate standard, it seeks the solution of all problems and the elimination of evil itself from a continuous onslaught against all traditions and all objective standards. In this it is a Christian heresy which seeks a religious end without having to undergo the religious experience.

To this degenerate and doomed type of democracy, Mr. Lippmann opposes another type which is represented by the English political system. The English type of democracy presumes an objective order within which the political process takes place. Majority rule cannot overthrow that order; it presupposes it. The principles of that order have been codified in documents such as Magna Carta, the

Declaration of Independence, the Bill of Rights of 1689, and the first ten amendments of our Constitution. Yet the better part of that order was never committed to writing. It lives on in what Lippmann calls "the traditions of civility" and has been formulated and applied in "the public philosophy." It is identical with that rational order which has been traditionally called natural law and upon whose principles all men once agreed, and can agree again, by virtue of their rational nature.

How can the belief in natural law and its effectiveness as a standard for political action be renewed? "In order to repair the capacity to believe in the public philosophy," answers Mr. Lippmann, "it will be necessary to demonstrate the practical relevance and the productivity of the public philosophy. It is almost impossible to deny its high and broad generalities. The difficulty is to see how they are to be applied in the practical affairs of a modern state . . ." (p. 115) applied in such a way that only the "wilfully irrational" can deny their validity and only the "wilfully subversive" can reject the obligations deriving from them.

The difficulty of restoring the public philosophy results from the positivist climate of opinion which cannot but be hostile to the assumption of objective standards not subject to the conditions of time and place. The modern age is no longer satisfied with ordering the political sphere by the standards of the public philosophy and thus establishing an uneasy and ever precarious balance between the good and the possible. Instead, "it promises, not the good life of this world, but the perfect life of heaven." It confuses the two realms of man's existence, that of this world with its contingencies and that of the transcendent world of the spirit. That combination of relativistic positivism and utopian perfectionism has destroyed the public philosophy and has rendered modern man powerless to order his political world by transcendent objective standards.

Since Mr. Lippmann sees the root of the evil primarily in the prevailing philosophy, the main remedy he suggests consists in the restoration of the philosophy which the prevailing one replaced: "I do not contend, though I hope, that the decline of Western society will be arrested if the teachers in our schools and universities come back to the great tradition of the public philosophy. But I do contend that the decline . . . cannot be arrested if the prevailing philosophers oppose this restoration and revival . . ." (p. 178). With this last word of Mr. Lippmann, I can have no quarrel. Yet I must doubt that it can be the last word.

This book is animated by a noble and moving faith, reminiscent of the rationalistic idealism of the eighteenth century, in the self-sustaining power of reason to transform the philosophy by which men live and, through it, their very lives. Mr. Lippmann believes that men in their political thoughts and actions can be "sincerely and lucidly rational," and he considers this rationality the very foundation of the public philosophy. Yet Herbert Butterfield, Reinhold Niebuhr, myself, and others have tried to show how much more ambiguous and involved the relations between reason and politics are than is suggested by this simple rationalistic faith. It must suffice here to point out that the public philosophy was not destroyed by its own rational deficiencies or by the hostility of the intellectuals, but—and Mr. Lippmann says as much--by the modern conditions and problems of life which the public philosophy, as it has come down to us, is unable to reflect and solve.

First of all, natural law, the form in which the public philosophy has been transmitted to us, has not only been the reflection of the objective standards of politics, but it has also always been a political ideology and predominantly an ideology of the status quo. In other words, the existing political order was identified with the objective and rational order. Yet when the existing political order lost its viability, natural law, through its intimate connection with it, lost its plausibility. It became a mere ideological tool by which partial interests and subjective opinions tried to establish their universality and objectivity. We cannot forget that experience, and no self-contained intellectual movement can obliterate its philosophic effects.

All political philosophy is concerned with the burning political problems of the day and is in turn a reflection, in the light of a truth which all ages have in common, upon the political experiences of the day before. The task of political philosophy in our age, then, is to apply the perennial truths of politics to the political world for the dual purpose of understanding it and of solving its problems. To this task Mr. Lippmann applies himself with outstanding success. Yet the restoration of a viable democratic order is not coterminous with that success being approved and shared by all rational men. As that order has been weakened and in places destroyed by its own defects, so its health can be restored only by political action remedying its defects. Political philosophy can hold up to society the mirror of its ills and contrast it with the ideal picture of health, hoping to mold thought and inspire action. Thus it is uneasily suspended between the consummated action of the past, which it reflects, and the hoped-for action of the future, which it propounds. It is its dilemma that it knows in a general way what ought to be done but cannot do it. There is its strength and its weakness, its victory and its defeat, and it should claim no more.

On the other hand, it is the dilemma of political action that it must act without being certain that what it does ought to be done. Political action without philosophy is blind; and even with philosophy it cannot help being shortsighted. For the gap between the general propositions of political philosophy and the concrete measures of political action must be bridged not by the logical deductions of a utopian rationalism but by the trial and error of political experience. The philosopher-king in whom the tension between philosophy and action is dissolved is an ideal which reality approaches only in the greatest of statesmen. In reality, the philosopher, that is, the political thinker, knows more than the king, that is, the political actor, and cannot act according to his knowledge. The king, even if he knew all the philosopher knows, would still not know for certain what action the concrete situation requires. No theoretical knowledge but only the experience of acting can teach him that. Yet even that experience will teach him only how to avoid the repetition of yesterday's blunder, not how not to commit a new one tomorrow.

Here, in this inescapable tension between reason and experience, between theoretical and practical knowledge, between the light of political philosophy and the twilight of political action, is indeed the ultimate dilemma of politics.

Index

Absolutism, 108, 112, 360, 363; legislative, 165
Acheson, Dean, 260
Adams, Charles Kendall, on political science, 10 ff.
Adams, John, on power, 247 f.
Adams, John Quincy, 285
Administrative convenience, 153
Administrative law, 123 ff., 168; and fourth branch of government, 133 f., 155, 162, 168; implied limitations, 155 ff., 168 f.; implied regulatory powers, 143 ff., 161, 168; interpretative regulations, 127 ff., 137 ff., 151 ff.; legislative regulations, 127 ff., 137 ff.; re-enactment rule, 140 f.; rule-making powers, 124 ff., 137 ff.; 157 ff.
Administrative state, 102, 115
Advertising, as substitute for democratic leadership, 328 ff.
Allen, A. C., 134
Alliances, crisis of, 202 ff., 332
America; see United States
American Civil War, 104, 244
American state system, 61
Anarchism, 346
Anticolonialism, 180 ff., 279
Anzilotti, Dionisio, 230
Appeasement, 261, 352
Arbitration treaties, interpretation, 222
Area studies: as academic discipline, 88, 91 ff.; and classical studies, 97; humanistic approach to, 96 f.
Aristocratic government, 106, 359, 363
Aristotle, 20, 22 f., 36, 38, 106, 281, 346
Art, modern, and political science, 24, 36 f.
Astronomy, as science, 370
Atlantic Charter, as ideology, 64
Atomic age, influence on foreign policy, 68 f., 74, 178 f., 254 f., 276 f.; see also Technological revolutions
Atomic weapons, "fourth-nation" problem, 69, 178 f., 279
Augustine, 38, 360
Austro-German Customs Union, 230
Autocracy, distinguished from totalitarianism, 109

Balance of power, 41, 47, 56 ff., 102, 178, 191, 196 ff., 225, 238, 258, 278
Baldwin, Stanley, and collective security, 77 f.
Balkanization, progressive, of world, 175, 179 f.
Bandung, Declaration of, 205
Barker, Sir Ernest, 25, 356
Beard, Charles A., on national interest, 69 f.
Belgium, neutrality of, 196
Bentham, Jeremy, on anticolonialism, 180, 266
Berle, A. A., 155
Bill of Rights, 379
Bipartisanship in foreign policy, 69, 297 f.
Bipolarity of power, 200 ff., 277 f.
Bismarck, Otto von, 49, 182, 250, 264, 324
Bluff, as principle of foreign policy, 332
Bluntschli, J. K., 21
Bodin, Jean, 36, 171
Bohlen, Charles, 250
Bonald, Louis, 367
Bonnecase, J., 213
Bradley, General Omar, 258
Brandeis, Louis, 214
Briand-Kellogg Pact, 216, 324 f.
Bright, John, 244
British foreign service, humanistic training, 97
Bryce, Lord, 19, 155
"Bulgarian Atrocities," 251 ff.
Burckhardt, Jacob, 368
Burgess, John W., and American political science, 12 f.
Burke, Edmund, 56; on political morality, 84 f., 250
Butterfield, Herbert, 380
Byrnes, James F., 249 f.

Calhoun, John, 38
Canning, George, 250, 271
Capitalism, 344, 347 f.
Cardozo, Benjamin, 214
Carney, Admiral Robert, 331

Carr, E. H., 341, 350 ff.
Carr, Robert K., 164
Castlereagh, Viscount, 250
Cavour, Count, 182, 242, 250
Cecil, Algernon, 86
Chamberlain, Neville, 352
Charles V, of Austria, 274
Checks and balances, as foundation of freedom, 121 f., 285 f.
Chiang Kai-shek, 329, 334
China: and Korea, 77; and nationalism, 181
Chinese revolutions, 290
Christianity, and Communism, 354
Church: and the national interest, 72; as political power, 361, 366
Churchill, Sir Winston, 49, 250, 257 f., 265 ff., 339; on Baldwin's foreign policy, 78
Civil liberties, as limits on majority rule, 113
Civilization: classical, as model, 97; as historical category, 370 ff.; Western, crisis of, 3 f., 375 f.
Clausewitz, Karl von, 256
Clemenceau, Georges, 182
Cobban, Alfred, 39, 377
Cobden, Richard, 244
Coexistence, policy of, 78
Cold War, 199 f., 278 f.
Collective security, 76 ff., 185, 192 ff., 201, 206 f., 259, 261 f., 351
Colonialism, new, 180 ff.
Columbia University, and early American political science, 11 ff.
Common good, 346, 362
Commonwealth of Nations, 61
Communism, 354; and freedom, 106 f., 177, 181 f.; influence on Soviet foreign policy, 83, 249 f.; and the national interest, 70 ff.; see also Totalitarianism
Comparative government, 34
Competition: freedom of, 119; political, essential to democracy, 110
Comte, Auguste, 213, 233, 372 f.
Congress: as expression of national sovereignty, 135; legislative powers, 124 ff., 134 ff.
Congress of Berlin, 251
Consensus: democratic, 289 f.; totalitarian, 109 ff., 289
Conservatism, 285 ff.

Constitution: function for legislation, 128, 130 ff., 156; implied limitations in, 164 ff.
Constitutionalism, 108, 113, 135
Containment, policy of, 78 f., 258, 277 ff.
Cooke, Alistair, 328
Cooley, Thomas McIntyre, 164 f.
Co-ordinate state, 50 ff.
Corporations, power, 102, 114, 119
Corwin, Edward S., 338
Cromwell, Oliver, 107, 250
Customary law, 223

Dante Alighieri, on popular will, 294
Davies, John Paton, Jr., 312
Declaration of Independence, 379
Delegation of legislative powers, 124 ff., 143 ff., 156, 162 ff.
Demagogy, as corrupted democracy, 293 f.
Democracy, 35, 108 ff., 134, 243, 289 ff., 293 ff., 353 f., 355 f., 359, 361 ff., 377 ff.; and advertising, 328 ff.; of ancient Greece, 293; capitalist, 344, 355; corruption, 293 ff., 367; decline in stages, 111 f.; decline in United States, 281 ff., 295 ff., 332 ff., 378; and diplomacy, 270 ff.; English and Jacobin type, 378 f.; and foreign policy, 302 ff., 324 ff., 332 ff.; imperfect, 109 f., 295 f.; and nationalism, 172, 181 f.; totalitarian, 109 ff., 355 f., 364; universality, 181
"Democratic centralism," 177
Deryng, Antoni, on science of international relations, 90
Despotism, new, 114 ff., 361
Dictatorship, and democracy, 355; see also Totalitarianism
Diplomacy, 262, 270 ff.; functions, 274 ff.; open, 270 f.
Disraeli, Benjamin, 250 ff.
Dodd, Walter F., 164 f.
Dostoevski, Feodor, 375
"Dual state," 315, 320
Due process, 231; compared to national interest, 65 f.
Duguit, Léon, 135, 223
Dulles, John Foster, 330 f.; conception of office, 299 ff.; on neutralism, 186
Dunning, W. A., 60

Economic power, concentrations of, 102, 114 ff., 119, 353 f., 367

Economics, development, 9, 15 f.; and politics, 116 ff.; self-sufficiency, 257
Economy: national, and government, 117 ff., 367; planned, 353, 367
Eisenhower, Dwight D., 185 f., 257, 282 ff., 295 ff., 315, 324, 327 ff.
Empire, moral valuation, 180
Equalitarianism, 107, 363
Equality of states, 59 ff.
Erich, Rafael, 330
Escapism, in American political thought, 62 ff.
European Coal and Steel Community, 68
European Defense Community, 330

Factual knowledge, distinguished from theoretical knowledge, 93 f.
Faguet, Émile, 239
Fair Labor Standards Act, 124 ff., 149 ff., 157 ff.
Fascism, 290, 347 f; *see also* Totalitarianism
Federalism, 59 ff.
Federalist, The, 21 f., 38, 120 f., 285
Feller, A. H., 81
Feudalism, new, 114 ff.
Foreign policy: democratic control, 326 f.; and moralism, 246 ff.; nature, 256 ff., 307 f., 324 ff.; and public opinion, 302 ff., 324, 326 f., 332 ff.; subversion in, 305 ff.
Formosa, defense of, 74, 329 f., 335
Fosdick, Dorothy, 86 f.
Foundations, influence on political science, 29
Four Freedoms, 347 f.; as ideology, 64
Fox, Charles James, 250
Francis I, of France, 274
Frankfurter, Felix, on constitutional interpretation, 155, 214
Free trade, 244
Freedom, 102, 104 ff., 120 ff., 239 f., 344 ff., 359 f., 363 ff., 378; of contract, 231; and nationalism, 170 ff., 176, 181 f.; and power, 104 ff.; of the press, 106
French Revolution of 1789, 1, 290; philosophy, 56, 182
Freud, Sigmund, and Western civilization, 3 f.
Freund, Ernst, 157, 159, 163
Functionalism, in international law, 224 ff.

Galileo, Galilei, 36
Gaulle, General Charles de, 205
Gellhorn, Walter, 123
General welfare: compared to national interest, 65 f.; and individual rights, 113
Germany: diplomatic solution of problem, 275; imperialism, 175; nationalism, 172, 175; Nazi, 355; resistance to Nazism, 285; West, rearmament of, 74
Gierke, Otto von, 21
Gladstone, William, 250 ff.
Gneist, Rudolph von, 21
Goethe, Johann Wolfgang, on justice, 43
Good Neighbor policy, 61, 83
Gouzenko case, 71
Government, atrophy, 288 ff., 378
Graham, Billy, 374
Gray, John Chipman, 216
Greece, in World War II, 269
Griswold, Erwin N., 142
Guillaume, General Augustin, 288

Haddow, Anna, 14
Haller, Karl Ludwig von, 285
Hamilton, Alexander, on national interest, 55, 71, 250, 285
Hamlet, 65, 312
Harcourt, Sir William, 303
Hart, James, 157
Harvard University, and early American political science, 12, 14
Hayek, F. A., 344
Hegel, Georg Wilhelm Friedrich, 285, 361, 372
Hegelianism, 21, 365, 373
Henry VIII, 67
"Higher law," doctrine of, 165
Historiography, 368 ff.
History: as ideology, 64; lessons, 258 ff.; and philosophy, 264, 368 ff.; and political science, 31, 35, 48 f., 67, 89, 368
Hitler, Adolf, 177, 264, 324, 353, 355
Hobbes, Thomas, 36, 358, 360; on origin of morality, 80 f.; on separation of powers, 133
Hobhouse, Lord, 154
Holloway, Vernon H., 86
Hoxie, Gordon R., 12, 14
Hudson, Manley O., 214, 230
Hull, Cordell, 250

Hume, David, on balance of power, 56
Humphrey, George, 283

Ideology, political, 4, 28, 30 f., 35 f., 43, 51 ff., 59, 64 f., 102, 207, 247 f., 356, 380
Imperialism: German, 175; new, 180; totalitarian, 199
Implied legislative powers, 143 ff.
India, foreign policy, 206 ff.
Indians, treatment, 64
Individual, and the state, 102, 114 ff., 359 ff.
Individual rights, and collective good, 113, 345 f.
Individualism, political, 112, 345 f., 361, 363
Indochina War, 331 f.
Interdisciplinary research, 94 f.
International law, 89, 210 ff., 354; and balance of power, 225; binding force, 219; and community of interests, 224 ff.; functional theory, 224 ff.; and international politics, 221 f.; interpretation, 218 ff., 232 f.; science, 210 ff., 229 f.; and social forces, 212 f., 219 ff.; two types, 228 ff.; validity, 215 ff., 226 ff.
International politics, theory of, 47 ff., 54, 58 f., 67, 69, 73 f., 98 ff.
International relations: as academic discipline, 88 ff., 97 ff.; revolutionary transformation, 102
International society, peculiarities, 47 f., 50 ff.
Interpretation, identical with legislation, 128 ff., 168
Isolationism, 63, 248, 256, 261, 272, 274
Italy, foreign policy, 74, 77

Jackson, Robert H., 125
Jefferson, Thomas, 64, 250
Jellinek, Georg, 21, 215
Jouvenel, Bertrand de, 341, 358 ff.
Judicial review, 156
Justice, 43, 218, 361; minoritarian and equalitarian, 106 ff.

Kant, Immanuel, 375; on separation of powers, 133
Kaplan, Abraham, 19 ff.
Kaufmann, Erich, 223
Kautilya, 36, 48, 56, 67
Kelsen, Hans, 21, 213, 223
Kennan, George, concept of political morality, 85 f.

Kersten, Charles J., on "liberation" policy, 78
Keynes, Lord, 356
Khrushchev, Nikita, on German problem, 186
Kierkegaard, and Western civilization, 3
Knowland, William F., 337
Koenig, Msgr., on political morality, 86
Korean War: and collective security, 194 f., 261 f.; and the national interest, 76 ff.

Laband, Georg, 21
Labor unions, power, 102, 114, 119
Laissez faire, 353
Laski, Harold, 24, 341 ff., 377
Lasswell, Harold, 19 ff.
Lauterpacht, H., 213 f.
League of Nations, 351, 356; and neutrality, 192 f., 196 ff.; sanctions against Italy, 77, 197
League of Nations Covenant: interpretation, 216, 221 f.; validity, 226, 228
Le Fur, Louis, 223
Legalism: in constitutional interpretation, 123, 155 ff., 168; in foreign policy, 73, 301 f.; in international law, 211, 234
Legislative process, hierarchical structure, 128 ff., 135 ff., 143 f., 166
Legitimacy, democratic, 112 f.
Leibniz, Gottfried Wilhelm, 171
Leighton, Alexander H., 86
Lenin, V. I. Ulyanov, 353
Letwin, Shirley R., 86
Lex, concept, 134
Liberalism, 112, 248, 256, 343 ff., 352 f.; collectivist, 113; contradicted by political reality, 112 f.; decline, 16 f., 113 ff., 343, 348 f.; dilemmas, 113, 120, 343, 348 f.; individualistic, 112; and nationalism, 171; as safeguard of democracy, 111 ff.; utopian, 285, 350
"Liberation" policy, 78 f., 329
Liberty; see freedom
Lincoln, Abraham: as conservative, 80, 285; on freedom, 104, 106, 113; on prudence, 84
Lippmann, Walter, 330, 341, 377 ff.
Locarno treaties, 221, 227
Locke, John, 21 f.
Logical positivism, 19, 23
Louis XIV, 361

Loyalty, national, 309 ff., 322 f.
Lundstedt, A. V., 223

MacArthur, General Douglas, 262, 335
McCarthyism, 285, 316 f.
Machiavelli, 19 ff., 48, 206, 250 f., 294, 357
McIlwain, Charles Howard, 155
Madison, James, 71, 250
Maginot line strategy, 263
Magna Carta, 378
Maistre, Joseph de, 367
Majority rule, 35, 107 f., 110 ff., 362; limited by liberalism, 112 f., 115, 378; tyranny, 110 ff., 363 ff., 378
Man, modern image, 3, 374 f.
Mansfield, Mike, 331
Mantoux, Paul, on science of international relations, 90
Marshall, General George, 257
Marshall, John, 60, 119, 144 f., 152, 155, 164 f.
Marsilius of Padua, 360
Marx, 353 f., 372 f.; and the Western tradition, 2, 4
Marxism, 170, 242, 256, 347 ff., 356
Mass media of communication, 102, 106, 109
Mazarin, Jules, 250
Mazzini, Giuseppe, and nationalism, 172, 182
Meinecke, Friedrich, 55
Merson, Martin, 316
Methodology, in political science, 18 ff., 31, 36, 101, 368
Metternich, and nationalism, 172
Michelangelo, 375
Michels, Roberto, 19 ff.
Michigan, University of, and early American political science, 10 ff.
Military, self-sufficiency, 257, 267 f.
Mill, John Stuart, 266, 344 f.; on British foreign policy, 64
Minorities treaties, 174, 182
Mises, Ludwig von, 344
Monarchy, 133 f., 359, 361 f., 364 ff.; absolute, 171
Montgomery, Robert, 328
Moore, Barrington, Jr., 19
Moralism, 63 f., 205 ff., 246 ff., 263 f.; and nationalism, 177, 180 ff.
Morality: as ideology, 51 ff., 247 f.; and law, 217 ff., 230 ff.; political, 50 ff., 74, 80 ff., 242, 245 ff., 253 ff., 261, 270 ff., 281 ff., 351, 357

Mores, and law, 217 ff., 230 ff.
Morgenthau, Hans J., 17, 27 f., 81 f., 123, 191, 196, 206, 223, 226, 230, 235, 286, 325, 327
Morley, John, 183
Mowrer, Paul Scott, on balance of power, 56
Müller, Adam, 357
Munich settlement of 1938, 352

Napoleon I, 353, 355, 361; and nationalism, 172, 176, 182
Napoleon III, and nationalism, 172
National Industrial Recovery Act, 125, 153
National interest, 50 ff., 54 ff., 65 ff., 73 ff., 85, 351; usurped by sectional interests, 69 ff.
National minorities, 173 ff., 182
National security, and individual rights, 113
National self-determination, 171 ff., 182, 353, 355; modified by power, 173 ff.
National state: historic relativity, 67 f.; justification, 178; obsolescence, 180, 354 f.
Nationalism, 52 f., 170 ff.; hostile to international order, 173, 179 f.; and individual rights, 174, 182; obsolescence, 178 ff.; as political religion, 176; as tool of political power, 173, 175, 181 ff.; of twentieth century, 175 ff., 354 f.; Western conception, 170, 177, 180 ff.; in World War I, 172 f., 176 f.; in World War II, 175
Nationalistic universalism, 176, 183, 199
NATO, 205, 263
Natural law, 212 f., 218, 379 ff.
Natural science, as model for political science, 17 f., 240 ff.
Nehru, on neutralism, 188
Neutralism: concept, 185 ff.; different types, 200 ff.; as escapism, 201 f.; moral, 205 ff.; political 202 ff.; as reaction to bipolarity, 202
Neutrality: and balance of power, 191, 196 ff.; and collective security, 192 ff.; concept, 185 ff.; in League of Nations, 192 f., 196 ff.; legal status, 188 ff.; obsolescence, 198 ff.; in United Nations, 186, 192 ff.; and war, 188 ff.; in World War I, 191
"New order," 175
Niebuhr, Reinhold, 356 f., 380

Nietzsche, Friedrich, and Western civilization, 3
Nihilism, political, 285
Nixon, Richard, on neutralism, 186 f.

Oppenheim, L., 213 ff.
Opposition: decline of, 297 f.; in American political system, 336 ff.

Pareto, Vilfredo, 234
Parsons, Father Wilfred, on political morality, 85 f.
Pearson, Lester, 330
Penn, William, 49
Perfectionism, political, 240, 242 ff., 379
Philosopher-king, dilemmas, 381
Philosophy: crisis, 3 f., 9 f.; and political science, 32 f.
Pitt, William, 250
Pius XI, on political morality, 86
Pius XII, 86
Plato, 21 ff., 36, 38, 106, 375, 377; and the problem of truth, 4, 8, 42; on relations between philosophy and politics, 7 ff.
Pluralism, American: cultural, and area studies, 92 f.; economic, as purpose of American government, 117, 120 ff.; influence on foreign policy, 83; political, 107, 112, 289
Poland: foreign policy, 74; and nationalism, 173
Political economy, 42, 116
Political influence, as element of economic competition, 117 ff.
Political philosophy: conflict in modern, 54 f.; conflict between tradition and contemporary world, 1 ff., 101 f.; decline, 2 ff., 341, 356; distinguished from ideology, 4; and empirical science, 20 ff., 32 ff.; and practice, 9, 380 f.; restoration, 3 f., 101 f., 377 ff.; see also Political theory
Political science, American, 9 ff., 16, 23 f., 27 ff., 34 ff.; curriculum, 12 ff., 40 ff.; as description, 17; as empirical science, 17 f., 19 ff.; as empirical theory, 26, 37 ff.; five methodological positions, 15; identical with theory, 32 ff.; as ideology, 35 f.; importance of philosophy for, 32 f.; moral commitment, 27 ff., 42 f.; as normative theory, 40; origins, 9 f.; social ambivalence, 27 ff.

Political theory: as academic discipline, 24 ff., 34 f., 377; decline, 16; nature, 19 ff., 32 ff., 56, 88, 250 f., 377, 380 f.; see also Political philosophy; Political science
Politics: displaced by economics, 256; displaced by the military, 256 ff., 269; escape from, 237 ff., 246 ff., 272 f., 281; modern conception, 3; nature, 259 ff., 270 f., 281 ff.
Positivism, 33, 379; legal, 211 ff., 233
Pound, Roscoe, 223
Power, 30, 33, 37 ff., 50 ff., 61 f., 88, 100, 104 ff., 239 ff., 246 ff., 253 ff., 258 ff., 351 ff., 358 f., 361 ff., 366 f.; private concentrations, 102, 114 ff.
Pressure groups, 35, 118 f.
Pride, and politics, 254, 262 ff.
Propaganda, and foreign policy, 356
Proudhon, Pierre Joseph, 244
Prudence, essential to political morality, 84, 254
Psychoanalysis, 3 f.
Public administration, 16
Public opinion: and democracy, 293 ff., 302 ff., 332 ff.; nature, 333 ff.

Quantification, in political science, 18 f.

Radin, Max, 134
Ranke, Leopold von, 49
Rationalism, 350 f., 380 f.
Ray, Jean, 226
Realism: in international law, 223 f.; and morality, 80 ff., 270; political, 54 f., 65, 67, 73, 75 ff., 206, 249 f., 285, 350 f., 357
Reality, modern devaluation, 4
Reason of state, 55, 250
Reform, as applied theory, 49, 89
Reformation, 360
Relativism, political, 101, 110, 112, 368, 379
Religion: and civilization, 375; crisis, 3; and national interest, 72; and politics, 374; return to, 373 ff.; return to, in United States, 374
Religiosity, distinct from religion, 374 ff.
Revolution, of twentieth century, 353 f.
Richelieu, Duke de, 250
Robbins, Lionel, 348
Robson, W. A., 38
Rodin, Auguste, 375
Roman law, 220, 232

Romanticism, political, 357, 367
Roosevelt, Franklin D., 267
Roosevelt, Theodore, on powers of president, 108
Root, Elihu, on delegation of legislative power, 156
Rousseau, Jean-Jacques, 21 f., 239 ff.; and the Western tradition, 2
Russian revolutions, 290

St. Pierre, Abbé de, 49
Salisbury, Lord, on national interest, 67, 86
"Salt-water fallacy," 181
Scalapino, R. A., on Asian neutralism, 205
Scelle, Georges, 217, 223
Schmitt, Carl, 357
Schumpeter, Josef, 348
Scientism, 240 ff., 368
Secrecy, in government, 289 f.
Secretary of State, functions, 299 f.
Self-interest, enlightened, distinguished from national interest, 74 f.
Semantics, general, 19
Sentimentalism, in foreign policy, 73
Separation of powers, 123 f., 133 ff.; as implied limitation, 165 ff.
Sin, as corruptiveness of power, 108, 247, 254
Social sciences: development, 9, 15, 19, 93, 235; nature, 93 ff., 210, 235, 240 ff., 368 ff.
Sociology: development, 15 f., 19; of history, 369 f.; of law, 212 f., 219 ff.; political, 41 f.
Sophocles, 375
Sorel, Georges, II, 24
Sovereign power, 133 f.
Sovereignty, 344, 364; divine, 359 ff.; dynastic, 170 f.; popular, 360 f.
Soviet Union: challenge, 356; colonialism, 181; as democracy, 355 f.; in eastern Europe, 79; foreign policy, 82 f.; freedom in, 348; imperialism, 175, 268; and Korea, 77; national interest, 71 f.; and nationalism, 177, 181; nationalities policy, 177; as supranational state, 355; underestimation, 263 f., 288
Spengler, Oswald, 372 f.
Spinoza, Benedict, 360
Staley, Eugene, 348
Stalin, Joseph, 49, 260, 267, 355

State: as menace and protector, 114 ff., 120; modern, power, 359 ff., 367; as umpire, 116
Statesmanship, as applied theory, 49 f., 58 f.
Stebbing, L. Susan, 86
Stein, Gertrude, 20
Subversion, in United States, 70 ff., 305 ff.
Suez crisis, 301, 303
Sulzbach, Walter, 348
Sumner, William Graham, 234 f.
Supranational organization, need for, 69
Switzerland: federal structure, 60 f.; neutrality, 186, 191, 196 f.

Taine, Hippolyte, 367
Tannenbaum, Frank, 56 ff.
Taylor, Henry, 285
Technological revolutions: philosophic effects, 2; political effects, 68 f., 102, 178 f., 184, 199 f., 203, 243 f., 276 f., 287, 367
Third Force, 198, 204 ff.
Thucydides, 49, 67, 264
Tocqueville, Alexis de, 19, 367
Tolstoy, Leo, on modern history, 31
Totalitarianism, 37 f., 106 ff., 244 f., 256, 287, 315, 317 f., 345 ff., 353, 378; democratic claims, 2, 106, 109; and law, 213; and nationalism, 177, 182
Toynbee, Arnold, 341, 368 ff.
Treason, in America, 63, 70 ff., 309 ff.
Treaty of Versailles, validity, 226, ff.
Truman, Harry, 267, 330
Truman administration, and Korean War, 77 f.
Truth, problem of political, 4, 28 ff., 35 f., 42 f., 67, 95 ff., 101 f., 105 ff., 289, 325 f., 349, 377
Tucker, Robert W., Jr., 55
Two-bloc system, 200 ff., 207, 277 ff.
Tyranny, as unlimited freedom, 111, 114, 363 f.

Ulpian, 134
"Unconditional surrender," 267
United Nations: as alternative to national interest, 72 f., 244, 268, 272 f.; diplomacy, 273; as ideology, 64; and neutrality, 186, 192 ff.
United States: decline of prestige, 321 f., 332; economic system, 119 f.; federal structure, 60; government,

economic functions, 117 ff.; misunderstanding of democracy, 281, 295, 332 ff.; and nationalism, 181; party system, 336 ff.; political tradition, 285 ff., 336 ff.; presidency, 295 ff., 304; principles of government, 321 ff.; security policies, 305 ff.; as world power, 62
United States Department of State, decline, 303 f., 318 ff.
United States foreign policy, 258 ff., 287 ff., 296 ff., 324 ff.; "agonizing reappraisal," 330; toward China, 334 f.; conception, 256 ff., 267 ff.; conduct, 299 ff., 306, 324, 327, 332 ff.; experience in, 248; great issues, 54, 57 f.; in Indochina War, 331 f.; "new look," 330 f.; tradition, 56 ff.; in Western Hemisphere, 61
Utopianism, political, 54 f., 67, 73, 75 ff., 206, 285, 350 f., 356 f., 362, 381

Vagts, Alfred, on balance of power, 56
Verdross, Alfred, 223

Vico, Giambattista, 372
Viner, Jacob, 348
Visscher, Charles de, 330

War: as continuation of foreign policy 256 ff., 267 f.; and the national interest, 74 f.
Washington, George, 55, 71, 248
Watkins Frederick, 42
Webster, Sir Charles, 89
Willoughby, W. W., 164
Wilson, Charles, 283
Wilson, Woodrow, 49, 86, 177, 182, 243, 250, 285, 355; on American foreign policy, 57 f.
Winslow, E. M., 348
World Federalists, 49
World government, 243 f., 272
World revolution, 353
Wright, Quincy, 211

Yalta agreement, 263, 324 f.

Zimmern, Sir Alfred, 89, 217